# HIGH AND MITRED

Dr. P—s—y.          Dr. P—n—h.          Dr. Gl—d—st—n.          Ld. Sh—f—ts—b—y.

## CONGÉ D'ÉLIRE-IUM.  A CASE FOR THE DOCTORS.

*Uneasy bedfellows: Pusey and Shaftesbury jointly oppose Gladstone's nomination of Frederick Temple as Bishop of Exeter (see page 93).*

Bernard Palmer

# HIGH AND MITRED

*A Study of Prime Ministers as*
*Bishop-Makers 1837 – 1977*

First published in Great Britain 1992
Society for Promoting Christian Knowledge
Holy Trinity Church
Marylebone Road
London NW1 4DU

*To my wife Jane,
who provided the idea and the title,
leaving me to write the book*

British Library Cataloguing-in-Publication Data

CIP data for this book is
available from the British Library

ISBN 0-281-04594-1

Typeset by Pioneer Associates, Perthshire
Printed in Great Britain by
The Cromwell Press, Melksham, Wiltshire

# Contents

# Foreword

*by the Rt Hon. Sir Edward Heath,* KG MBE MP

The make up of the episcopal bench is not only of deep interest and sometimes concern to the rest of the clergy and the members of the established Church of England, it is also an endless source of fascination to many of the general public who have, in fact, little understanding of the workings of our institutions.

The ever-growing influence of the media – press, radio and television – and its preparedness to publicize every aspect of the church's affairs has involved our fellow citizens, whether they like it or not, in a personal assessment of the procedures involved in all such appointments.

There can be no doubt that this is a healthy development provided that a proper balance is maintained between the various interests involved. This must not just be left to the scaremongering of the tabloid press.

However, to secure a full understanding amongst both churchgoers and non-churchgoers it is essential to have an elucidation of the principles involved in such appointments as well as a description of the means of sustaining them.

Bernard Palmer has spent his lifetime at the centre of the discussion of such ecclesiastical matters, as did his family before him. No one is better qualified to describe the history of the episcopal bench and its members. In *High and Mitred* he does so with clarity and wit, shaped by knowledge and wisdom.

I commend this book to the ever-growing body of people taking a personal and indeed practical interest in our Church and its leaders.

# Acknowledgements

In addition to those specifically mentioned in the Preface I should like to express my gratitude to the Rt Hon. Sir Edward Heath, and the Rt Hon. Lord Callaghan of Cardiff for responding so readily to my request for information on their own bishop-making practice while Prime Minister. The two other surviving (at the time of writing) pre-1977 premiers, the Rt Hon. Lord Home of the Hirsel and the Rt Hon. Lord Wilson of Rievaulx, were sadly not well enough to help me directly, though Lord Wilson referred me to the relevant chapter of his book, *The Governance of Britain*.

I should also like to thank Robin Catford, the current Prime Minister's Secretary for Appointments, and his predecessor, Colin Peterson, for helpful background advice in connection with the book; the Rt Rev. Gerald Ellison for sending me a copy of the text of his Anthony Bevir Memorial Lecture of 1980; the Rt Rev. E. J. K. Roberts for explaining the unique circumstances of his nomination by *two* prime ministers; the principals of a number of theological colleges for checking my lists of their episcopal alumni; Judith Maltby of Salisbury and Wells Theological College and the Rev. Noel Pollard of Ridley Hall for background information concerning the colleges; the Canterbury Press, Norwich, for letting me have an advance proof copy of Edward Carpenter's *Archbishop Fisher* (which was not published until after my own manuscript had to be finalized) and for giving me permission to quote extensively from the *Church Times*; Dr P. E. Hughes, Archivist of the Church of England Record Centre, for unearthing some missing consecration dates from their collection of *Crockfords*; and Mrs Pat Bancroft, Librarian of Lichfield Cathedral, for information concerning the elusive Bishop Bowstead.

The extensive quotations from George Bell's *Randall Davidson* (1935) are published by permission of Oxford University Press.

I am grateful to JAK and the *Evening Standard* for their permission to use the cartoon reproduced on page 270. I spent several hours at the Mary Evans Picture Library and the Westminster Reference Library researching into back numbers of *Punch* to find the cartoons reproduced elsewhere in the book.

Last but not least, I should like to thank my wife for transmuting my own imperfect typescript into an impeccable fair-copy for the publishers – and for much-needed encouragement along the way.

# List of Illustrations

# Preface

As Editor of the *Church Times* from 1968 to 1989 I had frequently to report the appointment of new bishops in the Church of England and to carry articles and letters critical of the system by which they were appointed. Over the years I became well versed in the arguments for and against the existing system. This came to an end effectively in the summer of 1977, with the transfer of the initiative in making nominations from the prime minister to the Crown Appointments Commission (CAC). In retirement I have had the leisure to make a prolonged study of the whole fascinating business; and this book is the result of that study.

It seemed to me that, though there was much published material on the subject, it was scattered too widely to provide a complete and readily accessible picture; and that therefore to assemble as much as possible of the available material within the covers of a single volume might be a worthwhile exercise. My book makes no pretence of being a work of original scholarship. I have shamelessly plucked other men's flowers to provide a survey of the whole field of English episcopal appointments from the beginning of Queen Victoria's reign in 1837 to the establishment of the CAC in 1977. I chose the start of Victoria's reign as a suitable launch-pad, as most of her prime ministers and not a few of the bishops they appointed are widely known. Chapters at the beginning and end of the book deal with the evolution of the system up to 1837 and with the various twentieth-century proposals to reform it, culminating in the 1976 Church–State concordat which set up the CAC. A postscript deals briefly with the premiership of Margaret Thatcher, during which the new system gradually got into its stride.

In order to keep the book within reasonable bounds I have had to omit various categories of bishop from my survey. These include all overseas bishops (as in India) appointed by British prime ministers; all English suffragan bishops (who were in effect chosen by the bishop of the diocese in which they were to minister); and the handful of bishops of the Church of Ireland who were nominated by British premiers between 1837 and the disestablishment of that Church in 1871. I *have*, however, included all bishops of Welsh dioceses up to the disestablishment of the Church in Wales in 1920, as those dioceses formed part of the province of Canterbury and may therefore be regarded logically as part of the Church of England. Deaneries and those canonries which were Crown appointments I have also excluded for reasons of space, except where particular appointments proved controversial and therefore deserve a mention. At the end of each chapter I have included a list of all nominations to diocesan bishoprics made by the prime minister in question. A Statistical Table of Bishops at the end of the book gives an alphabetical list of all diocesans appointed during the period 1837–1977, with various details about each.

A full list of books consulted appears in the Bibliography. I am especially indebted to Owen Chadwick, whose expertise on the subject of my study is unrivalled – and can be seen to advantage in his two-volume survey of *The Victorian Church* and in his masterly biographies of Hensley Henson and Michael Ramsey. And, like so many other dabblers in the byways of church history, I also owe a great debt to the late George Bell for his *Randall Davidson*, from which I have shamelessly plundered (as from Owen Chadwick) much rich treasure. Finally I must record my gratitude to my namesake, Dr Richard Palmer, the Lambeth Palace Librarian, for kindly allowing me to delve into the many volumes of archiepiscopal correspondence in his care. The letters to and from prime ministers included in these volumes have provided me with invaluable source-material for the second half of my book.

Bernard Palmer
*Charminster, Dorset*
*January 1992*

# PART ONE

# THE QUEEN'S ENGLAND

## 1

## God v. Caesar

On 27 March 1991 George Leonard Carey, until recently Bishop of Bath and Wells, walked into the London City church of St Mary-le-Bow. An hour or so later he came out of the church as Archbishop of Canterbury and Primate of All England. Between his ceremonial entry and exit had come the archaic legal ceremony of having his 'election' by the Dean and Chapter of Canterbury formally 'confirmed', thus transforming him from a mere archbishop-elect into an actual and fully functional archbishop.

The ceremony epitomized the extraordinary way in which the Church of England goes about the business of choosing its chief pastors, the bishops. Unlike every other member Church of the worldwide Anglican Communion, it fails to elect its bishops in the popular sense. Instead they are nominated by the sovereign on the advice of the prime minister – the process of 'election' by the dean and chapter of the diocese being an empty formality. This is the price the Church must pay for its 'established' status as part of the fabric of the State and for the privilege of having twenty-six of its forty-four diocesan bishops in the House of Lords. Though the premier now plays a far less significant role in the bishop-making process than in the past, he or she is still a part of it. This infuriates opponents of the system and leads to regular calls for the Church to be disestablished. In fact such calls are likely to be ignored. Governments have far too much on their plate nowadays to risk the enormous and time-consuming upheaval that disestablishment of the Church of England would involve. Successive modifications in the Church–State set-up over the past thirty years have given the Church far greater freedom to order its own affairs than it enjoyed in the first half of this century. Until recently the appointment of bishops by the prime minister was the principal remaining source of grievance: but here the sting has been largely removed with the setting up of the Crown Appointments Commission. The State, through the prime minister, may still nominally appoint the bishops, but it has retained the shadow without the substance.

The form of the 'confirmation' ceremony for Archbishop Carey was much the same as it was when originally established by the Appointment of Bishops Act 1533. Legal archaisms abounded. 'I porrect', intoned the Canterbury Diocesan Registrar as he made use of the old ecclesiastical lawyers' term for tendering or submitting a document. And the Archbishop of York, acting as chairman of the royal commission of nine senior bishops overseeing the arrangements, embarked on the reading of a series of 'schedules'. The first intimated that, if anyone objected to the election, it was now too late to say so. The second pronounced any objectors – meaning 'all and every opposer (if any there be) who would object against the validity of the said Election' – to be 'contumacious'. Dr Carey himself was described as 'a man both prudent and discreet, deservedly laudable for his life and conversation'. At the end of the ceremony he was declared to be in the 'real, actual and corporal possession' of his office.[1]

The new primate's subsequent enthronement on 19 April was, from a strictly legal point of view, a non-event, albeit a colourful and picturesque ceremony. He was described at one point in the service as 'by divine providence' Archbishop of Canterbury. The human intermediary had been the former prime minister, Margaret Thatcher. She had chosen Dr Carey's name from the list of two submitted by the Crown Appointments Commission and had passed it on to the Queen, who had approved it. The presence of Mrs Thatcher's successor, John Major, in the congregation as an honoured guest underlined the prime minister's role in the process of bishop-making. But, since the reform of the procedure in the late 1970s, that role had become a mere shadow of what it had been in the past. Up until the summer of 1977 the prime minister of the day had been the initiator of the process by which bishops of the established Church of England were chosen. He might, and almost always did, consult church opinion at the highest level. Latterly his secretary for appointments had taken an increasingly active part in the process. But his had been the key role in that process. The Archbishop of Canterbury might press for a particular man to be nominated, and the premier might often agree; but he could always propose a candidate of his own, and the final choice lay with him.

From the summer of 1977 onwards all that changed. Under the agreement reached with Prime Minister James Callaghan the initiative in the matter passed to the newly-minted Crown Appointments Commission, a fourteen-strong body representative of the Church. It was this body which decided on the names to be submitted to the Queen for her approval. Two names were to be submitted, if necessary in the Commission's order of preference, and the prime minister could choose whichever he preferred – not necessarily the first. So he retained a limited freedom of choice; and, if he felt uneasy about both names, he could ask the Commission to propose a further name or names. But, under the new concordat, he could not propose a name of his own. Towards the end of this book we shall consider the stages by which the growing dissatisfaction with the traditional method of choosing bishops led to such a basic alteration in the system. But the book's main purpose is to describe the working of that system during the last hundred and forty years of its life and the way in which prime ministers used and in some cases abused it. But first the basics of the old system need to be described.

A bishopric is technically a Crown appointment, meaning an appointment made by the sovereign acting on advice tendered by the prime minister of the day. Informal discussions may well have taken place before the formal submission of a name; but, once the prime minister's advice has been formally tendered, the sovereign is constitutionally bound to accept it. The candidate's name is then passed on to the dean and chapter of the diocese concerned, with instructions to 'elect' him as their diocesan bishop. Failure to elect the Crown's nominee exposed potentially disobedient clerics until recently to the severe penalties prescribed by the Statutes of Praemunire: possible imprisonment and confiscation of goods. Failure by a chapter to elect would result in the Crown's appointing its nominee by letters patent.

The ceremony of election is followed by that of confirmation – which takes place by custom in the church of St Mary-le-Bow in London. This is a purely legal ceremony, usually conducted by the Vicar-General of the province concerned – Canterbury or York. Its purpose is to enable the representatives of the Crown to satisfy themselves that the election has been carried out without irregularities and that the bishop-elect appearing at the confirmation really is the man chosen by the sovereign. Occasional attempts in the past to object to the Crown's nominee on doctrinal grounds have always been overruled. Once a bishop-elect has been 'confirmed', he possesses jurisdiction over his diocese. He can license and institute clergymen and appoint them to benefices.

He can exercise discipline. But, unless he is already in episcopal orders, he can neither confirm nor ordain.

The grace to perform these key episcopal functions is bestowed by consecration, which is carried out by the archbishop of the province, assisted by at least two diocesan bishops of the same province. Like election, consecration constitutes a formal safeguard against any alleged abuse of the royal supremacy. Just as, theoretically, a dean and chapter could decline to elect the Crown's nominee, so, theoretically, an archbishop could refuse to preside at a consecration. In fact no such gauntlet has ever been thrown down. Very occasionally a handful of canons have declined to vote as required, and very occasionally bishops have refused to assist at a consecration. But always in such cases a majority of canons have played ball and a quorum of bishops has been found ready to consecrate, so a showdown has been avoided.

The final stage in the process of appointment is when the new bishop pays homage to the sovereign. Homage relates to the temporalities of the see – in modern terms, its income from the Church Commissioners. The ceremony of enthronement has no legal significance, though it is the stage in the whole process of which the public, or rather the church public in the diocese concerned, is most aware, since it takes place in the cathedral, the mother church of the diocese, and is witnessed by a large congregation. It provides the new bishop with an opportunity to make a ceremonial entry into his domain and formally to address his flock for the first time.

The process of appointing bishops within the Church of England has developed over a long period of time. Before the Norman Conquest bishops were usually nominated by the king and confirmed by the Witenagemote (the national council or parliament). It was Archbishop Anselm who secured from Henry I the right of cathedral chapters formally to elect the royal nominee; though, as the election then took place in public, it would have been dangerous to turn him down. King John gave the chapters the right of free election (the meaning of the phrase in Magna Carta, *Ecclesia Anglicana libera sit*, 'Let the Church of England be free'), but it was a right that was never really effective. Occasionally a chapter would jib at a wholly unsuitable candidate – like Henry III's half-brother Ethelmar, proposed by the King for the see of Winchester, who was under the canonical age of twenty-three. Henry was exceedingly cross with the uncooperative monks who formed the chapter. He summoned them to hear a sermon preached by himself, in the course of which he denounced them and hinted at unspeakable penalties if they persisted in their opposition. Ethelmar was duly elected.

In practice the main opposition to the king, if it came at all, came from the pope. Sometimes chapters would appeal to Rome if they disapproved of the royal candidate for a bishopric; and, in the thirteenth century, the popes intervened actively and were able to appoint to a large number of English dioceses themselves. This led to frequent disputes between kings and popes. Eventually they came to an arrangement by which the king nominated a candidate and asked the pope to approve his choice. The pope then ratified the nomination as if it was his own. Occasionally the pope objected to a royal nominee, and some hard bargaining ensued – with perhaps, in the end, a compromise candidate being chosen. But, for the most part, the king got his way and was responsible for the majority of nominations to vacant sees. The pope retained the shadow but the king the substance of power, though he was always scrupulous in paying lip-service to the pope's nominal right to have the last word.

With the Reformation the pope's right to interfere, however tenuously, in the affairs of the Church of England lapsed. The power of the Crown to appoint bishops became absolute, and there was no longer any need to defer to a final court of appeal in Rome. The procedure to be followed was laid down by a statute, the Appointment of Bishops Act of 1533. Under the terms of that Act the Crown sent the chapter of the vacant diocese a 'licence to elect' (*congé d'élire*) the person named in an accompanying 'letter missive'. If the chapter failed to elect the royal nominee within twelve days, the Crown proceeded to nominate by 'letters patent'. If the chapter refused to elect or the archbishop subsequently to consecrate, they were liable to the penalties of *praemunire* (the title of various fourteenth-century statutes: the Latin word means 'to forewarn'), by which the offenders were put outside the king's protection and their lands and goods were forfeited. There was nothing new in the fact that the king could appoint bishops. As the report of the Joint Committee on Crown Nominations to Ecclesiastical Offices put it in 1920:

> What was a novelty in this was not the recognition of the King's rights, or the system of the *congé d'élire*, accompanied by the Letter Missive, which practically gave the Crown the right of appointment, but the coercive methods to be employed if necessary, subjecting a recalcitrant chapter or archbishop to the penalties of *praemunire*, and providing by statute for a method of filling a vacant see should the chapter fail to elect a nominee of the Crown.[2]

The king might appoint bishops, but even a monarch as autocratic as Henry VIII might sometimes distrust his own judgement and seek the advice of his close confidants. There is evidence that names were submitted to him by the Secretary of State. Henry's son, Edward VI, was a minor, and episcopal appointments during his reign were made on the recommendation of the Council. Elizabeth I was advised by Cecil, who was himself advised by Archbishop Parker. Charles I was advised by Archbishop Laud, and Charles II by a six-strong commission (consisting of the Archbishop of Canterbury, the Bishop of London and four laymen) which submitted its recommendations to the King via the Secretaries of State. William III, with his limited knowledge of the Church of England, also made use of a commission – in his case composed of the Archbishops of Canterbury and York and five bishops. Their brief was to 'recommend persons for ecclesiastical preferment to the end that the names of such persons may be presented to the Crown by one of our principal Secretaries of State that the royal pleasure may be further known therein'.

Queen Anne managed without a commission. She usually acted on the advice of her ministers, though occasionally she appointed bishops on her own initiative. By this time, nearly two hundred years after the Reformation breach with Rome, the royal advisers were beginning to resent this occasional urge on the part of their royal mistress to go it alone. There was an occasion in 1707 when two sees, Exeter and Chester, were vacant and the Whig ministers were not consulted. The Queen, having made both appointments, wrote afterwards to the Duke of Marlborough: 'I do assure you that these men were my own choice. They were certainly very fit for the station I design them; and indeed I think myself obliged to fill the bishops' bench with those who will be a credit to it and the Church.'[3] The protests, however, were effective enough to deter the Queen in future from acting without ministerial advice.

With the arrival in 1714 of the Hanoverian George I, who had no knowledge of either the English language or the English Church, the scenario hardened into the formal pattern that was to remain (with modifications) more or less constant until the setting up of the Crown Appointments Commission in 1977. The responsibility for appointing bishops now passed definitely to the prime minister, who was only very rarely overruled by the sovereign. The best-known case of such an overruling occurred during the reign of George III. When the Archbishop of Canterbury died in 1805 the Prime Minister, William Pitt, recommended the Bishop of Lincoln, George Tomline, to succeed him. But, as soon as the King received Pitt's proposal, he rode over to Windsor and offered the post to his old tutor, Manners Sutton, who had been both Bishop of Norwich and Dean of Windsor since 1794. Pitt was not best pleased. He protested strongly against the King's 'apparent disregard of his nomination of the Bishop of Lincoln to succeed to the archbishopric of Canterbury. He entreats your Majesty humbly to reflect that such a recommendation appears uniformly to have been graciously accepted for a long course of time in every instance.'⁴ George III appears to have got the message, as he did not offend again during the remainder of his reign.

His son and successor, George IV, also received a rap over the knuckles from the then Prime Minister, Lord Liverpool, when he too attempted to act on his own initiative. The King, at the request of Lady Conyngham, had appointed her son's tutor, Mr Sumner, to a canonry at Windsor. When Liverpool discovered this, 'he got into his carriage and went down to the king to state that, unless he was allowed to have the distribution of this patronage without any interference, he could not carry on the Government and would resign his office if Sumner was appointed. The man was only a curate, and had never held a living at all.'⁵ The threat was effective.

I have now arrived at the start of my chosen period: the accession of Queen Victoria in 1837. The prime minister's formal right to have the last word in the choice of all new bishops was now firmly established. Paradoxically, however, Victoria had such strong views of her own where appointments were concerned that she would often argue the toss with the premier of the day – and sometimes got her way. But the arguments were almost always carried on during the preliminary stages and before the formal submission of a name was made; and sometimes the accompanying correspondence was entrusted to Deans of Windsor, secretaries and other intermediaries, the Queen and successive prime ministers pulling the necessary strings. The Queen never disputed the premier's right to have the last word, even though she might grumble at having to concede it to him. Victoria's reign (or at least the early part of it) was in fact the prime ministerial heyday, when premiers could if they chose ignore the wishes of Archbishops of Canterbury and go their own sweet way (hoping that it would also be the Queen's).

Anthony Trollope paints the picture only too accurately in the opening chapter of *Barchester Towers*, when Archdeacon Grantly is hoping for the succession to his dying father às Bishop of Barchester. But the government was tottering to its fall, and it was a question of whether it would die before the bishop. 'No probable Prime Minister but he who was now in, he who was so soon to be out, would think of making a bishop of Dr Grantly.'[6] But alas for the archdeacon's hopes! He is on the point of sending off a telegram to Downing Street to announce his father's death when the news arrives of the fall of the government. 'Thus terminated our unfortunate friend's chance of possessing the glories of a bishopric.' The Trollopian situation, though fictional, curiously foreshadowed the real-life situation in 1868, eleven years after the publication of *Barchester Towers*, when the succession to the archbishopric of Canterbury would have turned out differently had the dying Longley lingered on till Gladstone rather than Disraeli was Prime Minister.

At that period in Victoria's reign the political element in episcopal appointments, though less marked than in former years, had still to be taken into account. And it was this aspect of the system that made it increasingly distasteful to its critics. (At the beginning of my period the choice of bishops was often unashamedly partisan; and my first prime minister, Melbourne, made no bones about filling the vacant sees with men of his own political views.) I shall consider at a later stage the growing feeling in the Church at large that the system left much to be desired, and examine the work of the various commissions which, during the middle years of the twentieth century, sought ways of reforming it – work which culminated in the Church–State concordat of 1976. But the body of the book will be concerned with the way in which prime ministers from Melbourne to Callaghan operated the system as it existed, and developed it in their own individual ways.

# 2

# Episcopal Whigs

*Viscount Melbourne: Prime Minister*
*18 March 1835 – 30 August 1841*

William Lamb, 2nd Viscount Melbourne (1770–1848), *was*
*educated at Eton and Trinity College, Cambridge. He entered the*
*Commons as MP for Leominster in 1806, joining the Whig*
*opposition under Fox. After a long spell of comparative obscurity*
*which saw the collapse of his marriage to Lady Caroline Lamb,*
*the lover of Lord Byron, he was Chief Secretary for Ireland under*
*Canning and Home Secretary in the government of Earl Grey,*
*whom he succeeded as Prime Minister in 1834. Apart from a*
*brief interlude in 1834–5 when Peel was Premier, he held the*
*post until the fall of his government in 1841. A combination of*
*eighteenth-century man of the world and romantic philosopher*
*(whose hobby happened to be theology), he is best remembered*
*for his influence over the young Queen Victoria, whom he*
*delighted to instruct in the principles of monarchy.*

'Damn it, another bishop dead!' is the remark attributed to Lord
Melbourne on hearing the news of a vacancy he would now have
to fill on the episcopal Bench.[1] But he took his powers of
patronage seriously. He might be driven by exasperation at a too-
importunate suitor to exclaim, 'Confound it, does he want a
Garter for his other leg?'; or (of a dim Scots peer), 'Give him the
Thistle! Why, he'd eat it!' Yet, when it came to ecclesiastical
appointments, he was not only painstaking but knowledgeable.
When, for instance, he was interviewing Connop Thirlwall, the
distinguished historian and theologian to whom he had just
offered the see of St Davids, he was able to boast, as he pointed
at a pile of folio editions of the Fathers: 'I take a great interest in
theological questions, and I have read a good deal of those old
fellows. They are excellent reading and very amusing; some time
or other we must have a talk about them.'[2] One cannot imagine
Lloyd George or Winston Churchill making that sort of remark.

But of course Melbourne would never allow his personal
predilections to get in the way of his political principles when it

came to the distribution of mitres. *What were those principles?*
Melbourne headed a Whig administration; and, at this stage of
Queen Victoria's reign, it was only to be expected that a Whig
premier would wish to fill vacant seats in the House of Lords
with men likely to support him politically.

But Melbourne declined to be too rigid in this respect – or at
least, when he went on public record, he was careful to avoid the
appearance of rigidity. In a letter to the Archbishop of Canterbury,
William Howley, on the Thirlwall nomination (19 July 1840) he
went out of his way to emphasize his own sweet reasonableness:

> While I feel myself bound to recommend for promotion
> clergymen whose general views upon political matters coincide
> with my own, I am most anxious not to advance any man
> whose doctrines are not in unison with those of the Established
> Church, or even whose promotion would be disagreeable to the
> great body of the clergy.[3]

Thirlwall was a liberal theologian, and Melbourne himself was
that way inclined. The Evangelicals he regarded as hypocrites
and bigots. The Tractarians, whose presence was just making
itself felt at Oxford, he found hard to fathom. He once complained
to Lord Holland:

> I hardly make out what Puseyism is. Either I am dull, or its
> apostles are very obscure. I have got one of their chief
> Newman's publications with an appendix of four hundred and
> forty-four pages. I have read fifty-seven and cannot say I
> understand a sentence, or any idea whatever.[4]

A far cry, evidently, from the crystal-clear Fathers! But at least
the liberal theologians were easier to follow (or so Melbourne
thought); they were open-minded in their conclusions; and, most
important of all, they tended to be Whig in politics, and were
therefore likely to vote on his side in debates in the Lords. So his
own inclination was to appoint liberal-minded men as bishops.

But, in his later appointments, he played for safety, as a result
of having burnt his fingers badly over an academic nomination in
1836, the year before our period opens. The post in question was
the Regius professorship of divinity in the University of Oxford.
The successful candidate was Renn Dickson Hampden, the man
who was to figure in an even stormier controversy eleven years
later, when Lord John Russell nominated him to the see of
Hereford. Among the reasons given by Melbourne for offering
Hampden the Oxford chair was his reputation for 'a liberal spirit
of enquiry, tempered by due caution'.[5] Melbourne may have
genuinely thought Hampden 'cautious', or he may have been

whistling to keep his courage up. But alas for his hopes! By 1836 Hampden had already blotted his copy-book badly in at least two respects. He had delivered a course of Bampton Lectures which were anti-dogmatic in tone and, in particular, cast doubts on the doctrine of the Trinity. And he was also the author of a liberal pamphlet, *Observations on Religious Dissent*, which, in the opinion of John Henry Newman, tended 'altogether to make shipwreck of Christian faith'.[6] The result can be imagined. The University was up in arms, High Churchmen and Low making common cause against the threat of infidelity in their midst. Newman and Keble organized a petition to the Crown which was signed by no fewer than seventy-three college tutors. The Crown itself, in the person of William IV, found itself in a tricky position. Up till now the King had never heard of Hampden. So, when Melbourne had written to him seeking his consent to the nomination but saying nothing about the nominee, he had given that consent automatically by return of post. There was therefore nothing he could really do in the matter, apart from protesting to the Premier about his having been kept in the dark. So the appointment was dully gazetted, and Melbourne was able to ride out that particular storm. But the wind had been sown; and it was left to a successor, as we shall see, to reap the whirlwind.

Melbourne had learnt his lesson, and for the future made sure of a candidate's theological orthodoxy before recommending him for a mitre. No better example of his new spirit of caution can be found than his handling of Connop Thirlwall, to whom he eventually offered the see of St Davids in South Wales and who was to turn out to be among the most distinguished appointments of his premiership. For all his distinction, however, Thirlwall's copy-book was blotted. He had had to resign his assistant tutorship at Trinity College, Cambridge, in 1834 following his denunciation of compulsory attendance at chapel. Even worse, he had caused controversy at Cambridge by his translation of Friedrich Schleiermacher's commentary on St Luke's Gospel, a work of dubious orthodoxy. In fact Melbourne had turned down Thirlwall for the see of Norwich in 1837 precisely because the two bishops to whom he had sent the translation for approval had reported unfavourably on certain passages in its preface.*

---

*The bishops had in fact qualified their disapproval. In a letter to Archbishop Howley (19 July 1840) Melbourne wrote: '[They] told me that there were in the preface some passages respecting the inspiration of the New Testament which they considered objectionable, but at the same time they seemed to think that the errors, considering the time and circumstances in which they were committed, were not of such magnitude as to bar the promotion of a man of so much learning and ability. This also is my opinion.'[7] Time had evidently marched on!

But that had been only a year after the Hampden controversy; and no doubt Melbourne had felt that, in the light of this double episcopal caution, he had better play for safety. But it was now 1840. The Hampden controversy was well in the past. Moreover, he had by this time received a second (or rather third) opinion on the orthodoxy or otherwise of Thirlwall's translation of Schleiermacher. The recommendation came from Charles Buller, a Radical friend of both Melbourne and Thirlwall who pleaded the latter's cause with the Prime Minister. On Melbourne's complaining that Thirlwall was 'not orthodox in that preface to Schleiermacher' Buller retorted that he thought Thirlwall sufficiently orthodox for a bishopric. They then adjourned to Melbourne's library, where they spent the morning searching the church Fathers for precedents for Thirlwall's opinions.[8] At last Melbourne declared himself satisfied, even though the Archbishop of Canterbury, Howley, accepted the nomination with a bad grace. Since leaving Cambridge Thirlwall had been beavering away at an eight-volume history of Greece in the obscurity of a Yorkshire rectory. Melbourne now assured Howley that he had 'heard from all quarters' that Thirlwall richly deserved promotion. Howley, who disliked both Whiggery and religious heterodoxy, 'hummed and hawed a great deal, but, finding himself out-Bishopped, was fain to make the best face he could and gulped the pill'.[9]

So the offer of St Davids was made. It reached Thirlwall's home when he was on a walking tour; and, in those leisurely times, it took several days before a friend finally tracked the lucky nominee down to an obscure village inn. At first Thirlwall wanted to refuse the offer; but his friends (including Thomas Carlyle) pressed him to accept, and eventually he called on the Prime Minister to deliver his acceptance. When he arrived Melbourne was still in bed, sipping chocolate and surrounded by letters and papers – including those folio editions of the Fathers to which reference has been made. He hastened to reassure (or to warn) Thirlwall:

> I only wish you to understand that I don't intend if I know it to make a heterodox bishop. I don't like heterodox bishops. As men they may be very good anywhere else, but I think they have no business on the Bench . . . I sent your edition of Schleiermacher to Lambeth, and asked the Primate to tell me candidly what he thought of it; and look, here are his notes in the margin; pretty copious, you see. He does not concur in all your opinions; but he says there is nothing heterodox in your book.[10]

So Thirlwall was in the clear; and he occupied his remote Welsh see for the next four-and-thirty years. But he was too far from London to make the best use of his talents, and so tended to find himself out on a limb. His friends might praise him for his calm and judicial intellect and for his sense of duty, but Palmerston told Queen Victoria in 1861 that he was inefficient; and the Dean of St Davids remarked to Samuel Wilberforce in 1854 that, though the clergy were proud of their bishop's reputation for scholarship, they found him cold and reserved. In fact his episcopal duties dried Thirlwall up completely as a creative writer. He would have agreed with Archbishop Whately of Dublin, who once exclaimed, plucking at his lawn sleeves: 'I don't know how it is; but, when we have these things on, we never do anything more.'[11]

Melbourne, meanwhile, had had other sees to fill besides St Davids. Few of his nominees made much of a mark, though Thomas Musgrave, who was whisked out of the deanery of Bristol in 1837 after only a few months there to become Bishop of Hereford, was later translated to York by Lord John Russell. Three of Melbourne's later appointments were to the same diocese, Sodor and Man (i.e. the Isle of Man). But then this was considered a poor see both in financial terms and because of its geographical remoteness, so it often became a stepping-stone to higher things. (There was a move to merge it with the diocese of Carlisle in the 1830s, but this fell through.) The third Manx nominee was Thomas Vowler Short, who before his consecration had been a tutor at Christ Church, Oxford, and who was a friend of many of the leaders of the Oxford Movement. One of these, Edward Bouverie Pusey, was a favourite pupil who always acknowledged his influence and held him in affection and respect. Pusey was less well disposed to another Melbourne nominee, Philip Shuttleworth, who, after much unsuccessful jockeying for a see, was eventually appointed Bishop of Chichester in 1840* but lived to enjoy his reward for only fifteen months. Shuttleworth, as Warden of New College, Oxford, had been a vigorous opponent of the Oxford Movement; and Pusey thought he saw in his early removal from the earthly scene a 'token of God's presence in the Church of England'.[13]

It was the shadow of Hampden which caused Melbourne to be cautious in his later episcopal appointments. It was that same

---

*Shuttleworth was a worldly don who invented a mahogany railway to carry decanters of port across the senior common-room of his college. 'I know little of him myself', Melbourne told Lord John Russell, 'and what I do know I do not like very much.'[12]

shadow which deterred him from offering a bishopric to Thomas Arnold, the famous Headmaster of Rugby, whose claim was a strong one. But Arnold, like Hampden, was a liberal in theology, and to have made him a bishop would have enraged the Tractarians and unleashed a fresh storm of controversy. 'What have Tory churchmen ever done for me', Melbourne once exclaimed, 'that I should make them a present of such a handle against my government?'*[14] So he played safe by and large, advancing mainly Whig sympathizers and moderate churchmen to the episcopate. Thirlwall was his riskiest choice – made, as we have seen, only after considerable agonizing: Keble complained about it in a letter to Newman. In the event most of his nominees played fair by him. Henry Pepys, for instance, always voted in the House of Lords in favour of the chief Liberal measures, though he only spoke twice – on ecclesiastical questions of small importance. Thomas Musgrave was a decided Liberal in politics, though without any admixture of party spirit. George Davys, who before his appointment to Peterborough acted as a tutor to the young Princess Victoria, took no active part either in ecclesiastical controversy or in politics.

Melbourne made no bones about his need for his bishops to be Whigs, and he was careful to probe a candidate's political sympathies as well as his pastoral and academic capabilities. A typical Melbourne enquiry was described thus by Charles Lushington (no doubt with his tongue in his cheek):

> 'Is he a good man?'
> 'An excellent man; he is a most accomplished theologian, an exemplary clergyman, and is truly beloved throughout his district . . .'
> 'Aye, aye, I understand all that; but is he a good man – is he a good Whig – will he vote for the Irish Corporation Bill?'[16]

But Melbourne could never rely absolutely on bishops appointed by him necessarily supporting him with their votes in the Lords. Irish church matters were a constant source of disagreement. He once complained to Charles Longley (at that time Bishop of Ripon): 'I am continually subjected to the reproach of having disposed more ecclesiastical patronage than any other minister within so short a period, and of having so arranged it, as neither to secure one steady personal friend, nor one firm supporter of

---

*Melbourne put his objections in a slightly different form when writing to the Bishop of Norwich, Edward Stanley (24 August 1840): 'I have a high opinion of Dr Arnold . . . but Dr Arnold has published some indiscreet opinions . . . and these opinions would, I own, render me unwilling to name him for a professorship of divinity, or any science connected with divinity, in the University of Oxford.'[15]

my own principles and opinions.'[17] On another occasion he remarked that he had always had much sympathy with Saul: 'He was bullied by the prophets just as I have been by the bishops, who would, if they could, have tied me to the horns of the altar and slain me incontinently.'[18]

But, amid all the slings and arrows of prime ministerial bishop-making, there was always one source of consolation – the opportunity to oblige one's friends. Lord John Russell, Melbourne's political colleague, had a half-brother in orders with the peculiar Christian name of Wriothesley. On two occasions, at Lord John's request, Melbourne nominated Lord Wriothesley Russell to a bishopric: Lichfield in 1839, Chichester in 1840. On each occasion Lord Wriothesley declined the offer ('Wrio is most dogged and determined in his *Nolo episcopari*,' said Melbourne); but it must have been gratifying to the Premier to have been in a position to have made it.* A little earlier he had thought of Lord Wriothesley in connection with the vacant deanery of Exeter:

> There is much application for it, and . . . writes in the greatest anxiety, saying that they want a man of the firmest character and the greatest abilities to cope with that devil of a bishop [Henry Phillpotts], who inspires more terror than ever Satan did. If it is in the gift of the Crown Wrio shall have it, and I wish you would write and tell him so. I think his aristocratic name and title will be of advantage to him in his contest with the Prince of Darkness, of whom, however, it must be said that he is a gentleman.[19]

**Nominations to bishoprics (under Queen Victoria) 9 (7 first appointments, 2 translations)**

*First appointments:*

(1) 1837: Thomas Musgrave to Hereford.
(2) 1838: James Bowstead to Sodor and Man.
(3) 1839: George Davys to Peterborough.
(4) 1840: Philip Nicholas Shuttleworth to Chichester.
(5) 1840: Henry Pepys to Sodor and Man.
(6) 1840: Connop Thirlwall to St Davids.
(7) 1841: Thomas Vowler Short to Sodor and Man.

*Translations:*

(1) 1840: James Bowstead to Lichfield (from Sodor and Man).
(2) 1841: Henry Pepys to Worcester (from Sodor and Man).

*'Wrio' never held a bishopric, or indeed any major ecclesiastical office. He never rose higher than rector of Chenies, Buckinghamshire, and canon of Windsor.

# 3

# A Man of Principle

*Sir Robert Peel: Prime Minister*
*6 September 1841 – 29 June 1846*

*Sir Robert Peel, 2nd Baronet (1788–1850), was the eldest son of a rich Lancashire cotton-manufacturer. He was educated at Harrow and Christ Church, Oxford, where he took a double first. He was elected a Tory MP in 1809 and soon became a minister. He was successively Under-Secretary for War and the Colonies, Chief Secretary for Ireland and Home Secretary under Lord Liverpool: as Home Secretary he launched the Metropolitan Police, whose members were soon nicknamed 'Peelers' or 'Bobbies'. Under Wellington he became Leader of the House of Commons. He was briefly Prime Minister in 1834–5, but his main premiership lasted from 1841 to 1846. His final year in office was overshadowed by fierce controversy over the repeal of the corn laws. His Corn Law Bill was eventually carried, but a few days later he was defeated on an Irish Bill and resigned. Peel was an able financier, effectively acting as his own Chancellor of the Exchequer, and a capable administrator who introduced many important domestic reforms. He was also noted for his intellectual honesty, and for his willingness to sacrifice his own interests and those of his party if he thought that they conflicted with what was necessary for the public welfare. The same tendency soon became apparent in his ecclesiastical appointments.*

Peel, who succeeded Melbourne as Prime Minister in September 1841, may have been poles apart from his predecessor politically, but the two men had at least one thing in common: their dislike of extremes in religion. Like Melbourne, Peel was a Broad Churchman who found himself out of sympathy both with Tractarians and with ultra-Evangelicals; and he too favoured moderates in the exercise of his ecclesiastical patronage.

Unlike Melbourne, Peel was no amateur theologian; but he was sustained by a genuine and sincere religious faith. An example of his faith was quoted in *The Times* a few years after his death. It was a prayer which had been sent to him by a Nonconformist minister during the Corn Law crisis of 1846, when Peel was under severe attack; and it was found among the personal possessions in his dressing-room. The Victorian public was quick to agree with *The Times* that Peel's retention of the prayer meant that he had found its words inspiring. In part the prayer read:

> Great and Merciful God, Ruler of all nations, help me daily to repair to Thee for wisdom and grace suitable to the high offices whereto Thy Providence has called me. Strengthen, O Lord, my natural powers and faculties, that the weighty and solemn interests with which Thy servant is charged may not greatly suffer through weariness of body and confusion of mind. Deign, I beseech Thee, to obviate or correct the ill-effects of such omissions or mistakes in my proceedings as may result from partial knowledge, infirmity of judgment, or unfaithfulness in any with whom I may have to do.[1]

But Peel was too reserved by nature to wear his heart on his sleeve. His faith, though sincere, was undogmatic. He had no use for extremes of churchmanship, either high or low, and so attracted the scorn or the apprehension of extremists. The Evangelical Lord Ashley, for instance, who was to achieve wider fame as the philanthropist Earl of Shaftesbury, mistook Peel's reserve for religious indifference. A few months before the start of his first brief premiership (12 July 1834) Ashley had written in his diary: 'Humanly speaking, I can see nothing worse than that Peel should be called to the helm of affairs.'[2] Seven years later (24 July 1841) his diary records the confirmation of his fears: 'His love of expediency, his perpetual egoistry, his dread of an immovable principle, his delight in the praise of men . . . a well-turned phrase of compliment and eulogy from John Russell or Macaulay will attract him more than "Hast thou considered my servant Job?"'[3] This was unfair. Peel was far from unprincipled, though his principles were those of the undogmatic, middle-of-the-road churchman – or 'central bigot', as a later age might have called him. So, to an enthusiast like Ashley, he might appear merely weak and woolly. In fact Peel had a great devotion to the Church of England as such, and took endless pains to promote its interests. During his first premiership in 1834–5 he had launched the Ecclesiastical Commission, the body which was to last for over a hundred years until its merger in 1948 with Queen Anne's Bounty to form the present-day Church Commissioners. He defined his government's aims in religious affairs in a letter he wrote in 1842 to John Wilson Croker,* a privy councillor to whom he used to turn for ecclesiastical advice: 'The sense of the Government should be in favour of that which is reasonable and just, in favour of the Church of England. Protestant principles as they have been understood for the last hundred years, the via media between Popery and Dissent.'[5]

But Peel's championship of the Established Church was never uncritical. To the Bishop of Exeter, Henry Phillpotts, he had written in 1834: 'All mere political considerations . . . are as nothing in my mind, compared with the great object of giving real stability to the Church in its spiritual character.'[6] He was only too well aware of the need for many more churches to be built in London and in the centres of industry in the Midlands and North. 'I do earnestly ask', he enquired in 1835 of the Bishop of Durham, William Van Mildert, 'whether it be fit that the great manu-facturing towns and districts of the country should be left, as to the means of spiritual instruction, in their present state.'[7] And he was quick to put theory into practice. His New Parishes Act of 1843 allowed the Ecclesiastical Commission to form, on the authority of an order in council, new parochial districts in heavily populated areas. Such districts were for long known as 'Peel parishes'. They received no direct government subsidy and were financed largely out of private enterprise. In 1843 Peel gave £4000 from his own pocket (four-fifths of his annual salary as PM) for building new churches in London and other centres of industry.†

Peel's handling of church patronage signalled a distinct change of tack from that of Melbourne. No longer would men be appointed to high ecclesiastical office mainly on grounds of political affiliation. Henceforward promotion was to be made unashamedly on merit. Perhaps not entirely so, for, where two potential candidates were of equal talents but opposite parties, Peel would

---

*Croker lived at Alverstoke, Hampshire, the parish of which Samuel Wilberforce, later Bishop of Oxford, was for long the incumbent. Wilberforce appeared to be in two minds about this particular parishioner. In 1838, when he suspected Croker of blocking his admission to the Athenaeum, he called him a 'clever dung-feeder'. But two years later, writing to his brother Robert, he remarked: 'I really think that I have never heard him make an unkind remark on any one. He is very attentive at Church.'[4]

†Peel's amazing generosity was the subject of a eulogistic paragraph in *The Standard* (11 October 1843). After noting that the Prime Minister had now given away his entire annual salary (£4000 for church building, £1000 to the Education Fund) the paper declared: 'We admire and respect Sir Robert Peel in all his relations, but in this instance we have real pride in presenting the Prime Minister of England to the nations of Europe.'[8]

choose the Tory. But, other things being equal, learning, pastoral zeal and professional ability were likely to gain promotion for a cleric rather than mere political usefulness. In a letter written in September 1845 Peel was able to assure the Archbishop of Canterbury: 'My desire is to place on the Bench the divines best entitled by professional character and merit to preferment.'[9] To an English dignitary who had asked for a substantial living in addition to his present post, Peel replied (5 April 1843): 'I do not consider patronage as the means of gratifying private wishes of my own. It would be a complete departure from the rule to which I have always adhered. All patronage of all descriptions, so far from being of the least advantage personally to a Minister, involves him in nothing but embarrassment.'[10] And when John Merewether,* the Tory Dean of Hereford, who had been promised a bishopric by the dying King William IV, reminded Peel of the royal pledge, he was told that the Prime Minister's principles precluded him from attaching weight to any considerations other than those of professional character.[11]

Admittedly Peel distrusted the Tractarians, so anyone flying unashamedly Tractarian colours could not expect preferment. But even here he was not completely above suspicion. In 1843 he had assured Ashley that he held Tractarianism 'in horror'; but, three years later, Ashley was wondering if that dislike was wholehearted. Peel 'disliked the forms but not the tenets', Ashley complained in 1846.[12] Certainly the Tractarians themselves regarded Peel as totally out of sympathy with their movement; and their then mouthpiece, the *British Critic*, castigated him in July 1841 as 'a nullity in any question in the least connected with religion'. His whole career, the paper alleged, had been 'one continual defalcation'; though it conceded his 'great weight in questions of malt, registration and sugar'. One applicant to Peel for a living took care to state: 'I am no Puseyite.'[13] But, though he never promoted an out-and-out Tractarian, Peel rarely made an anti-Tractarian appointment.† He had little use for the Tractarian leaders, however. He suggested that Newman would be better advised to go openly over to Rome rather than, in effect, to act as a snake in the Anglican grass. Newman took a mild revenge by

---

*It was this same Dean Merewether who was to address to Lord John Russell in 1847 an immensely long letter protesting against the choice of Renn Dickson Hampden as Bishop of Hereford: a letter which drew from Lord John a devastating 36-word reply. See Chapter 4.

†Peel told the Bishop of Lincoln, John Kaye, who was helping him to fill two ecclesiastical professorships at Oxford, that decided opponents of the Puseyites might add to the dissensions of the University.[14]

ridiculing Peel's ideas in letters to *The Times* appearing under the pseudonym 'Catholicus'.

The majority of Peel's appointments were 'safe, solid and dull',[14] though there were one or two exceptions to the rule, e.g. Samuel Wilberforce and William Buckland. But solidity did not necessarily rule out merit. John Lonsdale, for instance, who was appointed to Lichfield in 1843, is described in the *Dictionary of National Biography* as the 'perfect model of justice, kindness, humility and shrewd sense', even though his 'absorption in strictly ecclesiastical labours prevented his taking that leading part as a ruler of the Church at large for which he was qualified by his abilities, prudence and moderation'. The Archbishop of Canterbury assured Peel: 'In the opinion of all who know him a better appointment could not have been made'.*[15] In fact Lonsdale had accepted the nomination only after being assured that it had already received the *imprimatur* of the Archbishop himself and of the Bishop of London, Charles Blomfield, whom Peel had consulted. And it was in his willingness to consult the Archbishop as a matter of course when making a major ecclesiastical appointment that Peel differed from Melbourne, who had relied mainly for advice on unofficial Whig sources.

Blomfield was another confidant to whom Peel turned regularly. There was a real *rapport* between the two men; and the resemblance between them struck a contemporary so forcibly that he called Blomfield an 'ecclesiastical Peel'.[16] The Bishop had for long regarded Peel as the one man on whom the Church could ultimately rely. Peel had an equal respect for his friend; and indeed actually wrote to Blomfield in 1842 to offer him the archbishopric of Canterbury, which he erroneously believed was about to fall vacant.[17] He never hesitated to pour out his heart to Blomfield. When he was drawing up a short list in 1843 of 'eminent men' from among whom to select a new Bishop of Lichfield he told him that he would omit from the list 'Dr Pusey and other divines of his peculiar party in the Church'.[18]

On only one occasion was Peel suspected of having made a definitely party appointment. The nominee was Ashurst Gilbert, who was appointed Bishop of Chichester in 1842 in succession to the short-lived Shuttleworth (see previous chapter). Gilbert's claim to fame, or rather to the gratitude of the Prime Minister, was the key part he had played in the controversy surrounding

---

*Lonsdale was a scholar who was said, while still an undergradua᷃ᵗ Cambridge, to write the best Latin since the age of Augustus. 'In intellectual powers', says the *DNB*, he was 'inferior to no prelate of his time except Thirlwall.' Moreover, 'belonging to no party, he deserved and obtained the confidence of all.'

the election of a successor to John Keble as Professor of Poetry at Oxford. But in fact Gilbert had not been Peel's first choice for the vacant bishopric. The favoured candidate had been none other than Samuel Wilberforce,* at that time Archdeacon of Surrey and already *persona grata* to the Royal Family and one of Prince Albert's chaplains. The objection to Wilberforce was not his comparative youth (he was then only 36), but the conviction that he was too sympathetic to the Tractarians to warrant promotion to the Bench. At least such was the verdict of Wilberforce's diocesan, Charles Sumner, who had been asked by Peel 'what is the real state of Mr Wilberforce's opinions in matters connected with the theological differences at Oxford'. So he was passed over on this occasion. Peel wrote to Archbishop Howley: 'I am sorry for the impediment to the selection of Archdeacon Wilberforce – but I feel the force of the Bishop of Winchester's observations.' But this was considered by those in the know to be a merely temporary setback. At the start of Peel's premiership Wilberforce had received an assurance from his friend James Stephen that 'Sir R. Peel would *quam citissime* call me *episcopari*'. And Lady Lyttelton, who had heard him preach at Windsor in 1842, wrote that 'everybody says he will be a bishop'.[19]

But to return to the contest for the poetry chair at Oxford and the part played in it by Wilberforce's supplanter as Bishop of Chichester. The rival candidates were Isaac Williams, a minor poet who had himself written three of the *Tracts for the Times* and was thus identified with the Puseyites; and James Garbett,† a translator of classical verse and a literary critic. Williams was put forward by the Fellows of Trinity College and Garbett by those of Brasenose. The Principal of Brasenose was Ashurst Gilbert, who led the campaign in favour of Garbett. Intense passions were aroused both in the university and outside it. The contest soon ceased to concern itself with the poetical talents of the rival candidates and became an ecclesiastical dog-fight, with Tractarians and anti-Tractarians locked in verbal combat. Objective observers considered Williams the stronger candidate;

* Wilberforce was the third son of William Wilberforce, the philanthropist and advocate of the abolition of the Slave Trade. By this time he was a widower, his wife Emily having died in 1841 a month after giving birth to her sixth child (and four years after the death of her sister Caroline, wife of the future Cardinal Manning). Wilberforce's famous nickname of Soapy Sam was said by his enemies to derive from his oily nature and by himself from his ability always, when in hot water, to come out of it with clean hands.

† Garbett succeeded Manning as Archdeacon of Chichester on the latter's secession to Rome in 1851. He was an uncle of Cyril Forster Garbett (1875–1955), successively Bishop of Southwark and of Winchester and Archbishop of York.

PUNCH, OR THE LONDON CHARIVARI.—October 16, 1858.

## SOAPEY SAMUEL KISSES THE ROD.

*Samuel Wilberforce, eventually appointed Bishop of Oxford, attempts to live down his reputation for favouring the Tractarians.*

but a straw poll conducted before voting-day claimed that 921 votes had been promised to Garbett and only 623 to Williams – who withdrew his name a week before the election. Gilbert had his reward. His appointment to Chichester was announced in the papers the day following Williams' withdrawal. Peel assured his critics that he had selected Gilbert on merit, and not because of his connection with the poetry contest. The public may or may not have believed him. Certainly Peel could appreciate Gilbert's academic prowess. They had both been among the five undergraduates who, in 1808, had obtained firsts in classical Greats.*

Meanwhile Wilberforce continued to labour away as Archdeacon of Surrey – and to await the preferment that he felt was bound to come. Peel heard his praises sung on every side. His friend Croker wrote to him:

> Wilberforce is a charming man in society, a most excellent parish priest, one of the best preachers I ever heard, of competent scholarship, of a very deep yet cheerful piety, and very active and intelligent in temporal matters, and one who will, I doubt not, make a very good bishop. He has, I think, something of his father's restlessness, and seems, on the whole, to want a little of that *aplomb* and dignity which we see, for instance, in the Bishop of London. But these qualities would be no doubt developed by the episcopal character, and I should say, as far as my judgment goes, that you may safely, both as to Church and State and to your own reputation, make him a bishop when you will.[20]

That letter was written in February 1842, only a few weeks after Peel had considered, but rejected, the idea of making Wilberforce Bishop of Chichester. A year later he again thought of Wilberforce for what he hoped would be a vacant see, this time Oxford. His plan was to translate the sitting tenant, Richard Bagot, to Lichfield, vacant by the death of Bishop Bowstead. In the event Bagot declined to move; but in fact Peel had already decided against the archdeacon. 'I may have Wilberforce's name mentioned to me', he wrote to the Bishop of London (in a reference to the possibility of the Queen, who was pro-Wilberforce, putting his name forward); but 'I do not think his appointment to Oxford

---

*Gilbert soldiered on at Chichester for the next twenty-eight years, dying in the bishop's palace there in 1870 at the age of 83. Two years previously he had interdicted the Rev. John Purchas from conducting ritualistic services in St James's Chapel, Brighton, thereby initiating the long process of legal wrangling which culminated in the famous Purchas Judgement of 1871.

would be advisable.' Blomfield agreed, and told Peel he thought Wilberforce young enough to wait.[21]

The waiting period was not long. Wilberforce was already high in the royal favour and, as one of Prince Albert's chaplains, a frequent and popular preacher at both Claremont and Windsor. So it was not surprising that, when in 1845 the Dean of Westminster, Thomas Turton, was made Bishop of Ely,\* the Queen should favour Wilberforce's promotion to the vacant deanery. On this occasion she clashed with the Prime Minister, who would have preferred William Buckland, Professor of Geology at Oxford. Peel wrote to the Queen (22 March 1845): 'There would be public advantage in selecting for the Deanery of Westminster a divine of irreproachable life and sufficient theological attainments, and at the same time eminent as a man of science. It strengthens the Church to have such men occasionally selected for preferment.' After putting forward Buckland's name as his first choice† Peel hedged his bets by adding that, as Her Majesty might wish the deanery to be offered to Archdeacon Wilberforce, 'Sir Robert Peel would most cheerfully withdraw any other claims that might interfere with his.'[23] The Queen did so wish, as she told the Premier two days later: 'As Sir Robert has asked the Queen whether she would like to see Archdeacon Wilberforce succeed to the Deanery of Westminster . . . she must say that such an arrangement would be *very satisfactory* to us, and the Queen believes would highly please the Archdeacon.'[24]

So Wilberforce found himself one rung higher on the ladder of ecclesiastical preferment – and he had not long to wait before he found himself higher still. In September 1845 Bagot at last agreed to be translated – to Bath and Wells. He was by now only too eager to move. As Bishop of Oxford during the stormiest years of the Oxford Movement he had been forced, reluctantly, to play a part in its history. (He treated the Tractarians with marked courtesy, though he deplored the 'lamentable want of

---

\*Turton was a vigorous controversial writer well known for his taste in the fine arts and for his interest in church music. He was another bishop who soldiered on into extreme old age – though, the *DNB* discreetly remarks, 'for several years preceding his decease increasing infirmities precluded him from the active discharge of his episcopal functions'.

†Buckland succeeded Wilberforce as Dean of Westminster. Although dismissed by Ashley in his diary (17 November 1845) as a 'joking geologist who has hardly ever preached and whose language oftentimes borders on the profane', he was a colourful character who used to go around with a bag of bones and fossils and whose dining-room sported tanks of snakes. At Westminster he devoted his spare time to improving the local sanitary arrangements and to studying the diseases of the potato. He went mad after three years in the deanery.[22]

judgment' often exhibited in their writings.) He now needed a rest.* Peel put aside the hesitations he had felt two years ago and recommended Wilberforce to the Queen as Bagot's successor. 'My desire is to place on the Bench the divine best entitled by professional character and merit to preferment', he wrote to Archbishop Howley (26 September 1845). His offer of the diocese was received by Wilberforce on 14 October – and was at once accepted with the customary protestations of the candidate's unworthiness: 'I assure you that I feel most unfeignedly my own lack of qualification for such a post: yet I cannot, when so selected, for a moment doubt as to the duty of accepting it.'[25]

A less inhibited response to Peel's offer came in a letter Wilberforce wrote the same day to his friend Louisa Noel. After reporting the news of the offer and that 'Her Majesty had most cordially acquiesced in the suggestion', Wilberforce continued:

> Ah! dearest sister, when you and I have talked of such matters, how different has it looked from what it does now! I thought I knew my unworthiness of such a post; but now I see that I never felt it at all. My soul is penetrated with a thrilling sense of it. Yet you will understand how, without real inconsistency, I yet feel I could not decline the offer so made. I have written to accept it . . .[26]

To his diary Wilberforce confided the same night: 'I had wished for this, and now it comes it seems *awful*.'[27] But, whatever qualms he may have felt at the time of his appointment, he was to prove one of the ablest bishops of the century and to have fully justified any doubts *Peel* may have felt as to the wisdom of the choice.

Even the high-principled Peel was not entirely free from the taint of nepotism. Melbourne had twice endeavoured without success to appoint a colleague's half-brother to a vacant bishopric. Peel found himself in the embarrassing position of appointing his own brother to a vacant deanery. In fact the initiative in the matter came from the Queen herself. She wrote to Peel from Windsor on 12 June 1845:

> The Queen understands that the Deanery of Worcester has become vacant by some new arrangement. Believing that Sir

---

*Bagot's health had been ruined by what the *DNB* tactfully calls 'the excitement of the previous years'. Soon after leaving Oxford he suffered from a 'temporary mental derangement' (presumably a nervous breakdown); and his see was for a time administered by the Bishop of Gloucester and Bristol. By the time of his death in 1854, however, he had recovered sufficiently to be able to cross swords with one of his archdeacons, George Denison, the famous Tractarian controversialist.

Robert Peel's brother, Mr John Peel, has a fair claim to such preferment, but being afraid that Sir Robert would perhaps hesitate to recommend him on account of his near relationship to him, the Queen wishes to offer herself this Deanery, through Sir Robert, to his brother.[28]

The Prime Minister was also assured by the Archbishop of Canterbury that the Bishop of Worcester and members of the cathedral chapter were all hoping that the Prime Minister's brother would be their next dean. 'A similar feeling exists among the canons of Canterbury should there be a vacancy there', the Archbishop added.[29] Peel evidently felt that it would be unnecessarily high-minded to snub both Queen and Primate; so the offer of the deanery of Worcester was made to John Peel – and gratefully accepted.

**Nominations to bishoprics 5 (4 first appointments, 1 translation)**

*First appointments:*

(1) 1842: Ashurst Turner Gilbert to Chichester.
(2) 1843: John Lonsdale to Lichfield.
(3) 1845: Thomas Turton to Ely.
(4) 1845: Samuel Wilberforce to Oxford.

*Translation:*

(1) 1845: Richard Bagot to Bath and Wells (from Oxford).

# 4

# For Ever Hampden

*Lord John Russell: Prime Minister*
*6 July 1846 – 26 February 1852*

Lord John Russell, 1st Earl Russell (1792–1878), *was the third son of the sixth Duke of Bedford. He was educated at Westminster School and Edinburgh University and entered Parliament as a Whig. He served as Home Secretary and Colonial Secretary under Melbourne and, after Melbourne's defeat in 1841, led the opposition against Peel, whom he succeeded as Prime Minister in 1846. After his own defeat in 1852 he accepted a seat in Aberdeen's cabinet and later served as Colonial Secretary and then as Foreign Secretary under Palmerston. On the latter's death Lord John, who had been created Earl Russell in 1861, served a second brief premiership (6 November 1865–5 July 1866), but resigned after the failure of his Reform Bill. He was an obstinate but plucky man, full of self-confidence but lacking in subtlety.*

'My Lord, the Crown has no *right* to force a Bishop on the Church whom the Church has just right to reject as a "setter forth of erroneous and strange doctrines contrary to God's Word" . . . Forbear, my Lord, while you have yet time! Persist not in your rash experiment!'[1] The impassioned plea came from Henry Phillpotts, Bishop of Exeter. It was addressed to Lord John Russell, who had succeeded Peel as Prime Minister in the summer of 1846. Its occasion was Lord John's nomination of the Reverend Professor Renn Dickson Hampden to the bishopric of Hereford in the autumn of the following year: that same Hampden whose original elevation to the Regius chair of divinity at Oxford in 1836 had made life so uncomfortable for Melbourne. The nomination was to prove controversial beyond Lord John's wildest fears. The Archbishop of Canterbury had described it as potentially explosive even before it had been officially announced. It was to cause a furore throughout the Church of England – and to dash the prospects of Bishop Samuel Wilberforce's higher preferment for many years to come. And it taught Lord John –

like Melbourne before him – to be more cautious in his future nominations.

How did Lord John come to stir up such an ecclesiastical hornets' nest? Primarily through his strong desire to promote liberal and Protestant theologians, wherever possible, to the episcopate. According to his first biographer, Spencer Walpole, he acted throughout the Hampden affair on the highest motives and for what he honestly believed to be the good of the Church. But, like both his immediate predecessors, he distrusted the Tractarians as a divisive influence in the Church. When supporting the Manchester Bishopric Bill in Parliament in 1847, though he expressed a sincere desire to see the Church of England 'united in harmony and concord', he also trusted that the Church's Protestant character 'would be maintained by its bishops and its clergy for ever'.[2] He was himself a sincerely religious man. He was a regular communicant in the Church of England, though he had never been confirmed and regarded confirmation as an unnecessary barrier to receiving communion. He attended either parish churches or Dissenting chapels.* When making ecclesiastical appointments he might seek advice or receive it unsought, but would often disregard it.

In the Hampden case the omens were unpropitious. Lord John was only too well aware of the storm that had greeted Melbourne's nomination of Hampden in 1836. On that occasion the University had declared its lack of confidence in the new professor as a teacher of theology by absolving students from the duty of attending his lectures. An attempt six years later to persuade the University to rescind its decree of 1836 had been unsuccessful. Hampden was therefore very much *persona non grata* to the Church at large; and it would be a rash prime minister, or one supremely confident in the rightness of his own judgement, who would risk upsetting the ecclesiastical apple-cart by appointing to the Bench a cleric of such questionable orthodoxy. Lord John could certainly not pretend that he had not been warned. When he had initially thought of Hampden as a potential bishop it was the newly-founded see of Manchester that he had had in mind for him. He had sought the advice of Archbishop Howley on the nomination. The Primate had given Hampden only a qualified clearance. Nothing in his writings since his appointment as

---

* Or neither! His second wife records a remark he made to her one Sunday while they were sitting quietly at home: 'It conduces much to piety not to go to church sometimes.'[3] Russell's fervent Protestantism may have been a reaction to the Tractarian ceremonies introduced into his parish church at Knightsbridge by the Rev. W. J. E. Bennett.[4]

professor had appeared to him objectionable, he told Russell, but he had some doubts as to his judgement and discretion.

Then came a change of plan. On 5 November 1847 the death occurred of the ninety-one-year-old Archbishop of York, Vernon Harcourt.* Russell decided to translate one of Melbourne's bishops, Thomas Musgrave of Hereford, to the vacant see. 'It is of such consequence', he told Queen Victoria, 'to have an Archbishop of York who will, like the late Archbishop, avoid quarrels and crotchets, and live peaceably with all men.'[6] (He had in fact first sounded Maltby of Durham for the archbishopric, but Maltby had refused.) So he now had a second vacant see to fill; and he decided to offer Hampden Hereford rather than Manchester. When he announced his decision to Howley, however, the Primate, while raising no specific objection, warned him that the appointment would cause a great outcry. A fortnight after the offer had been made Howley wrote to Russell in much stronger terms:

> When I last saw your Lordship in Whitehall Place I observed that the promotion of Dr Hampden might probably cause some expression of feeling. *Explosion*, I think, was the term I used; but I had then no conception of the degree of excitement which it would occasion. From what has come to my knowledge I collect that a majority of the clergy of all degrees, whatever the difference may be on other points, concur in strong condemnation of this appointment . . . If I had anticipated so decided a movement I should have expressed my apprehensions in much stronger terms to your Lordship.[7]

Lord John replied to the Archbishop the following day (27 November). He expressed regret that the outcry over the appointment had been 'greater than you expected', but attributed it chiefly to the Tractarians: 'to that portion of the clergy who share Mr Newman's opinions but have not had the honesty to follow Mr Newman in his change of profession' (i.e. into the Church of Rome). He continued:

> I confess I am not surprised that such persons should dread to see a man on the Bench who will actively maintain Protestant doctrines. So long as a bishop is silent and winks at their attempts to give a Roman Catholic character to the Church of England they are not alarmed; but when they see a man

---

*A month after he had fallen into an ornamental pool in his garden at Bishopthorpe following the collapse of a wooden bridge over it. 'I think we've frightened the frogs', he observed to his chaplain – and went on to preside at a dinner party that evening.[5] He had served almost forty years as archbishop.

promoted who has learning to detect and energy to denounce their errors they begin to fear that confessions, and rosaries, and articles taken in a non-natural sense, and monkish legends of saints, will be discouraged and exposed.[8]

The Prime Minister, in other words, looked on Hampden not only as a liberal-minded theologian but as a Protestant scourge with which to chastise the Tractarian traitors in their midst. In response the Archbishop pointed out that those opposed to the appointment included many non-Tractarians, and that Hampden would therefore be well advised to make a public declaration of his firm belief in the doctrines of the Church.

The full force of the opposition now hit Lord John, in the shape of a public remonstrance from thirteen out of twenty-five bishops on the English Bench. Twelve out of the thirteen had been appointed by Tory prime ministers. They included Blomfield of London, Charles Sumner of Winchester, Phillpotts of Exeter and Wilberforce of Oxford. The Primate himself was not among the signatories; nor was Sumner's brother John, Bishop of Chester (who, two months later, was to succeed Howley as Archbishop). But it was a formidable opposition for the Premier to face; and such a public remonstrance against an episcopal nomination was quite without precedent. The letter read:

My Lord,
We, the undersigned Bishops of the Church of England, feel it our duty to represent to your Lordship, as head of Her Majesty's Government, the apprehension and alarm which have been excited in the minds of the clergy by the rumoured nomination to the See of Hereford of Dr Hampden, in the soundness of whose doctrines the University of Oxford has affirmed, by a solemn decree, its want of confidence. We are persuaded that your Lordship does not know how deep and general a feeling prevails on this subject; and we consider ourselves to be acting only in the discharge of our bounden duty both to the Crown and to the Church when we respectfully but earnestly express to your Lordship our conviction that, if this appointment be completed, there is the greatest danger both of the interruption of the peace of the Church and of the disturbance of the confidence which it is most desirable that the clergy and laity of the Church should feel in every exercise of the royal supremacy, especially as regards that very delicate and important particular, the nomination to vacant Sees.[9]

The thirteen signatories declared themselves to be Lord John's 'very obedient and faithful servants', but he was unimpressed.

The key sentence in his forceful reply to the remonstrants read as follows:

It appears to me that, should I withdraw my recommendation of Dr Hampden, which has been sanctioned by the Queen, I should virtually assent to the doctrine that a decree of the University of Oxford is a perpetual bar of exclusion against a clergyman of eminent learning and irreproachable life; and that, in fact, the supremacy which is now by law vested in the Crown is to be transferred to a majority of the members of one of our universities.[10]

The Prime Minister claimed (untruly) that 'many of the most prominent among that majority' had subsequently joined the Church of Rome. He added that he could not 'sacrifice the reputation of Dr Hampden, the rights of the Crown, and what I believe to be the true interests of the Church, to a feeling which I believe to be founded on misapprehension and fomented by prejudice'.

Two days after the dispatch of this letter Bishop Phillpotts of Exeter, who was said to have been the brain behind the episcopal remonstrance, addressed to Lord John the personal plea quoted at the beginning of this chapter. In the course of his letter he referred to the 'foul provision' of the statute of Henry VIII which gave the Crown the power to imprison any dean or chapter which declined to elect the Crown's nominee. The statute itself Phillpotts dismissed as the 'Magna Charta of Tyranny'. Queen Victoria was not amused when this was reported to her. She wrote to Russell: 'The Bishops behave extremely ill about Dr Hampden, and the Bishop of Exeter is gone so far, in the Queen's opinion, that he might be prosecuted for it, in calling the Act settling the supremacy on the Crown a *foul act* and *the Magna Charta of Tyranny*.'[11] *The Times* thought Lord John's shots had got home, but had its own reservations. 'His Lordship has floored the Bishops, it is true. But *cui bono*? Why floor them? What if he should have floored the Church of England and himself too?'[12]

The Queen was not Lord John's only ally. Bishop Maltby of Durham, who had only recently declined the Prime Minister's offer of the archbishopric of York, wrote to congratulate him on his 'sagacity as well as courage' in promoting Hampden. He had never found in any of the professor's writings 'the slightest ground for the attack, except that he had chosen for a subject one in which it would be difficult for the most careful writer to avoid stumbling upon some expression at which ignorance or bigotry could not but cavil'.[13] An unsuspected defender of the appointment was the ultra-zealous Lord Ashley, who was an unofficial (and self-appointed) adviser to the Prime Minister on ecclesiastical affairs. Ashley admitted in his diary entry for 13 December that Lord John had not in fact consulted him about this particular appointment, though he had asked Ashley subsequently what he thought about it. 'I replied, "I should not, had I been Prime Minister, have made the appointment myself; but, now that it is made, I venture to say that more good than evil will, I think, come out of it."' Hampden's nomination as Regius Professor had been 'infamous'; 'but during the last four or five years he has written and published very beautiful and orthodox discourses.'[14] So Hampden's earlier indiscretions were now forgiven!

A weightier reply to the remonstrance of the thirteen bishops took the form of a counter-petition in Hampden's favour signed by 250 members of the University. Among them was Archibald Campbell Tait, the future Archbishop of Canterbury. Although he had no liking for Hampden's 'frigid and somewhat shallow ʾnd uninspiring theology', he saw nothing very unorthodox in his opinions and thought that he had been unjustly abused. In a letter to his brother James, Tait conceded that Lord John would have done much better not to have appointed Hampden in the first place; but 'I am fully of the opinion that no case of heresy can be made out after the explanations in Hampden's subsequently published writings.'[15]

A key role in the controversy was played by Samuel Wilberforce. In addition to his chair of divinity Hampden also held the living of Ewelme, in the diocese of Oxford, and as an incumbent came under Wilberforce's episcopal jurisdiction. When the appointment to Hereford had first been announced the Bishop had been appalled. 'I deeply lament it', he told Prince Albert's secretary (16 November). 'I cannot conceive *what* was Dr Hampden's recommendation . . . Unless Lord John Russell wished for an opportunity of shocking the young confidence of the Church in him, I cannot conceive why he should have made it.'[16] But Wilberforce now found himself having to deal with the matter as Hampden's diocesan. He began by asking the Prime Minister to appoint a tribunal to weigh the 'specific charges of disqualifying unfitness' made against Hampden. By this time Russell had replied to the remonstrance of the thirteen bishops and was in no mood to brook further delay. 'It is obvious', he told Wilberforce, 'that this is a question which may lead to interminable controversy . . . So that Dr Hampden may be kept suspended between the cap and the mitre for years, to the infinite amusement of the idle crowd but to the detriment of the Church and of the Royal Supremacy'.[17] The request was refused.

Wilberforce's next move was to sanction a suit brought against

Hampden by three fellow-incumbents of the diocese under the Church Discipline Act of 1840. One of the two main grounds for suspecting Hampden's orthodoxy was the series of Bampton Lectures he had delivered in 1832. In the lectures he had attacked various theological words and phrases as a screen artificially interposed to separate later Christians from the simplicity of the early Church. The purpose of the lawsuit was to decide, in the provincial Court of Arches, whether the lectures were guilty of heresy. But soon Wilberforce began to have second thoughts about the wisdom of his action. He was assured by Provost Hawkins of Oriel that Hampden was ready to revise the lectures for any future reprint, removing any expressions which might be obscure or liable to misinterpretation. Moreover, said Hawkins, Hampden had told him that copies of his *Observations on Religious Dissent* – the second main ground against his orthodoxy – were now being sold without his permission. After re-reading the lectures at leisure Wilberforce told his friend Louisa Noel on 29 December that, though they contained 'a good deal that was disagreeable, a great deal that was obscure', they nevertheless included nothing heretical.[18] Since he did not consider the lectures heretical and the *Observations* had now been withdrawn, Wilberforce felt himself unable to authorize legal proceedings against Hampden and therefore withdrew his consent to the proposed reference to the Court of Arches.

His immediate reaction must have been one of relief. He had earlier told Miss Noel that the entire Hampden affair was '*very* painful' to him. 'It is so like hunting a man down that I am at times sick at heart, and feel I could do anything to show him how I hate persecuting him.'[19] Wilberforce went on to forecast, however, that his role in the affair would cost him the confidence of the Queen. He was only too right. His signing of the original remonstrance had offended her, and his later decision to withdraw his agreement to a prosecution failed to restore him to her good graces.* Moreover, to those in the Church at large who were unversed in the theological and legal subtleties that had brought about his change of heart, Wilberforce appeared in the unattractive light of an episcopal turncoat. Nor did his seeming vacillation help him towards higher preferment. When his second cousin John Bird Sumner succeeded Archbishop Howley at

---

*On hearing the news of Bishop Wilberforce's death in 1873 (from a fall from his horse) Queen Victoria wrote to Gladstone: 'The Queen admired and liked him *most before* he became a Bishop, and before he leant so much to those High Church views which did harm, and which are so great a misfortune to the Church.'[20] Prince Albert had told another prime minister, Lord Aberdeen, in 1855: 'He does everything for some object.'

Canterbury early in 1848 Wilberforce complained to Louisa Noel: 'I feel if it had not been for the Hampden controversy *I* should very probably have been put there . . . I have rather a sad feeling as if I had made a great mistake and thrown away a means of usefulness.'[21] It was many years before he received further preferment; and he was never to reach the top of the ecclesiastical ladder.

The scene now shifts to Hereford, whose dean and chapter had to obey the royal command to elect Professor Hampden as their new bishop or else face the consequences. The dean – that same John Merewether who had been promised a bishopric by William IV but had failed to persuade Peel to redeem the pledge – was firmly against the appointment of Hampden on the grounds of his allegedly heretical views. He bombarded Lord John with letters explaining his objections. He memorialized the Queen to no effect. A final desperate missive running to three thousand words or so and stuffed with the fruits of his historical researches brought the following tart rejoinder from the Prime Minister on Christmas Day:

> Sir,
> I have had the honour to receive your letter of the 22nd instant, in which you intimate to me your intention of violating the law.
> I have the honour to be your obedient servant,
> J. Russell.*[23]

Three days later, on the feast of the Holy Innocents, the election took place in Hereford Cathedral. Dean Merewether read a long prepared statement recording his dissent. One of the four canons residentiary also voted against Hampden. The other three canons residentiary and eleven prebendaries voted for him; the remaining dozen prebendaries failed to turn up. Hampden was declared elected, though the Dean, stubborn to the last, refused his traditional right to affix the chapter seal to the certificate of election.

But even that was not the end of the affair. The election had to be confirmed at a ceremony in St Mary-le-Bow, London, before Hampden could legally be declared Bishop of Hereford. A crowd of objectors turned up at the church, but their objections were

---

*No doubt he lived to regret his *jeu d'esprit*, which *The Manchester Guardian* said could 'only be characterised as worthy of himself'. The paper pontificated: 'Lord John Russell has within the last six weeks destroyed, with an unparalleled rapidity, all notions that may ever have been entertained of his fitness for the position of premier.'[22]

ruled out of order. They then applied to the Court of Queen's Bench for a *mandamus* compelling the Archbishop of Canterbury or his vicar-general to hear the objections. The case was fully argued in court. In the end the four judges were equally divided, so the *mandamus* was refused. Any last hope that Howley might refuse to consecrate Hampden was dissipated with the death of the Archbishop on 11 February, the day before his eighty-third birthday. His successor, Sumner of Chester, who had refused to sign the remonstrance against Hampden, consecrated him on 26 March in the chapel of Lambeth Palace. Sumner was assisted by three 'Whig' bishops: Llandaff, Norwich and Worcester.

Hampden's subsequent career was an ecclesiastical non-event. He laboured blamelessly in his rural diocese for the next twenty years, but never again hit the headlines. Nor did he cause any more disturbance to anyone by allegedly heretical utterances.*

The Hampden case is of crucial importance in any consideration of the role of the prime minister in the process of bishop-making. The furore may seem now to have been out of all proportion to the issues involved, but it seemed real enough at the time; and it curiously foreshadowed (even to the actual see involved) Lloyd George's nomination of Hensley Henson seventy years later – and, in modern times, Margaret Thatcher's choice of David Jenkins as Bishop of Durham. Certainly it caused the first serious rumblings against the system of Crown appointments. Gladstone, in a letter to Bishop Blomfield (31 January 1848), advocated a 'substantial check' being placed on the prime minister's power to create bishops on his own initiative; and Archdeacon Robert Wilberforce suggested to his brother, Bishop Samuel, that, failing a reform of the present system, the sooner they 'cut the cord' (i.e. left the Church) the better.[24] The Archdeacon later followed his own advice by joining the Church of Rome.

One would have supposed that, after the uproar caused over Hampden, Lord John would have played for safety in his future appointments. But, though he never again blotted his copy-book to quite the same extent, he still managed to offend influential sections of church opinion by his choice of new bishops. Nine out of ten of his episcopal nominations were of Low or Broad

---

*In the course of a brief but catty obituary notice the *Church Times* (2 May 1868) observed: 'Dr Hampden did only one thing after his promotion . . . he remembered the Apostolic saying that the man who fails to provide for his own household is worse than an infidel, and consequently he bestowed the best living in his diocese on a gentleman unknown save as his son.'

Churchmen.* Wilberforce complained to Gladstone (26 December 1851) about Russell's 'miserable appointments' and of the 'weakening of the bishops' just influence by the introduction of such men as Lord John has put amongst us'.[25] On the other hand Ashley (who had succeeded his father in 1851 as Earl of Shaftesbury) waxed lyrical. When Lord John resigned in 1852 he wrote to thank him for 'many excellent and invaluable appointments in Church matters. No Prime Minister has ever surpassed you; nay, I do not believe, has equalled you. There may have been an exception or so, but I speak of the mass of your nominations. May the recollection of them be a comfort to you in after-life, as the fact will be honourable to your name!'[26]

Shaftesbury was lucky to be able to approve so many of Russell's appointments because his advice, though freely proffered, was not always taken. Indeed he had complained to the Prime Minister on 2 November 1849: 'Dear Russell, It is quite manifest that you hold my opinions, ecclesiastical and religious, in supreme contempt . . . Nevertheless, you have always been so kind and good-humoured in allowing me to state what I think.'[27] In fact Russell tended to go his own way when choosing bishops and not to take advice from anyone, even the Archbishop of Canterbury, on a systematic basis. Perhaps his closest confidant was the Prince Consort – whose wife, after all, was nominally responsible for the appointments. And it was the Prince who encouraged him to appoint so many men of learning both to the Bench and to cathedral posts. But of course they were always Broad or Low Churchmen, never (or hardly ever) remotely High. Here at least Russell and Shaftesbury found themselves at one: in their detestation of the Tractarian influence in the Church of England. No Puseyite could hope for promotion under Russell, any more than he could have hoped for it under Melbourne or Peel.

Lord John showed his true colours in the famous letter he addressed to the Bishop of Durham on the 'Papal aggression' of 1850: the Bull of Pope Pius IX dividing England into twelve sees and appointing Nicholas Wiseman as Cardinal Archbishop of Westminster. The letter was bad enough in its contemptuous dismissal of the Roman Catholics for their 'mummeries of

---

*The exception was Thomas Vowler Short, who was sympathetic to the Oxford Movement and the friend of Pusey and other Tractarian leaders. Short was translated from Sodor and Man to St Asaph in 1846, following the discovery of a flaw in the Act of Parliament which would have united the Welsh see to that of Bangor.

superstition'. But it was equally offensive to the Tractarians by
its cavalier reference to

> clergymen of our own Church who . . . have been most forward
> in leading their flocks 'step by step to the very verge of the
> precipice'. The honour paid to saints, the superstitious use of
> the sign of the cross, the muttering of the liturgy so as to
> disguise the language in which it is written, the recommendation
> of auricular confession, and the administration of penance and
> absolution – all these things are pointed out by clergymen of
> the Church of England as worthy of adoption . . . What then is
> the danger to be apprehended from a foreign prince of no great
> power compared to the danger within the gates from the
> unworthy sons of the Church of England herself?[28]

By far the most significant vacancy Lord John found himself
having to fill was the archbishopric of Canterbury itself. As we
have seen, the aged Howley had died in February 1848, a few
weeks before he would have had to decide whether or not to
consecrate Hampden. Russell's field of choice was circumscribed,
in that thirteen bishops were ruled out automatically as having
signed the remonstrance against Hampden. They included a
number of the most influential figures on the Bench. Of those
who had *not* signed some were too ancient and others too modern.
After canvassing two or three names, including Lonsdale of
Lichfield and Pepys of Worcester, the Prime Minister's choice
eventually fell on Sumner of Chester.

Apart from his reluctance to condemn Hampden, the great
thing about John Bird Sumner (and the quality above all to
recommend him to Lord John) was his fervent Protestantism.
The son of a country parson, he had come, while an undergraduate at King's College, Cambridge, under the influence of
Charles Simeon, who helped to harden him in the Evangelical
mould. He hated Tractarianism and denounced it as 'the work of
Satan'. He had been the first bishop to condemn the Oxford
tracts. He told his clergy that the movement was undermining
the foundations of the Church of England; and he stigmatized 'the
bad faith of those who sit in the Reformers' seat and traduce the
Reformation'.[29] It was hardly surprising that he should have been
*persona gratissima* to both the Queen and Prince Albert, who
pressed his claims on the Prime Minister. Lord John must have
felt that he had backed the right horse when, in 1850, Sumner
personally instituted the Rev. G. C. Gorham to the rectory of
Bramford Speke, in the diocese of Exeter, after the diocesan,

Henry Phillpotts, had declined to do so on the grounds of Gorham's allegedly heretical views on baptismal regeneration.*

Sumner's fourteen-year reign at Lambeth was characterized by a general indecisiveness. He may have pleased the man in the pew by ambling around with an umbrella under his arm, but he was despised by many High Churchmen as weak and woolly. Sidney Dark called him a 'virulent Protestant'; but his Protestantism was less obtrusive at Lambeth than it had been at Chester. 'What is to be done with such a Primate in many ways so mischievously good?'[30] enquired Samuel Wilberforce of Gladstone in 1851. 'Kindly and popular but generally ineffective' was the general verdict on Sumner as Archbishop. How much more exciting would things have been had Wilberforce not ruled himself out of court by his ambivalent role in the Hampden affair!

Even after Hampden, theological liberals were still nominated to the Bench. In 1849 Russell appointed Samuel Hinds† as Bishop of Norwich. The following year he complained to a friend: 'The man I have heard most against next to Hampden is Hinds. The Bishop of Oxford did all he could to raise a storm against him. This is the way in which bigots try to prevent liberal men from rising in the Church.'[31] But Hinds was not in the same league as Hampden theologically speaking, and there was never any serious risk of his being unseated. The Russell bishops were mostly 'remarkable for the depth of their learning while all of them were distinguished for the breadth of their views', remarks his first biographer approvingly.[32]

Tractarian eyebrows would certainly have been raised at such a tribute being paid to at least one Russell nominee: James Prince Lee, first Bishop of the newly-created see of Manchester.‡ Before

---

*Gorham took proceedings against Phillpotts in the Court of Arches, but lost his case. He then appealed to the Judicial Committee of the Privy Council, who declared in his favour. The case aroused intense passions and led to the secession to Rome of, among others, Henry Manning and Robert Wilberforce, brother of the Bishop of Oxford.

†Hinds was of West Indian ancestry, having been born in Barbados and connected in early life as a missionary with the Society for the Conversion of Negroes. He was for some time Principal of Codrington College, Barbados, and later a domestic chaplain to Archbishop Whately of Dublin – who vainly pressed his claims on Russell for the succession to Hampden as Regius Professor of Divinity at Oxford.

‡Lee's episcopate had got off to an unfortunate start. When his appointment was announced charges were made against his private character by a Birmingham surgeon, Thomas Gutteridge, who accused him of corruption and drunkenness during his headmastership. In a pamphlet Gutteridge claimed that Lee would drink two or three bottles at a sitting and then make himself quickly sober by wrapping wet towels round his head.[33] Lee successfully sued Gutteridge for libel.

his consecration Lee had been Headmaster of King Edward's School, Birmingham, among his pupils being three future eminent Victorian prelates: E. W. Benson, J. B. Lightfoot and B. F. Westcott. But he seems to have brought a whiff of the schoolroom with him into the episcopal study; and even the *Dictionary of National Biography* allows that he was 'thought, not without justice, to be despotic and to pursue pedagogic methods'. Let the last, admittedly biased, word lie with the *Church Times*, which had been founded in 1863 to propagate the ideals of the Oxford Movement. In a leader (28 October 1865) on Russell's likely succession as premier to the late Lord Palmerston, the paper took the opportunity of a hefty side-swipe at the unfortunate Lee, now in his eighteenth year as Bishop of Manchester:

> We imagine that it would be difficult to explain why Dr Lee became a Bishop, except that Lord Russell so willed it . . . He had had little or no experience in the work of the ministry, he was destitute of all but the shallowest smattering of theological learning, and he was not conspicuous for personal piety; but he was a classical scholar, and a *protégé* of Lord Russell's, and he became Bishop of Manchester. It was a stroke of good fortune for Dr Lee, but it was a positive calamity for the Church.

**Nominations to bishoprics 10 (7 first appointments, 3 translations)**

*First appointments:*

(1) 1846: Walter Augustus Shirley to Sodor and Man.
(2) 1847: Robert John Eden to Sodor and Man.
(3) 1847: James Prince Lee to Manchester.
(4) 1847: Renn Dickson Hampden to Hereford.
(5) 1848: John Graham to Chester.
(6) 1849: Samuel Hinds to Norwich.
(7) 1849: Alfred Ollivant to Llandaff.

*Translations:*

(1) 1846: Thomas Vowler Short to St Asaph (from Sodor and Man).
(2) 1847: Thomas Musgrave to York (from Hereford).
(3) 1848: John Bird Sumner to Canterbury (from Chester).

# 5

# The Sin of Sarum

*Earl of Aberdeen: Prime Minister*
*28 December 1852 – 1 February 1855*

*George Hamilton Gordon, 4th Earl of Aberdeen (1784–1860), was educated at Harrow and St John's College, Cambridge, succeeding to the earldom in 1801. After serving as ambassador at Vienna he entered political life as a Tory, holding cabinet office under both Wellington and Peel. He was Foreign Secretary from 1841 to 1846, but resigned with Peel. He was in opposition for the next six years, succeeding the Earl of Derby as Prime Minister in 1852. But his coalition ministry of Whigs and followers of Peel declined in popularity owing to its mismanagement of the Crimean War, and he resigned after a successful Commons vote of censure against his government. Aberdeen was notably fair-minded in his dealings with the Church of England. His premiership saw the revival of the Convocation of Canterbury (a provincial assembly of the clergy), dormant since 1717.*

Lord Aberdeen is among the least known of Queen Victoria's prime ministers. During a premiership of little more than two years he nominated only four bishops. But one of these four appointments was significant in that the Queen, after formally approving it, had second thoughts about the suitability of the nominee – by when it was too late to do anything about it. The episode taught the Queen to be more cautious in future, and not to accept her prime minister's nominations without probing extensively into the names put forward. Henceforward her role in the bishop-making process was no longer to be that of a royal rubber-stamp. Premiers after Aberdeen often had to engage in prolonged tussles with the Queen before they got their way; and in quite a few cases they failed to get it.

The Queen herself was fully aware of her constitutional position in relation to the Church (though on one occasion she had to be corrected by Disraeli for describing herself as its 'head' rather than as its 'supreme governor'). And it was through the part she played in the appointment of its leading officials, and particularly of its bishops, that she was able to exercise a real influence on its fortunes. Among her published letters are many which show the extent of that influence and of her intimate knowledge of the individuals concerned. She was personally acquainted with many leading ecclesiastics. And in two notable Deans of Windsor – Gerald Wellesley (1854–82)* and Randall Davidson (1883–91) – she had confidential advisers whose business it was to keep her fully informed on church matters and who, when a potential bishop's name came up, could brief her on the candidate's suitability for the post. So the Queen could prove a formidable opponent if her judgement on a bishop-designate happened to clash with the prime minister's.

Where her own religious views were concerned the Queen was a strong Protestant – and fully conscious of her coronation oath to 'maintain the Protestant Reformed Religion established by law'. She was thus firmly opposed to the Tractarians and all they stood for, as of course to the Roman Catholic Church itself. 'The Govt and many people in this country', she complained to Lord Granville, 'seem to the Queen to be totally blind to the alarming encroachments & increases of the R. Catholics in England & indeed all over the world. The Pope was never so powerful & the Queen is quite determined to do *all* in her power to prevent this.'[1] She also strongly approved of the Broad Church position, which she once described to Gladstone as 'the only true, enlightened, Christian and intellectual view of religion which exists'.[2] Spiritually she seems to have been most at home when attending services of the (Presbyterian) Church of Scotland. This gave great offence to Tractarians and led to the frequent gibe that Her Majesty changed her religion north of the Border.† No doubt Lord Aberdeen, as a Presbyterian, would have had a particular attraction for her for that very reason.

In fact Aberdeen was no ultra-Protestant bigot. He was conspicuously fair in his ecclesiastical appointments – so much so that the narrowly Evangelical journal, *The Record*, once

---

* Wellesley, a nephew of the Duke of Wellington, turned down Aberdeen's offer of the see of Bath and Wells in 1854, shortly before accepting the deanery.

† A typical comment in the *Church Times* (16 November 1877) read: 'The painful fact that "the Supreme Governor" of the Church of England is becoming an alien from its faith and discipline has received another confirmation. We read in the *Glasgow Herald* that on Sunday week the Queen and Princess Beatrice communicated at Crathie parish church. The Princess of Wales was also present, but we are glad to say that her Royal Highness would have nothing to do with the business.'

stigmatized him as a 'popishly-inclined-puseyite-presbyterian'.[3] Today he would be lauded as an ecumenist, if not an ecumaniac. Certainly the Tractarians had nothing to fear under his premiership. The High Church Gladstone declared on more than one occasion that he would never have consented to serve in Aberdeen's government if he had not thought that the interests of the Church of England would be as safe in the hands of the Presbyterian Aberdeen as they had been under his short-lived predecessor as premier, the Anglican Derby.[4] Some High Churchmen disliked the whole idea of a coalition of High Church Peelites such as Gladstone with Erastian Whigs, and others could never stomach a Presbyterian being responsible for Anglican appointments. On the whole, though, the High Church element in the Church of England approved of Aberdeen's fairmindedness and looked back on his premiership as a brief golden age for the Church. 'For Church matters how dark a prospect!', Samuel Wilberforce wrote in his diary on hearing of Aberdeen's defeat in 1855. 'The only Government which could or was minded to be fair to the Church overthrown, because six miles of road not made from Balaclava to Sebastopol.'[5]

Aberdeen's general attitude to ecclesiastical appointments was summed up in a letter he wrote to Queen Victoria on the subject in reply to a complaint from the Queen. She had discovered – too late – that a candidate whose nomination to a bishopric she had approved* was credited with 'extremely High Church' views. Aberdeen explained:

In all matters connected with the Episcopal Bench, Your Majesty will never receive from him [i.e. the writer] recommendations of any but such as he is satisfied possess true moderation of character and opinions. Provided these qualifications exist, Lord Aberdeen is indifferent to what party in the Church such persons may incline. He thinks it would be unwise and unjust to exclude good men in consequence of a tendency either to High Church or Low Church; although he would at once equally reject those holding High Church doctrines which lead towards Popery and Low Church opinions tending to fanaticism, and to bring the Church of England into contempt.[6]

Aberdeen might pay lip-service to the Queen's anti-Tractarian prejudices, but his essential fair-mindedness was never far below the surface. His choice of the moderate John Jackson as Bishop of

---

*W. K. Hamilton. See below.

Lincoln was widely approved, even the Highish Samuel Wilberforce thinking it 'quite a respectable appointment'.[7] And when he translated Lord Auckland, the former Robert Eden, from Sodor and Man to Bath and Wells in 1854, he stipulated that the bishop-designate should 'neither persecute Mr Bennett nor prosecute Archdeacon Denison'.[8] Both W. J. E. Bennett and G. A. Denison were Tractarians. Bennett had fallen foul of the authorities for his ritualistic practices while a parish priest in London. Denison had crossed swords with the previous Bishop of Bath and Wells, Bagot, and there was now a temporary lull in the litigation: Aberdeen had no desire to see it renewed.

The particular appointment which so annoyed the Queen was jocularly referred to by Gladstone as the 'sin of Sarum'.[9] The see in question was Salisbury ('Sarum' being its Latin name). The successful candidate was Walter Kerr Hamilton, who had at one time been a private pupil of Thomas Arnold. While at Oxford he had come under the influence of the Tractarians, and he continued a High Churchman to the end of his life. In 1841 he had been appointed to a residentiary canonry of Salisbury Cathedral and for the next thirteen years ministered there with marked success, becoming a close friend of the bishop, Edward Denison. And it was Hamilton whom, in a letter dictated from his deathbed, Denison recommended to Aberdeen as his successor.

At first the Prime Minister demurred. Instead he offered the see to John James Blunt, a scholar of vast erudition who currently held the Lady Margaret chair of divinity at Cambridge. But Blunt turned the offer down, on the ground that, at close on sixty, he was too old for the job; so Aberdeen offered it to Hamilton instead. He did so with some reluctance, because he was aware of Hamilton's Tractarian sympathies. But Gladstone pressed Hamilton's claims – and indeed was equally assiduous in pressing Hamilton to accept the offer after the canon had dithered in an agony of indecision in case his High Church views might cause offence in the diocese. In the end he agreed; the offer of the see was formally made and accepted; and it was at *this* stage that the Queen at last became aware that a potential Tractarian snake was being infiltrated into the pure Anglican grass of Salisbury. In an anguished outcry to Aberdeen she complained that, much to her distress, she was hearing 'from *all sides* that he [Hamilton] is considered extremely High Church in his views'.[10] But she had missed this particular boat, though the episode taught her to be more careful in future. The full extent of her refusal to take names on trust, especially from the High Church Gladstone, is revealed in fascinating detail in letters of the period – and also in one of the great Victorian diaries: that kept by Hamilton's son Edward, who served as one of Gladstone's private secretaries during his second premiership of 1880–5. We shall hear more of these tussles with royalty as we come to consider the Queen's relations with future prime ministers.

**Nominations to bishoprics 4 (3 first appointments, 1 translation)**

*First appointments:*

   (1) 1853: John Jackson to Lincoln.
   (2) 1854: Walter Kerr Hamilton to Salisbury.
   (3) 1854: Horatio Powys to Sodor and Man.

*Translation:*

   (1) 1854: Robert John Eden, Lord Auckland, to Bath and Wells (from Sodor and Man).

# 6

# His Master's Voice

*Viscount Palmerston: Prime Minister*
*10 February 1855 – 20 February 1858*
*18 June 1859 – 18 October 1865*

Henry John Temple, 3rd Viscount Palmerston (1784–1865), *was educated at Harrow and St John's College, Cambridge. He succeeded in 1802 to his Irish peerage and five years later entered the House of Commons. Between 1809 and 1828 he served as Secretary for War under various Tory prime ministers, and later (having by now joined the Whigs) as Foreign Secretary under Grey and Melbourne. He went into opposition during Peel's second premiership (1841–6), but resumed office as Foreign Secretary under Lord John Russell. He served as Home Secretary in Aberdeen's coalition government, and replaced Aberdeen as Premier following his chief's mismanagement of the Crimean War. Apart from a sixteen-month interlude in 1858–9 he remained as Prime Minister till his death in 1865. Palmerston's cheerful common-sense and firm handling of international issues endeared him to the electorate and ensured his personal popularity. He knew little about ecclesiastical affairs and relied for advice mainly on his friend Lord Shaftesbury. As a result there was a pronounced Evangelical bias among his church appointments.*

Palmerston's bishop-making differed from that of his predecessors in that it was done largely, as it were, by proxy. Previous prime ministers had usually taken advice before choosing a candidate, even if they had often disregarded it. Palmerston had one supreme adviser, Shaftesbury, to whose views he almost invariably deferred, so that before long Shaftesbury came to be known as 'the bishop-maker' and to find himself in an unrivalled position as an ecclesiastical *éminence grise*. Loose ties of kinship helped to establish him in that position. He was a stepson-in-law of the Prime Minister, his wife being the daughter of Palmerston's wife by her first marriage. The two men were thus linked by ties closer than those of ordinary friendship; and, as Palmerston knew little and Shaftesbury a great deal about church matters, it is hardly surprising that the latter's influence in the field of ecclesiastical appointments came to be equally great.

If we are to believe Shaftesbury, Palmerston's ignorance of religious matters was profound. Writing to his son Evelyn, Palmerston's future biographer, a fortnight after the start of his premiership, Shaftesbury voices the fear that the new prime minister's ecclesiastical appointments will be 'detestable' and that, in theology, 'he does not know Moses from Sydney Smith':

> The vicar of Romsey, where he goes to church, is the only clergyman he ever spoke to; and, as for the wants, the feelings, the views, the hopes and fears, of the country, and particularly the religious part of it, they are as strange to him as the interior of Japan. Why, it was only a short time ago that he heard, for the first time, of the grand heresy of Puseyites and Tractarians![1]

Palmerston may not have been quite as ignorant as Shaftesbury made out, but he certainly tended to oversimplify the party divisions in the Church of England. Thus, in a letter to his cabinet colleague Sir Charles Wood (20 November 1856), he claimed that two-thirds of the population of England and Wales were Churchmen and one-third Dissenters (presumably including Roman Catholics); and that the Churchmen were themselves split into two factions, High and Low:

> The High Church are few in numbers and are found chiefly in the higher classes; the different degrees of Low Church, or at least of those who are against the High Church, are numerous among the higher classes, and one may say universal among the middle and lower classes of Churchmen. The dignitaries of the Church who are of the High Church Party are verging towards Papacy, and are in constant antagonism with their Low Church brethren and with all the Dissenters. The dignitaries who are of the Low Church School are more forbearing towards their High Church brethren and are at peace with the Dissenters.[2]

This crude classification of Anglicans as either Low Church goodies or High Church baddies may have been imbibed at second-hand from Shaftesbury; but it helps to explain why Palmerston was perfectly happy to endorse the nomination of so many Evangelicals to the episcopate. Not that Shaftesbury imagined to begin with that Palmerston would take his advice. On 6 February 1855, while Palmerston was still in the process of forming his government, he poured scorn on the idea in an entry in his diary:

> People will begin to expect that Palmerston's Church nominations will differ much from Aberdeen's, being influenced by my opinion. There could not be a greater error. He has never in his life, and never will, so long as he has breath, consult me on anything. It is not very likely that he will consult anybody; but, if he do, it will not be one connected with the Evangelical party.[3]

In fact Shaftesbury was being far too modest about his powers of persuasion. Almost from the start he found himself the Prime Minister's chief confidant on church appointments. 'I had rather take your advice than that of all the bishops put together', he records Palmerston as having said to him on one occasion.[4]

Before considering the lines along which Shaftesbury exercised his quasi-prime ministerial patronage, we must allow Palmerston to say a few words on his own behalf. In a letter he wrote to the Earl of Carlisle, then Lord-Lieutenant of Ireland (17 August 1862), he observed that he had never considered ecclesiastical appointments as patronage to be given away for grace and favour, or for personal or political objects. 'The choice to be made of persons to fill dignities in the Church must have a great influence on many important matters; and I have always endeavoured, in making such appointments, to choose the best man I could find, without any regard to the wishes of those who may have recommended candidates for choice.'[5] This emphasis on 'goodness' is brought out by Shaftesbury in an appendix he contributed to his son Evelyn's life of Palmerston, published in 1876. '"If the man is a good man", he often said, "I don't care what his political opinions are. Certainly I had rather not name a bishop who would make party speeches and attacks on the Government in the House of Lords; but, short of that, let him do as he likes."' Shaftesbury goes on to quote a further remark Palmerston had made to him about his luck in having no sons, grandsons or nephews to 'stuff into the Church'. 'So far as all *that* is concerned, I can do what I think right.'[6]

So much for Palmerston's own views on his appointments. But what of Shaftesbury's? In a series of entries in his diary soon after Palmerston's death he lays down the broad guidelines which governed his, or rather the Premier's, appointments. He stresses Palmerston's anxiety that his bishops should be 'good men, active, zealous, and sound members of the Church of England'. In the matter of church appointments, he claims,

Palmerston was conspicuous for 'justice, propriety, impartiality, and freedom from merely political views'. But, in putting forward candidates for Palmerston's approval, Shaftesbury adds that he always took into account the Prime Minister's position as a public man and the peculiar difficulties with which he had to contend. He therefore proposed only those names which Palmerston and he could both defend, not those 'which could be defended by myself alone'.

Shaftesbury's anti-Roman prejudices soon make their appearance in his retrospective apologia. Palmerston, he claims,

> regarded any approximation to Popery, Popish doctrines, and Popish practices, with special dislike and even fear. From the commencement I obtained his full assent that, on all occasions, men should be selected who would be moderate and decent in their language towards Nonconformists, and civil in their personal intercourse with them. He felt, as I did, the folly, nay the iniquity, of haughty sacerdotal bearing, of vituperative epithets, of clerical despotism, towards the body of Dissenters; he saw too, and resolved if he could to obviate, the danger of such an ecclesiastical arrogance.[7]

In other words, when Palmerston and Shaftesbury spoke of the desirability of making 'good men' bishops, they really had their eye on men who would be nice to Nonconformists.

But Shaftesbury was not only against High Churchmen: he was equally suspicious of Broad Churchmen. Believing as he did in the infallibility of Scripture, he deplored Rationalist endeavours to bring the Bible down to the level of any other book. 'How', he asked in a letter to the Duchess of Argyll, 'does it differ from the Koran?'[8] Rationalist attempts to take account of modern trends in scholarship and strip the Bible of divine inspiration ended up by stripping Christ of his divinity and man of his hope. A God limited in power was all but an absurdity in Shaftesbury's eyes.

From distrust of a particular class of learned men it was an easy step to distrust of learned men as such – at least where promotion to the Bench of Bishops was concerned. Professors, tutors and college dons were not in Shaftesbury's opinion men fitted for episcopal duty: 'The knowledge of mankind and experience of parochial life are not acquired in musty libraries and easy-chairs.' Practical divinity was one thing, speculative divinity another; 'and the accomplishments that make an active and useful bishop are purchased at the cost of that learning which would make him a theological champion, armed at all points and ready on all occasions.'[9] So, Shaftesbury wrote to

Palmerston late in 1856, candidates for bishoprics need not be concerned with 'profound and minute research, detailed scholarship and the power of keeping pace with the theological literature of the times'; nor need they occupy themselves with current heresies and theological problems in the manner of German professors. The Shaftesbury-type bishop would have acquired a knowledge of all that was 'primarily necessary' before he was thirty. He would be a man of activity and experience of parochial life who could live on friendly terms with his clergy and concern himself with the spiritual and temporal interests of the working classes. Such active but unacademic paragons would, Shaftesbury assured Palmerston, 'rivet the Church in the affections of the people, secure the Establishment, and promote true and sound religion'.[10]

The only clerics whom Shaftesbury would allow to dwell in ivory towers of academic theology were cathedral deans. It was they, but definitely *not* bishops, who might 'read and write without interruption, eat deservedly of the bread of the Church, and defend her and the truth against all Assailants'.[11] This was the theory behind Shaftesbury's bishop-making. In practice it was to work out rather differently as far as the emphasis on non-academics was concerned. The Shaftesbury–Palmerston bishops included two ex-headmasters, three Oxbridge college heads and three professors of divinity. It is to be presumed that not all these gentlemen had closed their minds to further theological knowledge before they were thirty.

Shaftesbury may have persuaded himself that non-learned bishops would 'rivet the Church in the affections of the people'. Others were unconvinced by such arguments. Queen Victoria, for one, liked at least *some* of her bishops to be learned. She asked Palmerston in December 1860 not to confine his selection of new bishops to 'respectable parish priests', but to bear in mind that the Bench 'should not be left devoid of some University men of acknowledged standing and theological learning'. The Bench, in the Queen's view, would be seriously weakened if, in controversies on points of doctrine agitating the Church, 'no value were attached to the opinions at least of some of those who are to govern her'.[12]

Palmerston was unrepentant. In the course of a hard-hitting reply to the Queen he minced no words about the role of the bishop as he saw it:

Viscount Palmerston would beg to submit that the bishops are in the Church what generals of districts are in the Army: their chief duties consist in watching over the clergy of their diocese, seeing that they perform properly their parochial duties, preserving harmony between the clergy and the laity, and softening the asperities between the Established Church and the Dissenters. For these purposes it is desirable that a bishop should have practical knowledge of parochial functions, and should not be of an overbearing and intolerant temperament. His diocesan duties are enough to occupy all his time, and the less he engages in theological disputes the better.[13]

The sting in this particular letter came in the tail. Palmerston assured the Queen that 'much mischief has been done by theological bishops' – and, if the Bench were filled with men like the Bishop of Oxford (Wilberforce) and the Bishop of Exeter (Phillpotts), 'there would be no religious peace in the land'. Palmerston had made a similar remark four years earlier to Prince Albert, when asked to comment on a memorandum on episcopal appointments drawn up by the Dean of Windsor, Gerald Wellesley. In the memorandum the Dean had claimed that prime ministers had too often selected 'very inferior specimens, *safe men*'. Palmerston had agreed that 'men of very moderate capacity have too often been chosen for the office of Bishop', but had stressed the risk inherent in a more daring approach. He suggested that the two 'most able' bishops, Wilberforce and Phillpotts, 'would be better if their abilities were less'.[14]

During a reign of power which (allowing for the sixteen-month interregnum in 1858–9 when Derby was Premier) lasted for over nine years Palmerston found himself with an exceptionally large number of vacant dioceses to fill. He was able to nominate bishops for no fewer than nineteen English sees (as many as his three immediate predecessors combined), of whom thirteen were first appointments; his six translations included an Archbishop of Canterbury and two Archbishops of York. In addition he filled six Irish sees and ten English deaneries. His early episcopal nominees were almost all Evangelicals, representing that party in the Church to which Shaftesbury's wholehearted allegiance was given. Shaftesbury had recommended them to Palmerston precisely because they *were* Evangelicals. In his diary he explains: 'I could not foresee the duration of his power, and I was resolved to put forward men who would preach the truth, be active in their dioceses, be acceptable to the working people, and not offensive to Nonconformists. He accepted my suggestions on these very grounds, and heartily approved them.'[15] The emphasis on Evangelicals attracted attention all the more because of their neglect by previous prime ministers. As Owen Chadwick neatly puts it: 'The profession of evangelical opinion had until this moment erected a fence against preferment. In February 1855 the fence collapsed and reappeared as a ladder. Everyone was surprised; none more surprised than the evangelical clergy.'[16]

Of course Palmerston had sometimes to turn his ear to other counsellors, causing his confidant-in-chief many anxious moments. When the see of Gloucester and Bristol fell vacant in June 1856 Shaftesbury pictured the adherents of Christianity on one side of Palmerston and those of Belial on the other. If a 'Neologist' (i.e. Broad Churchman) were appointed, said Shaftesbury, it must be taken as a sign that 'God is wrath unto us: and He will most justly, tho' fearfully, cast us off as a filthy rag'.[17] On this occasion all went well. The Evangelical Charles Baring was appointed: a 'blessed appointment', said Shaftesbury ('to God be all the glory').[18] There was admittedly a political spin-off on this occasion. Shaftesbury confided to his diary after the nomination of Baring to Gloucester and Bristol and of Montagu Villiers, the Evangelical Rector of Bloomsbury, to Carlisle: 'His two bishops, whom I named to him, have brought him unbounded popularity; and well they might. Will he not believe that my next advice will be of the same character?'[19] These particular candidates had a further point in their favour: they were members of influential Whig families. Baring was the younger brother of Melbourne's chancellor of the exchequer; Villiers was the younger brother of the Earl of Clarendon, who served as Palmerston's foreign secretary.[20] Both men were later appointed Bishop of Durham, Baring succeeding Villiers in the see on the latter's premature death and carrying out a massive work of church extension in the diocese during his eighteen-year episcopate.

If Palmerston's first two episcopal appointments had attracted popular applause, another of his early choices proved more controversial. The nominee was Robert Bickersteth, who had succeeded Hamilton as Treasurer of Salisbury Cathedral; and he was *not* Shaftesbury's first choice for the see of Ripon. The trouble was that Palmerston felt that he had to nominate a Cambridge graduate, since all his earlier appointments had been Oxford men. He therefore turned down Shaftesbury's candidate, a canon of Wells, and suggested the Dean of Hereford instead. At first Shaftesbury was nonplussed, as he could think of no Cambridge man with whom to trump the Dean. Then he discovered that one of the candidates on his own episcopal short list, Bickersteth, *was* a Cambridge graduate after all and persuaded the Prime Minister to adopt him instead of the Dean. But the appointment excited astonishment and apprehension in the Church at large. Charles Greville recorded in his diary his feeling that it was neither fair nor prudent. 'It will exasperate the moderate High Churchmen and set them strongly against a Government which appears determined to shut the doors of ecclesiastical preferment against all but the Lowest Churchmen.'[21] Even the Queen was disapproving. She was prepared formally to ratify the appointment, but warned the Prime Minister that it would be looked upon as a 'strong party one', as Bickersteth was a leading Low Churchman. She advised him in future to 'remove any impression of the Church patronage running unduly towards party extremes'.[22]

In fact Palmerston (via Shaftesbury) was already hedging his bets. He had translated the moderately High Church Charles Longley* to Durham in the autumn of 1856. And about the same time he invited Archibald Campbell Tait† to be Bishop of London. Tait was Broad Church; but, believing that this school of thought ought to be represented, Shaftesbury selected him as (in the words of his diary) 'the mildest among them' and (as he told Tait's sister, Lady Wake) 'by very much the best' of the dangerous followers of Thomas Arnold. But there were other points in Tait's favour. He had been the most active member of the royal commission appointed by Lord John Russell to reform the University of Oxford and sweep away many of its abuses. He had been a success for the previous six years as Dean of Carlisle. More especially he had been the object of nationwide sympathy when, in the spring of 1856, he had lost five of his six small daughters in a scarlet-fever epidemic. The Queen was among the foremost sympathizers, and all in favour of promotion for Dean Tait in his bereavement. This was no doubt the crucial factor in persuading Palmerston to promote a man not yet in episcopal orders to a diocese second in importance only to Canterbury. On receiving Palmerston's offer, Tait recorded in his diary, he resolved to 'take an hour of prayer' on subjects which included 'that I may not act rashly, seeing that I have no doubt of accepting the offer . . . that I may be kept from worldliness in every form'.

---

*Longley had been Bishop of Ripon since 1836, and his oath of allegiance at the act of homage following his consecration had been made to William IV. No sooner had he risen from his knees than the King had suddenly adjured him in a loud voice: 'Bishop of Ripon, I charge you, as you shall answer before Almighty God, that you never by word or deed give encouragement to those d— — —d Whigs who would upset the Church of England.'[23]

†Tait was a Scot and was brought up as a Presbyterian. He had been born club-footed and had had to wear special tin boots in boyhood. On his first visit to London at the age of nineteen he took a walk through Lambeth and, on being asked the reason, replied: 'Well, I wanted to see how I shall like the place when I get there.'[24] He became Archbishop of Canterbury in 1868.

'This is certainly *not* the post which I should ever have dreamed of for myself,' he modestly added.[25]

High Church reaction to the first five Palmerstonian bishops was mixed. Gladstone complained to Wilberforce that there was visible in the Prime Minister's ecclesiastical appointments Shaftesbury's 'haughty and domineering spirit'.[26] Wilberforce himself was equally bitter. 'Lord Palmerston's wicked appointments meet us at every turn,' he told Gladstone. The government was one 'which every sound Churchman feels insults the Church almost every time it has to recommend to the Crown for a bishopric'.[27] Not perhaps *every* one. Edward Bouverie Pusey, the Tractarian leader, is credited by Shaftesbury in his diary with remarking about Palmerston's appointments that, 'if all were not such as he could have wished, all, at any rate, were in the interests of religion'.[28] The same line was taken by the *Church Times* when, in an editorial (28 October 1865) comparing Palmerston's episcopal nominees with those of Russell, the paper conceded that the former, however bigoted and narrow-minded they might be, at least were 'unquestionably men of holy lives and fervent piety, and full of zeal and earnestness in labouring in their Master's cause according to the light vouchsafed to them'. Palmerston himself was unmoved by complaints about his appointments. His selection of bishops, he told the Queen, 'has been much found fault with by the High Church, Puseyite and semi-Catholic Party', but had 'given great satisfaction to the nation at large . . . The people of this country are essentially Protestant; they feel the deepest aversion to Catholicism, and they see that the High Church, Tractarian, and Puseyite doctrines lead men to the Church of Rome.'[29]

In February 1858 Palmerston was defeated in a Commons vote and resigned. He was out of office for sixteen months; and, when he resumed the premiership in June 1859, he brought a number of prominent Peelites into the government, the most notable among them being Gladstone. This dilution of the milk of pure Whiggery also led to a modification of his policy on ecclesiastical patronage, since some of the new ministers – again notably Gladstone – were High Churchmen; and a policy of appointing too many Low Church bishops would obviously cause problems. As Shaftesbury, writing after Palmerston's death, put it in his diary:

After his junction with the Peel party he observed to me, 'I should like to be a little cautious in the selection of bishops, so as not unnecessarily to vex my colleagues, some of whom are very high. It is a bore to see angry looks, and have to answer questions of affected ignorance. This must not stand in the way of fit men, but, if we can now and then combine the two, so much the better.'[30]

Gladstone's position was certainly a difficult one. In a letter he wrote to Bishop Wilberforce of Oxford (17 June 1859) shortly before becoming Chancellor of the Exchequer he sets out the constitutional proprieties as he sees them:

I believe that I should be either setting a bad precedent or following an equally bad example were I to make my opinions on Lord Palmerston's past exercise of Church patronage the criterion of my political opposition or support. Any suggestion to that effect if made to me I must decline. The head of a Ministry would compromise both his dignity and his duty were he willing to enter into any compact on such a subject.[31]

Shaftesbury himself was full of forebodings for the future following the 'evil of Tractarians in a Cabinet'. He felt that

Gladstone, S. Herbert and the D. of Newcastle have power by a single word, or a cold look, to shake him [Palmerston] from his purpose . . . They will, I fear, go on setting aside by a species of veto all proposed until they have driven him in very weariness to appoint a man of their own; and that will be either a Puseyite or a Rationalist, one, to them, as good as the other; for their object is not real worth, but a defeat of the Evangelicals.[32]

In fact Shaftesbury's fears were premature. For the first year or two of the new government no significant change in policy was apparent; and no party extremists, either Puseyite or Rationalist, were appointed at any time during Palmerston's second period of office. 1860 saw the nomination of the unashamedly Evangelical Samuel Waldegrave to Carlisle; and of Joseph Wigram, regarded by some as an Evangelical though by others (including Shaftesbury himself) as a moderate High Churchman, to Rochester.

Wilberforce complained to Gladstone about Waldegrave's promotion. So did Bishop Hamilton of Salisbury, in whose diocese Waldegrave had served for sixteen years: his relations with him, he told a friend, had been more difficult than with almost any other of his clergy.[33] Palmerston justified the appointment in a letter he wrote to his cabinet colleague, Sidney Herbert, who had challenged him on the subject. His choice of Waldegrave, he told Herbert, had been largely influenced by the Bishop of London,

Tait, a former Dean of Carlisle. From his knowledge both of the man and of the diocese, Tait had said, he thought that Waldegrave would be better suited to the diocese than any other of the potential candidates mentioned.[34]

The case of Wigram is interesting, in that he was not Palmerston's first choice. The original selection had been the Headmaster of Harrow, C. J. Vaughan, who, as Master of the Temple and Dean of Llandaff, was later to achieve fame as a noted trainer of ordinands – 'Vaughan's doves'. Unfortunately, while at Harrow, he had had a homosexual affair with one of his pupils. The pupil had confided in a fellow-pupil, John Addington Symonds, and Symonds had rashly told his father. Symonds senior now threatened Vaughan with exposure unless he resigned his headmastership at once and promised never to accept any important ecclesiastical post.* Vaughan agreed to leave Harrow, and did so. But then came the offer from Palmerston of the vacant see of Rochester.† Vaughan was tempted by the prospect of a seat in the House of Lords to accept. When Symonds heard the news he warned Vaughan by telegram of immediate public exposure unless he withdrew his acceptance. Vaughan bowed to the inevitable and wrote to Palmerston asking to be excused.[36] The offer of the diocese went instead to Wigram, who ruled his diocese blamelessly, his principal phobias being clergymen who played cricket or grew whiskers.[37]

The key appointment during the Palmerston years was that of a successor to J. B. Sumner as Archbishop of Canterbury. Here Gladstone and Wilberforce were united in their preferred candidate – though Wilberforce, as will be seen, was not entirely disinterested. Sumner died on 6 September 1862. The following day Gladstone, in a letter to the Prime Minister, set out his thoughts on the succession. He suggested that Palmerston's choice should fall on 'someone who from moderation as well as piety

---

*Vaughan's wife was the sister of Arthur Stanley, the future Dean of Westminster. In an impassioned interview with Symonds she flung herself on her knees and implored him to have mercy on her husband. Symonds declined to do so. However, he raised no objection when, in 1869, Vaughan was appointed Master of the Temple – or perhaps he did not regard this as an 'important ecclesiastical post'. By 1879, when Vaughan became Dean of Llandaff, Symonds was dead.

†There is surely a discrepancy here. Phyllis Grosskurth ascribes Palmerston's offer of Rochester to Vaughan as having been made in 1863 – not 1860, the year in which the see fell vacant. But Shaftesbury says in his diary entry for 1 November 1865: 'Twice under my advice he [i.e. Palmerston] offered a bishopric to Dr Vaughan, of Harrow, and was, in each case, refused.'[35] Possibly Vaughan was also offered the see of Gloucester and Bristol, which *did* fall vacant in 1863.

and learning should carry real weight not with any party in particular, but with the Church at large'. There was only one possible candidate, in Gladstone's view – and that was Longley, whom Palmerston had translated from Durham to York only two years previously, and 'whose praise for wisdom and goodness is in all parts and all borders of the Church'.[38] Wilberforce agreed. But, he suggested, should Longley prove unacceptable to the Prime Minister, then the late Primate's brother, Charles Sumner, might do instead. 'He is a capital administrator', Wilberforce told Gladstone, 'an Eton scholar of that old school dying out amongst us, entirely good, sound on all main points of faith, a gentleman, and a man of surpassing prudence.' In short, 'I believe that, if we are not to have thorough churchmen, he would be far the best man among us.'[39] But Wilberforce need not have bothered to pull out all the stops on behalf of Sumner, as Longley was chosen. And that left York vacant – and who better to fill York than Wilberforce himself?

He pinned all his hopes on the force of Gladstone's advocacy with the Prime Minister. Even before Longley had been appointed he had written to assure his friend that, should a vacancy arise at York, he would be only too happy to fill it. He pointed out that the Wilberforces were a Yorkshire family and that, if a Yorkshireman with a Yorkshire power of moving the masses and 'getting at the Methodists' were chosen as Archbishop, there might be a true revival of the Church and the faith in the North:

> To you in solemn secrecy I may say that it was Lord Aberdeen who placed this vision before me. Then for *you* – *the* one thing your warm friends want at Oxford is one definite, tangible proof that at least you *can* fix your mark somewhere for the Church's good on a great appointment – It seems, humanly speaking, as if all the next great strength of our Church life now trembled in the balance. May the Lord direct the hearts of rulers aright.[40]

With reluctance, because he thought another suggestion coming from him might be counterproductive, Gladstone agreed to press Wilberforce's claims on the Prime Minister. He did so in a long letter sent from his home at Hawarden on 28 September. Wilberforce, he said, was 'probably the first preacher of the day in the Church of England'. He was a prudent administrator, a conciliator of the High and Low Church parties in his present diocese, 'on principle as well as by nature social', and altogether 'one of the great Bishops, necessarily few, who leave their mark upon their Church and upon the history of their time'. Furthermore, Gladstone assured Palmerston, his promotion would be very agreeable to the Queen.[41] But it was not to be. The day before Gladstone dispatched his letter Palmerston had offered the vacant bishopric to Tait of London.

Tait was reluctant to leave his present diocese, where he was by now well established, and wrote to decline the offer. The Prime Minister attempted to make him change his mind: 'The duties of the Archbishop of York, though more commanding and extensive in their range and nature, are nevertheless not so personally harassing.' Tait was adamant. He appreciated the Premier's kind motive in offering him a chance to move to a post 'at once of greater dignity and of less work', but he might find the distant and untried duties at York less congenial.[42] 'For you to give up London for York', wrote his sister, Lady Wake, 'would have seemed to me like a man making a second marriage while the first wife and family were not only yet living,' but possessed all the husband's thoughts and affections.'[43]

That ruled out Tait, so what other candidate was on offer for York? Certainly not Wilberforce, in Palmerston's view (Gladstone's advocacy notwithstanding). His suspicion of Wilberforce's High Church proclivities was sufficient to make the Bishop of Oxford a non-starter. Palmerston tentatively suggested translating Waldegrave of Carlisle, but the Queen was unenthusiastic: Waldegrave was 'excessively Low Church' in sympathies, she claimed (rightly).[44] She came up with two counter-suggestions: Philpott of Worcester and Thomson of Gloucester and Bristol. The Prime Minister plumped for Thomson.* Wilberforce was furious: Thomson had been his curate at Cuddesdon and was possessed, in Wilberforce's opinion, of talents far inferior to his own. Thomson's rise had indeed been rapid. After six years as Provost of Queen's College, Oxford, he had been appointed only the previous year to Gloucester and Bristol. But his first official act as a bishop had been to preach in Gloucester Cathedral at a memorial service for the Prince Consort – and the sermon had touched the Queen's heart. Out of a host of similar addresses it had been the one which had moved her most profoundly. In the retrospective words of the *Manchester Guardian* (26 December 1890), 'the Bishop's fortune was now made.'[46] So it was not perhaps quite so surprising that a comparatively unknown cleric should have been appointed Primate of England.

Nevertheless, Thomson's promotion was not universally

---

* Thomson's wife, Zoe, used to tell their children that Palmerston had suggested one name after another to the Queen for the vacant archbishopric. Each was rejected in turn. At last in exasperation he is supposed to have said: 'Here, Ma'am, is an entire list of the Bishops, from the oldest to the youngest.' 'I'll take the youngest', the Queen replied. And so Thomson was chosen. He would then have been 43.[45]

popular. Some High Churchmen were alarmed. They viewed him as an Evangelical who was being sent by Shaftesbury to put down Ritualistic teaching and worship in the North. The *Record* was pleased for this very reason – and relieved that Palmerston had not been beguiled by the 'siren eloquence of the Bishop of Oxford'.[47] The choice of Thomson was particularly unpopular in Yorkshire, where the general feeling was that Wilberforce should have been chosen. The *Hull Advertiser* had earlier urged the clergy of the diocese to petition for his translation on the ground that he was a Yorkshireman 'with Yorkshire feelings and traditions'.

The outgoing archbishop, Longley, was sympathetic. He told Wilberforce that he had indulged until the last the hope that he would succeed him – 'tho' I knew what the force of prejudice was and how possible it was that my hope might be disappointed'. Wilberforce himself reported to Gladstone: 'Cool, calm men whom I have in this past week been with in Yorkshire expressed in the very strongest language both their disappointment at my not having been appointed and (to use W. Beckett's words) their sense of "the affront" of the actual appointment.' Disraeli commented in a memorandum the following year that, if Gladstone, who had argued Wilberforce's case so forcefully, had threatened to resign on the issue, he must have won the day.[48] For Wilberforce the knife was twisted still further in the wound when he learned from the Dean of Windsor, Wellesley, that, had Tait accepted York, Wilberforce would have been offered London.[49] As it was, he had to wait a further seven years for preferment – and then it was only as far as Winchester.

Occasionally Palmerston managed to choose a bishop of whom *all* spoke well. Such was Edward Harold Browne, the Norrisian Professor of Divinity at Cambridge, who was nominated to Ely in 1864. The Dean of Ely wrote with delight to the candidate at having to 'certify to H.M. the election of the very man whom I should have decided to elect had there been no terrors of *praemunire* to help my decision'.[50] We shall hear more of the blameless Bishop Browne.

An appointment later in 1864 led to a further brush between the Prime Minister and his Sovereign. The diocese was Peterborough and Palmerston's nominee Francis Jeune, Dean of Lincoln. Now Jeune had only been appointed to the deanery a few months before. The Queen therefore wrote to Palmerston to suggest that his promotion to the Bench would be premature, 'and would give an appearance of special selection hardly justified by any extraordinary pre-eminence'.[51] She suggested two other names. Palmerston was annoyed at this attempt by the Queen to overrule him and proceeded to lecture her about the constitutional position. 'Viscount Palmerston', he wrote to her on 29 April, 'regrets to find that your Majesty has some objection to Doctor Jeune's appointment, and a preference for other persons not named by Viscount Palmerston.' The sting of this particular missive came towards the end, when the Premier observed tartly:

> All that the first Minister of the Crown can do is to pick out for ecclesiastical dignities men whom he has reason to believe fit for the posts to be filled, without at all undertaking that other persons, if they had a duty of advising your Majesty, might not in the crowd find others who might in many respects be equally fit; but the responsibility of advising your Majesty must rest with somebody, and it happens to rest with the First Lord of the Treasury.[52]

The only person who might complain about the appointment, Palmerston added, might be Dr Jeune himself, 'to whom the removal may be a cause of expense'.

He was certainly not going to be dictated to by the Queen on this occasion, he told Shaftesbury. 'She fancies, poor woman, that she has peculiar Prerogatives about the Church because she is its Head, forgetting that she is equally Head of all Institutions of the Country.'[53] The Queen was exceedingly cross, but decided to bite the bullet. It would be very disagreeable to her to answer Lord Palmerston's letter, she wrote to him, 'or to prolong a discussion which has taken a tone so different from that in which Lord Palmerston is in the habit of addressing her'. She therefore sanctioned Jeune's appointment – 'though she still considers the double promotion of a clergyman, within six months, to a Deanery and to the Bench to be so unusual as to require to be founded upon some very pre-eminent claims'.*[54]

Only a few weeks later the Queen again found herself crossing swords with her prime minister. This time the appointment was a minor one: the rectory of St Margaret's, Westminster. She asked Palmerston to submit more than one name. He agreed, but pointed out that 'this in some degree implies a Reference of a Recommendation by one of your Majesty's responsible advisers to the judgement of your Majesty's irresponsible advisers in such matters'. The Queen was not amused. She expressed surprise at

---

*The Queen conveniently forgot that, nineteen years before, an exactly parallel situation had arisen in respect of Samuel Wilberforce, whose appointment first as Dean of Westminster and six months later as Bishop of Oxford she had approved without demur. But then perhaps Wilberforce's double promotion had been founded on 'some very pre-eminent claims'.

the tone of Palmerston's remarks. 'He can never pretend that the Sovereign has not the right, as everyone else has, to ask anyone she chooses about any person who is recommended . . . The Queen makes it a rule, as the Prince did, to make enquiries in various quarters.'[55]

We come now to the last of Palmerston's episcopal appointments, and to the only one which was unashamedly political. On this occasion it was a case of Gladstone's nominee supplanting Shaftesbury's. The vacant see was Chester and the successful candidate William Jacobson, who had succeeded Hampden as Regius Professor of Divinity at Oxford (and who had, incidentally, been one of the Queen's two preferences as against Jeune for the see of Peterborough). Jacobson was a High Churchman of an old-fashioned sort, and therefore not the sort of man whom Shaftesbury would have chosen. But he happened to be chairman of Gladstone's election committee at Oxford (Gladstone represented the University in the Commons); and his promotion would therefore strengthen Gladstone's interests. Palmerston had already approved Shaftesbury's nominee, Archdeacon Prest of Durham; but, when he received a letter from Gladstone pressing the claims of Jacobson ('a man of earnest piety, enjoying universal respect'), he was prepared to think again. A few days later he told Gladstone that he had written to the Queen to recommend 'the Son of Jacob' for the vacant bishopric. Gladstone replied with an effusive letter of thanks. 'I am sure that this appointment will do you no dishonour; rely upon it, the children of Abraham and Isaac, and the children of all the tribes of this many-coloured world, will be well pleased . . .'[56] Shaftesbury was less well pleased. He described Jacobson as a 'cold, comfortless preacher with few Episcopal qualities'. But he agreed to the appointment on the ground that, though inferior to Prest, Shaftesbury's own candidate, Jacobson was *absolutely* fit, thoroughly respectable and beyond any hostile criticism'.[57] He later changed his mind about Jacobson's fitness when the new bishop 'speedily gave offence' by his hostility to the Nonconformists in his diocese.[58]

Palmerston's long premiership ended only with his death on 18 October 1865 at the age of eighty-one. It was Shaftesbury, rather than an ordained clergyman, who administered the Protestant version of the last rites to him on his deathbed. Among the many obituary notices that in the ultra-Protestant *Record* was noteworthy in that it gave the departed statesman an entirely clean bill of spiritual health. Although, thirteen years before, it had dismissed the Duke of Wellington as an 'old heathen', it pulled out all the stops where Palmerston was concerned. As Bishop

Thirlwall wrote to his friend Lord Houghton, the former Richard Monckton Milnes:

> The *Record* . . . grants Palmerston absolution for all that was most honourable and useful in his life . . . in consideration of his having made so many Low Church Bishops and Deans. At the end of such a life he might well have been content with the Elysian Fields and the company of the Duke, as a *pis-aller*. But that he should be admitted into the *Record*'s paradise, to be singing its hymns and enjoying its conversation for all eternity, must be more than he could ever have hoped for himself, or his friends for him.[59]

The Palmerston–Shaftesbury policy on bishop-making might be dismissed by the *Saturday Review* as 'flinging mitres to third-rate professors of ignorance and obscurantism'.[60] But at least all those appointed during their joint reign were 'good men'.

**Nominations to bishoprics 19 (13 first appointments, 6 translations)**

*First appointments:*

  (1) 1856:  Archibald Campbell Tait to London.
  (2) 1856:  Henry Montagu Villiers to Carlisle.
  (3) 1856:  Charles Baring to Gloucester and Bristol.
  (4) 1856:  Robert Bickersteth to Ripon.
  (5) 1857:  John Thomas Pelham to Norwich.

  (6) 1860:  Joseph Cotton Wigram to Rochester.
  (7) 1860:  Samuel Waldegrave to Carlisle.
  (8) 1860:  Henry Philpott to Worcester.
  (9) 1861:  William Thomson to Gloucester and Bristol.
(10) 1863:  Charles John Ellicott to Gloucester and Bristol.
(11) 1864:  Edward Harold Browne to Ely.
(12) 1864:  Francis Jeune to Peterborough.
(13) 1865:  William Jacobson to Chester.

*Translations:*

  (1) 1856:  Charles Thomas Longley to Durham (from Ripon).

  (2) 1860:  Charles Thomas Longley to York (from Durham).
  (3) 1860:  Henry Montagu Villiers to Durham (from Carlisle).
  (4) 1861:  Charles Baring to Durham (from Gloucester and Bristol).
  (5) 1862:  Charles Thomas Longley to Canterbury (from York).
  (6) 1862:  William Thomson to York (from Gloucester and Bristol).

# 7

# Derby Days

*Earl of Derby: Prime Minister*
*25 February 1858 – 18 June 1859*
*6 July 1866 – 25 February 1868*

*Edward Geoffrey Stanley, 14th Earl of Derby (1799–1869), was Prime Minister for three brief periods which together totalled less than four years. In his first premiership (28 February–28 December 1852) he appointed no bishops. Educated at Eton and Christ Church, Oxford, he entered the Commons in 1821 as a Whig and was Chief Secretary for Ireland under Grey. In 1834 he switched to the Tories and from 1841 to 1844 was Peel's Colonial Secretary. He moved to the Lords as Lord Stanley in 1844 and succeeded to the earldom on his father's death in 1851. During his three brief ministries Disraeli was the dominant figure, master-minding the Reform Bill of 1867 and succeeding his chief on the latter's resignation through ill-health in 1868. Though not outstanding as a statesman, Derby was a renowned orator, fine classical scholar and keen sportsman.*

> *The brilliant chief, irregularly great,*
> *Frank, haughty, rash – the Rupert of debate.*[1]

Thus Edward Bulwer-Lytton, who served as Colonial Secretary in Derby's second administration of 1858–9, lauded the future Prime Minister (then plain Edward Stanley) for his speeches attacking Daniel O'Connell. Disraeli too compared Derby with the Royalist cavalry leader during a Commons speech in 1844: 'The noble Lord is the Prince Rupert of Parliamentary discussion.' Derby had an early opportunity of exercising his eloquence on an ecclesiastical issue when, as Chief Secretary for Ireland, he had devised and carried through the Commons in 1833 the notorious Church Temporalities Bill. It was that Bill which, by a series of mergers, reduced the number of sees in the Church of Ireland from twenty-two to twelve. After its enactment it was denounced by John Keble in his Assize Sermon of 14 July 1833 – from when the Oxford Movement is traditionally dated. Derby could hardly have imagined that his Bill would set light to the Tractarian fuse; though, like a number of other premiers, he was deeply interested in religion. He was a devout churchman who is said to have read 'most impressively' at the prayer services held in his private chapel at Knowsley, and he considered the Church of England to be a vital part of the British way of life. But he was also a doughty Protestant. He once stated that the Reformation was among the greatest blessings ever bestowed on England, and he regarded the Tractarian innovators with the deepest suspicion. He favoured simplicity in church services and had little sympathy with Anglican clergymen who introduced 'novelties' into their services. As for the Roman Catholics, he once complained during a parliamentary debate that the spiritual character of their religion was 'overloaded with that which is merely external and apparent to the senses'.[2]

The general drift of his religious ideas he gave on the eve of the general election of 1857 in a comment on the church appointments nominally made by Palmerston but actually recommended by Shaftesbury – which, by and large, Derby approved. He had, he said, 'no sympathy with what are called Tractarian views', and could 'conceive nothing more dangerous, nothing more detrimental to the interests of the Church of England than the preponderance of the Tractarian party'. At the same time he declined to 'throw himself into the other extreme' and to give his sympathies to 'pseudo-Liberalism and latitudinarianism'. He respected the labours, energy and piety of many of the Dissenters, but confessed that his sympathies, feelings and affections were with 'that party which, with their Bible for their guide, with the ancient fathers of the Church and the modern lights of the Reformed Church as the commentators and assistants, are more ready to inculcate upon their hearers the practical precepts than the abstract doctrines of religion'.[3] But, for all his Protestantism, Derby was fair-minded and against any sort of an anti-Ritualistic witch-hunt. In 1862, when in opposition, he told the Queen's secretary that the widespread feeling against Ritualism 'has led to many clergymen being stigmatized as High Churchmen who are no more so than I am myself . . . and on whom H.M. could not interpose Her veto without causing serious injury and creating great dissatisfaction'.[4]

Derby had no episcopal vacancies to fill during his first premiership in 1852, and only three in his remaining two ministries; so he had not much opportunity to develop a policy of his own. Nor did he have a 'grey eminence' breathing down his neck, as had Palmerston with Shaftesbury. His 1859 nomination of James Campbell to Bangor was at least long-lasting: Campbell soldiered on in his see for the next thirty years. The second Derby appointment could be said, in a sense, to have been a reward for services rendered. In 1853 Derby had been installed as Chancellor of Oxford University; and, in accordance with custom, an inaugural ode in his honour had been composed by the Professor of Poetry at the University and recited at the installation ceremony. The Professor of Poetry at the time happened to be one Thomas Legh Claughton, who, when not occupied with his university duties, was serving as Vicar of Kidderminster, a post he held from 1841 to 1867. So his nomination in 1867 to the bishopric of Rochester was seen by some as a belated thank-offering on the part of the Chancellor.

Derby's final appointment, that of George Augustus Selwyn to Lichfield, was much the most significant. Selwyn – like Derby an Old Etonian, though ten years his junior – had gone out in 1841, at the age of only thirty-two, to be Bishop of New Zealand. He had laboured there with conspicuous success for the past quarter-century. In 1867 he had come back to England to attend the first Lambeth Conference, at which he was among the two or three outstanding participants. Derby, searching for a successor to the late John Lonsdale at Lichfield, noted Selwyn's quality and offered him the see (having previously offered it to J. B. Lightfoot, the future Bishop of Durham, who declined it). But he had to fight hard to persuade him to accept it.

The Prime Minister's letter arrived on 12 November 1867. Describing the immediate sequel to his friend Sir William Martin, Chief Justice of New Zealand, Selwyn wrote at the end of the month: 'Without taking advice, but after prayer for guidance, I declined the offer by return of post, and supposed that the matter would end there.' But it did not. The Archbishop of Canterbury had written to him, Selwyn told Martin, urging him to reconsider his decision – and, when originally sent to New Zealand, he had promised Longley's predecessor obedience 'in all things lawful and honest'.

> My own desire to return to New Zealand is so strong that I cannot altogether trust my own judgment on a question of conscience. If I were to go upon my own will, I could decide in a moment. On Sunday I am to go to Windsor, and the Dean of Windsor [Wellesley] leads me to think that the Queen may speak to me on this subject. If this should be so, the principle of obedience will again come into operation.[5]

In his letter to the Prime Minister Selwyn had based his refusal of the offer of Lichfield primarily on the fact that 'the native race to whose service I was first called requires all the efforts of the few friends that remain to them', and that the organization of the Church in New Zealand was still incomplete. But Longley had told Selwyn that 'no advantage that can accrue to the Church in New Zealand by your remaining there will be comparable to the benefit you will thus confer on the Church at home'. Selwyn felt himself torn between conflicting loyalties. 'As a matter of promotion conferred by the civil power, I had no hesitation in refusing the Bishopric of Lichfield', he wrote to Longley. But, 'as a soldier of the Church, I shall probably feel bound to do whatever my commander-in-chief [i.e. the Queen] bids me.'[6] As his wife put it in a letter to a friend: 'He could refuse Lord Derby's offer, as he owed no duty there and acknowledged no call. But the Archbishop shook him to the core; for he has ever obeyed when he has recognized the duty. And then came the personal desire of the Queen.'[7] In the end the principle of obedience was too strong for Selwyn. The Queen (more or less) commanded, and he felt he must bow the knee. On 9 January 1868 he was enthroned in Lichfield Cathedral. He spent the first half of the year in his new diocese, but returned to New Zealand for the second half in order to wind up his affairs there.

The whole episode of Selwyn's struggle with his conscience comes as a refreshing reminder that not all Victorian clerics were consumed by ambition. As the Queen remarked in her journal for 1 December 1867, the day of Selwyn's visit to Windsor:

He is a very earnest man, devoted to his missionary work in New Zealand and to the natives . . . He said 'It will be a great change to me after my wild life in the hills.' I do indeed pity him, for the exchange to the Black Country, where there will be no romance, no primitive races, but the worst kind of uncivilised civilisation, will be most trying.[8]

A less attractive side of the Queen's character was exhibited towards the end of Derby's life, when he was wondering whether, because of his poor state of health, he ought to hand over to Disraeli. His son, Lord Stanley, recorded in his political journal his father's distress at the lack of any expressions of sympathy or regret in the Queen's curt note telling him he ought to resign at once. 'I am not surprised', Stanley adds, 'but he has always entertained some illusions about her . . . She is civil to persons in power under her whose good will contributes to her comfort (and not always to them): but sees no reason for wasting civility on those who can no longer be of use to her.'[9]

**Nominations to bishoprics 3 (2 first appointments, 1 translation)**

*First appointments:*

  (1) 1859: James Colquhoun Campbell to Bangor.

  (2) 1867: Thomas Legh Claughton to Rochester.

*Translation:*

  (1) 1867: George Augustus Selwyn to Lichfield (from New Zealand).

# 8

# A Dizzy Descent

*Benjamin Disraeli: Prime Minister*
*27 February – 2 December 1868*
*21 February 1874 – 27 April 1880*

Benjamin Disraeli, Earl of Beaconsfield (1804–81), *was the son
of Isaac D'Israeli, an Anglicized Jew, but was baptized into the
Christian Church in 1817. He was educated privately and trained
as a solicitor. After travelling for three years in the East (1828–
31) he turned to writing: both novels and political pamphlets. In
1837 he entered Parliament as MP for Maidstone: he was howled
down during his maiden speech, but warned his audience that
the day would come when they* would *hear him. By 1842 he was
already leading the 'Young England' group of radical Tories and
four years later, on Peel's fall from power, became uncrowned
leader of the Conservative Party. He increased his reputation as a
parliamentarian during his many years in opposition to the
Liberals. His great chance came in 1867 during the third Derby
administration, when he piloted through a radical Reform Bill
which added two million voters (mainly factory workers) to the
electorate. On Derby's retirement in 1868 Disraeli succeeded him
as Prime Minister, but was soon forced out of office and, for the
next five years, led the opposition to Gladstone. His second
administration (1874–80) established his reputation as a statesman. He acquired for Britain a controlling interest in the Suez
Canal, proclaimed Queen Victoria Empress of India, annexed the
Transvaal and brought back 'peace with honour' from the 1878
Congress of Berlin. On the domestic front he successfully
sponsored a number of progressive social measures. He was
created Earl of Beaconsfield in 1876, but was defeated in the
general election of 1880. He wrote a number of influential political
novels, including* Coningsby *and* Sybil, *in which he preached the
gospel of radical Toryism. Like Melbourne, Disraeli was a
favourite of the Queen's – in spite of frequent differences of
opinion over ecclesiastical appointments.*

'Ecclesiastical affairs rage here. Send me Crockford's directory; I must be armed.'[1] The *cri de coeur* came from Benjamin Disraeli. He was writing from Balmoral to his secretary – and finding himself much in need of the indispensable clerical reference-book for his verbal tussles with Queen Victoria over the choice of new bishops. The appeal is symptomatic of Disraeli's ignorance of church matters. But this was hardly surprising in view of his background and upbringing.

His parents, in spite of their Jewish origins, had been agnostics. He had himself been educated at a Unitarian school, though he had been baptized and confirmed into the Church of England. He worshipped regularly in his parish church at Hughenden, Buckinghamshire, and made his communion at Easter. His Christianity may have been on the hazy side, and he could sometimes be flippant – as when he reputedly told the Queen: 'I am the blank page between the Old and the New Testament.'[2] Samuel Wilberforce, the bishop whom he knew best but with whom he enjoyed a love–hate relationship, wrote to a friend after a meeting with Disraeli in 1867: 'He is a marvellous man, not a bit a Briton, but all over an Eastern Jew . . . He *always* speaks as if he did believe in the Church.'[3] But his ignorance of church ways is brought out in an anecdote recorded in the biography of A. P. Stanley, Dean of Westminster. The Dean met the Prime Minister in the street one Sunday late in 1876 and invited him into the Abbey to hear a sermon by F. W. Farrar, whom Disraeli had just made a canon. To an informed churchman the experience would have been nothing out of the ordinary: to Disraeli it was an Arabian Nights adventure to be piloted into the Abbey to hear a popular preacher. 'I would not have missed the sight for anything', said the Premier, 'the darkness, the lights, the marvellous windows, the vast crowd, the courtesy, the respect, the devotion – and fifty years ago there would not have been fifty persons there.'[4] Perhaps, in spite of all his deviousness where the Church was concerned, Disraeli was after all, as he observed during the famous Oxford debate on Darwinism in 1864, 'on the side of the angels'.

Nevertheless, to knowledgeable churchmen, his ignorance must sometimes have appeared profound. 'Send me down tomorrow the Clergy List', he wrote to his secretary at the height of the McNeile controversy (see below). 'I don't know the names and descriptions of the persons I am recommending for deaneries and mitres.'[5] Disraeli had never moved in ecclesiastical circles, and found his lack of personal knowledge of the leading clerics of the day a handicap in his selection of new bishops and deans. Not

PUNCH, OR THE LONDON CHARIVARI.—December 10, 1864.

## DRESSING FOR AN OXFORD BAL MASQUÉ.

"THE QUESTION IS, IS MAN AN APE OR AN ANGEL? (*A Laugh.*) NOW, I AM ON THE SIDE OF THE
ANGELS (*Cheers.*)"—Mr. Disraeli's *Oxford Speech, Friday, November 25.*

*Disraeli on the side of the angels.*

that he lacked advisers only too anxious to make good the gaps in his knowledge. Chief among these was the Lord Chancellor, Lord Cairns, an Evangelical churchman who tried to play Shaftesbury to Disraeli's Palmerston, though with limited success. Bishop Wilberforce and other High Churchmen attempted to influence the Prime Minister in an opposite direction. Lord Derby, Disraeli's predecessor as PM, was always happy to advise when required. And the Queen herself, with her wide experience in ecclesiastical matters, was to prove a formidable adversary when her views on a candidate's suitability clashed with her Prime Minister's.

Disraeli's motives in his exercise of church patronage were blatantly political. Shaftesbury wrote in his diary for 22 August 1868: 'I cannot trust him [Disraeli] for an instant. His word is worthless, and he has not an atom of principle.'[6] Four months later Wilberforce, writing to the Archbishop of Dublin in the aftermath of his failure to be promoted to either Canterbury or London, complained bitterly: 'Wholly unprincipled men like Disraeli are content to use religion, as they would any other precious thing, as an instrument of obtaining ever so short a tenure of place at the cost of ever so entire a sacrifice of that which they so use . . . His whole idea is to use the Church to keep himself in office.'[7]

Disraeli certainly gave every appearance of being motivated mainly by electoral considerations. That shrewd observer Dean Wellesley advised the Queen a year after the start of Disraeli's second ministry: 'Mr D'Israeli's letters confirm the Dean in the notion that he will never wittingly propose to your Majesty for high preferment a clergyman of the Liberal party. He regards the Church as the great State-engine of the Conservatives and that any appointments with regard to its future reformation will weaken him politically with his followers.'[8] As we shall see, Tait, who *was* a Liberal in politics, was promoted to the primacy on the insistence of the Queen and against the wishes of the Prime Minister. Disraeli certainly made no bones about his partisanship where ecclesiastical vacancies were concerned. 'Another deanery!', he wrote to his secretary at a moment when a decanal decease coincided with a political crisis. 'The Lord of Hosts is with us!'[9] But he was having to modify his enthusiasm after his defeat by Gladstone in the general election of November 1868. 'Bishoprics, once so much prized, are really graceless patronage now', he complained to Derby. 'They bring no power.'[10]

The Queen still preferred Broad Churchmen to either High or Low. 'It is by such [moderate] appointments alone', she told Disraeli in 1874, 'that we can hope to strengthen the very tottering fabric of the established Church. The extreme Evangelical school do the established Church as much harm as the High Church.'[11] Disraeli himself thought that it was the Low Church interest that needed to be placated most. This view was based on his reading of the ecclesiastical barometer. 'The country, I am convinced, is, almost to a man, against the High Church party', he wrote to Lord Stanley in August 1868. 'I don't know who is for them, except some University dons, some youthful priests and some women; a great many, perhaps, of the latter. But *they* have not votes yet.'[12] He made the same point a few days later in a letter to the Queen: 'There is no sort of doubt that the great feature of national opinion at this moment is an utter repudiation by all classes of the High Church party. It is not only general: it is universal.'[13] But, if the Queen agreed with Disraeli that High Church was bad, she was not prepared to concede that Low (that is, extreme Low) Church was much better. 'It will *not* do', she lectured the Premier from Lucerne (7 September 1868), 'merely to encourage the ultra-Evangelical party, than wh. there is none more narrow-minded, and thereby destructive to the well-being and permanence of the Church of England . . . The Queen feels bound to ask for moderate, sensible, clever men, neither Evangelical nor Ritualistic in their views, to be appointed to the high offices in the Church.'[14]

Disraeli was not prepared to submit to the royal preferences without a struggle. When the Queen presented him in 1875 with a list of suitable nominees for bishoprics, deaneries and canonries he wrote back to explain that, for political reasons, he could not favour the names on the list, most of whom were Broad Churchmen. 'The great mass of the Conservative party, in and out of Parliament, view the Broad Church school with more suspicion and aversion than they do the Ritualists', he told the Queen. If he named men on her list, 'a disruption of the Cabinet would inevitably take place'.[15] But, however fierce their squabbles over ecclesiastical appointments, the Queen was never cross with her Prime Minister for long. After she had got her way over the Peterborough vacancy in 1868 she wrote in her journal: 'Mr. Disraeli will, I think, make good Church appointments, as he sees the force of my arguments in favour of moderate and distinguished men.'[16] Disraeli, for his part, was prepared to play ball with the Queen. 'Everyone likes flattery', he remarked to Matthew Arnold, 'and, when you come to royalty, you should lay it on with a trowel.'[17] He did just that.

His trouble was that, in dealing with Crown appointments, he failed to follow a consistent policy. His tendency to seesaw was remarked upon by Dean Wellesley in a talk he had with Bishop Wilberforce after the appointments to Canterbury and London in

1868. Wilberforce in his diary reports the Dean as saying: 'Disraeli has been utterly ignorant, utterly unprincipled: he rode the Protestant horse one day; then got frightened that it had gone too far and was injuring the county elections, so he went right round and proposed names never heard of. Nothing he would not have done.'*[18]

During his two premierships, which lasted just under seven years in all, Disraeli awarded thirteen mitres. But five of these, including the prestigious appointments to Canterbury and London, were bestowed during his first premiership of only nine months; and it was this period that saw his sharpest differences of opinion with the Queen, who disputed three out of the Premier's five choices and got her way on each occasion. Matters moved on to a far more even keel during the second and much longer period of office, during which Disraeli was ennobled and, as Lord Beaconsfield, basked in the royal favour.

He got off to an uncontroversial start in 1868 with the appointment of the Vicar of Leeds, James Atlay,† to succeed the late R. D. Hampden at Hereford. Atlay was a hardworking parish priest of moderately High Church views. He got on well with Anglicans of all schools of thought, though Disraeli told the Queen soon after his appointment that he had been 'denounced, tho' erroneously, as a creature of the Bishop of Oxford, a prelate who, tho' Mr Disraeli's diocesan, he is bound to see is absolutely in this country more odious than Laud'.[21] According to the *DNB* Archbishop Benson praised Atlay (posthumously!) as 'the most beautiful combination of enthusiasm, manliness and modesty'.

With his next appointment Disraeli made an unashamed bid to curry favour with the Evangelical wing of the Church. The Protestant cat he was to put among the pigeons was Hugh McNeile, a seventy-three-year-old canon of Liverpool well known for his extreme anti-Roman and anti-Tractarian views. McNeile had already been brought to the Prime Minister's attention as a potential Bishop of Hereford whose appointment 'would make the Protestant party fight like dragons for the Government'.[22]

---

*When *Lothair*, in which he himself was portrayed, was published in 1870, Wilberforce wrote: 'My wrath against D[israeli] has burnt before this so fiercely that it seems to have burnt up all the materials for burning and to be like an exhausted prairie-fire – full of black stumps, burnt grass, and all abominations.'[19]

†Atlay has achieved immortality of a kind in the pages of *Kilvert's Diary*. At a confirmation service in 1870 he mistook a clergyman friend of Kilvert's for a candidate because he wore no gown and had arrived late with his single candidate, a farmer's daughter. Atlay insisted on confirming both together, ignoring the cleric's protests and 'seeming to think he was dealing with a refractory, ill-conditioned youth'. Kilvert adds: 'The whole Church was in a titter.'[20]

Hereford was no longer vacant, but the deanery of Ripon was the next best thing. Disraeli put McNeile's name before the Queen (who was holidaying at Lucerne) on the ground that it was 'highly important at the present moment that sympathy should be shown with the Evangelical party in the Church'.[23] He went on to argue that the choice of McNeile would help him politically in two Lancashire by-elections that were pending. Such special pleading put the royal back up; and the Queen only consented to McNeile's appointment with great reluctance. As was to be expected, it received a mixed press. Lord Cairns declared that 'nothing more politic could occur at the present time'. To Lord Derby the nomination appeared 'rather a hazardous bid for the extreme Low Church'.[24] The Dean of Chichester, Walter Hook, described it as an insult to orthodox Christians.[25] The Queen told Disraeli that it was '*not* liked by *moderate* men'.[26] And even one correspondent who rejoiced at the news complained that, though a deanery was all very well for McNeile, a bishopric would have been even better.[27] Disraeli himself considered the choice of McNeile a real coup. He wrote to Derby from Perth on 18 September: 'I was really surrounded by hungry lions and bulls of Bashan till that took place, but, since, there has been a lull, and an easier feeling in all quarters.'[28]

Over the choice of a Dean of Ripon the Queen had yielded, though reluctantly. Over the next appointment, that of a new Bishop of Peterborough, she dug in her heels – and eventually got her way. In spite of his brave talk about bulls of Bashan Disraeli must have felt qualms about suggesting another Protestant quite so militant for the vacant see. Wilberforce warned him that a series of appointments like McNeile's would alienate moderate church opinion – and that influential clerics like Dean Hook were now wavering in their support of Conservative parliamentary candidates. Disraeli therefore hedged his bets by proposing a moderate Evangelical, Canon Champneys of St Paul's, to the Queen. He told her (correctly) that McNeile's appointment had rallied the Protestant party, but (incorrectly) that it had 'been received by the other sections with no disfavour or cavil'. The new prelate, he now insisted, 'should be one of unquestionably Protestant principles'.[29] The Queen was un-impressed by his arguments. She considered Champneys an 'insignificant Low Churchman' and pressed for an alternative. The best the Prime Minister could do in reply was to suggest two names, of which Champneys was one and the other (also an Evangelical) Archdeacon Hone of Worcester. The views of both, he assured Her Majesty, were, 'tho' inevitably decided, temperate and conciliatory in their application' (which could hardly have been said of McNeile's). 'Doubtless neither of these appointments would please the sacerdotal school', he added, 'nor even satisfy the philosophic . . . but they would be received with respect alike by Ritualist or Rationalist; and with confidence and joy by the great body of your Majesty's subjects.'

But not by Her Majesty! Disraeli had, earlier in this letter, reverted to the unashamedly political tone of his ecclesiastical nominations. The passage reads:

> He [the writer] thinks that, with the more ardent [Evangelicals] satisfied by the tardy recognition of McNeile and the calmer portion, now alarmed and irritated, encouraged and soothed and solaced by such an appointment as that which he indicates, we might get over the General Election without any violent ebullition: and, even if another vacancy were to occur in the interval, a man more conformable with your Majesty's views might be advanced, if your Majesty could fix upon one.[30]

Her Majesty had indeed fixed upon one – but it was for the present vacancy, not a future one. The cleric she wanted for Peterborough was the Dean of Cork, William Connor Magee: a 'very clever man', she told the Premier, 'and the finest preacher the Queen has ever heard out of Scotland'.[31] Disraeli, apparently, knew little or nothing about this paragon, though Magee was already making a name for himself as one of the greatest orators and most brilliant conversationalists of the day – and, before September was out, was to hit the newspaper headlines through a sermon appealing to the Church of England to come to the help of her Irish sister, now threatened with disestablishment. Disraeli weakly suggested to the Queen that the new bishop ought to be an Oxford man. 'She suggested the Dean might be one', he told his secretary; 'but I had no book to refer to, and I am not sure whether Crockford, shortsighted Crockford, biographises the Irish clergy.' One great objection, he added, was that Magee's appointment 'would give us nothing'. But a Cabinet colleague, the High Church Lord John Manners, had independently proposed Magee's name for the Prime Minister's consideration, on the ground that it would satisfy all parties.[32]

Disraeli gave way, awarding the deanery of Lichfield as a consolation prize to Champneys. And he added a droll touch to his letter offering Magee the vacant see. The Irishman had recently written to Disraeli asking him, when choosing a new Dean of St Paul's, 'to give him one of the appointments that might be vacant in so doing'. The Premier began on the first page of his reply by refusing Magee's modest request and then, when he turned over the leaf, made the offer of the bishopric. His biographer observes: 'It was wise and politic of the Premier, in the hour of danger to the Irish Church, to mark the unity of the Churches by recommending an Irishman for an English see.'[33] It was the first such appointment since the Reformation; and Magee was to justify his choice in a sense by making one of the finest speeches ever heard in the House of Lords when he attacked the Bill proposing the disestablishment of the Church of Ireland.

And now comes the climax of Disraeli's ecclesiastical tussles with the Queen: the key appointments to Canterbury and London. The saga began with the death of Archbishop Longley at the end of October 1868. There were a number of potential successors in the wings. Samuel Wilberforce was always a possibility, though he was by now so critical of Disraeli that his promotion was unlikely while Disraeli remained Prime Minister. (Wilberforce's own diary entries of the period imply that he was not expecting to succeed Longley.) Bishop Tait records in his diary his feeling 'almost certain that the Archbishop of York [Thomson] would be appointed to Canterbury and the Bishop of Oxford to York'.[34] Another possibility was the Bishop of Ely, Harold Browne. His biographer records a conversation between a friend of the bishop's and a Cabinet minister (both unnamed). The minister remarked: 'It is quite incredible, the number of letters I and others in the Cabinet have received from every part of the country urging the nomination of your friend the B————p of E—y.' The anonymous friend replied: 'Well, he is the very man. He is liked by all classes, and would be popular with all parties. He is a thorough gentleman, which is not the case with *every* Bishop, and he has that in him, both spiritually and intellectually, which would ensure his rising to the height of any emergency.'[35] Browne's star, however, was not yet sufficiently in the ascendant: he was to be, as we shall see, a much stronger candidate when Canterbury next fell vacant. In the event the winner in the present primatial stakes was neither Thomson, nor Wilberforce, nor Browne. But neither was it Disraeli's own front-runner.

The Queen got her oar in first. On the very day (29 October) on which she heard the news of the death of the 'worthy and amiable' Longley she wrote to Disraeli from Balmoral urging the appointment of Tait to succeed him. 'The Queen thinks there is *no* one so fit (indeed she knows of no one who WOULD *be fit*) than [*sic*] the Bishop of London, an excellent, pious, liberal-minded, courageous man, who would be an immense support and strength to the Church in these times.' Surprisingly (viewed from a present-day consideration of the respective responsibilities of Canterbury and London) she adds: 'His health, which is not good, would be benefited by the change.'[36] Disraeli had meanwhile proposed a name of his own (the letters in fact crossed): the Bishop of Gloucester and Bristol, C. J. Ellicott. He gave his reasons in a letter to Derby (marked 'Secret') four days later:

> My Church policy was this: to induce, if possible, the two great and legitimate parties to cease their internecine strife, and to combine against the common enemies: Rits and Rats. This could only be done by a fair division of the patronage . . . As I did not want a very High Churchman, or an Evangelist [sic], for Archbishop, the materials from which I could select were very few. I was disposed in favour of the Bishop of Gloucester, whom I don't personally know, but was pleased by his general career since your accession to office, and also by a correspondence which he held, subsequently, with me, arising out of the Ritual Commission. It seemed to me very desirable that the new Primate should not be mixed up with all the recent controversies and clerical fracas, which have damaged all concerned in them.[37]

Tait of course was a Broad Churchman and Ellicott a strong Conservative politically – which added to their attractions in the eyes of their respective sponsors. But neither Queen nor Prime Minister was impressed by the other's candidate. The former immediately asked the Dean of Windsor for his opinion of Ellicott – and it was far from flattering. 'He [the Dean] thinks your Majesty may fairly begin by positively declining the Bishop of Gloucester. He has a miserably thin, weak voice, and no dignity of manner . . . He is an amiable, insignificant man, talking constantly and irrelevantly, with some book learning.' If that was the kind of bishop the Prime Minister wanted, said the Dean, Browne of Ely was a better specimen. He went on to extol Tait. 'He is the only one among the *greater* Prelates who is trusted by the *Laity*, and he would also be welcomed by a large body of the Clergy . . . His labours deserve the comparative repose [i.e. of the Primacy!] . . . If Mr Disraeli will not have London, he should produce something better than Gloucester.' The Dean ended his long screed with some remarks about Wilberforce:

> The Dean is very sorry that Mr. Disraeli appears to have taken up such exaggerated prejudices respecting the Bishop of Oxford. These he has got from the Bishop of Gloucester . . . Mr Disraeli might safely send him to York should the other [i.e. Thomson] be moved, or to Winchester if vacant. But the Dean

does not *wish* York to be moved. It may be a necessity. He is better than Gloucester.[38]

The next day the Queen wrote to Disraeli, reiterating that Tait was the '*only* fit man' to succeed Longley. 'The Bishop of Gloucester and Bristol, though a very good man, has not the knowledge of the world, nor the reputation and general *presence* (which is of so *great* importance in a position of such very high rank, constantly called upon to perform all the highest functions in connection with the Sovereign and Royal Family).'[39] Disraeli continued to resist the royal bait. Having explained to Derby his reasons for preferring Ellicott, he now received from the former Premier an ambivalent note: 'I cannot agree with H.M. that the Bishop of London would be either a popular or a judicious selection.' Ellicott, on the other hand, 'has a foolish voice and manner which make him appear weaker than I believe he really is'. Derby suggested Browne as a compromise; but Disraeli retorted that he would gain nothing by proposing his name, 'while H.M. will only be annoyed'. The Bishop of Oxford was quite out of the running, he added, 'so great is the distrust of him by the country'.[40]

Meanwhile he continued to argue with the Queen against Tait. In a letter of 4 November he wrote: 'Mr Disraeli finds him, as an Ecclesiastical statesman, obscure in purpose, fitful and inconsistent in action, and evidently, though earnest and conscientious, a prey to constantly conflicting convictions' (in fact just like Disraeli himself when it came to church appointments). Moreover, 'there is in his idiosyncrasy a strange fund of enthusiasm, a quality which ought never to be possessed by an Archbishop of Canterbury, or a Prime Minister of England' (this was presumably a dig at Gladstone). The most dangerous feature in Tait's character, said Disraeli, was 'the peculiar influence which Neology has had upon his mind'. In short, Tait had forfeited the confidence of both High Churchmen and Evangelicals, 'and is only looked up to with curious and unquiet hope by the Romanising or the Free-thinking Clergy'.[41] Having said which, Disraeli had just about shot his bolt.*

The Queen persisted in her opinion that Tait would be 'the

---

*Disraeli's use of flowery language even when differing from the Queen no doubt helped to endear him to her. He ended this particular letter: 'His [Disraeli's] idea of the perfect relations between the Sovereign and her Minister is, that there should be, on her part, perfect confidence; on his, perfect devotion. In the blended influence of two such sentiments, so ennobling and so refined, he sees the best security for your Majesty's happiness, and the welfare of the realm.'

proper person, indeed the only proper person', to succeed the late
Archbishop. Should the Prime Minister still object to him, she
would 'more gladly' see the promotion of the Bishop of Ely
(Browne), the Bishop of Lincoln (Jackson) or the Bishop of
Lichfield (Selwyn) than the Bishop of Gloucester, whose
promotion could 'under no circumstances be approved'. She had
always heard these other bishops well spoken of as 'men
distinguished for piety and learning and moderation of opinion'.[42]
By this time, however, Disraeli felt that to persist in pressing for
Ellicott in the face of the Queen's opposition would only enrage
her, and that her alternative suggestions were not meant to be
taken seriously. So he gave in as gracefully as possible. The
formal offer to Tait was dispatched on 12 November and accepted
the following day. On emerging from his final interview with the
Queen Disraeli exclaimed to Lord Malmesbury: 'Don't bring any
more bothers before me; I have enough already to drive a man
mad.'[43]

The irony of the whole affair is that, if the dying Archbishop
Longley had only lived for a few weeks longer, Gladstone rather
than Disraeli would have been Prime Minister at the time of his
death. And in that case, almost certainly, the palm would have
gone to Wilberforce rather than to Tait.

There remained London, Tait's present see, to fill – and here
again Disraeli was unlucky. His choice was Christopher
Wordsworth, Archdeacon of Westminster and a nephew of the
poet. But the Queen objected, on the ground that the candidate
lacked experience and that there were other bishops with stronger
claims. She suggested Jackson of Lincoln as a better choice – and
Jackson it eventually was. Many people in the Church had thought
that it would be Wilberforce. If Disraeli had taken Derby's advice
and proposed him to the Queen instead of Wordsworth, she
might well have agreed. Lord John Manners, writing to Disraeli
two years later, asked him why he had not suggested Wilberforce
for London. Disraeli replied that he was constantly being told
that public opinion throughout the country would have resented
the appointment – and would have visited its displeasure at the
polls on the government responsible for it.[44] There was another
and more cogent reason. Within a few hours of Longley's death
had come the announcement that Wilberforce's only daughter
Ella and her husband Henry Pye had been received into the
Roman Catholic Church. A translation at this moment of a
bishop whose three brothers and now whose daughter and son-
in-law had all gone over to Rome might not have gone down well

with the church public. But Wilberforce would have had to be very philosophic to conceal his disappointment at being passed over – and he noted the reactions of other leading clerics. 'The Archbishop of York chagrined manifestly', he confided to his diary on 15 November; and, four days later: 'Bishop of Gloucester very fierce about ecclesiastical appointments, especially as to Lincoln for London . . . I trying to discipline myself, but feeling the "affront", as dear Randall said.' Later the Dean of Windsor told him: 'He [Disraeli] alone prevented London being offered to you. The Queen . . . would have agreed to you . . . You cannot conceive the appointments he proposed and retracted or was overruled . . . He had no other thought than the votes of the moment; he showed an ignorance about all Church matters, men, opinions, that was astonishing . . . thoroughly unprincipled fellow. I trust we may never have such a man again.'[45] Wilberforce summed up his feelings in a letter to Sir Charles Anderson: 'I am afraid my dear children and friends will be disappointed. For myself, I really thank God; it very little disturbs me. I in my reason apprehend that by the common rule in such matters I had no right to be so treated; but I am really thankful in feeling so cool about it.'[46]

As for Wordsworth, he had *his* consolation prize: the bishopric of Lincoln. No doubt the Queen considered that the lack of experience which, in her view, disqualified him for London would matter little to the Lincolnshire peasantry. In the event he had to be persuaded to accept even *this* reward. When he received Disraeli's offer of the see he was at first inclined to turn it down. But he was on his way to stay with E. W. Benson, the Headmaster of Wellington and future Archbishop of Canterbury; and Benson persuaded him to change his mind and accept. Which was just as well, as it proved to be a mitre that fitted. Even the *Church Times*, which dismissed Jackson (21 November 1868) as 'one of the least distinguished of living prelates, one of the most helplessly incompetent of administrators',* wrote of his projected successor at Lincoln that 'we may cheerfully admit his learning, piety, and general orthodoxy'. Admittedly it spoiled the complimentary effect by adding that 'these qualities are marred by his fanatical hatred of the whole Roman Church and by the hereditary belief in his

---

*The *Church Times* had it in for poor Jackson. In the course of the same leader it declared: 'There is no prospect of the Bishop of Lincoln ever rising to the occasion. He will be more of a nobody at Fulham than even at Riseholm; and, if even the bucolic parsons of the fens and wolds have learnt that their diocesan is neither theologian nor ruler, it may well be supposed how soon the whetted intellects of London will detect him.' And more to the same effect!

own personal infallibility'. But at least the paper considered Wordsworth 'a safe person in any dispute against the Rationalizing [i.e. Broad Church] party'.

Disraeli's second premiership of just over six years (1874–80) was an anti-climax as far as church appointments were concerned. It was, however, an eventful period ecclesiastically, in that it saw a determined attempt to put down Ritualism through the courts. Much of the 1874 parliamentary session was spent by Disraeli (urged on by the Queen) in forcing through the Public Worship Regulation Bill in the teeth of fierce opposition. The fight, in the Prime Minister's words, was against the 'Mass in masquerade' – and it was to lead to a number of Anglo-Catholic priests being sent to prison for defying their bishops over matters of ceremonial in church. This attempt to regulate the externals of religion by means of the law was to fail eventually; but it kept the ecclesiastical pot boiling throughout Disraeli's second ministry. The period saw a further eight nominations to bishoprics; but, by and large, all went smoothly in comparison with the excitements of the 1868 premiership.

The most significant appointment, in that it was a stepping-stone on the road to higher things, was that of Edward White Benson to the newly-founded see of Truro, which had been carved out of the huge diocese of Exeter. After an assistant mastership at Rugby Benson had gone in 1859 to be Headmaster of Wellington, a public school which had been founded to perpetuate the memory of the great Duke and many of whose pupils were the sons of army officers. Its first patron was Prince Albert; and the Queen's subsequent close association with the school led to her getting to know Benson and admiring his quality. He left Wellington in 1873 to become Chancellor of Lincoln Cathedral. Three years later he was sounded informally as to whether he would accept the bishopric of Calcutta. After agonizing for days he decided against, mainly on the grounds that acceptance would mean leaving behind his six children to be educated in England. However, in December of the same year (1876), the offer of Truro arrived from the Prime Minister; and though, as he told his friend Joseph Lightfoot, '£3000 a year does not really seem adequate for a person without private fortune',[47] he was prepared to obey this particular call – especially as it was the desire of the Queen that he should accept it. Indeed she had pressed his claims on the Prime Minister, who complained to his friend Lady Bradford:

I am very busy trying to make a Bishop of Truro. Nothing gives me more trouble than the Episcopacy. There are so many parties, so many 'schools of thought' in the Church.* Cornwall is full of Dissenters, like a rabbit warren . . . And yet the dissenting pastors . . . are no longer popular with their flocks. So there is an opportunity for an adequate man.

Benson was obviously 'adequate', so Disraeli (by this time formally the Earl of Beaconsfield) was able to report to Lady Chesterfield four days later: 'I think I have got a good man' [for Truro]. Among those who had urged Benson's promotion was Disraeli's High Church friend, Gathorne Hardy. The Premier told Hardy immediately after dispatching the formal offer to Benson: 'You have made a bishop'.[49] Dean Church, who arranged his consecration service the following April in St Paul's Cathedral, told Benson: 'I hope you may be permitted to add in Cornwall another of the many victories which the revived English Church has achieved and which, in spite of disasters and menacing troubles, make it the most glorious Church in Christendom.'[50]

Disraeli had been happy to accept the Queen's recommendation of Benson for Truro because he was prepared to believe that he was a 'good man'. Indeed, throughout his second period of office, he relied less on party political considerations than in the first. And, so far as churchmanship went, he maintained a reasonable comprehensiveness, the Highish Benson and moderate Lightfoot being balanced by the Evangelical Thorold† and Ryle. He had to press for Lightfoot against the Queen's preference for her old favourite, Magee of Peterborough. Lightfoot had been a professor of divinity at Cambridge since 1861 and was widely acclaimed as among the foremost New Testament scholars of the age. He had declined the offer of the see of Lichfield from Lord Derby in 1867, but it was felt by many that he would make a first-rate Bishop of Durham.

Having given in once to the Queen over Magee, Disraeli was not going to be worsted a second time. Without denying Magee's

---

*The abundance of church parties was obviously a sore point with Disraeli. He wrote to Lady Bradford after the nomination of W. D. Maclagan to the see of Lichfield in 1878: 'I am glad you approve of the Bishop. It seems a success with all "schools of Church thought", *alias* Church nonsense.'[48]

†A. W. Thorold succeeded T. L. Claughton in 1877 as Bishop of Rochester after a portion of the diocese had been hived off to form the new see of St Albans under Claughton. The *Church Times* remarked bitchily (4 May 1877): 'The fact that Mr Thorold owes his canonry to him [Archbishop Thomson of York], and is besides his examining chaplain, amounts very nearly to a formal certificate of professional incompetence.'

abilities, he told her, 'No party has any confidence in him: his judgment cannot be relied on; he is vehement in opposite directions; and, above all, he is wanting in dignity of manner and mind.' Lightfoot, on the other hand, was an altogether superior article. 'The University of Durham, under his guidance, will exercise great influence on the ecclesiastical future, and on the formation of the religious mind of the rising generation.' Moreover (and here politics reared its head slightly):

> It is of great importance, to yr Majesty's Govt, that some mark of respect and recognition should now be shown to that powerful party of the Anglican Church which Lord Beaconsfield would describe as the 'right centre': those who, tho' High Churchmen, firmly resist, or hitherto have resisted, the deleterious designs of Canon Lyddon [sic] and the Dean of St Paul's [Church], who wish to terminate the connection between the Crown and the Church, and ultimately unite with the Greek Church. The Church Union is entirely under their control . . . No effort should be spared in preventing the orthodox and loyal High Church party being absorbed by these dangerous malcontents, who would support any candidate, even Bradlaugh, against your Majesty's Government.[51]

After Her Majesty had given way the Prime Minister piled on the flattery: 'Your Majesty's appointment of Canon Lightfoot to the see of Durham will add lustre to your Majesty's reign', he declared.

The final mitre to be bestowed by Disraeli was that for the new diocese of Liverpool. His choice was John Charles Ryle, a doughty Evangelical who once remarked that he had no love for 'men who had no distinct opinions: theological jelly-fish without bones, brains, teeth, or claws'.[52] The snag was that, only a fortnight earlier, Ryle had been nominated as Dean of Salisbury, though he had fortunately not yet been installed. So it represented a promotion of such lightning speed that the Prime Minister had to produce a cogent reason to convince the Queen. He came up with this masterpiece of special pleading:

> The people of Liverpool are very anxious about their new Bishop. The Tories subscribed the whole of the endowment, and built 'the palace'. Lord Sandon says his seat for Liverpool depends upon the appointment being made by your Majesty's present advisers. The whole city are most anxious that your Majesty should appoint the present Dean of Salisbury [Canon Ryle]. He is known at Liverpool, and has a great following. There would then be Salisbury for your Majesty's choice.[53]

By this time the Queen was prepared to take the honeyed words of her beloved Lord Beaconsfield on trust. Where, sixteen years before, she had jibbed at awarding a mitre to a dean (Jeune) who had been only six months in his deanery, she was now prepared to award one to a dean who could barely have begun unpacking his belongings in his new residence. But she agreed to Ryle's nomination, and he began his reign officially on 19 April. Eight days later, following his defeat by the Liberals in the general election, Disraeli resigned. He died the following year. On his deathbed he declined the offer of a visit from the Queen. He is reputed to have said: 'No, it is better not. She will only ask me to take a message to Albert.'

**Nominations to bishoprics 13 (10 first appointments, 3 translations)**

*First appointments:*

(1) 1868: James Atlay to Hereford.
(2) 1868: William Connor Magee to Peterborough.
(3) 1868: Christopher Wordsworth to Lincoln.

(4) 1874: William Basil Tickell Jones to St Davids.
(5) 1876: Edward White Benson to Truro.
(6) 1877: Anthony Wilson Thorold to Rochester.
(7) 1877: Rowley Hill to Sodor and Man.
(8) 1878: William Dalrymple Maclagan to Lichfield.
(9) 1879: Joseph Barber Lightfoot to Durham.
(10) 1880: John Charles Ryle to Liverpool.

*Translations:*

(1) 1868: Archibald Campbell Tait to Canterbury (from London).
(2) 1868: John Jackson to London (from Lincoln).

(3) 1877: Thomas Legh Claughton to St Albans (from Rochester).

# 9

# Back to Olympus

W. E. Gladstone: Prime Minister
9 December 1868 – 17 February 1874
28 April 1880 – 9 June 1885
6 February – 29 July 1886
18 August 1892 – 3 March 1894

William Ewart Gladstone (1809–98), *four times Prime Minister of the United Kingdom, was the Grand Old Man of Victorian politics and for fifty years a dominant figure in the House of Commons. The son of a Liverpool merchant, he was educated at Eton and Christ Church, Oxford (obtaining firsts in classics and mathematics), and entered the Commons in 1832 as Tory member for Newark. He held several junior offices under Peel, becoming Colonial Secretary in 1845 and following his leader into opposition when the Conservative Party split over the repeal of the Corn Laws and Peel resigned. After some years in the political wilderness Gladstone returned to office in 1853, becoming Chancellor of the Exchequer in Aberdeen's coalition ministry of Whigs and Peelites. He held the same post in Palmerston's second administration of 1859–65 and during this period transferred his full political allegiance to the Liberals. He succeeded Russell as leader of the Liberal Party in 1867 and became Premier for the first time at the end of the following year, having defeated Disraeli in a general election fought on the issue of Irish disestablishment. His first premiership saw both the disestablishment of the Irish Church and the seminal Education Act of 1870. After his defeat in the general election of 1874 he resigned the leadership of the Liberal Party and devoted himself to theological studies. But anger over Disraeli's failure to denounce the 'Bulgarian atrocities' committed by the Turks brought him out of his semi-retirement. He aroused the conscience of the nation and was swept back into power in the general election of 1880. His second premiership was dominated by Irish controversies, by the battle to extend the UK franchise and by British involvement in the affairs of Egypt and the Sudan – cul-*

*minating in the fall of Khartoum and the death of Gordon. After a brief interval of Conservative government Gladstone was returned to power for the third time in February 1886, but split the Liberal Party on the issue of internal self-government for Ireland and was again defeated. For the next six years he led the opposition to Salisbury's coalition of Conservatives and Liberal Unionists, but became Premier for the fourth and last time (aged 82) in August 1892. After successfully steering an Irish Home Rule Bill through the Commons but seeing it rejected by the Lords (who then held a power of veto) he resigned in March 1894, handing over the Liberal leadership to Rosebery.*

*Although Gladstone devoted his life to politics he could equally well have pursued a career in the Church, to which he was passionately devoted and on the affairs of which he was an acknowledged expert. He had originally intended to take holy orders, but had had to give up the idea in the face of his father's opposition. Religion, however, remained (along with politics) the dominant interest of his life – and was the driving force behind the lofty principles and unbending sense of moral duty which underlay his parliamentary activities and helped to mould him into becoming the greatest statesman of his age.*

'A vacant See is a great excitement to Mr G. Indeed I believe it excites him far more than a political crisis.'[1] Thus his secretary, Edward Hamilton, summed up Gladstone's reaction to the news of a bishop's retirement and the need to choose a successor. Disraeli too had often been excited at the prospect of another episcopal vacancy to fill. But *his* enthusiasm had been fired by the thought of possible electoral advantage if he could find the right man, whereas Gladstone acted on an altogether higher moral plane. This was hardly surprising in view of the two men's totally dissimilar attitudes to religion. Disraeli, though formally a member of the Church of England, sat lightly to the deeper obligations of Christianity and was woefully ignorant of many of the practicalities of Anglican affairs. Hence his approach to Church appointments was openly opportunist and blatantly political. He weighed vacant sees in terms of votes, whereas to Gladstone they provided opportunities, as he saw it, of serving the best interests of the Church.

Gladstone had imbibed his religion literally at his mother's knee, she being an ardent Evangelical. It remained 'by far the most important part of his life, in comparison with which politics were merely accidental and external'.[2] As an undergraduate he had brooded over the possibility of becoming a priest. He wrote to his father in 1830: 'I do not see how I am to persuade myself that any powers, be they the meanest or the greatest, can be *so* profitably or *so* nobly employed as in the performance of this sublime duty.' His father, however, thought otherwise – and persuaded him to aim at a political rather than an ecclesiastical career. 'You will allow me to doubt', he told his son, 'whether the picture your perhaps too sanguine mind has drawn would ever be practically realized.'[3] So Gladstone's role in the Church was to be that of a devout layman. 'His faith was to him', in the words of a friend, 'what the Nile is to Egypt, what sunshine is to the world.'[4] He went to church twice on Sundays, was a weekly communicant and taught in the Sunday school. But his was no Sundays-only religion. In his own household prayers were said twice daily – and sometimes he would preach to a congregation of his family and servants. As he dressed and undressed, he would read from a large Bible kept on his dressing-table.[5] He had a stern view on the need to use time properly and not to fritter it away. 'We should deal with our time', he advised his eldest son, 'as we see in a shop a grocer deal with tea or sugar, or a haberdasher with stuffs and ribands: weighing or measuring it out in proportions adjusted to that which we are to get for and by it.'[6]

Gladstone read widely in theology and church history – and himself wrote books and pamphlets on religious topics. He was the supreme example of an ecclesiastical layman, his appetite for acquiring knowledge being matched by his capacity to store it in his mind and bring it out as occasion offered. He had been brought up as an Evangelical, but was gradually converted to the ideals of the Oxford Movement and knew many of the leading Tractarians. He was never an extremist, however. He deplored the excesses of Ritualistic priests; but he equally deplored attempts to put down Ritualism by law and doggedly opposed the Public Worship Regulation Bill as, under Disraeli's sponsorship, it inched its way through Parliament. He regarded himself as a quintessential Anglican and took pride in the Church of England's claim to be the Catholic Church of the land.

This then was the man who was to choose the Church of England's bishops during two long and two short premierships which together totalled over twelve years. 'It is extraordinary the trouble he takes with making these clerical appointments', his secretary, Edward Hamilton, wrote in a diary entry for June 1882. 'I doubt if a Prime Minister ever was so conscientious on this matter before or took so much pains or had so much personal knowledge of individual clerics.'[7] Of this period another of Gladstone's secretaries, George Leveson Gower, wrote many years afterwards:

Whenever a Church dignitary happened to die – and we used to say that we thought that they did so on purpose to spite Mr G. – the whole business of State seemed to be put aside whilst he poured forth a perfect avalanche of letters inquiring at great length and in minute detail as to the comparative merits and claims of various clergymen for preferment. In fact he seemed hardly able to give his full mind to any other matter, however weighty or urgent, until this Bishopric, Deanery, or even Canonry were filled.[8]

Many of those letters, in that pre-typewriter age, would have been written out by the Prime Minister in his own hand and afterwards copied into a letter-book by one of his secretaries.

Gladstone was a High Churchman and the leader of the Liberal Party. But he cast his ecclesiastical net widely; and many of those trawled up in it were neither Liberals nor High Churchmen. As he put it to a friend: 'Saints, theologians, teachers, pastors, scholars, philosophers, gentlemen, men of business – these are not to be had every day; least of all are they to be commonly found in combination. But these are the materials which ought to be sought out, and put forward in the Church of England, if she is to stand the trials and do her work.'[9]

He once jotted down on a scrap of paper the qualities he looked for in a potential bishop. His list ran as follows:

Piety. Learning (sacred). Eloquence. Administrative power. Faithful allegiance to the Church and to the Church of England. Activity. Tact and courtesy in dealings with men: knowledge of the world. Accomplishments and literature. An equitable spirit. Faculty of working with his brother bishops. Some legal habit of mind. Circumspection. Courage. Maturity of age and character. Corporal vigour. Liberal sentiments on public affairs. A representative character with reference to shades of opinion fairly allowable in the Church.[10]

Political allegiance ranked sixteenth in the list of seventeen qualities considered by Gladstone to be desirable in a bishop: Disraeli would no doubt have put such allegiance in the first place. To at least one of his secretaries Gladstone, so far as politics were concerned, was 'rigidly impartial' in his church appointments. In the words of George Leveson Gower:

I had all but said 'too impartial', by which I mean that if a clergyman had shown himself active on the Liberal side it almost seemed as though this put him at a disadvantage. Since no corresponding feeling actuated Conservative Prime Ministers, to say the least of it, with regard to clergymen of their own political views, there was not much inducement to an able and ambitious clergyman to espouse the cause of Liberalism.[11]

This was taking too simplistic a view. Ever conscious of the minority representation of the Liberals in the House of Lords, Gladstone could not afford wholly to ignore political considerations. He made this plain in August 1869 when seeking a bishop for the vacant diocese of Bath and Wells. His favoured choice was Lord Arthur Hervey, a son of the Marquess of Bristol; and he invited a friend of Lord Arthur's to tell him in confidence 'what you think of his political leanings, a subject which, though I could never consent to make it paramount, I cannot in the office I now hold leave wholly out of view'. Eventually Hervey was given a clean bill of political health by Archbishop Tait: 'If not what is called in party language a Liberal, he is most truly liberal and enlightened in his views.'[12] This was enough for Gladstone, who appointed Hervey to the vacant see. The successful candidate was duly grateful, assuring Gladstone in after years that he had always been 'most generous in not claiming from me any political *obedience*', though conscious of the fact that 'it is to your kindness and friendship that I owe the possession of a vote in the legislature'.[13] As it happened, most of the bishops appointed by Gladstone during his first ministry were Liberals in the true political sense. But his second batch (1880–5) were mainly Conservatives – among them the new Archbishop of Canterbury, E. W. Benson. So Leveson Gower's comment, though not true of Gladstone's first premiership, could justifiably be applied to the later period.

Gladstone's general policy over episcopal appointments was to favour moderate men of every church party – and to divide his favours between the parties. His main problem was that, unlike Palmerston, he was unable to discover many Evangelicals distinguished enough, in his view, to deserve mitres. Hamilton, commenting on a claim by the *Pall Mall Gazette* that the Prime Minister was preferring too many High Churchmen as compared with Broad or Low Churchmen, conceded that the section which had received really scant favour had been the Evangelical school – 'the fact being that there are so few men of eminence among the Low Churchmen'.[14] Bishop Wilberforce agreed. The Evangelical school, he told Gladstone, was 'in its utter decadence'. He suggested that the Prime Minister might show his 'fairness and even-handedness' by awarding minor appointments to such Low Churchmen as he could find.[15] Hamilton (who was himself the son of the High Church Bishop of Salisbury who had been slipped under Queen Victoria's guard by Aberdeen) diagnosed Gladstone's mind thus in January 1884, when the search was on for a bishop for the new see of Southwell. 'What is evidently in Mr G.'s mind in view of other episcopal vacancies', he wrote in his diary, 'is to "do off" the Low and Broad Churchmen and then to follow them up by men like Dr Liddon and Canon King.'[16] Undoubtedly High Churchmen fared far better under Gladstone than under previous prime ministers – King, who was made Bishop of Lincoln, being a notable example. But they were by no means the exclusive recipients of Gladstone's ecclesiastical patronage; and he was quick to point this out when accused of favouring them unduly. To one such challenger in 1883 he replied that, of thirty 'important appointments' he had made, only eleven would probably be called High Churchmen. 'On further examination it will appear that High Churchmen, whom I take to be a decided majority of the clergy as well as a decided minority of my recommendations, have gone as a rule to the places of hard work and little pay.' He ended by observing that such terms as High, Low and Broad were 'rather repugnant' to him, 'but I use them as a currency of tokens with which it is difficult to dispense'.[17] The nub of the problem of episcopal appointments he put in a letter to his daughter Mary:

> It is to be borne in mind that they [the bishops] are so preferred not by a single force but by many. If I am one of them, so the particular diocese is another, the Queen a third, the Liberal Party a fourth. It is the resultant of all these forces which determines the choice. Men of the highest stamp as a class should undoubtedly be chosen, but it cannot be the highest man in the class.[18]

To show the pains taken by Gladstone over church appointments Hamilton recorded a conversation he had had with G. H. Wilkinson, the newly-appointed Bishop of Truro, concerning the choice of his own successor as Vicar of St Peter's, Eaton Square, now in the gift of the Crown. 'He told me that he should always regard his conversation on this appointment with Mr G. as among the greatest honours of his life; it was a real privilege and comfort to talk to a man like Mr G. who had the interests of the Church so much at heart.'[19]

In his letter to Mary Gladstone quoted above the Prime Minister had described Queen Victoria as one of the four 'forces' involved in the appointment of each new bishop. The Queen in fact was not so much a force as an obstacle who occasionally proved insurmountable. Throughout his premierships, and particularly during his second period of office (1880–5), she was to engage in frequent passages of arms with Gladstone. Part of the trouble lay in her jealousy of her Prime Minister. Hamilton in his diary tells of a letter he received from his master in which Gladstone

> opens his mind about the Queen and himself. She feels, as he puts it, aggrieved at the undue reverence shewn to an old man [Gladstone was then 74] of whom the public are being constantly reminded, and who goes on working for them beyond the allotted time, while H.M. is, owing to the life she leads, withdrawn from view. Hence comes a dislocation of the natural and just balance of popular interest.

Hamilton then puts his own gloss on Gladstone's letter:

> What he wraps up in guarded and considerate language is (to put it bluntly) *jealousy*. She can't bear to see the large type which heads the columns of newspapers by 'Mr Gladstone's movements', while down below is in small type the Court Circular. This is no unnatural feeling in a Sovereign, especially when the Sovereign is a woman . . . She finds Herself with a Prime Minister whose position in this country is unique and unlike that of anyone else of whom She has had experience, or of whom indeed any of Her predecessors had experience.[20]

The Prime Minister was certainly a hero to his secretaries, who sometimes felt that the Queen was not sufficiently appreciative of the efforts he made on her behalf. Leveson Gower draws a touching picture of Gladstone writing regular bulletins to her ('always couched in terms of the most courtly deference') on the proceedings of each sitting in the House of Commons:

> I remember once after a specially tiring and harassing debate witnessing a sight which to me was peculiarly pathetic. Mr Gladstone, paler even than usual and looking worn out with fatigue, sat late at night writing his letter to the Queen, unmoved by the habitual taunts and insults which were being hurled at him by the Opposition; and I could not help wondering whether the Royal recipient of that letter at all realized the depth and fervour of devotion with which the Crown and the Royal Family were unceasingly served by the greatest of her Ministers, in circumstances which might well have discouraged a less magnanimous and high-minded statesman.[21]

In fact the Queen's relations with Gladstone during his first premiership were far less acrimonious than they became later on.

No doubt she noted the contrast between his approach to church appointments and that of Disraeli, and appreciated the pains he was obviously taking to find the best man to fill each vacancy that arose. He was a close friend of the Queen's beloved Dean of Windsor, Gerald Wellesley; and the Dean was able to act as a valuable go-between in the discussions that took place on the claims of rival candidates. Gladstone was rather less intimate with the comparatively youthful Randall Davidson, who took over as Dean in 1883 after the death of Wellesley's short-lived successor. But the Queen herself continued to take a close interest in the filling of ecclesiastical vacancies. Davidson's biographer, George Bell, prints a memorandum drawn up by Davidson in 1906 (by when he had become Archbishop of Canterbury) to describe the Queen's practice in the matter:

> She did not like to wait until a recommendation should arrive from the Prime Minister before forming opinions of her own about the vacant position and the sort of man who was to fill it. I say the sort of man, for I always deprecated any endeavour upon the Queen's part to shift to her own shoulders the responsibility belonging to the Prime Minister, as representative of the English people, of nominating the particular man who should fill the vacant office . . . I always tried to impress upon her that the Prime Minister of his day holds office because he is the man the English people want to have in that position, and therefore we are bound to regard his judgment as expressing the contemporary judgment of the nation as a whole. This, though she admitted its truth, she used to regard as a rather troublesome dogma of mine.[22]

But the Queen, though she may have appeared at times to the diplomatic Davidson to sit lightly to the constitutional niceties, at least appreciated that different sorts of men might be wanted for different positions. 'I remember being struck', says Davidson in his memorandum, 'by hearing her blurt out, with reference to an appointment at Manchester: "The man seems to think he is making an appointment to Wells or Ely, and not to a great industrial capital."'

It is ironic that the only one of Gladstone's nominations to cause a public furore got past the Queen more or less on the nod. This was because the man in question, Frederick Temple, Headmaster of Rugby, happened to be a Broad Churchman, a class of cleric which had Her Majesty's full approval. It is also ironic that this particular appointment, which was to excite the fiercest controversy since the nomination of Hampden a generation earlier, should have been made by a churchman as orthodox as Gladstone. Temple was recommended to the Queen on 22 September 1869 for the see of Exeter (vacant at long last by the resignation of the aged Phillpotts) 'by reason of his very high character and remarkable abilities for administration and otherwise, and also of his probable influence in the House of Lords'.[23] (Temple was a Liberal.)

The objection to Temple's nomination was a straightforward one. He was the author of the introductory article to a notorious volume, *Essays and Reviews*, which had been condemned by the Convocation of Canterbury in 1864 as 'containing teaching contrary to the doctrine received by the United Church of England and Ireland in common with the whole Catholic Church of Christ'. In fact Temple's essay had been couched in more moderate terms than the others in the book: no one had impugned its orthodoxy, and it was supposed by many churchpeople not to have been included in Convocation's general anathema.* He declined, however, to pacify his critics by withdrawing his essay from subsequent editions of the book, but instead published a volume of his Rugby sermons so that the critics could re-read his essay in the context of his general teaching. This at least reassured the parents of Rugby boys, though one sixth-former, in response to an anxious enquiry from home, added his own personal reassurance: 'Dear Mother, Temple's all right; but if he turns Mahometan all the school will turn too.'[24] Admittedly the Headmaster happened to be a Liberal who backed Gladstone's move to disestablish the Church of Ireland; but, though his essay might have been indiscreet, he still, in the Prime Minister's eyes, possessed many of the qualities mentioned in his list as desirable in a bishop. Gladstone pointed out to the Bishop of Lichfield, George Selwyn, that Temple's responsibility prior to the publication of *Essays and Reviews* had been confined to his own contribution.

> The question whether he ought to have disclaimed or denounced any part of the volume afterwards is a difficult one, and, if it was a duty, it was a duty in regard to which a generous man might well go wrong. As regards his own essay, I read it at the time of publication and thought it of little value, but did not perceive that it was mischievous.[25]

* The essay which caused all the fuss was in fact a Rugby School address which had been reworked into an Oxford University sermon. Its subject was 'The Education of the World', comparing the growth of an individual with the growth of mankind. Though some of Temple's interpretations of biblical texts were questionable, the essay was basically inoffensive from the standpoint of orthodoxy.

Temple was nominated with the Queen's full approval, but Gladstone was under no illusions that the nomination would be unopposed. He had written to Archbishop Tait on 2 October, a few days before it was made public, to warn him that he was not so sanguine as to believe that it would pass 'without some noise';[26] and the expected noise was soon heard. Indeed so loud did it become that Gladstone even warned the Queen of the likelihood of some formal remonstrance being made or some other proceedings attempted in a bid to halt Temple's nomination. He added, however, that such proceedings were unlikely to be 'favoured by the more sober-minded even of those who disapprove', and that 'nothing has occurred to lead Mr Gladstone to regret his recommendation of Dr Temple to your Majesty'.[27]

The outcry against the nomination resulted in an uneasy alliance of High and Low Churchmen. A committee was formed to promote resistance to the appointment both inside and outside the diocese. The chairman of the committee was Shaftesbury and the vice-chairman Pusey: they were cousins, so their close personal relations made such an alliance between representatives of opposing religious camps that much easier. But Shaftesbury accepted the chairmanship of the committee with some reluctance, as he was under no illusions as to the motives of many of his fellow-Evangelicals. He wrote in his diary on 23 October:

> The Temple affair has revealed many things. It has revealed the utter indifference of the country at large: the coldness and insincerity of the bulk of the Evangelicals, their disunion, their separation in place and action. It has shown that they have much political and personal, and very little spiritual, Protestantism. They dislike the appointment because Gladstone made it, and they would not oppose it lest they should be found in concurrence with Pusey . . . It has revealed, too, their utter intolerance.[28]

Nevertheless, Shaftesbury had turned his hand to the plough, and he was to do his duty by the committee in spite of his private misgivings and his feeling that the very vehemence of the public protest might turn out to be counter-productive. He presented a memorial to the Prime Minister on behalf of the committee, urging him to retract his advice to the Queen to approve Temple's nomination. He told Gladstone that, while he respected Temple's personal character and talents, he felt that to have contributed to such a work as *Essays and Reviews* was an 'absolute disqualification for the profession and responsibilities of so sacred an office'. But Gladstone declined to act. He assured Shaftesbury that the appointment had been made in the firm conviction that it would tend to promote the true interest of religion.[29]

Meanwhile the uproar against it grew no less, and letters rained down on the luckless Tait urging him to interfere and have the nomination cancelled. 'The agitation in the diocese', wrote the Dean of Exeter, 'becomes stronger every day, and from all parts of the country I have letters about the sword of the Lord and of Gideon, exhorting us to go to prison' rather than obey the royal injunction to elect Temple. 'Matters are hourly growing more serious,' another critic wrote. 'The diocese of Exeter is fast approaching the boiling-point. Meetings are being held, organisations set on foot, and every preparation made for resistance. Can your Grace in any way interpose so as to prevent Gladstone pushing matters to an extremity?'[30] His Grace declined to interpose. He forwarded a bundle of protests to Gladstone, who, on returning them, observed sardonically: 'The movement against Dr Temple is, like a peculiar cheer we sometimes hear in the House of Commons, vehement but thin.'[31] In fact it was basically a clerical movement. Pusey might inveigh against the luckless Temple for having 'participated in the ruin of countless souls', and Bishop Trower might warn readers of *The Times* that Temple's consecration would be 'perhaps the greatest sin with respect to fidelity to revealed truth in which the Church of England has been involved since the Reformation';[32] but the laity by and large were little upset by the nomination. Bishop Browne of Ely estimated that nineteen out of every twenty laymen approved of it.

Temple's opponents, however, were determined to carry on the fight to the bitter end. So worried was Tait that the Dean and Chapter of Exeter might refuse to elect the Crown's nominee that he drafted a letter of reassurance making the point, among others, that the Prime Minister would never nominate an unworthy candidate. In the event he refrained from sending the letter, and the Chapter found itself seriously split. Temple was elected by thirteen votes to six, with four abstentions, a larger minority risking the penalties of *praemunire* (possible imprisonment and the loss of their goods and chattels) than had been the case even with Hampden twenty years earlier. The next stage was the confirmation of the election at St Mary-le-Bow church in London on 8 December. The situation was considered sufficiently grave for Temple's elder sister to be summoned to testify that her brother had been born in lawful wedlock (a bastard could not be a bishop). Lawyers for the opposition raised formal objections to Temple's election, but, as in the case of Hampden, the objections were overruled. The Vicar-General insisted that the royal mandate must be carried out.

Temple was now legally a bishop, but even this was not the end of the affair. He had still to be consecrated, and the controversy showed no signs of dying down. Eventually Tait was driven to defend the bishop-elect through a letter published in *The Times* (22 November). He affirmed his personal admiration for Temple, suggested that the popularity of Rugby as a school indicated a public confidence in its headmaster and, most significantly, claimed that Temple did *not* fall under the blanket Convocation censure of *Essays and Reviews*. But the Archbishop's letter was not all sweetness and light, and he fired a warning shot across Temple's bows. Expressing regret that the bishop-elect had not withdrawn his essay from the condemned volume long ago, he suggested that, as soon as Temple took up his duties at Exeter, he ought to make his theological viewpoint clear.[33] At this stage the Archbishop, exhausted first by the long battle over Irish disestablishment and now by the Temple controversy, suffered a stroke.* So the chief responsibility for Temple's consecration fell on the Bishop of London, John Jackson. Out of seventeen bishops in the province of Canterbury no fewer than nine objected to taking part in the ceremony – four formally (including Ellicott, Selwyn and Wordsworth) and five unofficially (including Magee and Wilberforce). Some of the dissidents appealed to the fourth canon of the Council of Nicaea, which required the consent of all comprovincial bishops to a consecration. But the Church of England's law did not recognize this particular canon and required the presence of a mere three bishops. Temple was duly consecrated in Westminster Abbey on 21 December 1869.

The final act in the drama centred on the Convocation of Canterbury. A few members, led by Archdeacon Denison, urged Convocation to register its objection to the appointment. But when, through a friend of Temple (but without Temple's approval), Convocation was informed of his intention to withdraw his essay from any further edition of *Essays and Reviews*, the motion was withdrawn.[35] The controversy then rapidly subsided. Temple (like Hampden) performed his episcopal duties to everyone's satisfaction; and his eventual promotion first to

---

*Tait's stroke (from which he soon recovered) caused the promotional wheels to whirl for a while. Gladstone had the Dean of Windsor in mind to succeed him, and even Wilberforce had a final flicker of ambition. He wrote to his son Ernest: 'Everyone takes for granted, without any foundation, that if he [Tait] is removed I shall go there. I pray God to keep me from all bad thoughts, and I do feel very quiet indeed about it.'[34]

London and then to Canterbury caused scarcely a ripple of protest. But, at the time that the controversy was at its height, the Prime Minister's political opponents had rejoiced. It had, Bishop Ellicott told Disraeli, done Gladstone a world of harm. 'I think if our party is watchful and prudent they may secure the whole of the Church party. Gladstone's best Church friends are now, I privately know, much against him.'[36] If this was so, he survived their hostility with ease.

Temple's nomination to Exeter was one of four which Gladstone had submitted to the Queen in a single batch on 22 September 1869. His list had been headed by the name of Samuel Wilberforce, who, he recommended, should be translated from Oxford to Winchester 'on account of his distinguished powers and great practical services'. So, in his sixty-fifth year, promotion had at last come to 'Soapy Sam'. But, though a senior see, Winchester was not the post for which he had really hoped. He had set his sights on the superior goals of York and London, and in each case had been disappointed. Winchester, in a sense, was a poor consolation prize for his twenty-four years' hard labour in the diocese of Oxford. Moreover, as he was quick to point out, materially he would be worse off from the change. The retirement of his predecessor, Charles Sumner, had only been made possible by the Bishops' Resignation Act, passed in 1869. Under the terms of that Act Wilberforce was required to make over to Sumner as a pension £2000 of the £7000 which was now the reduced income of the see. This left him with a mere £5000 – the same sum which he had been receiving as Bishop of Oxford, but with far greater expenses.

There was also a political twist to his translation, and he had to defend himself against accusations that it had come as a reward for his support of the government in pushing through the Bill disestablishing the Church of Ireland. In fact he had neither spoken nor voted on the Bill until it had gone into committee after the second reading. And, when amendments came up, he had voted more often against than for the government. But, although he might oppose the Bill on points of detail, he was for it in principle. He realized that Gladstone could claim the support of a large majority in its favour throughout the country, and he had convinced himself that a diehard attempt to defeat it would be futile. But, as a previous opponent of disestablishment, he now had to justify his change of tack to the Irish bishops – and persuade them to withdraw their opposition. This must be done privately (for obvious reasons):

I should lose all power of doing good in the matter if it were to seem that I deserted [the Irish bishops] in their difficulty; and this hindrance is aggravated by the way in which Disraeli has avenged the sin of my known affection to Gladstone in those recent ecclesiastical appointments which are likely to outlast my life, and which will give so easy a handle for attributing my action to personal pique.[37]

About this time Wilberforce had received a letter from Lord Lyttelton, Gladstone's brother-in-law. In effect, beneath a sea of verbiage, it had offered Wilberforce the see of Winchester in exchange for his backing for the Irish Church Bill. 'Now of course what I am saying and about to say cannot but have the look of suggesting a temptation to you to let personal motives have weight with you in a grave public question. I cannot help that, as it is irrelevant in the case.'[38] To what extent Gladstone inspired Lyttelton's letter remains a mystery. Lyttelton informed Wilberforce's biographer, Canon Ashwell, that he had written 'almost in Mr Gladstone's name'. Gladstone himself told Lord Granville that he had got Lyttelton to write to the bishop – 'of course not in my name'. Years later he told Reginald Wilberforce, the bishop's son, who had taken over the biography after Ashwell's death and had asked him about the Lyttelton letter:

My memory does not record any single instance in which your father's advancement to Winchester was associated even by the most censorious of men with political subserviency. It was a very small acknowledgment of his vast services to the Church of England . . . I have no recollection of Lord Lyttelton's having written 'in my name', but it is perfectly possible that I . . . may have encouraged the idea.[39]

The remaining episcopal appointments of Gladstone's first premiership excited little comment. Wilberforce enjoyed the enhanced prestige of his new see for only four years before he was killed by a throw from his horse while out riding. His successor was Harold Browne of Ely – 'a prelate of the highest character both for learning and for moderation',[40] Gladstone assured the Queen. One break with precedent was the appointment of Joshua Hughes to St Asaph in 1870 – the first appointment of a Welsh-speaker in the Principality since 1715. As an alumnus of St David's College, Lampeter, Hughes also provided a break in the Oxbridge pattern of appointments.

It was in the early years of Gladstone's second premiership that the ecclesiastical sparks once again began to fly – provoked

on several occasions by a difference of opinion with the Queen.
The first dispute arose over the deanery of Westminster, vacant
by the death of A. P. Stanley in July 1881. The Prime Minister's
choice was one of the late Dean's colleagues, Canon Alfred Barry.
He proposed Barry to the Queen. She telegraphed back from
Osborne: 'We earnestly ask you to pause about Canon Barry.
Would infinitely prefer Dean of Christ Church [Liddell] . . . The
former has not the social position or superiority over others he
should have.'[41] On making enquiries Gladstone discovered that
Liddell was unwilling to move. He therefore suggested some
further names: the Headmaster of Eton, J. J. Hornby; the Headmaster of Harrow, H. M. Butler; and the Lord Chancellor's
brother, Edwin Palmer. The Queen thought Butler the best of the
trio. Unfortunately he was a member of the Church Reform
Association, which was anathema to Gladstone, but she felt sure
that this particular difficulty could be overcome. If not, she
suggested G. G. Bradley, Master of University College, Oxford,
and 'very distinguished . . . Barry and Hornby decidedly inferior'.
Gladstone, who was himself veering towards Palmer, complained
to Dean Wellesley: 'Does she think the two positions of sovereign
and minister are to be inverted? This really cannot go on long,
with me at least.' Bradley might be 'distinguished', but he was
too much of a schoolmaster in Gladstone's view to make a good
dean. Though he still favoured Palmer, the Queen continued to
press for Bradley. Consenting at last, though with reluctance, he
complained again to Wellesley:

> If I am, in the view of the constitution, the person responsible
> for the appointment, it requires strong and exceptional
> considerations to justify me in not sustaining this opinion by a
> corresponding recommendation [of Palmer]. Still I feel that the
> Queen has a peculiar feeling on this case, founded on strength
> of personal attachment . . .[42]

So he gave way – only to find himself crossing swords with his
royal mistress less than a year later over the first episcopal
appointment of his new ministry. The bishop was needed for the
newly created see of Newcastle, and Gladstone proposed G. H.
Wilkinson, Vicar of St Peter's, Eaton Square (a parish which
included Buckingham Palace). The Queen strongly objected. She
had a horror of Wilkinson, Wellesley told the Prime Minister,
regarding him as a 'sentimentalist, half High, half Low Church,
and a most power-loving clergyman'. In vain did Gladstone bring
up a whole succession of episcopal big guns to support his
choice: the Archbishop of Canterbury and the Bishops of London,
Durham and Winchester all spoke highly of Wilkinson. The

Queen remained adamant in her dislike of Gladstone's nominee. 'It is surely possible that without a single prop in the opinion of any authority this egotism may give way', Gladstone wistfully suggested to Wellesley. The Dean, however, could offer little comfort:

> I cannot set this down to *egotism* because she cannot have any personal interest in that bishopric. But she had always been sincerely prejudiced against him [Wilkinson], as all women are in society who form a party against those clergy who – they fancy – exercise priestly power. The very influence which they exercise over their parishes turns against them. 'This mode of dealing with people', she says, 'is most objectionable.'[43]

Once again Gladstone gave in – and in due course submitted the name of Samuel Wilberforce's son Ernest to be the first Bishop of Newcastle. The Queen agreed. In the event all the fuss had been a waste of effort. When Gladstone sought a successor to Edward Benson as Bishop of Truro after Benson's translation to Canterbury the following year, he again recommended Wilkinson. On this occasion the Queen accepted his choice. 'She seems to have changed Her mind about Mr Wilkinson', Gladstone's secretary, Edward Hamilton, remarks in his diary. 'This is probably due in part to Her having seen Bishop Benson, whose visit to Osborne was excellently timed, coming as it did on the very day She received Mr G.'s recommendation.'[44] The Queen was still far from enthusiastic, however. Referring to Benson's visit in a letter to Gladstone the following day, she observed: 'All that he said in favour of Mr Wilkinson (who the Queen is *not* very partial to) for the *particular* See of Truro – which she had *also* heard from Mr Davidson – leads her to the conclusion that he should be appointed to *that* Bishopric, which she accordingly sanctions.'[45] One see's poison was evidently regarded as another see's meat. Hamilton later reports: 'The Queen was not taken at all with Bishop Wilkinson when he did homage.'

But this was in the future. Meanwhile another crisis had arisen with the death of Dean Wellesley in September 1882. This was a deep personal loss to Gladstone but even more so to the Queen, who had relied extensively on the Dean for advice and counsel on church matters. A difference of opinion at once arose as to whether the deanery of Windsor, with its close royal connections, was different from other church appointments in that the sovereign rather than the prime minister took the initiative in filling it.

The constitutional position was admittedly confused; but, to begin with, Gladstone stuck to his guns and, while admitting the personal nature of the appointment, insisted on his right to suggest names to the Queen. In fact he suggested two: Dean Liddell and Lord Alwyne Compton. But the Queen had already made up her mind – and was not having either of the prime ministerial candidates. She proposed her own nominee:

> What the Queen wants is a tolerant, liberal-minded, Broad Church clergyman who at the same time is pleasant socially and is popular with all members and classes of her Household, who understands her feelings not only in ecclesiastical but also in social matters – a good, kind man without pride. The Queen, after much thought and consideration, has thought of Canon Connor, who unites the different qualifications which the Queen has enumerated. She only regrets that he is not of higher social and ecclesiastical rank. But he is of good family and a thorough gentleman, and universally respected.[46]

Once again Gladstone found himself having to bow the knee to the Sovereign. 'I cannot be a party', he told the Queen's secretary, 'to establishing any precedents against my successor, but I will certainly, in deference to Her Majesty, withhold any nomination I might have been led to make; although it would have undoubtedly been made with the desire that it should be accommodated to Her Majesty's convenience.'[47] So Connor obtained what Hamilton later described as '*the* appointment of all ecclesiastical appointments, the most charming of all ecclesiastical berths'.[48] But he was not to enjoy it for long. He died on 1 May 1883 after only seven months in office, and the whole business had to be gone through again. The Queen's first choice this time round was William Boyd Carpenter, a canon of Windsor; but his recent marriage to a 'most respectable but still not socially distinguished lady' perhaps made him less desirable as a dean than as a canon. So, on reflection, her choice fastened on Randall Davidson, whose wife was a daughter of Archbishop Tait and who, though only thirty-five, had acquired a considerable knowledge of church affairs through having acted as secretary to his late father-in-law. The Queen found Davidson 'singularly pleasing both in appearance and manner, very sympathetic and evidently very intelligent, wise, and able'.[49] Gladstone hinted at Davidson's youth as an objection to the appointment, but the Queen brought forward Archbishop Benson in her support. Gladstone withdrew his objection. 'I should have submitted my scruple on the score of age to Her Majesty', he told her secretary, Sir Henry Ponsonby, 'had I not been estopped by the heavy artillery she was pleased to bring into the field, which reduced my little point to dust and ashes.'[50]

Like Russell, Palmerston and Disraeli before him, Gladstone found himself having to nominate a new Archbishop of Canterbury. Like Disraeli, he had to argue the case for his candidate with the Queen; but, unlike Disraeli, he got his way in the end.

For some months before his death on 3 December 1882 Archbishop Tait had been ailing, so that the question of his successor had long been on Gladstone's agenda. There were three serious candidates: Browne of Winchester, aged 71; Lightfoot of Durham, 54; and Benson of Truro, 53. A fourth candidate, or at least one whose name was often canvassed in the press, was the Dean of St Paul's, R. W. Church, a High Churchman whom Gladstone had appointed to the deanery in 1871; but he had already told the Prime Minister that the state of his health ruled out any possibility of the primacy. He remained in the background as an adviser, and indeed after the death of Dean Wellesley became Gladstone's principal confidant on ecclesiastical affairs. Two other possible candidates were Temple of Exeter (now considered a pillar of orthodoxy after his long-forgotten indiscretion over *Essays and Reviews*) and Woodford of Ely. But before long the field had narrowed to Browne, Lightfoot and Benson, and eventually to Browne and Benson – or, as it seemed to those most closely involved, youth versus age.

A fortnight before his death Wellesley had written to the Queen regarding the succession to Tait. Temple he dismissed out of hand ('There is a want in him, while very liberal, of dignity and refinement'). Benson he described as 'excellent and most liberal', but in the end he plumped for Browne: 'He is moderate, and a gentleman; and we want rest from our party spirit.'[51] Tait himself had appeared to hedge his bets. He had told Benson in September that he hoped he would succeed him; but by late November, only a few days before his death, he had changed his mind and told Davidson: 'I should be truly thankful to think it certain that the Bishop of Winchester would succeed me at Lambeth. He could do more than any other man to preserve the Church in peace for its real work against sin. I pray God he may be appointed and may accept the call.'[52] Davidson reported these words to the Queen, who was confirmed in her feeling that Browne would be the right man.

Gladstone thought otherwise. Though 73 himself, he felt that Browne, at 71, was too old. In a long memorandum to the Queen he suggested that the Bishop of Winchester was 'no longer equal to such duties as the Primacy would entail'. He recommended the Bishop of Truro instead.[53] At least he could not be accused of political motives. When it was rumoured that Benson was to be appointed, a critic complained to Gladstone that he was not only a strong Tory but had joined an election committee at Cambridge whose chairman had recently made a violent personal attack on the Premier. 'You have just supplied me with a strong argument in Dr Benson's favour', replied Gladstone. 'For, if he had been a worldly man or self-seeker, he would not have done anything so imprudent.'[54]

Meanwhile, however, he had to persuade the Queen to change her mind – and this took some doing. If Browne might be considered too old, Benson in the Queen's view was too young. 'She feels convinced', she wrote to Gladstone, 'that to place a man of only 53, excellent as he is, above all the other Bishops would create a very bad and angry feeling in the Church and that the Bishop of Winchester is far the fittest to be appointed now.' She suggested that Benson should go to Winchester instead – 'which is far harder work than the Archiepiscopal see'.[55] (The diocese then included much of South London, besides Hampshire, the Isle of Wight and the Channel Islands.) But she must have begun to have doubts on the score of Browne's fitness for Canterbury, because she now entrusted Davidson with a delicate mission: he was required to go down to Farnham and tackle Mrs Browne confidentially on the subject of her husband's health. Her diagnosis was cautious and guarded, and far from reassuring. By this time Davidson, though not yet Dean of Windsor, was already, like Wellesley, advising the Queen on church matters; so what began as a medical bulletin (13 December 1882) went on to answer a question the Queen had put to him: 'What would the feeling of the Bishops be, looking to the *possibility* of the Bishop of Truro being chosen?' He began by assuring her that Browne was probably the only bishop whose presidency, were his health known to be equal to it, would be popular with all his episcopal brethren. 'His gentle wisdom and unobtrusive learning have long commended him in a marked degree to all the Bishops, even to those who would naturally be most afraid of his supposed High Church views.' Next to him in the view of the episcopate, Davidson continued, would undoubtedly be the learned Lightfoot of Durham. 'His position is so unique a one, and his reputation in certain fields so unrivalled, that with two dissentients only among the Bishops I believe he would be received with emphatic favour as their chief.' As for Benson, 'I cannot recall a single instance, either at a Lambeth Meeting or in Convocation, in which he has met with anything but cordiality and admiration among the assembled Bishops' – though Davidson had to admit that there were three or four bishops who would 'feel hurt and angry at his appointment to the Primacy, and this it would tax all his remarkable geniality and grace and goodness to overcome'.[56]

The question-mark raised over Browne's health caused the Queen's allegiance to him to waver. At this stage came another letter from Gladstone pointing out that, with a single insignificant exception, no Archbishop of Canterbury over the past 220 years had been appointed at or over the age of seventy. Moreover, seven archbishops during this period had been appointed when they were under sixty and two when they were only fifty. The Queen was still, however, not prepared to give in without a struggle. On her instructions her secretary, Sir Henry Ponsonby, wrote to the Prime Minister claiming that she had learnt 'from a confidential and trustworthy source' [i.e. Davidson] that the Bishop of Winchester 'is really stronger at this moment than he has been for some time past' and was therefore capable of discharging the duties of a primate. (This was a royal gloss on Mrs Browne's cautious words about her husband's health.) The Queen, Sir Henry told Gladstone, admitted the disadvantage of Browne's age, but asked whether the offer could be made to him 'with full permission or even encouragement to him to decline'.[57] This was a risk which Gladstone was not prepared to undergo – after all, Browne might have declined to take the hint. So he stuck to his guns and again proposed Benson. The Queen at last agreed, though she asked the Prime Minister to soften any possible blow to Browne's pride by letting him know how highly he had been thought of and the reasons why he had not been offered the primacy. 'I am directly authorised by her Majesty', the 73-year-old statesman assured the 71-year-old prelate, 'to state that this [i.e. age] has been the single impediment to her conferring the honour, and imposing the burden, upon you of such an offer.'[58] Poor Browne voiced a certain amount of disappointment at having been passed over for a man eighteen years his junior, though there was little bitterness on his part. While his fate was still in the balance he had confessed to a friend that the primacy would bring fresh and greater anxieties and larger correspondence ('for which two secretaries would be absolutely indispensable'). Now that the die was cast, however, he wistfully wrote to the same friend:

> When Gladstone wrote to me that I was too old, I felt rather a blank. I had begun plans for mending matters, if possible, and their fall brought some disappointment. But I am thankful that God has so ordered it. I am (or at least soon shall be) too old for any great struggle, and no one knows what is impending. Benson's shoulders are broader and his strength unbroken.[59]

In the event Benson lived only five years longer than Browne – and the Queen was to see both of them into their graves. But Benson retained his vigour to the last, so Gladstone's choice was justified. Hamilton wrote in his diary at the end of the saga: 'The apprehended rumpus about the archbishopric ended in smoke.'[60] Gladstone was overjoyed. After a succession of defeats by the Queen on ecclesiastical nominations he had at last got his way over the greatest of all appointments. After it was over Dean Church, who had been the Prime Minister's confidant throughout, wrote to his friend Asa Grey: 'Never for hundreds of years has so much disinterested pains been taken to fill the Primacy – such inquiry and trouble resolutely followed out to find the really fittest man, apart from every personal and political consideration, as in this case. Of that I can bear witness.'[61]

Apart from one or two minor squalls, the remainder of Gladstone's second premiership passed without incident as far as ecclesiastical appointments were concerned. And, on the first occasion when he had to change his plans, the reason had nothing to do with the Queen. It was at the beginning of 1884 that he found himself with two sees to fill: Chester, vacant by the impending resignation of Bishop Jacobson and now much reduced in size since the creation of Liverpool as a separate diocese; and Southwell, a new see formed out of the dioceses of Lincoln and Lichfield and covering Nottinghamshire and Derbyshire. Chester presented no difficulty: William Stubbs, a Tractarian savant who had been made Professor of History at Oxford by Derby and a canon of St Paul's by Disraeli, was a suitable (if highly learned) candidate. 'He is known', Gladstone assured the Queen, 'for a singularly calm and judicial mind which, together with vast knowledge, has placed him in the first rank of living British historians, and perhaps even at their head.' Of his religious character 'Mr Gladstone need not speak particularly, as your Majesty may rest assured he will never knowingly recommend anyone for a Bishopric who falls short in this respect'.[62]

Southwell proved a harder nut to crack. This was because Gladstone discovered at the last minute that his original nominee had blotted his copy-book, so he had to recall his submission to the Queen by telegraph. The erring cleric was James Moorhouse, Bishop of Melbourne, Australia. He had been considered an ideal candidate for an English see, but it now transpired that he had committed the (for those days) unpardonable offence of inviting a Presbyterian to assist him in his church. Such a transgression (Edward Hamilton confided to his diary) Gladstone thought 'would be too much of a good thing for the Bishop of Lincoln',

Christopher Wordsworth, out of whose diocese Southwell had been carved.[63] So poor Moorhouse was put back on the shelf and other possible candidates taken down for inspection. Eventually the choice fell on the Headmaster of Winchester, George Ridding, son-in-law of the Lord Chancellor, the Earl of Selborne, and a 'deeply religious' cleric who, Gladstone told the Queen, was also a 'man of large, tolerant and sympathetic mind from whom all will receive justice, while his energy seems to fit him in a remarkable degree for the work of organising a new See'.[64] So, as a result of his successful running of a major public school, the headmaster was invited to adapt his talents to running the church life of two populous English counties.

The next see to be filled was Ripon, which fell vacant in April 1884 through the death of Bishop Bickersteth. The Prime Minister felt it was time to promote an Evangelical, so he again thought of Moorhouse. But alas, on enquiry, it transpired that he was still under a cloud because of his past indiscretion, so Gladstone had to look elsewhere. His choice of Canon Boyd Carpenter of Windsor was not popular with the Queen. She might not have cared for the canon as a possible Dean of Windsor because of his wife's lack of social distinction, but she valued the canon himself and was loth to lose him – and even complained to Gladstone that he had not accompanied his submission of the name with an explanation for his choice. Hamilton had to point out to the Queen's secretary that the reason for the omission was simply that the Premier had thought that, 'as Her Majesty was so well acquainted with Canon Carpenter, he would be troubling Her unnecessarily'.[65] The canon duly became Bishop of Ripon, but Gladstone had to bow to the royal wishes over the choice of his successor. His own nominee was the Headmaster of Harrow, H. M. Butler – that same Butler whom the Queen had seemed to favour at one time as a potential Dean of Westminster. But she now turned him down. Hamilton suggested a reason. 'She has such a horror of Mrs Josephine Butler' [an active social reformer especially concerned with the 'white slave traffic'] 'that it extends even to her brother-in-law', he wrote in his diary.[66] Gladstone withdrew Butler's name and substituted a new one in deference to the royal wishes.

He dug in his heels, however, in respect of another canonry – and won. The man in question was Malcolm MacColl, a cleric with a keen interest in politics whose eyewitness accounts of the atrocities committed by Turkish troops in 1876 against Bulgarian Christians had given valuable ammunition to Gladstone in his denunciation of Disraeli's indifference to those atrocities. He had originally thought of MacColl in connection with the canonry of

St Paul's, vacant by the elevation of Stubbs to the episcopate. On this occasion, however, as Hamilton noted in his diary, though no clergyman had done greater political service in his readiness to fight for anything in any Liberal cause, 'Mr G. feels that MacColl has hardly rendered sufficient *bona fide* service to the Church at large to justify his being offered such a high and conspicuous piece of ecclesiastical preferment as that of a London Canonry'.[67] However, a cathedral stall in the North of England was a different matter; and, when a canonry fell vacant at Ripon six months later, Gladstone proposed MacColl's name to the Queen. She was furious. 'The Queen', she wrote back to Ponsonby, 'will never consent to promote this man, as he is the originator of all the Bulgarian atrocities for which *mania* of Mr Gladstone we are now suffering. This must be stopped at once.' Ponsonby accordingly wrote to Gladstone to point out that 'H.M. is in a high state of indignation . . . She considers him [MacColl] the author of half the excitement about the Bulgarian atrocities and his trying to get up false stories about Turkish impalements founded on a bag of beans he saw on a pole.'[68] But on this occasion Gladstone stuck to his guns. The Queen, whispering 'I will ne'er consent', consented; and MacColl's canonry was duly gazetted.

We come now to the final batch of Gladstone's episcopal appointments – final, that is, except for the solitary promotion of Sheepshanks to Norwich in 1893 during his fourth premiership. The process began with the sudden death on 6 January 1885 of Bishop Jackson of London. Randall Davidson, now Dean of Windsor, was asked for his opinion on likely successors by the Queen's secretary. He suggested three possibilities to Ponsonby: Lightfoot of Durham, Temple of Exeter and Goodwin of Carlisle. ('No one of the three is *ideal* for the post, but all the three possess *many* of the necessary qualifications.') Davidson thought that Lightfoot stood 'indisputably first among the theologians and scholars of England' – and he combined with his scholarship and culture a 'wide liberality of thought and action in religious matters of which I am quite sure the Queen must approve'. His 'great *dis*advantage' was that he was unmarried, though Davidson doubted whether this ought to outweigh the other considerations. Temple, in his opinion, had 'entirely lived down the foolish cry once raised against his theological opinions, which have turned out quite "safe" after all'. Goodwin would be inferior to the other two candidates, but his 'huge fund of experience on all Church questions' would still make him an admirable Bishop of London.[69]

The Prime Minister himself favoured Temple rather than Lightfoot. Archbishop Benson was inclined to agree. He told

Davidson that Lightfoot's growing caution and concern with his own scholarly pursuits made him less than useful as a confidant. '"I can't advise" has become a fixed phrase with him . . . He is what you might call terrifically selfish in pursuit of utterly unselfish ends.' Temple, on the other hand, though he would often 'wound and bruise one without knowing it', could be depended on for 'hearty sympathy, outspoken counsel and any amount of time and trouble'. In the light of this verdict Davidson told Ponsonby that there was little to choose between Lightfoot and Temple, though the bachelorhood of the former 'would be a very serious drawback to a man who has already a shrinking from Society'.[70]

Meanwhile the Prime Minister, anxious not to act in the matter without the goodwill of the Archbishop of Canterbury, had sent Hamilton down to Addington* to sound out Benson on his views. The Archbishop was in full agreement over Temple as the best choice for London. He was less sure about Gladstone's choice of Canon Liddon of St Paul's to succeed Temple at Exeter. Liddon was a leading Tractarian divine who had been appointed by Gladstone to his canonry in 1870. In the Prime Minister's view, said Hamilton, he was one of the 'great powers' of the Church – 'one of the few who has associated a great thinking force with the masteries of a first-rate preacher; he is the first living champion of belief'.[72] Benson was less enthusiastic. Hamilton recorded in his diary:

> His Grace had some doubts as to whether Dr Liddon possessed the requisite qualities of personal conciliation, whether he would work in harmony with the Episcopal Bench . . . and whether he had the requisite administrative capacity. I have doubts myself (as I have told Mr G.) whether Dr Liddon would accept a See . . . I am afraid the Queen would be certain to raise considerable difficulties.[73]

Hamilton reported back to Gladstone, whose doubts were increased by rumours that Liddon had not been on speaking terms with Archbishop Tait. In the event the problem solved itself after Liddon had been privately sounded by the Dean of St Paul's and had expressed himself as 'wholly averse' to the idea of a bishopric.[74] So Liddon dropped out of the running; and Gladstone, still anxious to promote a High Churchman, replaced

---

*Addington, Hamilton noted disapprovingly in his diary, 'is situated in a beautiful park in a lovely country, but it is curiously benighted for a place within easy driving distance of London. It has no Railway Station nor Telegraph Office within 4 miles, and the post leaves at 3 o'clock in the afternoon.'[71] The former archiepiscopal palace is now the headquarters of the Royal School of Church Music.

him with Edward King, whom he had appointed to the chair of pastoral theology at Oxford during his first ministry. King in fact was a far better candidate than Liddon. He was a charismatic character whose winning manners and powers of ready sympathy ensured that he got on well with churchpeople of all schools of thought. By now, however, Bishop Wordsworth of Lincoln had announced his intention to resign; and it was to Lincoln rather than Exeter that King was appointed. Bishop Stubbs congratulated Gladstone on having made 'the best appointment since S. Anselm'.[75] By the time King died twenty-five years later he was already being hailed as a saint, so memorable had been his episcopal ministry.

For Exeter Gladstone chose Edward Bickersteth, a Low Churchman – or (as Davidson described him to Ponsonby) a 'most *liberal-minded* Evangelical, of no party bias whatever, a man acceptable to all who know him as a refined Christian gentleman'.[76] Admittedly he had only just been nominated to the deanery of Gloucester; but the Queen had evidently overcome her former dislike of double promotions in quick succession, as she raised no objection when Bickersteth's name was formally put before her together with those of Temple and King. All three episcopal nominations were approved. 'The Queen was much pleased by your excellent letter upon them', Ponsonby told the gratified Davidson.[77] After the three acceptances had arrived Hamilton noted in his diary: 'Thank goodness – there is for a moment an end of episcopal appointments, which, with Mr G.'s excess of conscientiousness, give more trouble than almost anything else.'[78]

But the trouble taken was noted and appreciated in the Church at large. Commenting on Gladstone's ecclesiastical policy when he laid down office for the fourth and last time, the *Church Times* observed (16 March 1894) that he had raised the standard of the episcopate beyond all expectations. The typical bishops of the day did not now owe their thrones to such qualifications as had drawn forth the sarcasms of Thackeray. 'It is no longer enough to have been the scholarly editor of Greek plays, or to have been a nobleman's tutor, or the travelling companion of a Royal Prince.' The ideal, said the paper, had been vastly raised. 'Whatever a man's other qualities may be, this merit is now expected of him: that he have, in the estimation of those who are responsible for the choice, that spiritual character which befits a Father in God.'

If this was perhaps piling it on a little, and being unfair to some of Gladstone's predecessors as PM, it was at least a tribute to his own unbending religious principles. Perhaps the last word here may lie with a twentieth-century scholar, Alec Vidler, who in *The Orb and the Cross* (1945) speculated on what might have happened if Gladstone had entered the ministry rather than politics as a young man and if *he* rather than Tait had been offered the archbishopric of Canterbury in 1868.

> After all, would not Gladstone's political achievements have been carried out, in one way or another, even if he had not been at the political helm? Whereas, if the Church had been under his leadership, history might have pursued a very different course, and it might be in a very different condition today.[79]

**Nominations to bishoprics 22 (18 first appointments, 4 translations)**

*First appointments:*

(1) 1869: George Moberly to Salisbury.
(2) 1869: Harvey Goodwin to Carlisle.
(3) 1869: Lord Arthur Charles Hervey to Bath and Wells.
(4) 1869: Frederick Temple to Exeter.
(5) 1869: John Fielder Mackarness to Oxford.
(6) 1870: James Fraser to Manchester.
(7) 1870: Richard Durnford to Chichester.
(8) 1870: Joshua Hughes to St Asaph.
(9) 1873: James Russell Woodford to Ely.

(10) 1882: Ernest Roland Wilberforce to Newcastle.
(11) 1883: George Howard Wilkinson to Truro.
(12) 1883: Richard Lewis to Llandaff.
(13) 1884: William Stubbs to Chester.
(14) 1884: George Ridding to Southwell.
(15) 1884: William Boyd Carpenter to Ripon.
(16) 1885: Edward King to Lincoln.
(17) 1885: Edward Henry Bickersteth to Exeter.

(18) 1893: John Sheepshanks to Norwich.

*Translations:*

(1) 1869: Samuel Wilberforce to Winchester (from Oxford).
(2) 1873: Edward Harold Browne to Winchester (from Ely).

(3) 1882: Edward White Benson to Canterbury (from Truro).
(4) 1885: Frederick Temple to London (from Exeter).

# 10

# Sarum Rites

*Marquess of Salisbury: Prime Minister*
*24 June 1885 – 28 January 1886*
*3 August 1886 – 18 August 1892*
*2 July 1895 – 11 July 1902*

Robert Arthur Talbot Gascoyne-Cecil, 3rd Marquess of Salisbury (1803–1903), *who led the Conservative Party for twenty-one years, became heir to the title only on the death of his elder brother in 1865. He was educated at Eton and Christ Church, Oxford, and became a Tory MP in 1853. He served as Secretary of State for India (1866–7) in the third Derby administration and again under Disraeli in 1874–8. (He had moved to the House of Lords on the death of his father in 1868.) He was appointed Foreign Secretary in 1878 and accompanied the Prime Minister (now Lord Beaconsfield) to the Congress of Berlin, where he began building his reputation as a statesman. He succeeded Beaconsfield as Conservative leader in 1881. His three premierships together totalled almost fourteen years, and he came to be recognized as one of the dominant figures on the European political scene. Salisbury was an aristocrat in the grand tradition, with a reputation for aloofness. But he enjoyed considerable intellectual powers – and indeed, as a young man, had augmented his income through journalism, his articles in the* Quarterly Review *providing a valuable guide to his political philosophy. He was also an informed and devout churchman who, like Gladstone, took immense pains over ecclesiastical appointments.*

Lord Salisbury, as Prime Minister, awarded no fewer than thirty-eight diocesan mitres, more than any other prime minister before or since. This was partly because his total period in office was longer than that of almost all his predecessors and successors; partly because the Church of England now had more dioceses than at the start of Queen Victoria's reign; and partly because, during Salisbury's three premierships, there was an exceptional crop of episcopal deaths and resignations. So, in addition to the preoccupations of national and international politics, there was usually something to keep the ecclesiastical pot boiling. This did not, as might have been supposed, provide the Prime Minister with a little light relief. As Lady Salisbury remarked to the Queen's secretary on one occasion: 'I always find that anything to do with the appointment of Bishops has a special power of worrying and tiring him.'[1] This may well have been due to excessive anxiety on Salisbury's part to do the right thing by the Church. His religious faith was sincere and profound, and to his contemporaries he often seemed as devout a churchman as his great political rival, Gladstone.

Like Gladstone, he was a convert to Tractarianism. He had gone up to Oxford two years after Newman's secession to Rome, and had allied himself to those friends of Newman's who had remained loyal to Anglicanism. In particular he clung to the dogmatism of the Tractarians. In articles written for the *Quarterly Review* in the 1860s he denounced 'that shapeless, formless, fibreless mass of platitudes which in official cant is called "unsectarian religion"', and claimed that the dream of undogmatic religion was 'too baseless to impose long upon educated minds'. But Salisbury's religion was essentially of the heart rather than of the mind. It was here that he would subordinate his intellect to his feelings and emotions. As Paul Smith puts it in his introduction to his selection from Salisbury's *Quarterly Review* articles:

> Vigorously though he might employ his rational and critical powers on the intellectual subtleties of theology, a subject in which he was strongly interested and where he was no more inclined than in other realms to follow authority, he insisted that the essential core of religion was a mystery, impenetrable to human intellect and intractable to precise definition and analysis. In the end, one believed or one did not, guided by moral feelings and perceptions beyond the reach of reason either to dissect or to subvert. Religious faith was for Salisbury the necessary sheet-anchor of his mind, and against it no current of sceptical examination could be suffered to run.[2]

In dealing with ecclesiastical appointments Salisbury found himself, like his predecessors, in constant disagreement with the Queen. Although he would sometimes defer to her suggestions, at other times he stood firm – and got his way. The Queen told Dean Davidson on one occasion that the Prime Minister was proving 'very obstinate about the Bishops . . . she fears Lord

Salisbury is *rather* narrow and old-fashioned, or his advisers are. Really it is very tiresome.'[3] And, only a few weeks before this, the Dean had recorded in his journal (28 December 1889):

> She thinks Lord Salisbury not very wise in his nominations and means 'decidedly to take the matter largely into her own hands, while leaving the initiative *always* with him'. Lord Salisbury, she said, 'is so sensible and liberal-minded in political matters, and so ready to give up the foolish points of old-fashioned Conservatism, that it is a great pity he should so lack liberality in his view of Church appointments'.[4]

Paradoxically it was Davidson himself who was to become the subject of one of the bitterest tussles between Sovereign and Premier when a disagreement arose over his suitability for a senior rather than a junior bishopric.

By this time politics were taking more and more of a back seat where episcopal appointments were concerned. Salisbury was a Conservative, but his nominees were of all political complexions. This was brought out during Rosebery's brief premiership in 1894–5. Rosebery was thought by the Queen to be showing political bias in his church nominations. Her secretary, Sir Arthur Bigge, asked him to be more careful in future, but Rosebery (through *his* secretary) hotly denied the allegation – which he claimed could be more fitly made about his predecessor. 'Lord Salisbury practically ostracised Liberal Churchmen', he told Bigge, 'and during the whole of his administration no one had a chance of preferment who was not a supporter of his Government. This, I think, would not be denied by Lord Salisbury himself.'[5] In fact it was rightly denied by Bigge on Salisbury's behalf. He pointed out in his reply that at least four of the late Prime Minister's episcopal nominees – Westcott, Creighton, Perowne and Davidson – could hardly be described as Conservatives. (Westcott in fact was considered half a Socialist, as was Gore, one of Salisbury's later appointments.)

Where ecclesiastical considerations were concerned the Queen's preference for Broad Churchmen clashed with the Prime Minister's feeling that sometimes a High or Low Churchman would be more suitable. When, for instance, the bishopric of Durham was vacant at the beginning of 1890 and the Queen was anxious to promote the 'Broad' Canon Westcott, Salisbury begged to differ. He told her then secretary, Sir Henry Ponsonby, that at this particularly critical time for the Church (Bishop King of Lincoln had been charged with Ritualistic practices and was being tried by the Archbishop of Canterbury himself), Westcott, as a Broad Churchman, would be less effective as a bishop than a

High or Low Churchman of 'moderate temper and views' who might be able to control his more violent High and Low Church brethren. The conflict between the two parties, in Salisbury's judgement, had become so hot that 'a trifle might kindle it into a dangerous flame'.[6] Later that year, after the Queen had got her way over Durham and was pressing Davidson on the Prime Minister as a suitable candidate for Winchester, he complained direct to the Queen:

> Lately a cry has been raised among the Evangelicals that Lord Salisbury has a prejudice against Evangelicals, and will not recommend them for promotion . . . Lord Salisbury fears that, if during one year both these great prizes in the Church, Durham and Winchester, are given to a Broad Churchman, there will be a painful feeling among the Evangelicals.[7]

The Queen was not impressed by this sort of argument. 'It only perpetuates the two rival and antagonistic parties in the Church, which we are all so anxious to obliterate, as it weakens the Church so very much; and we want to *strengthen* it.'[8] But at least she and her advisers agreed with Salisbury as to the reason for the apparent boycotting of Evangelicals – the absence of suitable candidates. As Davidson put it to a complaining cleric:

> It is a simple delusion to suppose that there is any disinclination on the part of the authorities to give due prominence, in Church appointments, to men who belong to the Evangelical School. The difficulty is to find the right men; and they must be men not only of piety, learning, and power, but of physical strength sufficient for the daily increasing burdens of Episcopal work.[9]

Salisbury, like Gladstone, was a High Churchman; and a number of his nominations, like his cousin Edward Talbot, were of that school. But, like Gladstone, he never allowed his personal preferences to colour his general policy on episcopal appointments, which was to maintain a balance between the various church parties. Had he made any attempt to do so he would have run into even greater difficulties with the Queen, whose dislike of Tractarianism and all its works was well known. As the ever-diplomatic Davidson put it in his journal at the height of the Lincoln trial: 'My business is to try to put the *good* side of High Churchmanship before her. She hears and thinks plenty on the other side without my help!'[10] The Queen's own ideas at this time on the principles which she thought ought to govern episcopal appointments were otherwise unexceptionable. 'The men to be chosen *must* not be taken with reference to satisfying one or the other party in the Church, or with reference to any political party, but for their *real worth*; we want people who can be firm and yet conciliatory, else the Church cannot be maintained.'[11] But at least she had no illusions (or perhaps she was being unduly cynical) in one respect. Writing to Davidson on his appointment to Rochester she said that, with one exception, she had 'never found people promoted to the Episcopate remain what they were before . . . The whole atmosphere of a cathedral and its surroundings, the very dignity itself which accompanies a bishopric, seems to hamper their freedom of speech.'[12]

As for the process of bishop-making, no wonder Salisbury found it both 'worrying and tiring'. He poured out his woes on one occasion to Talbot, who had just turned down the offer of the see of St Albans on the ground that he had been only two years in his present post:

> I am weary and at my wits' end. I have had three refusals of the see of Durham and I have not got a Bishop yet. It seems likely that I shall have to commence the same enlivening round with St Albans.* I should not mind if in any case the refusal was based on any solid, robust, practical reason. But they are all reasons of the type you have sent me in your letter. Possible Bishops are according to my experience divided into three classes:— (1) Those who, in my view, are not fit. (2) Those who seem to me fit and whom I am not allowed to ask, and (3) Those whom I am allowed to ask but who find some coy excuse for refusing. Forgive me for my mutinous spirit, but I am in despair.[14]

One can sympathize with Salisbury. With the Queen on one side and a reluctant candidate on the other, the bishop-maker's lot was not a happy one.

Salisbury found himself having to fill no fewer than thirty-eight episcopal vacancies during his three-part reign as Premier.

The first vacancy, appropriately the see of Salisbury, must have given him an idea of the problems involved. His original choice, which the Queen approved, was William Inge, Provost of Worcester College, Oxford (and the father of the future Dean Inge). Unfortunately the Provost declined 'most resolutely' to forsake the fleshpots of Oxford – 'in terms', Salisbury told the Queen, 'which would be unnecessarily strong if he had been asked to go to Sierra Leone'.[15] Salisbury's second choice – referred

---

*After Liddon's refusal (see below) it was eventually bestowed on John Festing – who, the Queen told Salisbury, 'though worthy cannot be called eminent'.[13]

to in correspondence simply as 'Dr B.' – was an old colleague and friend of the Prime Minister's whom the Dean of Windsor dismissed in a letter to the Queen's secretary as 'a kindly, amiable gentleman, but that is all!'. The Dean reported a caustic comment by 'one most competent judge' to the effect that Dr B's appointment would be a disaster: 'He has no claim; he preaches feebly, speaks in wearisome fashion; he has written nothing, done nothing, organised nothing.'[16] In the face of such a verdict it is hardly surprising that the Queen should have put her foot down and told Salisbury to think again. Luckily his third choice proved more acceptable: John Wordsworth, son of the Bishop of Lincoln and one of the leading scholars of the day (though, Archbishop Benson recorded in his journal, his 'self-opinion mars fatally an otherwise interesting character').[17]

After his baptism of episcopal fire Salisbury enjoyed a relatively trouble-free two years at the start of his second premiership. Perhaps his most notable nomination during this period was that of James Moorhouse to the see of Manchester. Gladstone, it will be recalled, had wanted to promote Moorhouse, then Bishop of Melbourne, to an English diocese, but had discovered that he had blotted his copy-book by having once invited a Presbyterian to assist him in church. Presumably the memory of that indiscretion was now sufficiently faded to allow it to be overlooked. At any rate Salisbury thought highly of Moorhouse, whose sermons had impressed him as a young man when living in the London parish of St John, Fitzroy Square. So the invitation was sent and accepted.

The Prime Minister's next major brush with the Queen over a church appointment came in the summer of 1888 – and it concerned the venerable Canon Liddon. Since Pusey's death in 1881 Liddon had been universally acknowledged by High Churchmen as their leader. Gladstone had appointed him in 1870 to be Dean Ireland Professor of Exegesis at Oxford and a canon of St Paul's. He was among the most eloquent preachers in the land. Though nearly sixty he now seemed ripe – especially to a High Churchman like Salisbury – for further preferment. So he pressed Liddon's name on the Queen for the vacant diocese of Oxford:

Lord Salisbury would be wanting in his duty if he did not state frankly his opinion that the exclusion of Canon Liddon from the Episcopate, or at least from the offer of it, is a severe measure which is likely to do harm to the Church of England. He is so much the most brilliant member of the Clergy of the Established Church that his being passed over is a conspicuous act of censure and punishment for which the members of the Church do not readily see the reason . . . If he is passed over on the present occasion, it must be taken as definitive; for Oxford is the place where he is best known and has most influence; and it is the intellectual centre of the Church.[18]

Unfortunately Liddon had also been prominent at the time of the Bulgarian atrocities in denouncing the inactivity of the Conservative government. So he was doubly anathema to the Queen, who had to swallow both his High Churchmanship and his political partisanship. She at once wrote to her secretary, Sir Henry Ponsonby: 'She is greatly opposed to Canon Liddon being made a Bishop, but Bishop of Oxford he must *never* be. He might ruin and taint all the young men, as Pusey and others did before him.'[19]

Dean Davidson also weighed in with advice and counsel. He kowtowed to Her Majesty to some extent ('Canon Liddon has very little sympathy for anyone outside his own line of thought, and that line is undoubtedly an extreme one'). But he pointed out the undesirability of an outright veto on a man 'so eminent as Canon Liddon and so distinctly recognised as a foremost champion of what is undoubtedly a large party in the Church of England, which may claim a sort of right to be fairly represented on the Episcopal Bench'. Luckily, the Dean continued, there was a way out: Liddon's poor health. It was largely on the grounds of health that he had declined the 'very easy post' of Bishop of Edinburgh two years before. 'Lord Salisbury should definitely assure himself, *and assure your Majesty*, that Canon Liddon is now in such vigorous health as to enable him rightly to undertake the extremely heavy and harassing duties of the Bishopric of Oxford.'[20]

Alas for Salisbury's hopes! He failed to get the necessary assurance from Liddon; so in the end he offered the see to Stubbs of Chester, who was duly translated. But he made one final effort on Liddon's behalf, two years later, when the diocese of St Albans fell vacant. He first offered the see to his cousin Edward Talbot, Vicar of Leeds.* But, when Talbot declined the offer, he asked the Queen for permission to offer it to Liddon instead – unconditionally. The Queen reluctantly agreed, and the offer was duly made – and, as might have been expected, declined. Six

---

*He told Ponsonby that he considered Talbot specially suited to this particular diocese, 'where there are a great number of gentry, and where such matters as manners and birth and connection assume a considerable importance'.[21] Talbot, an alumnus of Charterhouse and Christ Church, Oxford, and former Warden of Keble, was to become Bishop in succession of Rochester, Southwark and Winchester.

months later Liddon was dead – but at least honour had been satisfied.

Early in 1890, however, Salisbury found himself fighting a war with the Queen on another front; the succession to Bishop Lightfoot of Durham, who had died at the end of the previous year. The Queen pressed the claims of Canon Westcott, Regius Professor of Divinity at Cambridge and a scholar of equal eminence to Lightfoot, as his successor. For a long time the Prime Minister resisted these claims, though they were also being pressed by Archbishop Benson. He told Ponsonby that Westcott, 'as a learned man, would be thrown away as Lightfoot was thrown away. His time would be occupied in the petty details of diocesan administration; and his unequalled erudition would become useless to the world for want of leisure to produce it.' He also objected to Westcott as a Broad Churchman who would be unable to control the combative spirits of High and Low Church interests at a time of fierce ecclesiastical conflict. And he dismissed Westcott personally as 'a man of little personal influence, unimpressive, a bad presence, no hold over other men'.[22] He suggested instead Boyd Carpenter of Ripon, but the Queen was unenthusiastic. She reluctantly agreed to the see's being offered to two of Salisbury's alternative nominees, Walsham How of Wakefield and Jayne of Chester, but both men declined it. After further correspondence* and the consideration of more names, Salisbury eventually threw in the towel. As Davidson puts it in a memorandum drawn up after it was all over: 'At last they had an interview and long conversation at Buckingham Palace on Tuesday, March 4th, and at this interview the Queen again said to Lord Salisbury that she was surprised he didn't accept the notion of Dr Westcott for Durham, which she had throughout desired – *whereupon he consented.*'[24]

Quite why Salisbury should have resisted the royal arguments for so long remains a mystery. His arguments as put before Ponsonby are unconvincing. Westcott was a man of far more distinction than any of the other candidates proposed – and his episcopate was to be as notable as had been Lightfoot's. At any rate the Prime Minister's despondency over his defeat on this occasion was soon over. Davidson noted in his journal the Queen's amusement at Salisbury's reaction to the jubilation with which

---

* Salisbury even made the bizarre suggestion to Ponsonby that, if Westcott *must* be made a bishop, he should be sent to a 'small diocese' such as Chichester, which was likely to be vacant before long and which would not make such exhaustive claims upon his time. 'Westcott might have the bishopric without entirely shutting his library up.'[23] In fact Salisbury had failed to do his sums. Chichester had 380 parishes, Durham 235.

Westcott's appointment was received in the Church at large: 'He talks as if *he* had done it, instead of having opposed it with all his might for weeks!' A year or two later the Queen triumphantly sent Davidson a letter to herself from Salisbury in which, following Westcott's intervention in a coal strike, the Prime Minister took special credit to himself for (in Davidson's words) 'the acumen he had shown in selecting Westcott for that office'.[25]

In the course of his memorandum Davidson had remarked that, had Salisbury refused absolutely to nominate Westcott, the Queen 'would have pressed, or even insisted, on his appointing *me*'. And it was the question whether the Queen could be induced to release her beloved dean for a diocese, and if so *which* diocese, that was to dominate the behind-the-scenes ecclesiastical discussions during the early autumn of 1890.

As the son-in-law and confidant of the late Archbishop Tait, and as Dean of Windsor and the Queen's confidential adviser for the past seven years, Davidson was of obviously episcopal potential. The Prime Minister himself recognized this. After Talbot's refusal of St Albans he had considered offering the see to Davidson before Liddon. He told Ponsonby: 'His power of dealing with men is very great indeed . . . I have no doubt that in time he would establish an influence over the Church not unlike that which Bishop Wilberforce possessed towards the close of his life.'[26] Prophetic words! Dean Vaughan of Llandaff (he who had almost become Bishop of Rochester in 1860) also took up the cudgels on Davidson's behalf. He wrote to Ponsonby suggesting that the time had come for placing Davidson 'in a still more prominent station in the Church'.[27]

Davidson himself was feeling restless. He told Ponsonby (and Ponsonby told the Queen) that the archbishops and others had remonstrated with him for 'remaining in this quiet and comfortable place when others were doing their utmost for the Church and devoting themselves to work'. He would gladly go to St Albans, if asked. 'He believes that, being young and active, he could do good service in the East End of London, that he could stir up a national feeling in the Church.'[28] The Queen told Benson that, though her first impulse had been to say that she '*could not* give Davidson up', she now felt, in the light of representations made to her by 'people of influence and experience', that she could not from selfish motives ('though I *do* think *all underrate* the *importance* of his present position') refuse to allow his name to go forward for a bishopric.[29] The first hurdle was now removed; but at this point the subject had temporarily to be shelved for a practical reason. The Dean had consulted his doctor. 'It turns out that your Majesty was right in doubting whether the Dean of Windsor would be strong enough to undertake the severe work of the diocese of St Albans', Ponsonby told the Queen. 'He writes that he finds it would scarcely be advisable for him to be appointed to it . . . the regular duty of the diocese would be more than he has strength to accomplish.'[30] By this time, however, the Queen had the bit between her teeth. Far from wanting any longer to keep Davidson by her side, she was now coming round to the position that he should go to a senior rather than a junior diocese as soon as his health allowed. The senior see was Winchester, vacant by the resignation of the aged Browne, and it happened to include her own house at Osborne within its purlieus. This made it in her eyes the ideal see for Davidson.

Once again the scene was set for a head-on clash between Sovereign and Premier, as the man the latter had in mind for Winchester was Bishop Thorold of Rochester – though he was prepared to promote Davidson to Rochester in Thorold's place. The Queen at once objected. Thorold, she complained to Salisbury, was old and not strong, would be of no use as a speaker, and would probably not last long at his post. Davidson, on the other hand, would at once as Bishop of Winchester be eligible to sit in the House of Lords and would be a great help there in every way. 'If he were merely made a junior bishop like Rochester his power of help would be wasted, and it would perhaps be years before he got into the House of Lords.'[31]

The Prime Minister dug in his heels. If Davidson ('able but not, as yet, distinguished') were advanced to so high a dignity as Winchester, he said, 'it would be generally felt that excessive favour had been shown to him; and that his merit, so far as known to the public, did not correspond to it'.[32] Benson and Vaughan both wrote to Salisbury to press Davidson's claim to Winchester, but the Prime Minister was adamant. He refused to retract his nomination of Thorold; and on 23 September he formally submitted Davidson's name for the choice of either Rochester or Worcester (also vacant by this time).

The Queen was livid. Thorold she now dismissed as 'an old frail man of no particular talent'.* Why, she wanted to know, should Salisbury reject the advice of the Archbishop of

---

*An amusing picture of Thorold is drawn by Albert Baillie in his autobiography. Thorold, 'an ugly little man . . . had the manner of a person several times his size, and the effect was comic. He would drive up to a church, even in the worst slum in South London, in a dignified carriage and pair. His servant preceded him into the vestry with his bag, and laid out on a table all the appliances for his toilet: a looking-glass, ivory-backed hair-brushes, a bottle of scent, a clean pocket-handkerchief and lavender kid gloves.'[33]

Canterbury (who she knew had written to Salisbury in her support) as well as her own? She reminded the Prime Minister that, when they had been considering the choice of a new bishop for St Albans, the diocese in which his own house at Hatfield was situated, the Queen had raised no objection to his nomination of Liddon (*not*, as we have seen, the Queen's favourite cleric!). 'But in this case of Winchester, which borders on Windsor and includes Osborne, the Queen's personal wishes and convenience are overlooked.'[34]

It was all to no avail. Salisbury had given in over Westcott earlier that year, but he was determined to stick to his guns on the present occasion. Davidson's moral strength in the Church, he insisted, would not be increased 'by an unexplained rapidity of promotion'. Let him do his stint in 'one of the ordinary Sees', and he would then have a claim to proceed higher.[35] The Queen reluctantly gave way and approved the two nominations. But she was arguing with Salisbury to the last. 'It is a complete error that the Dean of Windsor is not known. He is better known than most clergymen are.'[36]

Faced with the choice of Rochester or Worcester, Davidson plumped for Rochester. Both sees were then among the most densely populated in the Church. Worcester included Birmingham: Rochester took in the whole of South London, with a population of almost two million. But Davidson knew it well from his Lambeth days; and he would still be conveniently near Windsor should the Queen continue to consult him (as of course she did). So Rochester it was. He stayed there only four years; but it was long enough for him to have established a claim to Winchester when, as the Queen had prophesied, the 'old and frail' Thorold finally passed to his rest. Salisbury, then at the start of his final administration, could no longer object to Davidson on the score of youth or inexperience, so was now quite happy to appoint him to the senior see. And Talbot, who had declined St Albans in 1890 on the ground of not having been long enough at Leeds, was now happy to succeed Davidson at Rochester.

But we are jumping ahead. The most important see which Salisbury found himself having to fill during his second ministry was York: and he had to fill it not once but twice. Thomson, who had held the see since 1862, died at the end of 1890; and at once the names of potential successors began to be bandied around. The Queen pressed for Westcott, whom Salisbury had accepted so reluctantly as Bishop of Durham, but this time the Prime Minister refused to be persuaded. For one thing, he pointed out,

Westcott had only recently been promoted. But a much more serious objection arose from the 'Socialist tendencies of the speeches he has made since he became a bishop'. The archbishopric, Salisbury reminded the Queen, was a great political as well as ecclesiastical position. To confer it on Westcott at a time when 'Socialism is so burning a question' would be a grave mistake. The Prime Minister thought little of the Queen's other tentative suggestions: Maclagan of Lichfield, Walsham How of Wakefield and Moorhouse of Manchester. He proposed instead Magee of Peterborough (whose eloquence she had so much admired in the past and whom she had pressed on Disraeli successfully for his present see and unsuccessfully, ten years later, for Durham). Salisbury mentioned Magee's eloquence. He also mentioned Magee's opinions on both political and polemical questions as being 'moderate and safe'. 'His ecclesiastical proclivities were at one time Evangelical; but they are so ill-defined that his elevation would give offence to no party in the Church.'[37]

The Queen was less enthusiastic. She was convinced that Magee was not very popular with his clergy; and Davidson, then still Dean of Windsor, confirmed this in a letter to Ponsonby, though he thought that this defect was far outweighed by Magee's other qualifications. A more serious snag, said Davidson, was his health: 'He is *sixty-nine* and has had terrible illnesses.' Davidson added a prophetic finale: 'If I were his wife or his son, I should not like him to accept so tremendous a burden in his present state of health.'[38] In spite of all the caveats, however, Salisbury insisted on Magee – and therefore had only himself to blame when, two months after his enthronement, the new Primate died of the effects of influenza. It was all to do again; and Salisbury took the easy way out by plumping for one of the names the Queen had suggested as alternatives to Westcott, Maclagan of Lichfield. He was to rule the archbishopric blamelessly for the next seventeen years.

Meanwhile a new Bishop of Peterborough had to be found to replace Magee; and here Salisbury settled for a scholar of renown: Mandell Creighton, since 1884 Dixie Professor of Ecclesiastical History at Cambridge. Creighton accepted only with reluctance. 'A bishopric is to me after the flesh a terrible nuisance', he wrote to a friend. 'But how is a man to refuse the responsibilities of his branch of the service? . . . Only, as hundreds of men are pining for such a post, and I was not, it seems mere contrariety.' To another friend he complained: 'My peace of mind is gone: my books will be shut up: my mind will go to seed: I shall utter nothing but platitudes for the rest of my life.' But at least he was honest with himself and confessed to his wife: 'The worst of it is, that I believe I should make quite a good bishop.' In this belief he was correct. He was to rise higher in the hierarchy, and was soon regarded as a potential archbishop. But a couple of years after his appointment to Peterborough he could still write of himself:

> My life has been that of a man who tries to write a book, and is the object of a conspiracy to prevent him from doing so. It is quite true that no one cares to read my book, but that has never interfered with my pleasure in reading for it.[39]

The book he was trying to write was a history of the Papacy. It was never completed, though the first five volumes were published over a twelve-year period (1882–94): its author worked himself into a premature grave before he was sixty. Davidson, who was consecrated jointly with Creighton in Westminster Abbey on St Mark's day 1891, delivered a posthumous verdict on his colleague's reputation for having no real hold on the dogmatic side of Christianity. 'This was due to his endeavour . . . to appear as a finished man of the world with social experience and social gifts, who could meet other men of the world on equal terms.'[40] But we must leave Creighton for the moment lamenting his abandoned books and endeavouring to come to grips with the work of a diocesan.

Not all Salisbury's episcopal appointments were well received, though the sniping was usually reserved for birds not of the critic's particular feather. The *Church Times*, for instance, which by and large had approved of most of the nominations of his second premiership (1886–92), minced no words in its disapproval of what were to prove the two final ones of that ministry: J. W. Bardsley to Carlisle and N. D. J. Straton to Sodor and Man. In the course of its strictures (1 January 1892) the Manx diocese itself came in for no little stick. Bardsley, though a 'very estimable specimen' of his [Evangelical] school, was also, in the paper's view, 'without distinction or eminence of any kind'. However, no one had quarrelled with his nomination in 1887 to Sodor and Man, a small and insignificant diocese and latterly a heritage of ultra-Protestantism: 'Surely Dr Bardsley's merits were well recognised by this call. We are not aware that Dr Bardsley has been other than an excellent bishop – for Sodor and Man.' But to translate such a man to Carlisle, a much more important diocese which had for years been under the care of a 'consistently High Church bishop, one of the ablest men on the Bench, a great organiser and a statesmanlike ruler to boot' – that was altogether too much! 'There can be no excuse for such a choice; certainly no excuse can be found in the needs and character of the diocese of

PUNCH, OR THE LONDON CHARIVARI.—March 26, 1892.

## SPRING TIME IN LEAP YEAR.

Salisbury. "DON'T YOU THINK, NEPHEW ARTHUR, WE'D BETTER *PLUNGE*—BEFORE WE'RE *PUSHED?*"

*Lord Salisbury with his nephew (and successor as Prime Minister), Arthur Balfour. The plunge was ill-judged, as Salisbury lost the election to Gladstone.*

Carlisle, which is thoroughly attempered to the steady Church-manship of its late ruler.' As for the unfortunate Bardsley's successor, 'little need be said . . . Archdeacon Straton, as Vicar of Wakefield, has made himself a name for partisanship of the ultra-Protestant interest . . . This is the sort of man who is to be made Bishop of Sodor and Man. But Wakefield is to be congratulated.'

The main ecclesiastical interest of Salisbury's last premiership centred on the choice of a new Archbishop of Canterbury to succeed Benson, who had died suddenly on 11 October 1896 while staying with the Gladstones at Hawarden.* Salisbury had no doubts himself: the obvious successor was the Bishop of London, Frederick Temple: unquestionably, he assured the Queen, the greatest man on the English Bench. 'His great liberality of thought, his energy, his piety, and his great intellect have won for him the confidence of all parties in the Church.' Admittedly there was the problem of Temple's age – at 75 he was four years older than Browne of Winchester had been at the time of Tait's death in 1882; and the Queen needed no reminder about the trouble that *that* particular difficulty had caused. Nevertheless, said Salisbury, it would be a slur on Temple if he were passed over and would be resented by many on account of his great merit. Anyway, Salisbury was convinced that he would not accept the post unless he felt satisfied that he could do the work. 'It is very likely that he will not accept it. If he refuses it, the fact that it has been offered to him should be allowed to transpire.' In the event of Temple's declining the offer, Salisbury added, the choice lay between Davidson and Creighton. The former had 'more the manners of society and the knowledge of men', but his health was bad and, at only 48, he was young for an archbishopric. 'He has done nothing to justify in the eyes of the public his rapid advancement, which is in consequence generally attributed to your Majesty's personal predilection for him.' Creighton, on the other hand, was 53 and in strong health; but 'his manner is not good', and it would be felt that his experience in office had been insufficient to justify his elevation over so many men of greater experience. On the whole Salisbury would choose Davidson, whose previous career and intimacy with Tait

---

* He had arrived the previous day after a visit to Ireland and had talked much with his host. On his way to church on the Sunday morning he stopped a lot on the way and got out of breath. 'As they all knelt to confess their sins a frightened Minnie [his wife] heard his death-rattle. They clustered round; the saying of the Lord's Prayer began, but, with no time for a parting word, Edward was dead . . . Gladstone said "It was a soldier's death – a noble end to a noble life".'[41]

gave him a 'moral and social power' in the Church which Creighton did not yet possess. But he would still prefer Temple to either.[42]

The Queen replied that she was unhappy about Temple's age – 'far too advanced to undertake such an arduous position'. (She was herself two years older than Temple.) Moreover, his eyesight was 'most defective: he can hardly see anything below him'. She dismissed Creighton as too junior a bishop and plumped for Davidson (who had actually been consecrated on the same day as Creighton!). The implication that it was her own partiality which had obtained him his promotion to date was 'extremely wrong and unjust. It is in fact quite the reverse.' However, if the Prime Minister thought it 'absolutely necessary' to offer Temple the primacy, maybe the offer could be made 'almost on the understanding that he would not accept it . . . She has no objection to its being known that the offer was made.'[43]

Salisbury continued to oppose Davidson's claims over Temple's. He again insisted to the Queen that the former's rapid advancement was a 'cause of some perplexity'. If he were now to be made archbishop, 'he will be thought to have gained the post entirely by favour; and such a suspicion, though very unjust, will detract most seriously from his authority and usefulness'. Far better, in Salisbury's view, to let Temple hold the fort for a few years. By then Davidson, having served his time in the diocese of Winchester, 'will be of a suitable age, and will be able to do great service to the Church'.[44] The Queen reluctantly agreed. But, when she heard that Temple had accepted the offer with alacrity ('I do not feel that I have any right to refuse the call which her Majesty has made upon me') and without a word specifically about his health, she complained in a cipher telegram to Salisbury: 'Am very much surprised and I must say disappointed at the Bishop of London's acceptance.' She told Davidson: 'I do not like the choice at all, and think the Bishop of London's presence eminently unsuited to the post.'[45]

In fact matters were to turn out exactly as Salisbury had prophesied. Temple, becoming increasingly more doddery as he grew older, lasted six years – and was succeeded by Davidson, who was by then recognized as a (youngish) elder statesman.

Meanwhile there was London to fill; and here again Davidson found himself the favoured candidate – favoured, that is, by the Prime Minister, in spite of his having been at Winchester for little more than a year. But, in suggesting Davidson to the Queen, Salisbury allowed himself a let-out: the state of Davidson's health ('for the work of London is much harder than that of Winchester'). He also acknowledged the 'relations of the See of Winchester to

Your Majesty . . . possibly Your Majesty may not wish to part with him'.[46] Her Majesty did not indeed so wish, and persuaded the Prime Minister to fall back on his second string, Creighton, whose translation to London was duly approved. In a telegram to Davidson she excused herself thus: 'Lord Salisbury wished for you to go to London but feared for your health. I said it must not be offered to you as it would be utter ruin to your health.'[47] So the Queen got her way on this occasion, while persuading herself that it was all for Davidson's own good!

A postscript to this episode came a little more than four years later, when Creighton's death (a week before the Queen's) again left London vacant – and again it was offered to Davidson, this time with the full approval of the new monarch, Edward VII. But Davidson's health was still not strong; and, after consulting his doctor ('I believe, if you go to Fulham, you run the risk of being incapacitated within a couple of years'),[48] he turned the offer down. The see was then offered to, and accepted by, the Bishop of Stepney, A. F. Winnington-Ingram, who was to rule it for the next thirty-eight years. Two years later Davidson's health was sufficiently improved for him to be able to accept the primacy from Balfour (Salisbury's successor as Premier) with a clear conscience.

The last episcopal appointment to be made by Salisbury was also to prove among the most significant: that of Charles Gore to the see of Worcester. Gore was a leading High Churchman whose independent mind, prophetic strength of character and desire to bring Catholic principles to bear on social problems brought a new strand into the Anglo-Catholic movement. But he was considered suspect in some traditionalist quarters for his attitude to Old Testament criticism: his editorship of *Lux Mundi*, a 'series of studies in the religion of the Incarnation', caused controversy on its publication in 1889, as did his own essay in the book on 'The Holy Spirit and Inspiration'. And, as the founder of the Community of the Resurrection, a body of monks based at Mirfield, he was highly suspect in Protestant quarters. So it was not to be supposed that the nomination would get by without protest; nor did it.

It caused immense interest in the Church at large, however. In general it received a warm welcome, though it was hailed in some sections of the press as 'Lord Salisbury's Latest Surprise'. As a canon of Westminster since 1894 Gore had established a reputation as a preacher; and his wide circle of friends included many persons of influence in both Church and State. Salisbury's motive in choosing him, according to Gore's biographer, G. L.

Prestige, arose largely from his awareness of Gore's importance as leader of an important section within the Church, and from his feeling that such leadership ought to be represented on the Bench.[49] Gore himself seemed genuinely surprised by the offer. 'I am dazed', he told his close friends. He had thought that his membership of such a body as the English Church Union, the main High Church organization, made such an offer impossible. In fact one of the first things he did was to resign from the ECU and from his office as Superior at Mirfield: he was released by the community from his monastic obligations. This did not, however, assuage the fury of the extreme Protestants. The Evangelical suffragan in the diocese of Worcester, Bishop Knox of Coventry, might praise Gore as the answer to prayer, as one of the most distinguished of the Church's sons, and as a man whose gifts were specially suited to the diocese's needs and difficulties. Others were not so accommodating. One Protestant lecturer claimed that Gore's was the most objectionable episcopal appointment since the Reformation. And a Protestant newspaper called on loyal churchmen to pray for the bishop-designate in a prayer beginning, 'O God, have mercy on this Romaniser', and ending, 'O Lord, open the blind eyes of this perjured priest before he becomes a Bishop.'[50]

The opposition soon went beyond mere words. Although Gore was elected on 27 December 1901 by the Dean and Chapter of Worcester, the election had still to be legally confirmed before he could become a bishop. And the confirmation ceremony, as had happened in the cases of Hampden and Temple, proved a minefield. On this occasion objections to Gore's election on doctrinal grounds were raised by members of the Church Association and other Protestant militants. As in the other two cases, however, they were ruled out of order by the Vicar-General, on the ground that questions of doctrine could 'under no circumstances be entertained at the business of a confirmation'. Two of the objectors then applied for a *mandamus* to the Court of King's Bench to compel the Vicar-General to hear the objections. The consecration had to be postponed (at Gore's insistence) to allow the objections and arguments to be heard. Luckily all went well. In a unanimous judgement delivered on 10 February the three judges dismissed the application, upholding the Vicar-General's contention that doctrinal objections were out of order at a confirmation ceremony. Gore was duly consecrated in the chapel at Lambeth Palace on 23 February, a month after the date originally fixed. All had turned out well; but it had been a dramatic start to an episcopate which was to have its full share of drama.

A political twist had been added to the nomination by the fact that it had been made by a Conservative premier whose political views were far removed from those of his nominee. Less than a fortnight before the official announcement Gore had protested publicly about conditions in the 'concentration camps' set up by Salisbury's government to provide temporary accommodation for Boer women and children in the closing stages of the South African War. The piquancy of the attack was that the man widely credited with responsibility for the war was the Colonial Secretary, Joseph Chamberlain, whose political power-base happened to be Birmingham, the chief city in Gore's new diocese. A writer in *The Review of Reviews* commented: 'Imagine John the Baptist appointed by Pontius Pilate to be bishop over Galilee when Herod was in his glory, and we have some faint idea of the nature of the appointment by which Lord Salisbury sent Canon Gore to be bishop of Birmingham.'[51] At least no one could contend after this that the Prime Minister was politically motivated in his award of episcopal mitres!

**Nominations to diocesan bishoprics 38 (24 first appointments, 14 translations)**

*First appointments:*

(1) 1885: John Wordsworth to Salisbury.
(2) 1886: Lord Alwyne Compton to Ely.

(3) 1887: John Wareing Bardsley to Sodor and Man.
(4) 1889: Francis John Jayne to Chester.
(5) 1889: Alfred George Edwards to St Asaph.
(6) 1890: Brooke Foss Westcott to Durham.
(7) 1890: John Wogan Festing to St Albans.
(8) 1890: Daniel Lewis Lloyd to Bangor.
(9) 1890: Randall Thomas Davidson to Rochester.
(10) 1890: John James Stewart Perowne to Worcester.
(11) 1891: Mandell Creighton to Peterborough.
(12) 1891: John Gott to Truro.
(13) 1891: Hon. Augustus Legge to Lichfield.
(14) 1891: Norman Dumenil John Straton to Sodor and Man.

(15) 1895: Edward Stuart Talbot to Rochester.
(16) 1895: Edgar Jacob to Newcastle.
(17) 1896: Hon. Edward Carr Glyn to Peterborough.
(18) 1897: John Owen to St Davids.
(19) 1899: Watkin Herbert Williams to Bangor.

(20) 1900: Francis James Chavasse to Liverpool.
(21) 1900: Herbert Edward Ryle to Exeter.
(22) 1901: Francis Paget to Oxford.
(23) 1901: Handley Carr Glyn Moule to Durham.
(24) 1901: Charles Gore to Worcester.

*Translations:*

(1) 1886: James Moorhouse to Manchester (from Melbourne).†

(2) 1888: William Walsham How to Wakefield (from Bedford).*

(3) 1888: William Stubbs to Oxford (from Chester).

(4) 1890: Anthony Wilson Thorold to Winchester (from Rochester).

(5) 1891: William Connor Magee to York (from Peterborough).

(6) 1891: William Dalrymple Maclagan to York (from Lichfield).

(7) 1891: John Wareing Bardsley to Carlisle (from Sodor and Man).

(8) 1895: Randall Thomas Davidson to Winchester (from Rochester).

(9) 1895: Ernest Roland Wilberforce to Chichester (from Newcastle).

(10) 1896: Frederick Temple to Canterbury (from London).

(11) 1896: Mandell Creighton to London (from Peterborough).

(12) 1897: George Forrest Browne to Bristol (from Stepney).*

(13) 1897: George Rodney Eden to Wakefield (from Dover).*

(14) 1901: Arthur Foley Winnington-Ingram to London (from Stepney).*

* Suffragan see.
† Overseas see.

# 11

# Birds of a Feather

*Earl of Rosebery: Prime Minister*
*3 March 1894 – 21 June 1895*

Archibald Philip Primrose, 5th Earl of Rosebery (1847–1929), *was the first prime minister since Aberdeen never to have served in the House of Commons. Educated at Eton and Christ Church, Oxford, he succeeded to the title on the death of his grandfather in 1868. He soon began to make a name for himself on the Liberal benches in the House of Lords, and was Under-Secretary at the Home Office from 1881 to 1883. He served as Foreign Secretary in Gladstone's last two administrations, succeeding to the premiership when Gladstone finally stepped down in 1894. But his period in office was brief; and he resigned the following year after a government defeat in the Commons. In 1896 he resigned the Liberal leadership, and during his political twilight became more and more conservative in his views. In retirement he devoted himself to writing, including a number of noteworthy political biographies. He served as the first chairman of the newly-formed London County Council and, as a leading racehorse-owner, was three times winner of the Derby.*

Lord Rosebery stood in the tradition of aristocratic radicalism, though his manner was too aloof to appeal to the masses. In politics he often appeared as a detached observer rather than as an active participant. This characteristic had been apparent from an early age. His tutor at Eton, William Johnson Cory, once wrote of the young Rosebery (in a much-quoted phrase) that he was 'one of those who liked the palm without the dust'.[1] And, for all his democratic pretensions, a friend was later to remark: 'Rosebery feels about Democracy as if he were holding a wolf by the ears.'[2] As Foreign Secretary he had allied himself with his party's imperialist wing, which hardly endeared him to the radicals. Indeed Rosebery's great rival for the succession to Gladstone, Sir William Harcourt, only agreed to serve under him as Leader of the Commons in return for an unprecedented package of special conditions which curbed Rosebery's freedom of action. It is hardly surprising that, as he grew older, he should distance himself more and more from his Liberal past.

Rosebery was a deeply religious man. As a boy he had shown precocious piety. When only fourteen he wrote to his mother of his shock at seeing one of the confirmation candidates in the school chapel laugh [presumably in a fit of nervous hysteria] as the bishop was laying hands on him. 'I think this was the most horrible thing ever thought of. Just when God was about to admit him to his table – laughing. I prayed, Mother, that I never should commit such an enormous sin . . . I cannot help feeling sure that God has sent me this Confirmation for my special good as it impressed me so much.'[3] As an adult Rosebery read the Bible daily. He read prayers (and often one of Newman's sermons) to his children on Sundays, and of course was a regular communicant. But there was a morbid streak to his religion. John Buchan, who knew him well in his later years, drew attention to its essentially gloomy character: 'Behind all his exterior urbanity and humour lay this haunting sense of transience, and, while to the world he seemed like some polished eighteenth-century grandee, at heart he was the Calvinist of seventeenth-century Scotland.'[4] In particular Rosebery had an obsession with death, and he would astonish people by rushing off to see the remains of his friends before they were buried.

His diaries include copious notes on services and sermons. Once, holidaying at Gastein in Austria, he wrote: 'How I love this simple church and service: bare as our kirks – no meretricious madonna – only the picture of Christ – the devout congregation of mountaineers. Read prayers all day at home.'[5]

Rosebery had little more than a year in which to mastermind ecclesiastical appointments. But, during this short period, he contrived to offend the Queen both on the general principle of his nominations and in respect of one particular appointment. Not that he relished controversy for its own sake. 'I am very homesick for the Foreign Office', he wrote to a friend during his second week as Prime Minister. 'I do not think I shall like any of the duties of my new position. Patronage is odious; ecclesiastical patronage distressing. It is in consequence, indeed, of a Dean having died that I dictate this from my bed.'[6]

The main cause of offence to the Queen lay in the allegedly political character of his appointments. Although only two bishoprics fell vacant during his fifteen months in office, he found himself having also to fill four deaneries and several canonries. The spark was applied to the tinder with his nomination of W. H. Fremantle, a strong Liberal, to the deanery of Ripon. Fremantle was the latest in a line of political Liberals chosen by Rosebery for church appointments. The Queen felt that enough was enough and caused her secretary, Sir Arthur Bigge, to make enquiries of Randall Davidson, now Bishop of Rochester. Davidson minced no words. He confirmed to Bigge that Fremantle was indeed a strong Liberal politically ('and eke ecclesiastically'), though he added in extenuation: 'He is a thorough gentleman in all ways, and this commends his Liberal sentiments to many who would not otherwise find them acceptable.' Nevertheless, said Davidson, should Rosebery nominate for the vacant deanery of Canterbury yet another strong political Liberal, 'I venture to think the Queen might with great appropriateness point out to him that he has been somewhat markedly political in his nominations'. The bishopric of Hereford, plus the deaneries of Hereford, Durham, Winchester and Ripon and canonries at both Westminster and Canterbury, had all been filled by men noted as Rosebery's political partisans ('though excellent in themselves'). Davidson's finale (strong by Davidsonian standards) ran: 'No recent Prime Minister has, I think, made his political bias quite so prominent in his ecclesiastical nominations.'[7]

Bigge, acting on this advice, passed on the necessary warning to the Prime Minister, who was not amused. Indeed Bigge's letter caused a 'terrific fulmination' from Rosebery, who replied via *his* secretary, George Murray. The reply, said Murray, was 'directed at your [Bigge's] innocent head but is intended ultimately to get lodgment elsewhere. Pray see that it reaches its destination. It represents a good deal of Lord Rosebery's wine infused into my water. In fact you may take it as expressing with great fidelity *his* opinions.'

In his reply Murray challenged Bigge's assertion that Rosebery's church appointments were 'too political':

> There is nothing he [Rosebery] dislikes so much as having to consider politics in such matters. He presumes, however, that it would not be expected that a deserving ecclesiastic is to be excluded from preferment because he happens rather to agree than disagree with Lord Rosebery in other matters. Those who disagree with him have at any rate had a long innings.

Murray, on the Prime Minister's behalf, went on to make the allegation about the political nature of Lord Salisbury's appointments to which reference has been made in the previous chapter. He also examined in detail the recent nominations of Salisbury's successor and claimed that all but one of eight nominees were either non-political, of unknown politics (Fremantle was included in this category) or else political 'opponents'.[8]

Bigge duly passed on this effusion to the Queen, with a note expressing surprise that Rosebery was 'so ignorant as to the politics of those whom he has lately submitted for preferment'. Davidson again insisted that many of the nominees were *'marked as political partisans'*. The series of eight recent Roseberian appointments formed, in his judgement, a consecutive *series*; and the nominees 'ALL belong to the distinctly and distinctively Liberal party in public affairs'.[9]

In his reply to Murray Bigge reproduced many of Davidson's points, and added that the Queen was not singling out Rosebery for criticism. She had criticized or vetoed, where necessary, names submitted by previous prime ministers. She had, generally speaking, entirely approved of Rosebery's nominations, but wished to call attention to the danger of prolonging unduly a series of appointments of men of whom many were considered by the outside public to be political partisans. Bigge ended by pointing out that at least four of the bishops nominated by Salisbury were certainly not 'supporters of a Conservative policy'.[10]

Both of Rosebery's episcopal appointments excited criticism – though for different reasons. The first was that of George Kennion to Bath and Wells in the summer of 1894. Kennion had been a contemporary of Rosebery at Eton and had risen to be Bishop of Adelaide. Rosebery had met him again during a tour of Australia in 1883–4 and had been much impressed: 'Fancy one's contemporaries being so shabby as to take a Bishopric and make one feel a hundred. But I forgive him: I believe he is both a saint and a man of business. I have rarely been so fascinated.'[11] The sequel to this happy meeting of old school chums occurred ten years later, when Kennion returned to England after resigning his bishopric. Some friends at the Athenaeum told him, half in fun, that it was his duty as a retiring colonial bishop to call on the Prime Minister to pay his respects. Kennion took the suggestion in all seriousness and left his card with the butler at Rosebery's house – it happened to be Derby Day, so the Prime Minister was at Epsom. When he eventually got home from the races he found his friend's card awaiting him; and, as he was at a loss to know whom to appoint to the vacant see of Bath and Wells and remembered how impressed he had been by Kennion in Australia, it must have seemed like an answer to prayer. The saintly and businesslike Old Etonian was duly appointed.[12]

The nomination did not, however, escape criticism from the

many in the Church who regretted that greater search had not been made by the Prime Minister among the talent already available at home. The *Church Times* spoke for others besides Anglo-Catholics in suggesting (13 July 1894) that the news of the appointment would be received with much disappointment. 'The circumstances of Colonial life and Church administration in lands beyond the seas are so different from those of England at home that it may be doubted whether they furnish a good training for the work of a strictly English see.' There were, in any event, 'at least a score of Colonial Bishops whom we could name with a record which would justify translation to England far better than that of Lord Arthur Hervey's designated successor'. Moreover, on this occasion, the paper seemed to detect the shadow of the old school tie:

> We fear that there is still some truth in the old saying that either private means or social influence are among the primary qualifications for high preferment among us. It must be clearly understood that in these democratic days such considerations are of comparatively small account. A modern Bishop is something more than a county magnate.

Rosebery's second bishop proved unpopular in a higher quarter and for a different reason. The man concerned was John Percival, Headmaster of Rugby and in most respects an admirable candidate. *But* he was in favour of disestablishment for the Church in Wales; and the diocese for which he was now suggested, Hereford, included thirteen Welsh parishes. The Queen smelt trouble at once, and wondered how she could avoid appointing Percival. The first step was obviously to ask the invaluable Davidson; and this Bigge was instructed to do, as the Queen 'will on no account appoint a Disestablisher'.[13]

In his reply Davidson admitted the gravity of the nomination. 'To place on the borders of Wales almost if not quite the *only* prominent clergyman in England who has declared himself in favour of Welsh Disestablishment is to run a grave risk.' But Davidson saw 'great difficulty' in the Queen's giving an absolute refusal on the single ground of the candidate's opinions upon one political question of the hour.

> Were the Queen simply to say, 'I will not have a man who is in favour of Welsh Disestablishment' (Dr Percival is not, I believe, in favour of disestablishment in England proper), I should fear that this might be regarded, and even represented, as equivalent

to saying that the Queen insisted that all Bishops must be of one political party.

Davidson suggested that the Queen might point out to the Prime Minister that Percival's advocacy of disestablishment would place him in 'grave difficulties' with his own clergy and ask him for some reassurance ('which he will find it difficult to give in any cogent form').[14]

Rosebery evaded the argument that Percival's views might make him unacceptable to his clergy by ignoring it. Instead he concentrated on the actual issue of church establishments, maintaining that they were 'apt to be injurious to national religion when carried on against the national will' (as in Wales) but 'can be properly maintained and justified when they are approved by the national will' (as in England). The presence of the English establishment in Wales was an 'offence and a stumbling-block. It is there very much what Gibraltar is to Spain, a foreign fortress placed on the territory of a jealous, proud and susceptible nation'. Percival's appointment, Rosebery told the Queen, would strengthen the church establishment in England and the real interests of the Church in Wales.[15]

The Queen, cross with the Prime Minister for ignoring her point about Percival's possible non-acceptability among his clergy, again sought Davidson's counsel. But all he could do was to repeat his previous points and advise the Queen to reiterate her objections on the lines of: 'It still appears to the Queen most undesirable to send to a diocese on the Welsh border, in which feeling on the subject runs so high, a Bishop who will find himself placed in opposition, from the outset, to almost all his people and distrusted by them on that account.'[16] The Queen took this advice, passing it on to the Prime Minister but leaving the final responsibility in the matter with him. Rosebery, however, stuck to his guns and offered the see to Percival ('It is extremely desirable that a Bishop of your opinions should be placed on the marches of Wales'),[17] who duly accepted.

In the event the fears of the Queen and her advisers proved to have been ill-founded. The clergy of the diocese of Hereford for the most part jogged along in seeming accord with their bishop. He lived long enough to see a bill for the disestablishment of the Church in Wales enacted, though not long enough to see it come into force.

Rosebery's religion took a bizarre turn at the end of his life. He instructed one of his servants to buy him a gramophone and told him that, when the moment of death approached, he was to play a record of the Eton Boating-Song. Whether he actually heard the haunting strains of the song – the words of which had been written by his old Eton tutor, William Cory – must be doubted. But it was a typical Rosebery gesture in the face of death.[18]

**Nominations to diocesan bishoprics 2 (1 first appointment, 1 translation)**

*First appointment:*

(1) 1895: John Percival to Hereford.

*Translation:*

(1) 1894: George Wyndham Kennion to Bath and Wells (from Adelaide, Australia).†

† Overseas see.

# PART TWO

# PREMIERS v. PRIMATES

# 12

# Philosopher–PM

*A. J. Balfour: Prime Minister*
*12 July 1902 – 5 December 1905*

*Arthur James Balfour, 1st Earl of Balfour (1848–1930),*
*succeeded his uncle, Lord Salisbury, as Premier on the latter's*
*retirement in 1902. Educated at Eton and Trinity College,*
*Cambridge, he had inherited an estate at Whittinghame, Scotland,*
*in 1869, together with an ample fortune. A life-long bachelor, his*
*freedom from family and financial worries helped him to preserve*
*an Olympian detachment amid the political hurly-burly and to*
*cement his reputation as a philosopher. Elected a Conservative*
*MP in 1874, he represented first Hertford and then, from 1885 to*
*1906, East Manchester. His kinship with Salisbury eased his rise*
*to power. From 1887 to 1891 he was Chief Secretary for Ireland*
*(where his ruthless policy won him the nickname 'Bloody*
*Balfour'). He was Leader of the House of Commons from 1895 to*
*1902 before succeeding to the premiership. He resigned in 1905*
*following a defeat in the Commons, but remained leader of the*
*Conservative Party till his replacement by Bonar Law in 1911.*
*He returned to office during World War I – as First Lord of the*
*Admiralty under Asquith and then as Foreign Secretary under*
*Lloyd George. In 1917 he issued the famous 'Balfour Declaration'*
*promising British support for a Jewish national home in Palestine.*
*He left the Foreign Office in 1919 to become Lord President of*
*the Council, and from 1920 to 1922 was British representative*
*on the council of the League of Nations. A philosopher of*

*distinction as well as a statesman, he was President of the British Academy from 1921 until his death. He was also a prominent member of the 'Souls', the aristocratic élite which was influential in both politics and the arts in late Victorian and Edwardian England.*

Salisbury's retirement from the premiership in favour of his nephew marks a pivotal point in the history of prime ministers as bishop-makers. For Balfour's assumption of office came only eighteen months after the death of Queen Victoria and the accession of Edward VII; and his first episcopal appointment, made a few months later, was that of Randall Davidson to the see of Canterbury. Just as the new monarch was to play a far less significant role than his late mother in the bishop-making process, so the influence of the new archbishop was to become proportionately greater in his role as adviser to a succession of prime ministers. By the end of his twenty-five-year reign, no premier would have ventured to nominate a bishop to whose appointment Davidson was irrevocably opposed.

How did the new sovereign regard *his* part in the process? No one would suppose from the published accounts of his life that the raffish Edward VII possessed the same passionate interest in ecclesiastical affairs as the late Queen – nor did he. But he was certainly not indifferent to them. Prince Albert's librarian, Dr Becker, had reported to his master as long ago as 1852 that the main features of the Prince of Wales's character included a 'profound religious feeling'.[1] The Prince was confirmed in St George's Chapel, Windsor, at the age of sixteen by Archbishop Sumner, the Queen herself reading aloud to him beforehand from the sermons of Dr Arnold. On the day before the ceremony the Prince had been cross-examined by the Dean of Windsor, Gerald Wellesley, and had shown a thorough knowledge of the catechism and sacraments.[2] Thereafter, in the words of one of his biographers, 'an unclouded and humble faith remained with him always and was an immense source of strength'.[3] He might not always live up to his faith, but he never lost it. 'I do not mind what religion a man professes', he once remarked, 'but I distrust him who has none.'[4] He was not averse to High Church practices, and in later life would accompany Queen Alexandra to services at All Saints', Margaret Street, the Anglo-Catholic citadel in London's West End.[5]

The King may have been a convinced and practising Anglican, but he was anxious not to offend the susceptibilities of other Christians. However, he found himself unwittingly at loggerheads with Roman Catholics on a number of occasions. The first was at the state opening of Parliament in February 1901, a month after his accession, when he had perforce to declare himself a Protestant in terms so crude as to provoke an immediate protest from Cardinal Bourne, the Roman Catholic Archbishop of Westminster. (Among other things the King found himself having to proclaim that 'the invocation or adoration of the Virgin Mary, or any other saint, and the Sacrifice of the Mass, as they are now used in the Church of Rome, are superstitious and idolatrous'.) The Cabinet agreed with the King that the terms of such a declaration were hardly in accordance with the 'public policy of the present day', but felt that any attempt to alter the law would provoke a public outcry against 'Popery'. So nothing was done at the time; and it was left to a future prime minister, Asquith, to introduce an Act soon after the accession of George V which satisfied Protestant prejudices without causing undue offence to Roman Catholics.[6]

King Edward was anxious not to identify himself too exclusively with Anglicanism. When King Carlos of Portugal and the Crown Prince were shot by Left-wing assassins in February 1908, he insisted on attending a requiem Mass in their memory at St James's Roman Catholic church in Spanish Place, having driven there with the Queen and an escort of cavalry. He ignored Protestant protests – but hedged his bets by attending an Anglican memorial service for the murdered monarch in St Paul's Cathedral the next day.[7] The row over the Spanish Place requiem, however, may have prompted his caution later that year during a Roman Catholic eucharistic congress in London. The Home Secretary, Herbert Gladstone (youngest son of the late Prime Minister), had rashly given permission for priests in vestments, led by the papal legate, to carry the Host in procession through the streets of London as an 'act of reparation' for the Reformation. The King foresaw the likely risk of a Protestant counter-demonstration and put pressure on the Prime Minister, Asquith. Eventually Cardinal Bourne was persuaded to eliminate the Host and the priests' vestments from the procession – and all was well.[8]

When it came to ecclesiastical appointments in the Church of England the King displayed a moderate interest – but nothing like the same concern that his mother had shown. At the time of his accession he had been asked by Randall Davidson, then Bishop of Winchester and Clerk of the Closet, whether he should continue the confidential recommendations for church appointments which he had been in the habit of offering the late Queen. King Edward assured him that he wished the correspondence to be maintained.[9] But, although he rarely argued with his prime ministers to the same extent that his mother had done, he still had a mind of his own where church appointments were concerned. Within a week of his accession he was already writing to the then Premier, Lord Salisbury, about a successor to Mandell Creighton as Bishop of London; and, though his first suggestion, Talbot of Rochester, was overruled by the Premier, his final nominee, Winnington-Ingram of Stepney, was the man eventually appointed. The following year the King contested a suggestion of Davidson's that colonial bishops should be eligible for appointment as cathedral canons – and got his way.[10] He was never as enamoured of Davidson as his mother had been, regarding him as too indecisive. In the summer of 1906 he noted at the foot of a letter which Davidson, by this time Archbishop of Canterbury, had written to him: 'This is a very "shilly-shally" letter from a good but not strong man either physically or morally.'[11] As we shall see in the next chapter, he disagreed with Campbell-Bannerman over the choice of a new Bishop of Chichester. And, just before his death in 1910, he pressed strongly and successfully for the appointment of his own nominee, Bertram Pollock, Headmaster of Wellington, to the bishopric of Norwich – the diocese in which Sandringham House, the royal residence in Norfolk, was situated.[12]

Balfour himself is one of the more intriguing of twentieth-century prime ministers. Throughout his long career he always contrived to stay aloof from the rough-and-tumble of politics. His tutor at Eton, the poet William Cory, wrote of him shortly before he left: 'He philosophizes in his youth: he will philosophize to the end.'[13] This forecast proved accurate. A future prime minister, Ramsay MacDonald, was to say of Balfour: 'He saw a great deal of life from afar.' And a still-later premier, Winston Churchill, observed: 'Arthur Balfour did not mingle in the hurly-burly. He glided upon its surface.' Churchill went on (à propos of Balfour's easy financial circumstances):

> Throughout his life the late Lord Balfour, fortunately for himself, still more fortunately for his country, was removed from the vulgar necessities. He never had to make any of those compromises, increasing under modern conditions, between an entirely dispassionate outlook upon affairs and his daily bread.[14]

Balfour was a Scot; and his broad and undogmatic outlook on religious matters was helped by the fact that he was half a Presbyterian. He had been confirmed in the Church of England while a schoolboy at Eton, and thenceforward was a communicant of that Church as well as of the Church of Scotland. He regarded himself as a member of both Churches – and had no sympathy with those who thought otherwise. He was devout in his personal religious practice. He attended his parish church regularly when at home at Whittinghame: after church on Sunday mornings he and his guests would walk home discussing the sermon and arguing about the tunes of the psalms. Every Sunday evening he would read family prayers (including ones from the Anglican liturgy and a chapter from the Bible, which he always chose himself). His biographer, Blanche Dugdale, remarks: 'His reading was rather slow, without dramatic emphasis, but bringing out every inherent shade of beauty and meaning. It deeply impressed all his hearers. It was impossible for attention to wander from it for a moment.'[15]

Balfour's religious tolerance was in many ways in advance of his times. In January 1901 he told an audience at Haddington celebrating the union of the Free and United Presbyterian Churches of Scotland:

Do not suppose I am an advocate for that colourless thing known as an undenominational creed . . . What I plead for is that Christian men should understand there is a permission to differ without these differences carrying with them into ecclesiastical life, into political life, or into private life, any other difference which should make common work for a common object impossible . . . The Church is, among other things, a practical organisation to carry out a great practical work. It is something more than an organisation to produce a body of school divinity.[16]

Where the Church of England was concerned, Balfour was a pessimist. He wrote to Edward Talbot, then Bishop of Rochester and one of his oldest friends, on 6 February 1903:

I confess to entertaining the gloomiest apprehensions as to the future of the Church of England. I can hardly think of anything else. A so-called 'Protestant' faction, ignorant, fanatical, reckless, but every day organising themselves politically with increased efficiency. A ritualistic party, as ignorant, as fanatical and as reckless, the sincerity of whose attachment to historic Anglicanism I find it quite impossible to believe. A High Church party, determined to support men of whose practices they heartily disapprove. A laity divided from the clergy by an ever-deepening gulf, and exercised by religious problems which the clergy cannot help them to solve. An Episcopate – but I will not pursue the subject . . .[17]

Fortunately for his peace of mind he was also a close personal friend of Randall Davidson, who had been of great help to him in the preparation of the Education Act of 1902 and whom he nominated to succeed Frederick Temple as Archbishop of Canterbury on 31 December of that year. The offer had in fact been confidently awaited, but was unexpectedly long in coming. Following the premature death of Bishop Creighton of London in January 1901 Davidson had been the only obvious successor to Temple. Because of his close connection with Queen Victoria and with three successive Archbishops of Canterbury he had a far more intimate knowledge of the Church of England than any of his episcopal colleagues. As he put it himself, 'I do know the ropes better than others.' Balfour realized this as well as anyone – but was strangely slow to say so. The reason was not far to seek. As Davidson subsequently put it:

> Balfour's idiosyncrasies in the way of not writing letters came out in a peculiar way. He told me, in a letter with reference to the series of appointments which would become inevitable, that it was his intention and wish to nominate me to the King for the Primacy; but he sent no further letter on the subject, and, although I had a long interview with Sandars [Balfour's secretary] in my bedroom at Farnham while I was laid up with influenza, I had literally no letter which conveyed to me any definite proposal in the matter, until I had actually to ask for such and then it came readily enough.[18]

The letter when it *did* come was brief and to the point. 'Death has been making sad havoc in the Church', wrote Balfour, 'and the consequent changes throw a heavy burden of responsibility upon the unfortunate Prime Minister. I mean to propose your name to H.M. for Canterbury. From conversations I have had with him, I have no doubt that he will agree. But what next?'

The answer to this not wholly rhetorical question was of course the choice of a successor to Davidson himself. And this and subsequent episcopal appointments were affected by the close relationship formed between Downing Street and Lambeth during Davidson's own much longer reign as Archbishop of Canterbury. Here the chief source of information is Bishop Bell of Chichester. As Davidson's resident chaplain from 1914 to 1924 he was in a unique position to know the workings of his master's mind, and the details of his policy and practice over episcopal appointments. And, in his magisterial life of Davidson published in 1935, he distilled the fruits of that knowledge.

Bell observes that no previous Archbishop of Canterbury could ever have exercised greater influence in the appointment of bishops than Randall Davidson. During his long primacy Davidson had to deal with seven prime ministers, three of whom were Presbyterians and one a Baptist. All seven, says Bell, realized their responsibilities in relation to church patronage. They gave careful attention to the Archbishop's recommendations – 'and never, in the many instances of episcopal nominations during twenty-five years, did they make a single appointment which they knew to be fundamentally objectionable to the Archbishop'. They did not necessarily take Davidson's advice about a man's fitness for a particular see; but, if he insisted that a particular man was wholly unsuitable for the office of bishop, 'no Prime Minister ever during these twenty-five years persevered with his name'. Some appointments were less satisfactory than others, Bell concludes (no doubt thinking of Hensley Henson), and some the Archbishop, left to himself, would not have made; 'but in every case the merits and qualifications of the person ultimately chosen were carefully and conscientiously considered, and there was no instance whatever of what could fairly be called a mere political job'.[19]

An interesting footnote to these observations was added by Bell more than twenty years later (21 May 1956) in a letter to David Stephens, the then prime minister's appointments secretary. It related to a discussion on the subject between the two men which had taken place a short while before – and, says Bell, 'there was a point in our talk which I should like to clear up':

> You were kind enough to speak of my Life of Davidson as your 'bible'. And I think you said that, if the Archbishop of Canterbury of the day stated that a particular clergyman was not in his judgment suitable for a bishopric, the Prime Minister would not think of appointing him. I said that this seemed to me to be going much too far, and that, if an Archbishop thought a particular clergyman unsuitable, reasons of a compelling kind ought to be given – for otherwise it might be unfair to the clergyman and also to the Church.

In fact Stephens was not really all that far out in his observation, because Bishop Bell in his letter goes on to quote the passages from his own book given above. But he adds significantly, in a reference to the Henson case:

> Archbishop Davidson was, as you know, pressed very hard by a regular combination of churchmen of different schools of thought to tell Mr Lloyd George that Henson was wholly unsuitable for the office of a Bishop, and fundamentally objectionable to himself. Davidson was no doubt perturbed by

the idea that Henson should be Bishop of Hereford, and knew that his appointment to any See would cause something of a storm . . . But he did not rule him out as a Bishop, nor did he say that he ought not to go to Hereford.

Bell told Stephens that Davidson was always most anxious not to allow his own private feelings, or even his failure to appreciate particular persons, to lead him to rule out anyone whom the prime minister might suggest. 'And he was anxious too that the comprehensive character of the Church of England should be reflected on the Bench – though he knew that this policy must involve the appointment of men whose gifts and talents, or points of view on Church organisation or doctrine, might be very different from his own.'[20]

In thanking Bell for his 'footnote' to their recent conversation Stephens wrote that 'I really meant no more than that the practice described in your Life of Randall Davidson was still, I believed, being followed today'.[21] The prime minister by then was Eden and the archbishop Fisher. What happened shortly afterwards when Stephens broke the Fisher rules and acted on his own initiative will be described in a later chapter.

The actual method adopted by Davidson in dealing with episcopal appointments developed into an established routine. As soon as a vacancy occurred he would speak or write about it to the prime minister and, if necessary, describe the general conditions of the diocese or suggest the type of bishop required. As a rule he would suggest the names of three or more people to be considered. He would also make his own enquiries as to names which might have been independently suggested to the prime minister and let the premier know what he thought of them. Bell comments:

> The two general impressions left on the mind, after reading the extensive correspondence and memoranda covering this quarter of a century, are, first, that, though like other human beings they might not always succeed, Prime Minister and Archbishop both did their best to find the most suitable men for the Bench of Bishops; and, second, that Archbishop Davidson exercised a predominating influence upon the character of that Bench.[22]

Perhaps the best way of indicating how the system worked in practice is to quote a typical letter of Davidson's, the predecessor of scores of others, relating to a particular see. It was written during the second year of his Primacy:

Lambeth Palace,
July 27, 1904

My dear Balfour,

You have asked for a letter from me expressing my view as to the fitness of Bishop Hoskyns (now Suffragan Bishop of Burnley) for the See of Southwell, about to be vacated by Bishop Ridding's resignation.

I do not myself know Bishop Hoskyns very intimately. But everything that I do know of him, and everything that I have heard, leads me to believe that he is just the man for these quiet Midland towns – and the strong testimony of the present Bishop of Manchester [E. A. Knox], a man whose opinions on ecclesiastical matters have never been other than Evangelical (in the technical sense given to the word), is absolutely reassuring as to Bishop Hoskyns' freedom from narrowness and from *partisanship* of a High Church kind.

He is a High Churchman wholly free from 'vagaries', and I can confidently recommend his appointment should you think it well to seek – and doubtless to obtain – the Sovereign's approval of your choice.

Randall Cantuar[23]

Hoskyns – the father of the well-known biblical scholar – was duly appointed.

Although he was Prime Minister for only three years and five months, Balfour had to fill no fewer than fifteen vacant diocesan bishoprics. The first of these, after the nomination to Canterbury, was Davidson's former see of Winchester. Here both Premier and Primate found themselves at one in their wish to translate Talbot of Rochester, the friend of both. But on this occasion difficulties of churchmanship proved too much for them. Public discussion of the likely candidates led to criticisms of Talbot for being too sympathetic to the Ritualists – and *The Times* weighed in with a hostile article. Balfour bowed to the critics and eventually offered Winchester to Ryle of Exeter – who had been the last of the seven names originally suggested to him by Davidson.[24] (Talbot did eventually go to Winchester – but not until 1911, after he had won his spurs and disarmed his critics with a six-year stint as first bishop of the new diocese of Southwark. Asquith was the prime minister responsible.)

At about the same time, following the death of the worthy but uneminent Bishop Festing, Jacob of Newcastle was translated to the vacant see of St Albans. This caused Davidson to remark significantly in a letter to Balfour: 'The King very clearly wants to have a personal say in all the appointments. He wholly approves of Bishop Jacob for St Albans.'[25]

A whiff of politics still occasionally appeared in regard to ecclesiastical appointments even in those comparatively regenerate days. When, for instance, Edmund Knox, the father of Ronnie Knox and a doughty Evangelical who was at that time Suffragan Bishop of Coventry, was offered the see of Manchester in September 1903, he accepted by return of post. 'No doubt some will think that I ought to have taken at least a week for consulting my friends and for prayer and meditation', he remarks cynically in his autobiography. 'But I knew well beforehand what my friends would say. I should simply be putting them to the trouble of writing complimentary letters . . . I should only have deceived myself and others if I had pretended to hesitate where my mind was already made up.'

The real reason for Knox's prompt acceptance was his fear that the government might fall and the offer be withdrawn by a new prime minister. 'Mr Balfour's position, at the moment, was extremely hazardous. The Tariff controversy had taken from his Cabinet, for opposite reasons, his two chief supporters, Joseph Chamberlain and the Duke of Devonshire. The King, at Marienbad, was already coquetting with Campbell-Bannerman.'[26] Balfour survived that particular little local difficulty and lived to nominate other bishops; but no doubt Knox recalled Disraeli's last-minute nomination, only a few days before he fell from power, of an Archbishop of Canterbury who would certainly *not* have been chosen by his successor, Gladstone.

Knox's diocesan at that time was Charles Gore, the Bishop of Worcester. And politics were to play a part in Gore's own translation to Birmingham the following year; the key figure in the drama being Joseph Chamberlain, who had resigned from Balfour's government to promote tariff reform by way of 'imperial preference'. Chamberlain was the senior MP for Birmingham and a keen supporter of the scheme to make that city, then in the diocese of Worcester, into a bishopric of its own. The scheme had the full backing of Gore; and Chamberlain agreed to sponsor the necessary Bishoprics Bill in Parliament on the understanding that Gore (whom he both respected and admired) should become the first Bishop of Birmingham. At the same time Talbot was trying to hive off part of his over-large diocese of Rochester and make it into a separate diocese of Southwark; and a single Bill was introduced to divide both sees.

At that time such Bills were liable to be blocked in the Commons by obstructive tactics on the part of MPs with a grievance to ventilate. Both Gore and Talbot were known sympathizers with Ritualism, and there was therefore a good chance of this particular Bill falling victim to Protestant prejudices. In the event Chamberlain, Gore and their supporters did a deal with the government. Early in 1904 Balfour had reluctantly consented to the appointment of a royal commission to enquire into 'alleged lawlessness in the Church', because the Whips had informed him that the government would be defeated if he did not. The 'alleged lawlessness' centred largely on the use of unauthorized ceremonial by Ritualists, and Balfour was therefore faced with a war on two fronts: Protestant anger if he failed to appoint a royal commission, Anglo-Catholic anger if he did. In the ensuing controversy a tit-for-tat arrangement was made. Gore undertook to secure High Church agreement to the appointment of the royal commission: Balfour, in return, promised the government's full backing for the Bishoprics Bill and moved the second reading in the Commons himself. An amendment was then moved from the Protestant side to the effect that, until the bishops put down Ritualism by stern and drastic action, it would be a grave error to increase their number.

In the course of the debate Chamberlain made a key intervention. Another MP had given detailed particulars of Ritualistic services held in one of the Birmingham churches. Chamberlain, speaking as a Nonconformist who objected to the practices described, nevertheless assured the House that the statement that the Church in Birmingham had been scandalized by Gore's appointment was entirely incorrect. Gore, he said, had won golden opinions from Nonconformists as well as from Anglicans: 'his moderate, generous, broad and religious influence is exercising the best effect upon the people of this city'. The Bill was passed. Gore declared afterwards: 'It is a mercy. It seems to bridge the interval between despair and hope. I wrote in gratitude to A[rthur] B[alfour] and he replied, owning to having had "moments of anxiety", in spite of being "quite resolved to pass the Bill".'[27]

A few months later Balfour nominated Gore for appointment as the first bishop of the new diocese of Birmingham.

**Nominations to diocesan bishoprics 15 (5 first appointments, 10 translations)**

*First appointments:*

(1) 1903: Archibald Robertson to Exeter.
(2) 1904: John William Diggle to Carlisle.

(3) 1905: Edgar Charles Sumner Gibson to Gloucester.

(4) 1905: Joshua Pritchard Hughes to Llandaff.

(5) 1905: Frederic Henry Chase to Ely.

*Translations:*

(1) 1903: Randall Thomas Davidson to Canterbury (from Winchester).

(2) 1903: Herbert Edward Ryle to Winchester (from Exeter).

(3) 1903: Edgar Jacob to St Albans (from Newcastle).

(4) 1903: Arthur Thomas Lloyd to Newcastle (from Thetford).*

(5) 1903: Edmund Arbuthnott Knox to Manchester (from Coventry).*

(6) 1904: Edwyn Hoskyns to Southwell (from Burnley).*

(7) 1905: Charles Gore to Birmingham (from Worcester).

(8) 1905: Huyshe Wolcott Yeatman-Biggs to Worcester (from Southwark).*

(9) 1905: Edward Stuart Talbot to Southwark (from Rochester).

(10) 1905: John Reginald Harmer to Rochester (from Adelaide).†

* Suffragan see.

† Overseas see.

# 13

# A Good Liberal

*Sir H. Campbell-Bannerman: Prime Minister
5 December 1905 – 8 April 1908*

Sir Henry Campbell-Bannerman (1836–1908) *succeeded Balfour
as the first of three Liberal prime ministers. The son of a Lord
Provost of Glasgow, he was educated at Glasgow High School,
Glasgow University and Trinity College, Cambridge. He first
entered Parliament in 1868, and held minor office under
Gladstone before becoming, in 1884, Chief Secretary for Ireland.
He was Secretary for War in 1886 and again in 1892–5, and
succeeded Harcourt as Liberal leader in 1898. His administration
– which included Asquith, Grey, Haldane and Lloyd George –
granted self-government to the defeated Boer republics, from
which act of generosity stemmed the Union of South Africa; but
some of its key domestic measures were either rejected or
substantially amended by the House of Lords. Campbell-Bannerman's failing health led to his handing over much of the day-to-
day business of the premiership to Asquith, who succeeded him
three weeks before his death.*

Campbell-Bannerman's wife Charlotte once said of him that the
truest praise one could give C.B. was that he was a 'really
perfectly good man'. They were a devoted couple, in spite of their
totally opposite temperaments. Henry was witty, sociable and a
*bon viveur*, Charlotte shy, nervous and without self-confidence.
But she had a strong influence over her husband in spite of her
diffidence. He consulted her whenever he had an important
decision to make and would call her his 'final Court of Appeal'.
When away from home he would write her affectionate letters
beginning with such phrases as 'My own darling diddy'. It was
on one such absence in October 1892, when he was at Balmoral
as the Queen's minister in attendance, that his duties included
driving to the parish church at Crathie ('My companions envied
me my nice fur coat', he told Charlotte).[1] He would have been
thoroughly at home in the church, for he had been brought up in
the established Church of Scotland and was a devout Presbyterian.

But he was tolerant in his religious views and often declared himself to be no dogmatist. This was just as well when, as Prime Minister, he found himself having to choose bishops for the established Church south of the Border. Here he placed great reliance on his devoted private secretary, Henry Higgs. 'I am a Presbyterian', C.B. would say, 'and I do not know even what is a Rural Dean. But Higgs knows all about these matters. He is a member of the Church of England and keeper of my Ecclesiastical conscience.'[2]

We know a fair amount about the motives that guided C.B. in his bishop-making, for some years after his death Higgs described them in the course of a private memorandum on the late Prime Minister's methods. On C.B.'s attitude to ecclesiastical appointments in general Higgs wrote:

I soon discovered that he had no objection to a Broad Churchman, but had little liking for the type of High Churchman who sails as near as possible to Roman Catholicism. 'What I dislike intensely', he said, 'is the idea of a mediating priesthood standing between the individual and his Creator, claiming to reserve sacraments and to have a right of introducing the laity to the Deity as if they were a privileged caste.'[3]

Apart from his dislike of Ritualists, C.B. also disapproved of candidates whose claims to preferment were based on birth and breeding or on their academic attainments. On one occasion he told Higgs:

I have no patience with professors of a religion founded by fishermen who think that the higher posts in the Church must be preserved for the highly-born and the highly-educated. I have little doubt that St Peter dropped his h's and that Our Saviour's Sermon on the Mount was uttered in the broadest Galilean dialect.[4]

On another occasion Higgs described as 'unpleasant' a remark made in a letter from Lord Knollys, King Edward's secretary, concerning the King's views on a particular nominee. 'I feel pretty sure', said Higgs, 'that these views are something like this – "Above all things get a gentleman!"'[5]

Further light on C.B.'s handling of church appointments is shed in a letter he wrote to a Newcastle Quaker, Spence Watson, whom he had consulted in connection with the choice of a new Bishop of Newcastle and to whom he now explained:

About Bishops! I take infinite pains in the matter, and my object is . . . (1) to strengthen the Episcopal Bench and upper dignitaries with broad-minded men; (2) to encourage hard-working, spiritually-minded men in humble positions by showing them that their views are not boycotted . . . As to secular politics . . . I am to appoint Liberals but to avoid extreme Ritualists – that is what I am told. But all the new school of Church Liberals are Sacerdotalists; while all the Evangelicals of mark are pronounced Tories. What is a poor devil to do?

He told Watson that it seemed to him most desirable, after the 'prolonged dose of High Churchmen' to which the Church had been subjected, 'to mark a more catholic (with a small c) spirit. Therefore I have appointed at Truro a broad and liberal Bishop, at Newcastle an avowed Evangelical, at Manchester a Low Church Dean, at Ely an Academical Scholarly Right-Centre Dean, each suited to his locality . . . I must peg away on my own lines, but we cannot find each quality in each new man.'[6]

Campbell-Bannerman was determined not to be a cipher where ecclesiastical appointments were concerned, but at least he went through the formalities of consultation. During his premiership he became friendly with Randall Davidson and frequently sought his advice over appointments, though the Archbishop complained that he seldom took it. C.B. admitted as much in a letter he wrote to Davidson in connection with the vacant bishopric of Chichester: 'I am using much freedom with you in always bothering you and, as you once said, never acting on your advice. But you will be lenient to my doubts and perplexities!'[7]

Davidson, who was used by this time to getting his own way, was nettled by this constant ignoring of his counsel. He complained to Knollys:

I have a genuine respect and regard for the Prime Minister. But he really is, in this branch of his responsibilities, a rather trying person. Whenever a vacancy arises he writes to me for advice and tells me how he looks to me for it. I give it to the best of my power. In this case I gave him – in response to his request – a whole series of names. He then lets things run on – and then asks me again . . . *Then* he writes a letter . . . recommending to the King a man who has many merits but who seems to me distinctly *not* the man for Chichester. Why did he consult me at all?[8]

In spite of these differences of opinion Premier and Primate remained on cordial terms with each other. 'He is a most sensible man', C.B. remarked of Davidson towards the end of his life. 'I say "sensible" because he thinks just as I do!'[9] On other subjects possibly, but definitely *not* on episcopal appointments. About one particular, however, there can be no argument: C.B. took infinite pains in each case to secure the candidate *he* regarded as the right man for the job. On one occasion Higgs commented to Knollys that, during a particular fortnight up in Scotland, he and his chief had carefully gone over scores of names, and that in the past two years he had himself compiled elaborate confidential dossiers of nearly six hundred clerics. 'He [Sir Henry] said to me: "Our hesitation arises from our being so *méticuleux*" – which is, of course, a fault on the right side.'[10]

At least the Archbishop was left in no doubt about Campbell-Bannerman's dislike of High Churchmen. In the course of a letter concerning the selection of a new Dean of St Paul's 'when the time comes' Higgs wrote to express grave doubts (on behalf of his master) about Canon Scott-Holland. The canon, he said, was in many ways 'marked out for the succession', but he was likely, given the opportunity, to introduce requiem services into the cathedral 'and to cause serious disturbances of a kind which everyone would wish to avoid'. Higgs concluded: 'The Prime Minister seems to regard the sacerdotal spirit rather as a touchstone between the Anglican and the Roman Catholic branches of the Church, and he is not likely, I imagine, to select any one who can fairly be described as a sacerdotalist.'[11] It was therefore no surprise to the Archbishop when, faced with the need to choose a bishop for the vacant see of Newcastle, C.B. should have decided to translate the ultra-Evangelical and definitely non-sacerdotal Bishop of Sodor and Man, Norman Straton. The appointment was apparently suggested to him by Lady Wimborne, but C.B. himself was impressed by photographs of the bishop preaching in the open air to large crowds in the Isle of Man. Straton was no scholar, nor did the choice of a bishop who was politically Conservative prove acceptable to all the Prime Minister's fellow-Liberals. But the strongest complaints about the appointment came from Anglo-Catholics objecting to Straton's Evangelicalism. These were voiced by their mouthpiece, the *Church Times*, which dubbed him (5 July 1907) 'an uncompromising Protestant who has somehow been made a Catholic prelate'. The paper thought that 'the feeling of Northumbrian Churchmen is scarcely one of unalloyed satisfaction . . . Their new Bishop's utterances on subjects which Catholics hold of importance would seem to justify the anticipation of troubles ahead in a diocese which has been happily free from such since its foundation.' The *Church Times*'s fears were justified, for, within a few weeks of his arrival in his new diocese, Straton was crossing swords with one of his clergy, the Rev. Vibert Jackson (later Bishop of the Windward Islands), on the subject of eucharistic vestments and other signs of Catholic ceremonial. But by now the Prime Minister had other ecclesiastical matters on his plate – in particular the need to fill the bishopric of Chichester, vacant by the death of Bishop Wilberforce the younger.

This episcopal vacancy gave C.B. a great deal of trouble. 'It is an exceedingly difficult place to fill', he complained to Davidson, and some parts of it 'would appear to be in an extraordinary state, for I am told that no fewer than seventeen Curates and Vicars have actually passed over to Rome within the last few years.' Where, the Prime Minister plaintively enquired of Davidson, was to be found the 'firm, capable, discreet, impartial hand to set things right?'[12] But C.B.'s assurance to the Archbishop that he 'was much depending on your advice' must have been written with his tongue in his cheek because, a week before, he had confided to his friend Sinclair that he did not find Davidson 'very sound or decided' in his judgement of men; and that, although 'I am going to write to Randy [i.e. the Archbishop], he is little to be [hoped] to'. Earlier in the letter he had told Sinclair that, though the diocese 'is in a frightful state and needs a . . . manly, sensible, conciliatory but firm man', he would not touch Cosmo Lang [Bishop of Stepney and a likely candidate] with a barge-pole. 'Say what you like he is in with the real sacerdotal lot, and, if it can be told of him that he refuses to go into his father's church, that is enough for me.'[13] When, a fortnight later, Davidson mentioned Lang as a possible candidate for Chichester ('far the most eminent Suffragan Bishop . . . though himself a decided High Churchman, he is a resolute upholder of order and loyalty'),[14] he can hardly have been surprised that his hint was ignored.

The Prime Minister first offered the vacant see to the Bishop of Wakefield, G. R. Eden ('I do not think a better man could be found for the place', he told Davidson),[15] but Eden declined – just as he had declined translation to Truro when offered it the previous year. C.B.'s next nominee rather confusingly had the surname 'Wakefield': H. Russell Wakefield, Rector of St Mary's, Bryanston Square, London. He had in fact been suggested by Davidson a little earlier as an outside possibility – 'He is not, as you know, a graduate, and that would startle some people. But I do not see that it is fatal if on other grounds the appointment is desired.'[16] By now, however, the Archbishop was having second thoughts about such an ostentatiously unacademic priest; and, when asked by Knollys on behalf of the King his private opinion of Wakefield's suitability ('H.M. does not himself think that the fact of Mr Wakefield having been twice Mayor of Marylebone is any particular recommendation.'),[17] he poured out his soul to the King's secretary:

> Russell Wakefield is a good and able man, an authority on civic matters and poor law and many other things and a reasonable and moderate Churchman, rather of the liberal school. An earnest man, with no follies or cranks that I know of. But he was educated for commercial life and has *no university degree* – and altogether is not a very refined or scholarly or cultured man.

If only the Bishop of Wakefield had accepted the Prime Minister's offer, said Davidson, then Russell Wakefield might 'very suitably' have succeeded him. 'He would, I think, have been acceptable among the middle-class Churchmen of Yorkshire towns, and would have got on well with them in all ways – as he is a really *good* and *earnest* fellow, and the lack which he has would have been no marked lack there.' Chichester, however, was different. 'Its clergy are of the more cultured and refined sort . . . Among these men R. W., with no University degree, no culture and rather a rough-and-ready reputation, would be quite out of place . . . He would be a square peg in a round hole in Sussex.'

The cautious Davidson ended his letter to Knollys by remarking that it would not do for the PM to be aware that he had said so much. 'Would it be poss. for his M. to suggest to the Prime Minister that, seeing how diff. a diocese it is, he could consult *me*! The fact that R. Wakefield has no degree might come quite naturally from you as a piece of knowledge which is evident from the files (like Crockford).'[18]

The King's ever-obliging secretary was quick to transmute the Archbishop's robust private views on the prime ministerial nominee into suitably diplomatic but nevertheless disapproving language. H.M., he told Campbell-Bannerman, while not doubting for a moment Mr Wakefield's excellence as a good and conscientious clergyman with moderate views, still did not consider him a suitable bishop for a largely rural diocese like Chichester – though he might do very well in an urban diocese, especially a Yorkshire one. 'The King is always very reluctant to disagree with any recommendation of yours, but he has his own views as to the qualifications required for the higher appointments in the Church, and he is afraid he must ask you to be so good as to submit the name of some other clergyman for the Bishopric of Chichester.' Knollys hedged the royal bets, however (and took up

Davidson's hint), by suggesting that Sir Henry might 'feel inclined to consult with the Archbishop of Canterbury on the question of Mr Wakefield's suitability for this particular See'. If the Primate took the same view as the Premier, 'the King, while still holding to his own opinion in the matter, will not then be disinclined to disregard two such high authorities as the Archbishop of Canterbury and the Prime Minister'.[19] The Primate did *not* take the same view as the Premier, so in the event Campbell-Bannerman reluctantly gave way – but not before Higgs had protested at the unconstitutionality of the King's attitude.

> The letter is a sinister document . . . the selection of a Bishop is an Act-of-State which the Reformation cut off from the Church and handed over to the Head of the Nation . . . Responsible as you are, your advice ought not to need the concurrence of the Primate. The constitution of the Church gives him no voice . . . It is bad enough that he should cripple your legislation without blocking your executive action.[20]

C.B. then toyed with the idea of translating Bishop Collins of Gibraltar, whom Davidson had already suggested to him as 'just the man for Chichester'.[21] But, after satisfying himself that, whether really sacerdotalist or not, poor Collins 'has widely the reputation of it, and that is a bar to his selection',[22] he abandoned the idea. Finally, after a proposal to translate Edward Talbot, formerly of Rochester and now of Southwark, had also come to nothing, the see was offered to and accepted by Charles Ridgeway, Dean of Carlisle. But there was a happy ending for the earnest but unrefined Russell Wakefield. He was appointed by Asquith in 1911 to succeed Gore as Bishop of Birmingham, where 'the lack which he has' proved not so marked a lack as Davidson feared that it might have proved among the cultured clerics of Sussex. As for Campbell-Bannerman, he complained to Lancelot Fish, the Anglican chaplain at Biarritz, where he was attempting to recover his health in the autumn of 1907 in the middle of the Chichester bishopric saga: 'Canon, I can leave behind me all public business except the affairs of your Church. These follow me everywhere.'[23]

**Nominations to diocesan bishoprics 4 (3 first appointments, 1 translation)**

*First appointments:*

(1) 1906:  Charles William Stubbs to Truro.

(2) 1907: Thomas Wortley Drury to Sodor and Man.

(3) 1907: Charles John Ridgeway to Chichester.

*Translation:*

(1) 1907: Norman Dumenil John Straton to Newcastle (from Sodor and Man).

# 14

# Search for Sages

## H. H. Asquith: Prime Minister
## 8 April 1908 – 5 December 1916

Herbert Henry Asquith, 1st Earl of Oxford and Asquith (1852–1928), *was the dominant figure among Campbell-Bannerman's cabinet colleagues and succeeded him as Prime Minister. A native of Morley, Yorkshire, he was educated at the City of London School and Balliol College, Oxford, and was then called to the Bar. He first entered Parliament in 1886 as Liberal MP for East Fife and served as Home Secretary under Gladstone and Rosebery. In his early years as Prime Minister he piloted a notable series of domestic reforms through the Commons, provoking (and winning) a struggle with the Lords over their power of veto. The other dominant issue of his premiership, still undecided at the outbreak of war in 1914, was Irish Home Rule. His policy over the war, however, was attacked as indecisive. Although he headed the coalition which replaced the Liberal government in April 1915 he was displaced as Premier by Lloyd George in December of the following year. Thereafter he slowly faded from the political scene, accepting a peerage in 1925. Apart from his various church appointments his principal ecclesiastical achievement was his Bill to disestablish the Anglican Church in Wales, hitherto included in the province of Canterbury, though the Bill did not finally come into force until 1920, by when he had fallen from power. In the words of Winston Churchill,*

> *Asquith was a man who knew where he stood on every question of life and affairs in altogether unusual degree ... There was also the sense of scorn, lightly and not always completely veiled, for arguments, for personalities and even for events which did not conform to the pattern he had with so much profound knowledge and reflection decidedly adopted.*[1]

'No branch of Asquith's activities as Prime Minister interested him more than that which relates to ecclesiastical patronage and appointments.' So say his official biographers.[2] They go on to quote a long testimony from Sir Roderick Meiklejohn, one of his private secretaries, to the same effect. Meiklejohn claims that Asquith was better informed on church matters than most other laymen. He was well versed in church history, had heard sermons from many noted preachers of the day and was the personal friend of many leading ecclesiastics. Meiklejohn records:

> It was my duty to put before him a short list of the persons considered most suitable for any particular post, and he weighed their respective claims with the most scrupulous care; and, while he was always ready to receive the advice of the Archbishop of Canterbury, with whom he was very intimate, it was invariably on his own unbiased selection that a name was submitted to the King.[3]

Even allowing for the natural bias in favour of Asquith from an official who later became a personal friend, he undoubtedly had a close working knowledge of the Church of England which he was able to put to good use during his time as Prime Minister. Although he lived only a mile away from Davidson at Lambeth Palace, he would often send him long letters, sometimes two or more a week, on the subject of ecclesiastical vacancies.

Asquith had two particular quirks. He disliked extreme High Churchmen on principle and he had a profound reverence for academics. According to Meiklejohn he was by temperament and upbringing strongly Protestant in feeling, 'retaining until the close of his life what many would regard as an old-fashioned antipathy to the Roman Catholic Church'.[4] But Asquith's Protestant bias was kept firmly under control when it came to selecting new bishops, and he was at one with Davidson in his anxiety to preserve a balance between the different schools of churchmanship on the Bench. When it came to intellectual attainments, however, he proved a marked contrast to his predecessor. Campbell-Bannerman, though sharing Asquith's dislike of Ritualists, had disliked equally the scholastic snobbishness which paid exaggerated deference to a candidate's academic record. For Asquith, on the other hand, scholarship was all-important. He once sent Davidson a list of thirteen bishops who had sat on the Bench in 1895 and all of whom had, before their elevation, been headmasters, professors or dons – and contrasted them with the lesser array of academic talent present on the Bench in 1913.[5] He took particular pride in nominating the scholarly W. R. Inge to the deanery of St Paul's.

Asquith's first episcopal appointment was also the most important he was called upon to make: that of a successor to

W. D. Maclagan as Archbishop of York. The northern primacy
was normally filled by the translation of a senior diocesan. On
this occasion, however, Asquith broke with tradition by choosing
a suffragan bishop for the post. Admittedly the suffragan in
question, Cosmo Lang of Stepney, was outstanding. Davidson
had described him to Campbell-Bannerman (during the search
for a new Bishop of Chichester) as 'far the most eminent
Suffragan Bishop . . . a man of first-rate ability, earnestness and
strength'.[6] Lang was also a decided High Churchman, and this
had put off Campbell-Bannerman. One might have supposed
that it would also have put off Asquith. But Lang was no fanatic
and, Davidson had assured the former prime minister, could be
relied upon to keep order in his province and not allow Ritualism
to get out of hand. Asquith needed little convincing. Writing to
Davidson on 1 November 1908, he was able to report on a recent
conversation he had had with King Edward about the succession
to York.

He asked me if I had thought of anyone; and I replied that,
without for the moment making any formal submission, my
judgment turned towards Stepney as the best available man,
and that I thought you were (to say the least) not disinclined to
favour such a choice . . . But, before I take any action in the
matter, I should be glad to know whether your second thoughts
set in the same direction. I confess that mine do.[7]

Asquith faced a minor embarrassment. By his choice of Lang
he had deliberately ignored the claims of a political supporter,
Percival of Hereford, the man whose original nomination by
Rosebery in 1895 had so annoyed Queen Victoria because of his
championship of Welsh disestablishment. Percival had occupied
his see for thirteen years and now hoped for preferment. He had
good reason to hope, for Campbell-Bannerman had given him a
broad hint that he would be translated to York as soon as the see
fell vacant. But Campbell-Bannerman was now dead and Asquith
reigned in Downing Street. Percival was 74 and Lang a mere 43.
Asquith felt bound to plump for the younger man – and did so.
But he felt sufficiently uneasy in conscience to write to Percival
(the only bishop who had voted for the government in the
controversy over the 1906 Education Bill) to excuse himself. He
told Percival that he had passed him over solely on the grounds of
age – at 74 he really was too old to take up new work of so
arduous a kind. Percival attempted to conceal his mortification
from the Prime Minister, though he told him of his disappointment at not being translated after his thirteen years in 'this Tory
backwater'. He expressed that disappointment to his friends in

more bitter terms. 'Asquith has sent me my obituary notice', he complained to the Dean of Bristol. And Prebendary Wynne Wilson wrote:

> When I saw him on the day of the announcement of Lang's appointment, he was less reticent than I ever knew him to be. He sketched some of his plans that he had in view, specially in relation to the new northern universities. Though his best friends knew he could not cope with the work, he himself did not yet feel the limitations of his age.[8]

To Cosmo Lang his own nomination to York apparently came as a complete surprise. His acquaintance with the Prime Minister was slight. It was also fraught with embarrassment, as he had caught sight of Asquith in St Paul's one afternoon after preaching a sermon almost identical to one he had preached at a service in another church at which the Premier had also been present. Lang might, however, have had a premonition that something was in the wind. Only a few weeks before the offer of York came from Downing Street he had received a cable telling him that he had just been elected Bishop of Montreal in Canada. He consulted Davidson as to whether he should accept and was eventually told: 'It is very difficult, but I am afraid I must advise you to refuse.' Davidson gave no explanation, but Lang felt bound to follow his advice and turned down the offer. A few days later Asquith's letter arrived – and all was made clear. After consulting Davidson and the Bishop of London, Winnington-Ingram, Lang formally accepted the offer. Some newspapers commented on his extreme youth for so high an office; and Queen Alexandra remarked that she had not hitherto thought herself old enough to be the mother of an archbishop.[9]

For almost twenty years Lang served as Archbishop of York while Davidson remained at Canterbury, and a close and warm relationship grew up between the two men. Both were Scotsmen, Lang himself being the son of a former Moderator of the General Assembly of the Church of Scotland; both were deeply suspicious of State interference in the affairs of the Church; and both were champions of episcopacy as opposed to the militant Presbyterianism of Scotland. Of their collaboration Lang wrote years afterwards that 'never before in history had this relation been more close and cordial. Indeed it was a co-operation so unprecedented that it seems in itself to be an event noteworthy in the long history of the Church of England.'[10]

Almost the last episcopal appointment made by Asquith during the reign of King Edward VII was also one in which Sovereign and Premier failed to see eye to eye. In the end the King got his way – but only after the Archbishop of Canterbury had entered the lists in his support.

The see in question was Norwich, which contained the royal residence at Sandringham and was therefore of particular concern to the King. His choice was the Headmaster of Wellington, Bertram Pollock, in whose appointment to the headmastership he had been personally involved as chairman of the school governors sixteen years before. The King continued to hold Pollock in high regard and on one occasion remarked to him that the Prime Minister had recommended him for high ecclesiastical preferment. 'But I said to him, "We cannot spare him".'[11] But, now nearing the end of his life, the King felt that it was time his protégé was promoted; and Norwich, with its royal connection, seemed a highly suitable choice. He indicated to Asquith, via his secretaries, that he would like the nomination to go to Pollock. Asquith disagreed. 'I am very indisposed to such an appointment, which might do well but has no sufficient merits to recommend it', he told Davidson. He suggested five other names, ending with a plea: 'If I am to resist Pollock, I must have your decided support.'[12]

The Archbishop felt, however, that on this occasion the King was entitled to have his way. Remarking that Asquith had failed to say *why* he was against Pollock, he pointed out that, though lacking experience of parish work and being reserved and perhaps shy, the headmaster was a man of very real power:

> I could not say that I think him the best possible man. On the other hand I could not endorse an opinion that he is unfit for such a position. His appointment would certainly cause surprise, as he is comparatively little known. But that proves little in his case . . . You realise, I am sure, that I should be the last to advocate your acceptance of a suggestion emanating from illustrious quarters simply *because* it so emanated. But, considering the interest which H.M. shows in Norfolk both in Church and county matters, I suppose you would feel him to be entitled to his say in regard to this appointment; and, although his 'say' is not exactly what mine would have been, it is not at all a bad 'say' – *me judice*.[13]

Asquith was evidently convinced, or else he felt that the issue was not important enough to be worth fighting over; so Pollock was duly nominated. But the Prime Minister was not usually so influenced by the Primate against his own judgement. A few months after the Norwich episode they were corresponding over the choice of a successor to Edward King as Bishop of Lincoln.

At the end of one letter Davidson added a postscript: 'I do *not* think [E. L.] Hicks would do for Lincoln, and I am doubtful if he would do for Truro if it became vacant.'[14] So he would not have been best pleased, a fortnight or so later, to receive the following brief note from Asquith:

> My dear Archbishop,
>
> After much and careful consideration I have advised the King, and he approves, that Canon Hicks should be appointed Bishop of Lincoln. I believe that he will make a really good thing of it.[15]

The serious exchange of views about filling vacancies on the Bench was leavened by the occasional light-hearted aside, e.g. (Asquith to Davidson, 9 April 1913): 'I have written to [A. A.] David making the offer [of Bristol, which he declined]. I don't think we could do better, though Bigge reports that he wears a moustache.'[16]

The King, Asquith adds, had agreed to this appointment also, but by now it was a different king, George V having succeeded his father on 6 May 1910. The new monarch was a great contrast to his predecessor – more stolid and serious-minded and altogether less flamboyant. He had been much influenced as a boy by his tutor, the Rev. John Neale Dalton, a rumbustious character (and father of the future Labour politician) who was later to soldier on for forty-six years as canon of St George's Chapel, Windsor. Prince George was confirmed in 1882 by Archbishop Tait, together with his elder brother, Prince Eddy, the Archbishop exhorting them: 'God grant that you, Sirs, may show to the world what Christian Princes ought to be.'[17]

Prince George showed to the world a simple faith based on the Bible. Ever since his two-year world cruise as a youth in HMS *Bacchante* (1880–2), when he first acquired the habit, he would read a chapter of the Bible each night. Every Sunday he would attend divine service according to the rites of the Established Church – as an Anglican in England and as a Presbyterian in Scotland. At Sandringham, after he had come to the throne, he was regularly elected as the people's churchwarden. 'But I bargained that I should not be expected to take the bag round', he remarked; 'I drew the line at that.' Visiting preachers were entertained in style, Dean Inge being met at Windsor on one occasion by 'a royal carriage drawn by two white horses and by an enormous omnibus to carry my handbag'.[18] Great care was taken in the selection of preachers. Soon after Hensley Henson, already a controversial figure in church circles, had been appointed Dean of Durham in 1912, Lord Stamfordham wrote to

Davidson on the King's behalf to enquire whether it was safe to invite Henson to preach at Windsor before their Majesties. 'Some people might be surprised', he told the Archbishop; 'a few I suppose would be shocked! But the King ought to belong to no party: and selecting him to preach would justify both the PM's selection and HM's approval.' Stamfordham expressed doubts as to whether such a controversial cleric would preach a sermon acceptable to his audience, but concluded: 'Such men in the Church should not be allowed to think that they are boycotted by the Court.'*[20] Preachers in general, however, had to observe certain elementary rules. Stamfordham warned a man on one occasion: 'Preach for about fourteen minutes. If you preach for less, the King may say you are too lazy to prepare a sermon; if you preach for more than fourteen minutes, the King may say that the man did not know when to stop.' Another visiting cleric wrote later that he had followed his usual custom of preaching at the gamekeepers and kitchenmaids – and had been warmly congratulated on his sermon by both King and Queen.[21]

The King shared Asquith's distaste for anything that smacked of Ritualism. A visiting preacher at Sandringham wrote afterwards: 'The King talked about the iniquities of Communists, the plight of farmers and the shortcomings of Anglo-Catholics. Said to me point-blank, "Are you an Anglo-Catholic?" I reassured him about that – told him I was more like a Quaker.'[22]

Although a sound, middle-of-the-road Anglican when in England, King George, like his father before him, was anxious not to offend the feelings of his Roman Catholic subjects. At the time of his accession he objected, as his father had done, to the crudely Protestant terms of the declaration he was required to make before Parliament – and on this occasion was successful in getting it watered down. There was some difficulty at first in finding a form of words which would offend neither Roman Catholics nor anyone else, but eventually Davidson came up with the innocuous formula: 'I declare that I am a faithful Protestant and will uphold the Protestant succession.' And it was these blameless words that the King was able to utter when he opened his first Parliament on 6 February 1911.[23]

Where Crown appointments were concerned he was always vigilant in making sure that the proper protocol was observed, and that successive prime ministers at least went through the motions of submitting names to the monarch as though it was

---

*Henson must obviously have won the royal approval. After his nomination as Bishop of Hereford six years later the King declared: 'I like Hensley Henson. He is a very nice fellow.'[19]

really up to him to accept or reject them. But of course he was well aware of the shadowy nature of his powers – and infinitely less bold than his grandmother in challenging names to which he might take personal exception. Thus, when the deanery of Windsor fell vacant in 1917, he would like to have appointed his old tutor, J. N. Dalton, to the post. But Dalton's autocratic and cantankerous behaviour as a member of the Windsor chapter since 1885 would have made such a promotion highly controversial; and the King was not sufficiently sure of himself to risk a clash with the Prime Minister over such a comparatively minor matter – even though, because of its royal associations, the sovereign had hitherto been tacitly allowed the last say in filling the deanery. In the event the post went to a godson of Queen Victoria, Albert Baillie, who had to put up with the tiresome Dalton till the latter's death, fourteen years later, at the age of ninety-one.[24]

The King did, however, score one minor victory: over the appointment to the bishopric of Ripon in 1911. This was proving a difficult see to fill. Asquith was looking for an Evangelical candidate (having in recent months filled no fewer than five vacant sees in the province of Canterbury with non-Evangelicals), and Evangelical clerics with strong powers of leadership were hard to find. Davidson saw the difficulty – though he also regretted the need to appoint yet another Evangelical to a northern bench of bishops already swamped with them – 'men of mark', as he told Asquith, 'but all of them lacking in any wide sympathy with other forms of Churchmanship than their own . . . It is hard on the Archbishop of York to be made to look like an extreme High Churchman merely because of the contrast with that big group.'[25]

It was at this juncture that the King entered the arena. Asquith, in a letter to Davidson, had remarked that he was just off to Balmoral and might be 'driven (somewhat reluctantly) to recommend Welldon' for the vacant see.[26] James Welldon, a former Headmaster of Harrow and Canon of Westminster who was now Dean of Manchester, had spent three years (1898–1901) as Bishop of Calcutta; and it was while in India that he had committed a (to the Royal Family) heinous offence. As soon, therefore, as Asquith mentioned his name at Balmoral as a possibility for Ripon, the King took umbrage. Stamfordham wrote at once to Davidson. 'The King says he *won't* approve the appointment', he began, and then mentioned a sermon preached by Welldon in Calcutta Cathedral on the death of Queen Victoria:

When referring to King Edward he exclaimed: 'As to her successor, if he is to be respected he must be respectable.' The King says this is sufficient bar to his being made Bishop of Ripon or anywhere else! . . . The King says: 'The Archbishop *must* give me some good names to suggest if Welldon is put forward.'[27]

Stamfordham went on to say that Asquith had admitted that he was not 'sweet' on Welldon. 'But evidently he is in a quandary, and politically he may suffer if he does not please the Low Church party.' Faced with a choice between the Devil in the shape of the King and the deep blue Protestant sea, Asquith decided to forget about Welldon. Eventually he did manage to find a blameless Evangelical, Thomas Drury of Sodor and Man,* whom he translated to Ripon. He told Davidson (who had concurred in the choice): 'I think the appointment of Sodor and Man to Ripon is the safest and wisest in the circumstances of the case. I heartily agree with what you say as to the present resourcelessness of the Evangelical party in men of light and leading.'[29]

A definitely *non*-Evangelical appointment made a couple of months before this had been the translation of Charles Gore from Birmingham to Oxford. Gore was politically a supporter of Asquith's, though a High Churchman and not therefore on the Prime Minister's own ecclesiastical wavelength. But he was a man of such obvious distinction that his claims could hardly be overlooked. He was the first name on the list of possibles for Oxford that Davidson sent to Asquith, who replied that he was thinking along the same lines. 'They must have a High Churchman, and he has all the obvious qualifications.'[30] Asquith added, however, that Gore might well refuse the offer; and he was indeed reluctant at first to accept. He told Edward Talbot that he had been voting for the government lately in the House of Lords, 'and that is a reason against accepting what I suppose would be considered "promotion" at this moment'.[31] His friends were divided about the desirability of a move, and gave him conflicting advice. Eventually he went up to Lambeth to consult Davidson. On his return he announced his decision: 'I have got to go.' And he went. At the end of his life he was asked by a priest who had received the offer of a bishopric whether the invitation of the authorities in itself constituted a call which could not be

---

*Sodor and Man was still regarded as being right at the bottom of the episcopal league-table (see page 13). When the by-now vacant see was offered to J. Denton Thompson, rector of Birmingham, Asquith remarked to Davidson: 'His lack of refinement and distinction would be a serious disadvantage elsewhere.'[28]

refused. 'No', said Gore, 'I don't think I would say that. I think they rather pounce on one. Yes, they do pounce.'[32]

A year or so after appointing Gore to Oxford Asquith nominated to the deanery of Durham a man with whom Gore was to cross swords in a big way five years later: Herbert Hensley Henson. Henson at that time was a canon of Westminster, living a mere stone's throw from the Prime Minister's house in Downing Street. The two men were soon on intimate terms; and Asquith was so impressed with Henson's quality that, in February 1912, he entrusted him with the task of preparing his daughter Elizabeth for confirmation. In October of that year he wrote to Davidson to suggest that the deanery of Durham – 'one of the prizes of the Church' – ought to be filled by a churchman of wide views and academic interests. Only two churchmen in his view had the right qualifications: Hastings Rashdall and Henson. Although Rashdall had the better title ('He is the only clergyman in the Church who, so far as I know, has real claims to philosophic distinction'), his published views 'might be too much of a shock for such an atmosphere'.[33] So Asquith plumped for Henson, and Henson was appointed. But the Prime Minister could have been under no illusions that his candidate would be risk-free. Two years earlier, when he had been toying with Henson as a possible candidate for the deanery of Lincoln, he had written to Davidson: 'It would be rather like sending a torpedo destroyer into a land-locked pool.'[34] The words were to prove, in another context, prophetic.

**Nominations to diocesan bishoprics 19 (11 first appointments, 8 translations)**

*First appointments:*

  (1) 1909: Bertram Pollock to Norwich.
  (2) 1910: Edward Lee Hicks to Lincoln.
  (3) 1911: Hubert Murray Burge to Southwark.
  (4) 1911: Henry Russell Wakefield to Birmingham.
  (5) 1911: James Denton Thompson to Sodor and Man.
  (6) 1912: Winfrid Oldfield Burrows to Truro.
  (7) 1914: John Edwin Watts-Ditchfield to Chelmsford.
  (8) 1914: Henry Bernard Hodgson to St Edmundsbury and Ipswich.
  (9) 1915: Herbert Louis Wild to Newcastle.
 (10) 1916: Frank Theodore Woods to Peterborough.
 (11) 1916: Lord Rupert Ernest William Gascoyne Cecil to Exeter.

*Translations:*

(1) 1908: Cosmo Gordon Lang to York (from Stepney).*
(2) 1911: Edward Stuart Talbot to Winchester (from Southwark).
(3) 1911: Charles Gore to Oxford (from Birmingham).
(4) 1911: Frederic Edward Ridgeway to Salisbury (from Kensington).*
(5) 1911: Thomas Wortley Drury to Ripon (from Sodor and Man).
(6) 1913: John Augustine Kempthorne to Lichfield (from Hull).*
(7) 1914: Leonard Hedley Burrows to Sheffield (from Lewes).*
(8) 1914: George Nickson to Bristol (from Jarrow).*

\* Suffragan see.

# 15

# Storm over Hereford

*David Lloyd George: Prime Minister*
*7 December 1916 – 23 October 1922*

David Lloyd George, 1st Earl Lloyd George of Dwyfor (1863–
1945), *the radical politician who displaced Asquith as Prime
Minister half-way through the First World War, was also the
man primarily responsible for placing the issue of Welsh disestablishment firmly on the Liberal agenda. He was born at
Chorlton-on-Medlock, Manchester, but, after his father's death
while he was still a baby, was brought up in a village near
Criccieth, Caernarvonshire. He was educated at the village school
and articled in 1879 to a firm of solicitors at Portmadoc. In 1890,
standing as a Liberal, he fought and won a by-election at
Caernarvon Boroughs, the seat he was to hold continuously until
he was raised to the peerage shortly before his death. He stood
firmly to the left of the party, and, as Chancellor of the Exchequer
under Asquith, threw his weight behind a programme of radical
social reform which culminated in the Old Age Pensions and
National Insurance Acts. He served as Minister of Munitions in
the coalition government of 1915–16, but became increasingly
restive over Asquith's handling of the war effort and in December
1916 displaced him as Prime Minister. He proved an outstanding
war leader, and after the Armistice played a key part in the
negotiations resulting in the Treaty of Versailles. In late 1922,
however, growing Conservative dissatisfaction with his handling
of Irish affairs led to their withdrawing their support from the
coalition and to his own resignation as Premier. Neither he nor
the Liberals ever returned to power. He himself was replaced as
Liberal leader in the Commons by Asquith until the latter's
ennoblement, but from 1931 onwards gradually withdrew into
the ivory tower of an elder statesman. Lloyd George was at his
best and most sincere as a social reformer and later as a patriotic
war leader, but he was thought by many to be lacking in principle.
His eloquence led to his being dubbed 'the Welsh wizard', but in
the end his wizardry failed to convince and he lost both power
and influence.*

Lloyd George took over the government of his country in the middle of the First World War. But, while the battle raged on the Continent, back in Britain churchmen appeared to be much more exercised over a domestic issue: the Prime Minister's nomination of the Dean of Durham to the see of Hereford. Asquith, as we have seen, had likened Hensley Henson to a 'torpedo destroyer entering a landlocked pool'. Owen Chadwick, in an equally vivid phrase, suggests that the decision to send Henson to Hereford was like 'sending an armoured car into an orchard of apple trees'.[1] But, where ecclesiastical affairs were concerned, Lloyd George would have been the first to admit his limitations.

Whereas Asquith had acted over church appointments as an informed Anglican, his successor, a Welsh Baptist who had lost his faith during his teens, knew little about the Church of England and relied to a large extent on advisers of varying ability. As an orator himself, he looked more to a prospective bishop's powers as a preacher than to his academic attainments or other qualities. As Davidson put it after a meeting with the Prime Minister in August 1917 at which the forthcoming vacancy at Hereford was discussed: 'He pressed with a good deal of fervour, and even pathos, the need of having good preachers among the Bishops.'[2] And Henson had already acquired a reputation as a preacher of the first rank.

Davidson had little faith in the Prime Minister's advisers. In those days the Premier had no private secretary concerned with appointments and nothing else. His ecclesiastical duties were handled by his ordinary secretaries as part of their routine business and without their necessarily possessing any specialist qualifications. Lloyd George's secretariat included no knowledgeable churchman like Gladstone's Edward Hamilton. Davidson likened the Downing Street team to 'an army of inexperienced and arrogant neophytes who perform their work inefficiently and offensively. These defects are at their worst in the particular case of ecclesiastical patronage.'[3] The most objectionable of a bad bunch was apparently a man called Sutherland, who, Davidson complained to the Prime Minister, treated church matters with contempt and ridicule. But Captain Ernest Evans, another official with whom the Archbishop had frequent dealings, was not much better – and sometimes showed a distressing ignorance of protocol in dealing with Crown appointments. On a slightly higher level was Ernest Pearce, a canon of Westminster who had helped Asquith over some of the lesser ecclesiastical appointments and now took on a more prominent role as principal adviser to his successor on church matters. Pearce thought Davidson too cautious in his attitude to appointments. He told Henson, with whom he was on friendly terms: 'Cantuar wants a quiet time, but it isn't good for religion in England that he should have it.' And, when Henson's name began to be discussed as a possibility for Hereford, Pearce warned him: 'You are well to the fore: so don't complicate matters by any irruption marked by your usual cogency.'[4]

The Hereford bishopric affair is well charted. The two most detailed and objective accounts are those by George Bell in his life of Davidson and by Owen Chadwick in his life of Henson. Any attempt to summarize the controversy must be based to a large extent on these two masterly narratives, of which Bell's is perhaps the more fully documented and Chadwick's the more colourfully written. Henson's own version of the affair, as given in his autobiography, is highly subjective, though not without interest in matters of detail.

The saga began with the announcement by Bishop Percival, in the summer of 1917, that he intended to resign his see of Hereford because of old age. This was an understatement. It was nine years since Percival had been considered by Asquith to be too old at 74 to be made Archbishop of York. He was now well over 80, and for the previous two years had been unable to do much work because of his infirmities. Davidson met the Prime Minister on 5 August to discuss the coming vacancy. At this meeting three names were mentioned: Michael Furse, Bishop of Pretoria; Albert David, Headmaster of Rugby; and Henson. The Archbishop told Lloyd George that he would greatly prefer David to either Furse or Henson, and the Premier took note of the preference.[5]

At this point it would be as well to consider *why* Lloyd George favoured Henson while Davidson was against him. Henson was undoubtedly an eloquent preacher. He was also a fine scholar, having been elected to a fellowship of All Souls, Oxford, at the age of twenty after matriculating as an unattached student at the University while still under eighteen. He had been vicar of the industrial parish of Barking in London's East End after a short spell as head of Oxford House, Bethnal Green, and before his move to a Westminster canonry. But he was theologically suspect – and never backward in coming forward to proclaim his views. Once a High Churchman, he had broadened out in matters of doctrine and church order and now interpreted the creeds in liberal terms. Most significantly, in the eyes of his opponents, he sat lightly to the key doctrines of the virgin birth and the physical resurrection of Christ. Davidson was only too well aware of the controversy that might well be sparked off by his nomination to a bishopric. He noted after his interview with the Prime Minister: 'I pressed with no uncertainty the difficulties and perhaps the public protests which would arise if he nominated Henson.'[6] To Lloyd George, on the other hand, Henson's alleged unorthodoxy mattered little when set against his oratorical powers and his championship of Dissenters – among whom he himself was technically numbered. He dismissed Davidson's warning as a cry of 'Wolf'. He had been impressed, however, by the Archbishop's suggestion that, if Henson was to be made a bishop, Hereford was the wrong diocese for him. It was a rural see, but all Henson's ministry had been spent in urban areas.

Lloyd George began to think of other possible dioceses for Henson. He sent Bishop Burge of Southwark to sound him out about the see of Bristol. But Henson told Burge that, as a man without private means, he could not possibly afford to accept such a poorly-endowed diocese. The next development was a letter from Burge to Henson telling him that he, Burge, had been offered the see of Hereford and that he would accept it if Henson agreed to accept his present see of Southwark. Again Henson declined to play ball. He told Burge that he did not believe his physical strength sufficient for such a populous industrial diocese as Southwark.[7] So Burge stayed put, and, at the third time of asking, Henson was invited to become Bishop of Hereford. But, before making the formal offer, the Prime Minister wrote again to Davidson to announce his intention. 'It is true', he said, 'that I should have preferred to propose him for a more urban and industrial diocese' [the two previous soundings of Henson for Bristol and Southwark were not formal offers]; 'but I believe he has never yet failed to devote himself eagerly to whatever work lay before him.'[8]

Davidson made one last effort to dissuade Lloyd George. It was not that he was against Henson's being made a bishop, he assured him ('I am anxious to make that point quite clear'), but that a large rural diocese did not seem the right place for a 'preacher and speaker with the particular sort of popular gifts which Dr Henson possesses'. Moreover, Davidson again warned the Prime Minister, his appointment at the present time would undoubtedly cause a storm. 'I confess that I should prefer in the interests of the Church of England that your own first nomination to the Episcopate should be of a less controversial kind.'[9]

Lloyd George paid no heed to the warning. He told the Archbishop that he believed that Henson had 'powers of adaptability' which would stand him in good stead at Hereford, and that 'he will be learning his job in what ought not to be a very hard school'.[10] His letter offering the see was disarmingly frank. 'It is not quite the diocese I should have chosen for you if there had been any choice', he told Henson, 'as I should prefer to see you grappling with the needs of some large and industrial population. Such a vacancy, of a more responsible character, may arise in due course; if so, I trust you will have pròved your powers of governance and guidance in such a way that I may have the privilege of suggesting your translation.'[11] Such a letter, hinting strongly at the offer of a second diocese on top of the first, was unusual, to say the least.

Henson wrote to the Prime Minister on 9 December, accepting the nomination. Two days later the news appeared in the papers and the storm broke. The most vocal opposition came from the Church of England's Catholic wing, the weekly organ of which was the *Church Times*. It so happened that the paper's editor at that time, Ernest Hermitage Day, lived just outside Hereford, so was in close touch with feeling in the diocese as well as in the Church at large. The *Church Times* voiced its outrage at the appointment in two rousing editorials. The first (14 December 1917), headed 'Unhappy Hereford', said that churchmen everywhere were entitled to ask what there was in Henson's record which might seem to justify his nomination to a see. 'His most fervent admirers would be at a loss to supply the answer.' Churchmen everywhere, the leader went on, were bound to register their protest against the appointment. 'It is one which everywhere will meet with opposition, not from one section of Churchmen only.' The following week the paper returned to the attack in an even stronger leader, headed 'The Hereford Scandal', which suggested that never within living memory had the feelings of churchmen been more stirred by an episcopal nomination:

> The letters which lie heaped upon our table are witness to the fact that all over the country Churchmen deeply resent the indignity which has been put upon the Church . . . The case is unique, since never before has a nomination been so resented, not only within the diocese immediately affected but far beyond it.

The case was not of course unique, in that a similar uproar had greeted Lord John Russell's nomination of Hampden, seventy years earlier, to this selfsame see of Hereford. Lloyd George's nomination of Henson was certain, however, to cause the 'storm' predicted by Davidson. The authorities might safely ignore the thunderings of the church press, but they could hardly turn a blind eye when a bishop of the stature of Charles Gore entered the lists on behalf of orthodoxy. On 14 December Gore sent to all his fellow-bishops in the province of Canterbury a notice to the effect that he proposed to make a 'formal protest' to the

Archbishop against Henson's consecration and inviting them, if they saw fit, to join him. He drew the bishops' attention to three of Henson's books and said that, failing a retraction by Henson or the cancellation of the consecration, 'I see no course *practicable* but to resign from the episcopate'.[12] Meanwhile the English Church Union, representing the Church's Anglo-Catholic wing, rallied its forces against the consecration. It lost the first skirmish in the battle, however, when the Dean and Chapter of Hereford met on 4 January 1918 to elect Henson as the Crown's nominee. Although ten prebendaries absented themselves from the meeting, fifteen out of the nineteen who were present voted in favour of the election and only four against. The previous day Gore had sent his 'formal protest' to the Archbishop – a document a thousand words long which was published in *The Times* of 10 January. The nub of the protest came in its second paragraph: 'I am driven to act as I am doing solely because his [Henson's] expressed beliefs touching the fundamental matters of faith seem to me incompatible with the sincere profession of the Creeds.' Gore then attempted to prove Henson's heresy by quoting from his published works and from utterances of the bishops as a body with which Henson's views did not appear to square. He painted a lurid picture of the 'disastrous consequences' of Henson's being made a bishop and entreated 'Your Grace and my brother bishops' to refuse him consecration.[13] From the Evangelical wing the Dean of Canterbury, Henry Wace, joined in the condemnation of Henson, his alliance in this matter with the Anglo-Catholics recalling the joint stand by Shaftesbury and Pusey against Frederick Temple's appointment as Bishop of Exeter nearly fifty years before.

The next stage in the controversy was the famous attempt by Davidson to persuade Henson to modify his views in some way – or at least to give his opponents ground for believing that he was more orthodox than they supposed. The full story of the attempt as seen from Davidson's angle is given by Bell.[14] In the course of an exchange of letters drafted by Davidson for publication Henson assured the Archbishop that, when he repeated the words of the Apostles' Creed, including the clauses relating to 'Our Lord's Birth and Resurrection', he did so '*ex animo* and without any desire to change them'. How much such a profession of faith really represented a retraction of his views on Henson's part remains a matter of argument. The great thing was that Gore could say, in the light of the statement, 'I consider myself now entitled to declare that Dr Henson believes what I thought he disbelieved, and affirms *ex animo* what I thought he did not affirm.' Gore withdrew his protest against Henson's consecration

– and a major obstacle was removed from Davidson's path. On the day on which Gore withdrew his protest Henson's election was confirmed at a formal ceremony in St Mary-le-Bow church. Two objections (one from Hermitage Day), alleging Henson to be a heretic and unfit for episcopal office, were ruled out of order and Henson was duly confirmed as Bishop of Hereford.

The final hurdle was the consecration itself. This took place in Westminster Abbey on 2 February, the Feast of the Purification. It was an uneasy occasion, a number of bishops having declined to take part. Their implied rejection of his future ministry bitterly hurt Henson. He complained in a letter to Davidson three days before the ceremony that their behaviour had made a 'deep and painful impression' on his mind, and that his personal relations with them in future were likely to be difficult. 'Obsessed with the ambition of securing a "clean bill of orthodoxy" from the English Church Union, they seem never to have given a thought to the inevitable, or probable, consequences of their action . . . I shall try to content myself with leaving their Lordships to the comfort of their consciences and the lasting satisfaction of their memory.'[15] In his diary Henson was even more explicit. 'They [the abstaining bishops] have done what they can to hinder my entrance on my episcopate; they have added enormously to my difficulties in starting my work; they have lent the sanction of their names to the campaign of calumny and insult which has been running its course for the past month.'[16] At the service itself ('stately and very solemn') Henson's mind, he says, 'was inevitably harassed by a half-expectation at the crucial points that some fanatic would break in with a protest or an insult'.[17] Luckily nothing occurred to mar the harmony of the proceedings. Fourteen other bishops (including eight diocesans) assisted Davidson at the actual consecration. The sermon was preached by Dean Inge, who called Henson his 'dearest friend'. The most embarrassed person present must have been William Hough, the former Archdeacon of Kingston, who was being consecrated at the same time as Henson for the suffragan see of Woolwich and who thus found himself unwittingly caught up in the drama of a controversy in which he had played no part.

One result of the Hereford affair was the first serious attempt to reform the system by which bishops were appointed. Critics of the system were increasingly asking why the Church of England's leaders should be chosen by someone who was not even an Anglican. Matters came to a head in the Convocation of Canterbury three months after Henson's consecration. The case for reform was put forcibly by Bishop Gore, who complained that the present position was intolerable. 'At any moment the highest officers of the Church could be appointed by one who, for the time, was its enemy.' The system might have worked well enough under previous prime ministers, said Gore, but the training of the present premier 'had not been such as to give him an intimate knowledge of what was going on in the Church of England and what its best interests were'. He ended by urging the Archbishop to appoint a committee to consider reviving a seventeenth-century precedent by which the Crown had agreed to be advised on the choice of bishops by a body of churchmen.[18]

Gore's proposal was predictably denounced by Henson. In a hard-hitting defence of the existing system he pointed out that the prime minister advised the Crown as the representative of the English people, and that it therefore made no difference whether he was a churchman, a Nonconformist or a secularist. He had access to the best advice and acted under conditions which, Henson claimed, made abuse almost impossible.[19] But Henson's eloquence failed to impress the Convocation. It agreed to the appointment of a joint committee 'to consider various proposals for the giving of more effective expression to the mind of the Church either previously to such [Crown] nominations or before they became final'.[20] The committee sat for eighteen months; but, while it was deliberating, a parallel attempt at reform was going on behind the scenes of Parliament itself.

The impetus for this was noted by Davidson in a memorandum dated 24 February 1918, when the echoes of the Henson controversy were still very fresh in his mind. He noted that Lloyd George admitted quite frankly that he had no time for ecclesiastical appointments, or adequate knowledge, 'and is not at all averse to the idea of getting some advice regularly given by those who can be regarded as representative Churchmen'.[21] Davidson then arranged for a group of Anglican MPs to beard the Prime Minister with a suggestion that it was unfair to expect a non-Anglican to decide ecclesiastical appointments without assistance. Lloyd George welcomed the idea and agreed to the general principle of consultation between himself and a group of five selected churchmen. At this point, however, Davidson effectively drew the teeth of the plan by insisting that the members of the group ought to be consulted independently and not as a committee. In a memorandum dated 3 March 1919 he noted:

> I pressed . . . that the Prime Minister should not feel bound to consult all of them on every occasion, and that what passed between him and them should be regarded as wholly private, and that therefore they should not be regarded as men holding

a sort of office of a representative kind. Their *raison d'être* and status would be simply this, five men whom Churchmen in the House of Commons recognise as suitable persons to whom individually the Prime Minister might turn so as to keep himself in touch with Church opinion.[22]

Davidson feared that, if the arrangement were to become formalized, the effect would be 'almost wholly mischievous'. But the result of his intervention ensured that the group was never more than a nebulous and ineffective body because it was never in fact allowed to act as a body; and it gradually faded away.

Meanwhile the joint committee of Canterbury Convocation had concluded its deliberations; and, in February 1920, it presented its report. The chief recommendation was for a 'Standing Committee of representative Churchmen' who would be empowered to bring before the prime minister the names of persons suitable for bishoprics and who might regularly be consulted by him before the submission to the Crown of nominees to such appointments. This proposal was a kind of foreshadowing of the Crown Appointments Commission. It was, however, rejected by the Lower House of Convocation, which substituted for it the following resolution: 'That his Grace the President be requested to approach the Throne in order to secure that the two Archbishops should be officially consulted by the Prime Minister before the submission of names by him to the Crown for nomination to any diocesan bishopric'.[23] At this point Davidson's native caution again reared its head; and, when the Lower House resolution was brought before the Upper House, he successfully moved the deletion of the key word 'officially'. 'If there is a great desire to make sure that consultation is taken with those whom the Church is supposed to trust, or does trust', he told the House, 'a Resolution to that effect would be quite harmless; but, if the consultation is made obligatory and official, I think that it must diminish the responsibility which rests on the shoulders of those who at present bear it.'[24] The resolution as amended was passed by both Houses of Convocation and forwarded to the Prime Minister, whose reply, dated 21 February, showed that Davidson had gauged the situation correctly. 'As you are aware', he told the Archbishop,

it has been my invariable practice, since I became Prime Minister, to invite your counsel, which you have at all times been kind enough to give me, upon all important appointments in the Church. Certainly in this case of Diocesan Bishoprics my recommendations to His Majesty have only been made after careful and anxious consultation with yourself, and in the case of Sees in the Northern Province with the Archbishop of York also.

By now the unofficial group of churchmen whom Davidson had urged should be consulted separately rather than as a body was in being; so Lloyd George was able to add at this point: 'It is also within your knowledge that I have in regard to all higher appointments taken the further step of seeking the opinion of a number of prominent Churchmen representing all shades of opinion.' He went on:

Whilst the Resolution therefore may appear to the public to partake of the nature of a criticism of the present procedure, it is in reality an expression of approval of the course which I have adopted. You do not ask for, and I could not assent to, an action which would derogate from the well-established responsibility which rests upon Ministers of the Crown in respect of the advice which it is their duty to tender to His Majesty.[25]

Lloyd George's reply was satisfactory to the extent that it went along with Convocation's request for consultation (albeit unofficial consultation) between prime minister and archbishops before each nomination to a diocesan bishopric, and that it confirmed that this was by now an established practice. It was unsatisfactory in that it gave no guarantee that the prime minister would necessarily follow the archiepiscopal advice. And it soon became only too apparent that this particular prime minister was prepared to take no notice whatever of pleas emanating from Lambeth and Bishopthorpe. It was exactly three months after his honeyed words to Davidson that he made the nomination that caused the scales to fall from the archiepiscopal eyes; and the man concerned was again Hensley Henson. The occasion was as follows.

In early May 1920 the death occurred of the Bishop of Durham, Handley Moule, in his eightieth year. Davidson wrote at once to Lloyd George urging the appointment of the scholarly Dean of Christ Church, Oxford, Tommy Strong, as his successor. What was his consternation, then, to receive a reply a fortnight later from the Premier's secretary, the egregious Capt. Evans, not only rejecting Strong's candidacy but suggesting instead the translation to Durham of none other than the Bishop of Hereford. Henson's return to his former pastures would in the Prime Minister's belief, said Evans, 'be generally acceptable'.[26] Davidson thought not – and hastened to say so. The nomination, he told Evans, would raise afresh a storm which had largely subsided. 'The

Prime Minister will not suppose that it is likely to be received with welcome by the Church at large, notwithstanding Dr Henson's capacity, eloquence, and the personal friendship with many at Durham.' And, mindful of the Prime Minister's bland words of three months previously, he added: 'I know the importance attached by Mr Lloyd George to the opinions of the Archbishop of the Province in such matters . . . and I await with some trepidation the expression of the Archbishop of York's views.'[27]

Cosmo Lang minced no words. He wrote to Evans on 26 May to say that he was receiving letters almost every day from 'all sorts and conditions of people in the Diocese of Durham' expressing the earnest hope that Henson would *not* be translated.

> I am persuaded that the appointment of the Bishop of Hereford would lead to disappointment, division and friction just at a time when the Diocese urgently needs being pulled together in a spirit of unity and good will. For these reasons I venture still to hope that the Prime Minister may be persuaded to recommend the Dean of Christ Church.[28]

To Davidson Lang wrote on the same day in even stronger terms, putting the nub of his objection to Henson's nomination thus:

> In view of the recent letter of the Prime Minister [i.e. that of 21 February] we shall of course be regarded as responsible in some measure for this appointment, and in view of what has been said it is really rather monstrous that he should ignore the united recommendation of the Dean of Christ Church by both Archbishops and persist in appointing another man against their clear opinion. This sort of thing reduces consultation with the Archbishops to a mere form.[29]

In the course of his letter Lang suggested to Davidson that, if Lloyd George persisted in nominating Henson, they should see if they could persuade the Monarch to put a spoke in the prime ministerial wheel. Davidson agreed. He wrote to Stamfordham, the King's secretary, on 31 May to enquire whether this was a case in which the King might bring personal pressure to bear or even exercise an actual veto.

> The Prime Minister has stated in a public letter that he consults the Archbishops in these matters, and this throws upon us a peculiar responsibility in the eyes of the public. It may be our duty to show what this 'consultation' amounts to. But I do not want to do that if I can help it, for it might mean a real breach with Downing Street.[30]

## THE BISHOP OF DURHAM.

*This is the man that rules the see*
 *Whose prelates once held princely station;*
*A HENSON he, but not to be*
 *Confused with LESLIE (no relation);*

*And with his Durham he will smile*
 *If by your largesse you deliver*
*Her noble pile, of Norman style,*
 *From tumbling right into the river.*

**MR. PUNCH'S PERSONALITIES.—LXV.**

*Herbert Hensley Henson: by now the former rebel had become a pillar of the Establishment.*

In the end more prudent counsels prevailed. The Monarch was reluctant to be drawn into the ring. A period of reflection no doubt revealed to both Archbishops that an agreement by the Prime Minister to consult them over a particular appointment was not quite the same as an agreement to appoint the person they might press on him against his own inclinations. Finally Lloyd George agreed to meet them at least a quarter of the way by nominating Strong to the see of Ripon, which was also vacant.

The interesting thing about this second Henson appointment is that the Archbishops were crying 'Wolf' without due cause. When the news of Henson's nomination was announced in June there was no great public outcry. Even the *Church Times* made only token sounds of disapproval (and, by the time he announced his retirement eighteen years later, was actually, albeit under a different but still Anglo-Catholic editor, singing his praises). So no storm blew up on this occasion; and even Frank Weston, the impetuous Bishop of Zanzibar, who had published a book in 1919 attacking Henson for heresy and who had been dubbed by Henson the Zanzibarbarian, became firm friends with him when they met at the Lambeth Conference the following year. However rash Lloyd George may have been in his original decision to nominate Henson to Hereford in 1917, by 1920 Henson had lived down his reputation for heresy and was almost respectable. He had proved a popular diocesan, except for a tiny and disgruntled minority; and his translation to a senior see (where he had been a popular dean), though displeasing to the Archbishops, was not therefore greeted with the public cries of indignation which they had feared.

Henson was not of course the only man to be nominated by Lloyd George to a vacant diocese. His other eighteen nominees included two future archbishops, Garbett and William Temple. Even his trusty adviser, Archdeacon Pearce of Westminster, received a bishopric.

The Prime Minister must have felt a certain embarrassment, however, in proposing Pearce in 1919 for the see of Worcester, as the offer might have been construed as a reward for services rendered. Pearce himself thought he had better consult Davidson as to the propriety of accepting the offer. In the words of George Bell:

He [Pearce] said that he had one great difficulty about the right answer to the Prime Minister's proposal. He had (he told the Archbishop) read all the files at 10 Downing Street relating to recent episcopal appointments, including all the Archbishop's letters, and never once had the Archbishop mentioned his name as a possible Bishop! The Archbishop, without a moment's hesitation, put his hand on Canon Pearce's shoulder and replied: 'My dear Pearce, you were always in the background!'[31]

Pearce's nomination was not received, however, with universal accord. In the Worcester Chapter it was attacked by Canon T. A. Lacey, an able but eccentric priest who was at that time a leading member of the editorial staff of the *Church Times*. Lacey was strongly opposed to the system of Crown appointments to bishoprics and determined to use the occasion of Pearce's nomination to register a personal protest against it in his own cathedral. When the *congé d'élire* arrived at Worcester, with the King's instruction to the Chapter to elect Pearce as bishop of the diocese, Lacey rose to propose a candidate of his own. The Dean and two other members of the Chapter dutifully voted for the Crown's nominee, but the remaining canon was too agitated to record his vote at all. Under the Worcester Cathedral statutes a two-thirds majority was necessary for a valid election. Lacey maintained that Pearce, with three votes out of five, had secured a majority of only sixty per cent and was therefore not *de jure* but only *de facto* Bishop of Worcester. He observed on a subsequent occasion: 'Far be it from me to disagree with my ecclesiastical superior, if indeed he be my ecclesiastical superior, a matter upon which I have the gravest doubts.'[32] Pearce's younger brother Edmund, incidentally, was to become the first bishop of the new diocese of Derby – but not until 1927, by when the elder Pearce had ceased to be an *éminence grise* at 10 Downing Street.

It was only a few months after Ernest Pearce's nomination to Worcester that the future Archbishop of York, Cyril Garbett, was appointed to succeed Hubert Burge as Bishop of Southwark, the heavily populated diocese (covering parts of South London and Surrey) of which Henson had fought shy. But, as vicar of the huge and prestigious parish of Portsea with a dozen curates under him, Garbett was used to hard work. The challenge of Southwark held no terrors for him. On hearing the news of Burge's resignation he is supposed to have said, 'I'm sorry for the man who goes there, whoever he is';[33] but he had no hesitation in accepting Lloyd George's offer when it arrived a few days later. In contrast William Temple, another future Archbishop of York (and afterwards of Canterbury), when offered the succession to Bishop Knox at Manchester in November 1920, asked for a few days in which to think over the proposal. He happened to be the son of Archbishop Frederick Temple; but he had also been the main inspiration behind the reformist Life and Liberty Movement (which had led to the setting up of the Church Assembly), and, as such, doubtless felt hesitant at first about accepting a proposal to join the Church establishment as a diocesan bishop. Davidson, Lang and Gore, among others, quickly overcame his scruples and urged immediate acceptance of Lloyd George's offer, which was duly given. Temple was now one rung higher on the ladder to Lambeth.

Apart from Henson, all Lloyd George's nominees to the episcopate were unexceptionable. His only remaining brush with Davidson was on a matter of detail connected with the proposed translation to Salisbury in 1921 of the Archbishop of Brisbane, St Clair Donaldson, in succession to F. E. Ridgeway. The initiative for this appointment had come from Buckingham Palace. The King knew Donaldson and approved of him. So, on the day in May on which the papers announced the death of Bishop Ridgeway, Lord Stamfordham wrote to Davidson on the King's behalf to press for Donaldson to succeed him. 'Please write to the Prime Minister', he urged; 'try and get him to agree and to cable to the Governor of Queensland and fetch Donaldson home as soon as possible.'[34] Davidson took up the cudgels as requested and sang Donaldson's praises in a letter to Lloyd George. 'A scholar, a gentleman and a man of very great personal charm and popularity', he enthused. Salisbury was just the diocese to tempt him back to England: 'a dignified See, historically and otherwise, therefore making it not in any way derogatory to Australia that he should come home to it . . . I should greatly value him as a counsellor and friend.'[35] Luckily Lloyd George shared the Archbishop's enthusiasm for Donaldson, so the offer was made via a cable to the Governor of Queensland. But here the rub arose. Donaldson enquired of Davidson whether acceptance would mean his having to return to England before the next meeting of the Australian General Synod in October. Lloyd George felt that he must come home almost at once or else refuse the offer. Davidson disagreed. He thought the request by Donaldson to delay his return by three or four months a reasonable one. But he had to write a powerfully persuasive letter to the Prime Minister before he got his way.[36]

The *Church Times* has been mentioned several times in this chapter, so perhaps one further reference will be forgiven. The occasion was the enthronement of the first independent Archbishop of Wales in St Asaph Cathedral on 1 June 1920. Lloyd George, who had spearheaded the movement for Welsh disestablishment, was among those present at the ceremony. He had also, the same day, attended an early-morning celebration of Holy Communion in the cathedral at which he and his wife had both communicated. Now the Prime Minister happened to be a Particular Baptist and Mrs Lloyd George a Calvinistic Methodist; and to Anglo-Catholics in those pre-ecumenical days inter-communion was a deadly sin. The *Church Times*'s fury therefore knew no bounds. In its issue of 11 June it denounced such 'open disregard of Church discipline on the part of the assembled Primates' and talked of the 'distress and bewilderment' caused to church men and women in Wales and England by such a grave lapse. 'No blame of course attaches to the Prime Minister, for he cannot be held, as would an unknown person, to have deceived the authorities by presenting himself as a communicant.' The villain of the piece, the paper continued, was the Archbishop of Wales – 'and, though we look for an explanation of this astonishing action, we have not much hope of it satisfying loyal Churchmen . . . Celtic impulsiveness cannot account for such action at eight o'clock in the morning.'

The last word in the matter must lie with Archbishop Davidson. After referring in his journal to a 'teapot storm in ecclesiastical circles of the *Church Times* sort', he continued: 'In my judgment the net outcome will be entirely good. He [Lloyd George] did not come [to St Asaph] to triumph, or to belittle what was happening, or to curry favour. He came as a religious man who, I imagine, had no conception that anyone would do other than welcome him'.[37]


**Nominations to diocesan bishoprics 20 (12 first appointments, 8 translations)**

*First appointments:*

(1) 1917: Herbert Hensley Henson to Hereford.
(2) 1919: Ernest Harold Pearce to Worcester.
(3) 1919: Frederic Sumpter Guy Warman to Truro.
(4) 1919: Cyril Forster Garbett to Southwark.
(5) 1919: William Shuckburgh Swayne to Lincoln.
(6) 1920: Arthur William Thomson Perowne to Bradford.
(7) 1920: Henry Herbert Williams to Carlisle.
(8) 1920: Thomas Banks Strong to Ripon.
(9) 1920: William Temple to Manchester.
(10) 1921: Albert Augustus David to St Edmundsbury and Ipswich.
(11) 1921: St John Basil Wynne Willson to Bath and Wells.
(12) 1922: Charles Lisle Carr to Coventry.

*Translations:*

(1) 1918: Huyshe Wolcott Yeatman-Biggs to Coventry (from Worcester).
(2) 1919: Winfrid Oldfield Burrows to Chichester (from Truro).
(3) 1919: Henry Luke Paget to Chester (from Stepney).*
(4) 1919: Hubert Murray Burge to Oxford (from Southwark).
(5) 1920: Michael Bolton Furse to St Albans (from Pretoria).†
(6) 1920: Herbert Hensley Henson to Durham (from Hereford).
(7) 1920: Martin Linton Smith to Hereford (from Warrington).*
(8) 1921: St Clair George Alfred Donaldson to Salisbury (from Brisbane).†

* Suffragan see.
† Overseas see.

# 16

# Conservative Comeback

*A. Bonar Law: Prime Minister*
*23 October 1922 – 20 May 1923*

*Stanley Baldwin: Prime Minister*
*22 May 1923 – 22 January 1924*
*4 November 1924 – 4 June 1929*
*7 June 1935 – 28 May 1937*

Andrew Bonar Law (1858–1923) *was born in New Brunswick, Canada, the son of a Presbyterian minister. His education was begun in Canada and completed in Scotland. He achieved success as an iron merchant in Glasgow, but retired from business in 1900 and was elected a Unionist MP. He was Parliamentary Secretary to the Board of Trade under Balfour, and in 1911 succeeded him (as a compromise candidate) as Leader of the Opposition. He served in the wartime coalition government first as Colonial Secretary and then as Chancellor of the Exchequer and Leader of the Commons. From 1919 to 1921 he was Lord Privy Seal. When the coalition fell the following year he became Prime Minister, but ill-health forced him to resign within seven months and he died five months later. A close friend of Lord Beaverbrook, Bonar Law achieved a reputation both for integrity and for mastery of detail.*

Stanley Baldwin, 1st Earl Baldwin of Bewdley (1867–1947), *was the dominant figure in British politics between the wars. Born at Bewdley, Worcestershire, the son of a wealthy steel manufacturer, he was educated at Harrow and Trinity College, Cambridge. For the next twenty years he served as junior partner in his father's business before succeeding him in 1908 as Conservative MP for Bewdley – the seat he retained until he was raised to the peerage on his retirement in 1937. He held junior office in the Lloyd George coalition and was Chancellor of the Exchequer under Bonar Law, succeeding him as Prime Minister in May 1923. A Commons defeat eight months later, however, led to his resignation and the formation of the first Labour government. That government was likewise short-lived, and Baldwin was back in office by the end of 1924. His second and longest administration was dominated by industrial problems, culminating in the General Strike of 1926. Baldwin gave way again to MacDonald in 1929, but two years later the Labour administration was replaced by a 'National Government' nominally headed by MacDonald but effectually dominated by Baldwin. He became Prime Minister for the third and last time in 1935. His handling of the Abdication crisis won general approval, but he hesitated over pressing forward a policy of rearmament that might have entailed electoral defeat. He retired amid universal plaudits, but, by the time of his death ten years later, had sunk low in the esteem of a nation which held him personally to blame for its unpreparedness for war. He was a man of cultured charm but given to indolence; in the telling phrase of one of his biographers, 'the general habit of his mind was ruminative rather than executive'.[1] A cousin of Rudyard Kipling, he was for many people the prototypical middle-class Englishman.*

Bonar Law was Prime Minister for only seven months, so had time for little more than professing his good intentions to the Archbishop of Canterbury. He promised Davidson that he would always consult him about episcopal appointments, though he might not necessarily agree with his recommendations. The one bishop he *did* have the opportunity to nominate, however, became one of the most influential figures on the Bench in the inter-war period. This was Arthur Cayley Headlam, a fine New Testament scholar and expert on ecumenism who achieved the rare distinction in 1921 of being made a Companion of Honour. (The only other bishop to become a CH was H. H. Williams of Carlisle in 1945.) Headlam's name was urged on Bonar Law both by Davidson and by the outgoing Bishop of Gloucester, E. C. S. Gibson. Headlam was pressed to accept the offer on all hands – and not least by his friend Henson, who spoke of the prospect of higher things to come. 'If you are offered the Bishoprick of Gloucester, *take it*. Your doing so will not prejudice, and probably would facilitate, your going to London, or to one of the Primacies.'[2] In the event Headlam, who was sixty at the time of his appointment to Gloucester, was never offered translation. He was considered as a possibility for Winchester in 1932, but his age was against him.

Bonar Law was already in poor health when he assumed the premiership. When he resigned it seven months later he was a dying man. But the approach of death could not persuade him to abandon the sceptical approach to religion which he had adopted for most of his life. He had been brought up in the Presbyterian faith of his father, who had emigrated from Northern Ireland in 1845 to minister in New Brunswick. But the content of that faith meant little or nothing to him, and he did not believe in a life after death. He was buried in Westminster Abbey (against his own expressed wish), his ashes being brought to the Abbey from St Columba's, Pont Street, the Presbyterian church in London of which he had been a nominal elder and at which his family had worshipped. It was left to Asquith to remark on the fittingness of having buried the Unknown Prime Minister by the side of the Unknown Warrior.

Bonar Law's successor, Baldwin, in the seven and a quarter years covered by his three premierships, proved to be among the most prolific of bishop-makers. His total of thirty-two diocesans was exceeded only by Salisbury (though it was equalled by Churchill). But his attitude to what Lloyd George had once described as 'one of the greatest responsibilities entrusted to me as Prime Minister'[3] was apparently open to criticism. Alan Don, the future Dean of Westminster, who served as chaplain and secretary to Lang in the 1930s, complained in his diary on one occasion: 'Baldwin came to talk over various ecclesiastical appointments – the Deanery of Salisbury and the Bishopric of Derby . . . Baldwin is more casual about such matters than Ramsay MacDonald and had evidently lost a long memorandum which C[osmo] C[antuar, i.e. Lang] sent him in July about the Salisbury Deanery.'*[5]

As befitted a middle-of-the-road Anglican, Baldwin disliked extremes of churchmanship; but he took care not to appoint men of the same theological mould. 'As your Grace is aware', his secretary, Geoffrey Fry, wrote to Davidson in November 1926, 'Mr Baldwin's great anxiety in the matter of higher preferment is to maintain so far as may be possible a fair and just balance between the various points of view.'[6] Davidson obviously feared, however, that dislike of extremism (what a later generation would have called 'Central bigotry') might be carried too far and, on the eve of his own retirement in 1928, put words into Baldwin's mouth. 'In the changes which are inevitable as following upon my

---

*The diary entry added that 'Jack Rawlinson is a strong candidate for the Bishopric'. Rawlinson was appointed, Henson (in whose diocese he served as an archdeacon) being among those who pressed his claims. The bishop he was succeeding, Edmund Pearce, was pithily summed up by Henson as 'not great or attractive or particularly interesting, but always sane, sensible and serviceable'.[4]

resignation', he wrote to the Prime Minister, 'you will wish I know to consider the bearing of what you do upon Church partisanship, if one may use the word. You would not wish that the reasonable High Churchman or the reasonable Evangelical should feel that they had been passed over, or that all the emphasis had been laid elsewhere than on their friends.'[7]

In fact Baldwin could have retorted to Davidson that he had appointed the superior of a religious community to a bishopric. This was Walter Howard Frere, a member of the Community of the Resurrection whom Baldwin had nominated as Bishop of Truro during his first premiership in 1923. Admittedly he had done so very much at the Archbishop's prompting. Frere, besides being a monk, was a leading authority on liturgical matters; and the reason for Davidson's wanting him to be a bishop was given in a subsequent letter he wrote to Frere:

> For a long time past I have felt strongly that the Church had been suffering from the fact that among Diocesan Bishops there was no one who could speak with responsibility on behalf of . . . Anglo-Catholicism, and yet be able to regard these questions largely, sanely and with the equipment of scholarly knowledge . . . We need someone whom the Prime Minister can fairly be urged to nominate as a man who carries the confidence of Churchmen generally, whether they are of his school or not . . . There is one man who does possess the qualifications which . . . seem to me to be essential, and you are the man.[8]

Frere had at first been reluctant to step into the breach. He had written to Davidson on 27 August 1923 to say that he had received the Prime Minister's offer but had begged Baldwin not to submit his name to the King, 'as I would not be able to accept nomination'. The reason, said Frere, was that he regarded his primary task as being to 'take a hand in recovering Community life for our Church'.[9] Davidson had then, in the letter quoted above, tried to persuade Frere to think again. Eventually he succeeded. Frere withdrew his 'somewhat impetuous refusal' of nomination to the see of Truro, and all was well. 'I adhere to my view', Davidson assured the Prime Minister, 'that the accession of Dr Frere to the Episcopal Bench is, at the present juncture of Church life, a very real advantage.'[10] In fact, in spite of Davidson's confidence that Frere would go down well with men of all schools of thought, his reign in Cornwall was by no means universally popular – and was to lead to the appointment of a successor of a very different theological stamp.

The chief appointment of Baldwin's second premiership (1924–9) was that of a successor to Davidson himself, who resigned in the summer of 1928 after twenty-five years as Archbishop of Canterbury. Luckily for the Prime Minister there was a tailor-made candidate waiting in the wings: Cosmo Lang, who had by now served almost twenty years as Archbishop of York and who had for long been Davidson's trusted confidant. An outside possibility would have been George Bell, who had served as Davidson's resident chaplain for ten years and was now Dean of Canterbury. Dean Inge wrote of him at the time: 'George Bell is a wonderful man. If I were Baldwin, I would pass over all the old bishops and send him to Lambeth. Everybody except Cosmo would be delighted.'[11] But such rapid promotion for a comparative junior not yet in episcopal orders would have been too long a shot even for so allegedly casual a bishop-maker as Baldwin, however much it might have pleased the progressive elements in the Church.

The Prime Minister paid several visits to Lambeth to talk things over with Davidson, besides seeing him in the House of Commons and in Downing Street. 'There is no parallel', Davidson recorded afterwards, 'to the speed with which these things have been settled. But the speed did not in the least mean carelessness or lack of trouble, for we have given hours to the matter and Baldwin has honestly grappled with the difficulties.'[12] These of course included the choice of a successor to Lang as Archbishop of York. Here the favoured candidate was the Bishop of Manchester, William Temple, a man praised by Lang for his 'marked ascendancy of mind, his large outlook, his vigorous personality, and his power of writing and of speech'.[13] Temple's lively concern with social and international questions and his progressive views made him an admirable partner to the older and more conservative Lang.

The actual mechanics of the translation were handled with Baldwin's customary aplomb. Lang had come up to London from York on 26 July to attend a garden party at Buckingham Palace. After the party he was told by Davidson that the Prime Minister was coming to Lambeth at 9.30 that evening and wished to see him. At that meeting Baldwin broke the news to Lang of his desire to translate him. Lang observed afterwards that he doubted whether any such offer had ever before been conveyed by word of mouth rather than by letter – and certainly not by a prime minister smoking a pipe. He asked for time in which to consider the proposal. 'No,' said Baldwin, 'it is inevitable. I won't hear of any refusal. You are the only man. Your one and only duty is to say Yes at once, and before I leave.' Lang duly said Yes. Davidson was then summoned to the study, and the three of them settled the other consequent appointments: Temple for York, Guy Warman to be translated from Chelmsford to Manchester and Henry Wilson, Rector of Cheltenham, to go to Chelmsford. 'It was quick work!', Lang commented.[14]

Four days later, at a similar after-dinner session at Lambeth, Baldwin offered Temple the see of York. 'I expect you know why I have asked you to come and see me', Baldwin remarked. 'I have my suspicions', said Temple. 'Well, what about it?' Again the answer was Yes. Meanwhile Davidson had been breaking the news to Mrs Temple and telling her of the future possibilities for her husband: perhaps succeeding Winnington-Ingram as Bishop of London and in due course passing on to Canterbury.[15] In fact Temple might have been sent to London first rather than to York if London had been likely to be vacant in the near future. But of that there was no hope. Winnington-Ingram, who had held the see since 1901, 'had clearly intimated', Lang recorded, 'that he was not disposed to resign or to take a less arduous Diocese'.[16] In fact he was to soldier on for a further ten years – which was a pity, as, after nearly thirty years of his popular but lax rule, the diocese of London was in a state of ecclesiastical chaos. Baldwin toyed at one time with the idea of offering York to Winnington-Ingram as the only means of prising him out of the see, but was politely dissuaded from using the northern primacy as a pawn in the episcopal game.

Another equally way-out possibility, much discussed in the press, was that of translating Henson to York from Durham.* But Henson's age and idiosyncrasies ruled him out. Brooding in his diary as to whether he would really wish for translation, he commented: 'I think that I desire the distinction of *refusing* a Primacy, and, perhaps, I resent the loss of consequence which my being passed over must needs involve.' And, after Temple's appointment had been announced and Henson had begun to receive letters of 'condolence', he added that, since Lang was 64 and he himself 65, a younger man was almost inevitable for York. 'Two sexagenarians, marching with equal strides towards senility, would never have done. Even our long-suffering parent,

---

*Henson had even been suggested as a possible successor to Davidson at Canterbury. A 1927 limerick produced by some Cambridge undergraduates as a parody of a letter to *The Times* read:

> Dear Sir, The affairs of the realm
> Demand a strong hand at the helm,
>   A hand, Sir, that I
>   Am prepared to supply.
> Yours faithfully, Herbert Dunelm:[17]

the *Ecclesia Anglicana*, could hardly have sustained the spectacle of *both* Primates doddering together.'[18] So Temple went to York and Henson remained at Durham.

George Bell may have been too young and too low in the pecking order to be a serious candidate for Canterbury in 1928. But his ecclesiastical pedigree was flawless and he was obviously destined for a bishopric before long. The offer of the vacant see of Chichester came in 1929 (it was the last to be made by Baldwin during his second premiership), though the candidate accepted only with reluctance.

Bell's claims were pressed by the new Archbishop of Canterbury in a letter of 24 February. He told Baldwin that in ordinary circumstances he would not have suggested moving Bell after only five years as Dean of Canterbury, where he was doing very well. But the next Lambeth Conference would be held the following year, and it was vital that Bell, who had been secretary of the previous Lambeth Conference and therefore knew the ropes as no one else did, should be present as a full episcopal member of its successor. There was no guarantee, said Lang, that some other diocese within easy reach of London would become vacant before the summer of 1930; and it would be wasting Bell's value in the counsels of the Church if he were relegated to some distant diocese ('such for example as Carlisle').[19]

Baldwin accepted the force of Lang's arguments and made the offer to Bell. His first reaction was to decline. He sought advice from his friends (including Davidson, who urged acceptance), but their advice was conflicting. Bell dithered for some time. On 19 March he wrote a letter declining nomination 'with great regret, and only after the fullest deliberation', but fortunately refrained from posting it. On the following morning, during prayers in the cathedral, he changed his mind and wrote to accept the offer.[20]

Bell was to receive another letter from Baldwin five years later – asking his advice about a new episcopal appointment. Ramsay MacDonald was Prime Minister, but by this time of a National Government in which Baldwin ranked as number two. So when, in the absence of the Premier through illness, it fell to Baldwin to make some of the preliminary enquiries about a new Bishop of Guildford on MacDonald's behalf, he had no hesitation in seeking Bell's advice. 'Mr Baldwin has discussed the question with the Archbishop of Canterbury', his secretary wrote, 'and two names are outstanding – (1) the Bishop of Dover [J. V. Macmillan, an uncle of the future premier] and (2) the Archdeacon of Surrey, Dr Blackburne . . . Mr Baldwin would be most grateful if your

Lordship could tell him which in your view is the better of the two.'[21] Bell cast his vote in favour of Macmillan, and Macmillan was duly nominated.

During his premierships Baldwin's relations with both Davidson and Lang remained calm and amicable, and no violent differences of opinion occurred to rock the Church–State boat. The customary pattern was maintained of the Archbishop suggesting two or more names for each vacancy that arose, perhaps after a preliminary discussion, and of Baldwin in his turn leaning over backwards to make sure that he had the Primate's goodwill in his final choice. A typical letter is that with which Baldwin's secretary, G. P. Humphreys-Davies, announced to Lang's chaplain, Alexander Sargent, his master's decision with regard to the vacant diocese of Bath and Wells. Dated 10 March 1937, it began by saying that the Prime Minister had been reflecting on his talk the previous day with the Archbishop and had concluded that the best of the names mentioned had been that of the Dean of Rochester, Francis Underhill [Davidson's other favoured candidate had been the Bishop of Blackburn, Percy Herbert]. The letter continued:

> If the Archbishop concurs, therefore, he proposes to set in motion the machinery of submitting Underhill's name to the Palace and offering him the succession to the See. I should be grateful if you could let the Archbishop know of the Prime Minister's provisional conclusion and ascertain whether His Grace concurs in the action proposed.[22]

The appointment was the last Baldwin was to make before his retirement at the end of May 1937. He was a genuinely religious man – and indeed, while an undergraduate at Cambridge, had spent at least one Easter at the Trinity College Mission at Camberwell and even toyed with the idea of ordination. His religious philosophy he once summed up in an address he gave to the British and Foreign Bible Society:

> If I did not believe that our work was done in faith and the hope that at some day, it may be a million years hence, the Kingdom of God would spread over the whole world, I could have no hope, I could do no work, and I would give my office over this morning to anyone who would take it.[23]

## Andrew Bonar Law

### Nominations to diocesan bishoprics 1 (first appointment)

(1) 1922: Arthur Cayley Headlam to Gloucester.

## Stanley Baldwin

### Nominations to diocesan bishoprics 32 (17 first appointments, 15 translations)

*First appointments:*

(1) 1923: Walter Frere CR to Truro.
(2) 1923: Walter Godfrey Whittingham to St Edmundsbury and Ipswich.
(3) 1924: Cyril Charles Bowman Bardsley to Peterborough.
(4) 1924: Leonard Jauncey White-Thomson to Ely.

(5) 1925: Charles Leonard Thornton-Duesbury to Sodor and Man.
(6) 1925: Edward Arthur Burroughs to Ripon.
(7) 1926: Bernard Oliver Francis Heywood to Southwell.
(8) 1927: Claude Martin Blagden to Peterborough.
(9) 1927: Ernest Neville Lovett to Portsmouth.
(10) 1927: Edmund Courtenay Pearce to Derby.
(11) 1928: William Stanton Jones to Sodor and Man.
(12) 1928: James Buchanan Seaton to Wakefield.
(13) 1928: Henry Albert Wilson to Chelmsford.
(14) 1929: George Kennedy Allen Bell to Chichester.

(15) 1935: Alfred Edward John Rawlinson to Derby.
(16) 1936: Frank Partridge to Portsmouth.
(17) 1937: Francis Underhill to Bath and Wells.

*Translations:*

(1) 1923: Frederic Sumpter Guy Warman to Chelmsford (from Truro).
(2) 1923: Albert Augustus David to Liverpool (from St Edmundsbury and Ipswich).
(3) 1923: Frank Theodore Woods to Winchester (from Peterborough).

(4) 1925: Thomas Banks Strong to Oxford (from Ripon).
(5) 1926: Percy Mark Herbert to Blackburn (from Kingston-upon-Thames).*
(6) 1926: Cyril Charles Bowman Bardsley to Leicester (from Peterborough).

(7) 1927: John Harold Greig to Guildford (from Gibraltar).†
(8) 1927: Harold Ernest Bilbrough to Newcastle (from Dover).*
(9) 1928: Henry Mosley to Southwell (from Stepney).*
(10) 1928: Cosmo Gordon Lang to Canterbury (from York).
(11) 1928: William Temple to York (from Manchester).
(12) 1928: Frederic Sumpter Guy Warman to Manchester (from Chelmsford).

(13) 1936: Charles Edward Curzon to Exeter (from Stepney).*
(14) 1936: Ernest Neville Lovett to Salisbury (from Portsmouth).
(15) 1937: Edward Sydney Woods to Lichfield (from Croydon).*

* Suffragan see.
† Overseas see.

# 17

# Hunting for Heretics

*J. Ramsay MacDonald: Prime Minister*
*22 January – 4 November 1924*
*8 June 1929 – 7 June 1935*

James Ramsay MacDonald (1866–1937) *was a tragic figure who, though twice Prime Minister, was eventually expelled from the Labour Party which he had helped to found. Born at Lossiemouth, Scotland, he was an illegitimate child and was brought up by his mother. He was educated locally. He went to London in 1884, becoming a political journalist and propagandist for Socialism. He was appointed secretary of the Labour Party in 1900 soon after its foundation. In 1906 he was elected MP for Leicester and five years later became Labour leader in the Commons. His pacifism in the First World War, however, cost him both the party leadership in 1914 and his seat in Parliament four years later. In 1922 he was re-elected to both the Commons and the leadership, becoming the first Labour Prime Minister on Baldwin's resignation in January 1924. Eight months later the desertion of his Liberal allies caused his government to fall, and for the next four and a half years MacDonald led the Labour opposition. He returned to power in 1929, but was able to avert financial disaster in 1931 only by allying himself with the Conservatives in a 'National Government'. A few of his colleagues remained loyal, but the majority regarded his action as a great betrayal; and he was expelled from the party of which he had been the principal architect. For the next four years he remained Prime Minister of a government in which 'National Labour' held only a handful of seats and which was dominated by the Conservatives. By June 1935, when he retired as Premier, his health and faculties were in rapid decline. He died at sea two years later while on a recuperative trip to South America. MacDonald's last years as a puppet premier (he was called 'Ramshackle Mac' by Lady Londonderry) provided a pathetic contrast to that earlier period of his life when he had been the rising hope of the Labour Party.*

MacDonald was a deeply religious man in an undogmatic sense, though never after childhood a regular churchgoer. He respected the different denominations as embodiments of the life of the Spirit, but cared nothing for creeds or ritual. He had been brought up at Lossiemouth in the Free Presbyterian Kirk. Its gloomy strain of Calvinism, however, conflicted with the rationalistic side of his nature. He is said to have enquired of his Sunday school teacher on one occasion how Elijah could have been translated to heaven in a chariot of fire, since the chariot's wheels would have had nothing but air to grip.[1] He described himself to his fiancée as a Unitarian, and she was also that way inclined. When they settled in England after their marriage he would sometimes read aloud from the Bible to their children on Sunday – apparently his sole concession to outward religious observance. He felt that Protestantism had become as formal as Roman Catholicism, and that its true spirit was now to be found in the Ethical Movement rather than in the churches. That movement's ideal was that 'of man as a rational being, fighting out his spiritual battles within himself, aided neither by the prayers of a priest nor the communion of a church, excepting in so far as man can aid man to noble effort'.[2]

This then was the person who, for almost seven years of his life, found himself charged with choosing the bishops of the Established Church of England. How did he set about what he might well have regarded as a distasteful or irrelevant task? The church authorities obviously had their misgivings. Early in MacDonald's first premiership a dinner was arranged at the house of Lord Parmoor, a devout churchman who was both a friend of Davidson and a friend and political colleague of MacDonald, in order to discuss the general question of ecclesiastical appointments. In a letter to the Archbishop immediately afterwards Parmoor summed up the position as he saw it:

> Nothing must be done which will weaken in any degree the responsibility of the Prime Minister in regard to these nominations. Nothing must happen which would allow a notion to become current that the Prime Minister had handed over his responsibilities to other people. I perfectly understand that he has no intention of doing so, but I am anxious that in whatever is done the facts should be made clear.[3]

It is apparent from Parmoor's letter that MacDonald intended to follow the by now well-established practice of consulting the two Archbishops and other churchmen about each episcopal appointment, but that such consultation would continue to remain entirely unofficial. In the event he took a great deal of trouble over appointments. Lang remarked on one occasion that he had never known a prime minister who took his responsibilities in the matter so seriously as did MacDonald;[4] and Lang's chaplain-secretary, Alan Don, also found him less casual than Baldwin in his attitude to this particular duty.

MacDonald's first ecclesiastical appointment was that of George Bell, Davidson's resident chaplain, to the deanery of Canterbury in 1924. (Bell, as we have seen, was to be advanced by Baldwin five years later to the bishopric of Chichester.) The nomination was preceded by some polite procedural lobbying. Dean Wace died on 9 January. At that time Baldwin was still Prime Minister, though, as a result of the recent general election, he no longer possessed a working majority – and his position was therefore shaky. He would have liked to appoint Bell, but felt that, though he had the formal right to do so, he ought first to consult his potential successor, MacDonald, who advised against it. MacDonald became Prime Minister on 22 January and eventually appointed Bell himself – but not before considerable lobbying on behalf of other candidates, notably H. R. L. (Dick) Sheppard, the charismatic Vicar of St Martin-in-the-Fields, who was to succeed Bell as Dean of Canterbury in 1929.[5]

The initial episcopal vacancy that MacDonald was called upon to fill was Birmingham in the summer of 1924. His first nominee was unexceptionable: Canon Peter Green, Rector of St Philip's, Salford, and one of the ablest parish priests in the North of England. Green asked the Premier, however, not to make him a formal offer, as he would be obliged to decline it.* Davidson begged him to change his mind, but Green was adamant. He reminded the Archbishop that for years he had been saying in speeches, books and articles that the thing needed in the Church was a new vision of the importance and dignity of parish work. 'If I took a bishopric people would say, "Oh, of course. He praises parish work till something better comes his way."' Parish work, in Green's view, was more valuable in the long run than conferences and committees. 'I believe I am by nature best suited for pastoral and mission work. Why then take another job? . . . My heart would not be in the job. I should all the time be "homesick for the gutter".'[7]

---

*Four years earlier Green had refused the offer of the see of Lincoln. He told Davidson on that occasion that he was uneasy about episcopal palaces and incomes. The Archbishop pointed to Lambeth Palace and asked him if he felt that it was wrong. Green replied that such things were lawful but, at least for him, not expedient. Davidson then remarked, after a moment's silence: 'Do you know, such a thought had never occurred to me before!'[6]

MacDonald had to think again. The next name on his list was that of F. L. Donaldson, a residentiary canon of Peterborough Cathedral who had played an active part in Labour politics and had been described as 'one of the only men who can really preach with success to a congregation of the Labour classes'.[8] But the possession of Labour credentials, however impeccable, was not an automatic passport to high ecclesiastical office. Some of MacDonald's nominees may well have been his political supporters; but, as his secretary told one importunate cleric, ecclesiastical preferment was never dependent on political opinions but only on spiritual gifts. And any of his political colleagues who suggested that support for the Labour Party was a sufficient qualification for a bishopric were politely told to think again. MacDonald decided against Donaldson – though he did get a reward of sorts later that year in the shape of the Westminster canonry vacated by the man eventually chosen for Birmingham: Ernest William Barnes, a former Master of the Temple.

Barnes was a distinguished mathematician and scientist who had been a Fellow of the Royal Society since 1909. His name had already come before MacDonald earlier in the year in connection with the vacant deanery of Carlisle, so was fresh in his mind. And the Prime Minister would have known of him as a wartime pacifist prominent in the Union of Democratic Control. Barnes's supporters were said to include William Temple, though the origins of the appointment were in Downing Street rather than in church circles. Davidson himself had misgivings – as well he might, seeing that Barnes was theologically suspect in some quarters of the Church. This was because of his theological liberalism. He was concerned to reconcile the claims of religion and science. More than twenty years later his rejection of the miraculous in his book, *The Rise of Christianity*, was to lead to a formal vote of censure by the Archbishops of Canterbury and York. But even now there were grounds for disquiet on Davidson's part. In a letter which seems with the benefit of hindsight to be an example of whistling to keep his courage up he wrote to Russell Wakefield, the outgoing Bishop of Birmingham (he whose lack of refinement and of a university degree had caused such an upset to the authorities in Campbell-Bannerman's day) to defend Barnes's appointment:

I imagine that there will be some protest, or even outcry, in regard to his nomination, but so far as I am aware there is no real justification for regarding him as a man unsound in the Faith. On the contrary, I think he is a very genuine Christian teacher though of course on liberal lines . . . The nomination is in no way mine, but I have seen no reason to protest against it and I have a very great regard for Barnes himself and I entirely approved of his acceptance of the nomination.[9]

Davidson's fear of an outcry was justified. Barnes's nomination was attacked from both the Anglo-Catholic and the Evangelical wings of the Church. The loudest noise came from the former, although Gore, the last-but-one Bishop of Birmingham, had assured the English Church Union that Barnes was not a heretic and would give Anglo-Catholics fair play. The *Church Times* was unconvinced by such an assurance and, even before the appointment was announced, had rushed to condemn it. Barnes's modernism was notorious, the paper alleged. He was the 'constant and not too fair critic of the Catholic Revival' and had had no experience whatever in parish work. 'Is the work of the Lord to be threatened by a Bishop from whom nothing can be expected but criticism and misunderstanding?' The following week, after the appointment had been made public, the paper returned to the attack (8 August 1924). 'So long as the most important ecclesiastical appointments depend upon the caprice of statesmen who are not members of the Church of England and who can only have second-hand knowledge of the needs of the Church and of the wishes of priests and laity', it thundered, 'we must expect to be astounded, disturbed and disappointed.' The editor of the *Church Times*, Sidney Dark, a left-wing journalist who would have been on MacDonald's political wavelength, felt sufficiently incensed at this first example of his episcopal patronage to pen a personal letter of protest. The Prime Minister defended himself vigorously and, in the course of his reply to Dark, declared:

I did not know that anyone could have objected to the appointment of Dr Barnes to the Bishopric of Birmingham and I have been told that it has been received with great approval. My only interest is to put men in high position in the Church who really believe in Christianity and who regard it as a spiritual power influencing thought and conduct. If any of the ecclesiastical sections object to my appointment, the only way out of the difficulty is for the Church to cut itself off from the patronage of the State.[10]

From the Evangelical wing the objections to Barnes were argued with equal force by the ultra-Protestant *English Churchman*:

He has won a name for himself not by his affirmations, but by his denials, of the great God-given verities of our faith. Such denials seem to be a passport to promotion in these strange days to which we have come. We cannot congratulate the Prime Minister upon his first attempt to fill a Diocesan Bishopric.[11]

The appointment was received with varying amounts of enthusiasm in the secular papers, though all realized that the new bishop's 'Darwinian' views were not likely to make him universally popular. However, his consecration on Michaelmas Day in Westminster Abbey and his enthronement in his cathedral three days later passed off without incident. The predicted storms came later, Barnes being involved in many passages of arms with Anglo-Catholic priests in his diocese over the precise degree of ceremonial that was to be permitted in their churches. And his teaching was denounced publicly by G. R. Bullock-Webster, a London City rector, during a service in St Paul's Cathedral at which Barnes was billed to preach. Bullock-Webster protested against the 'false and heretical teaching' by which in his public utterances Barnes had 'denied and poured contempt upon the doctrines and sacraments of the Holy Catholic Church'. The protest was made on 16 October 1927, but by then MacDonald was out of office. By the time he returned to power in the summer of 1929 he was an older and wiser man from the ecclesiastical as well as from the political point of view. Almost all his remaining episcopal nominations were not such as to excite adverse comment. Only with his final appointment of J. W. Hunkin to Truro in 1935 did he disregard the advice of Lang and other senior churchmen. But by then he was failing both physically and mentally. With Hunkin he paid too much attention to vested interests and became altogether too emotionally involved.

In the earlier part of his second premiership, however, he made a number of significant nominations, including those of Cyril Garbett to Winchester, Mervyn Haigh to Coventry, Alfred Blunt (of Abdication fame) to Bradford and, not least, the future archbishop Geoffrey Fisher to Chester.

Garbett at first refused translation to Winchester from Southwark, and had to be coaxed into changing his mind by Archbishop Lang. He had been Lang's first choice in the list of 'possibles' he sent to the Prime Minister, the other names being Headlam of Gloucester (but at 68 'he seems to me too old')* and H. H. Williams of Carlisle. Garbett, Lang told MacDonald, was

---

*Headlam's biographer says that 'the suggestion was made to him that he might like to move there' (i.e. to Winchester), but that 'for several weeks he simply could not make up his mind'.[12] This is puzzling, as obviously no premier was going to wait for weeks while Headlam dithered. The 'suggestion' must presumably have been an unofficial sounding – or else an example of wishful thinking.

PUNCH, OR THE LONDON CHARIVARI.—MAY 22, 1929.

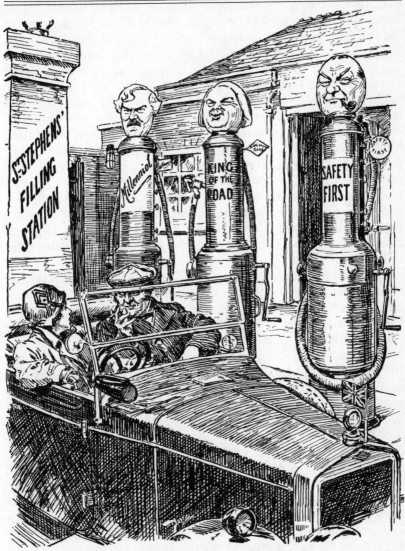

## THE SPIRITS OF THE HOUR.

WOMAN VOTER. "WHICH SHALL WE FILL UP WITH?"
JOHN BULL. "YOU CHOOSE, MY DEAR; YOU'RE DRIVING."

*MacDonald, Lloyd George and Baldwin limber up for the General Election of
1929 – won by MacDonald.*

at 57 'still in his prime' and, after having worked for thirteen years with 'unremitting energy in the difficult Diocese of Southwark', might welcome a diocese of less strain. 'It is important that he should be within easy reach of London, where his influence in the counsels of the Church and the position he has acquired in the House of Lords are important'.[13] Garbett admitted that Winchester was 'of all posts in the world what I knew I should like best', but thought at first that he ought to soldier on in his present diocese for a few more years. He was then told by both Premier and Primate that the real object of sending him to Winchester was to rest him before translating him to London when the lengthy reign there of Winnington-Ingram at last came to an end. As his biographer puts it, 'The prospect of being assigned to the task of cleansing that Augean stable – an even more herculean task than anything he had done in Southwark – was an incentive that Garbett could not possibly resist.'[14] He agreed to be, as it were, put out temporarily to grass; but his next promotion, when it came, was to be in an altogether different direction.

The nomination of Fisher to Chester came about largely through the efforts of Archbishop Temple. Fisher had been since 1914 Headmaster of Repton, the well-known public school in Derbyshire. Temple had been Fisher's predecessor as headmaster and was now chairman of the school's governing body. He pressed Fisher's claims on Lang, who bracketed him equal first with the Bishop of Gibraltar, Nugent Hicks, in his list of possible successors to H. L. Paget as Bishop of Chester. Lang dutifully sang Fisher's praises to MacDonald ('a man of very distinguished academic career at Oxford, with very broad sympathies . . . would probably make an excellent bishop'),[15] though he would really have preferred Hicks. He wrote to MacDonald's secretary, Neville Butler, after Butler had written to tell him that the post would go to Fisher: 'I am rather sorry for the Bishop of Gibraltar's sake that he has been passed over, as he finds the continuance of his present ceaseless travelling [the diocese covered all southern Europe] very bad for his health.'[16] (MacDonald made amends by appointing Hicks to Lincoln later in the year.) Fisher himself had no hesitation in accepting the Prime Minister's offer. He went through the motions of consulting Temple, but apparently wrote off to MacDonald before receiving Temple's reply. The reply, when it came, was suitably flattering. Temple wrote that he very much wanted to see Fisher in charge of a diocese. Of all the sees in the northern province, Chester would probably suit him best in its combination of town and country and in its brands of churchmanship. Temple stressed Fisher's power of mastering detail without losing sight of the main object of the exercise.[17] This talent was to stand him in good stead when he rose yet higher in the hierarchy of the Church.

Haigh's appointment as Bishop of Coventry was also made without the initial concurrence of Lang, who advised him against acceptance. In Haigh's case the objection was on practical rather than theological grounds. He had succeeded Bell as Davidson's chaplain and secretary and had continued to serve Lang as such. Lang thought that Haigh ought first to win his spurs as incumbent of some large parish. Moreover, the Archbishop was afraid lest the promotion of Haigh, following closely on that of Bell, would set a precedent, so that any future Lambeth chaplain would think that he had an automatic right to a mitre. Haigh was undeterred by the archiepiscopal scruples. After thinking and praying about the offer he decided to accept it – with Lang's eventual goodwill. Among the many messages of congratulation he received was one from Baldwin, who confessed that he had 'set my heart on seeing you at Worcester [as successor to Bishop Pearce], but it was not to be'. In the absence of Lang through illness Haigh's consecrator-in-chief was Winnington-Ingram, by whom he had, as a little boy many years before, been pushed round Amen Court on a bicycle.[18]

MacDonald's final appointment, which was to prove second only to that of Barnes in the controversy it aroused, was the nomination of the Archdeacon of Coventry, Joseph Hunkin, to the see of Truro. The difficulty arose because Hunkin's predecessor, Frere, as was only natural for a member of the Community of the Resurrection, had shown especial favour to Anglo-Catholics in the diocese. This had alienated Protestant opinion, which now urged the appointment of an Evangelical successor. Hunkin's cause was pressed by Haigh as his diocesan. Writing to Lang after Frere's resignation had been announced, he pointed out that Hunkin was a Cornishman of old Cornish family and would love to return to Cornwall. 'Of course I realize that for Hunkin to follow Frere might well set all Anglo-Catholics by the ears. But . . . the Prime Minister might have courage enough to take the obvious risks involved.' If the Prime Minister were so minded, the letter ended, 'he should not be dissuaded'.[19]

MacDonald needed little persuasion. Lang sent him a memorandum listing seven possible candidates for the vacant see. The list included Sir Edwyn Hoskyns, the New Testament scholar, and A. E. J. Rawlinson, the future Bishop of Derby; Hunkin was number four on the list.[20] But the Prime Minister responded four days later with a counter-memorandum. This dealt with principles rather than with personalities and revealed the fact that MacDonald had 'walked a good deal about Cornwall, talking to all sorts of people', so that he could claim a certain amount of inside knowledge concerning the see. He told Lang that the diocese was at present divided into two rival camps. One side was pleading that, while Frere's appointment had been a great mistake, it would be an equal mistake to choose a successor of the opposite theological hue. 'Their plea is, "Do not make too sharp a break".' The other side claimed that Frere's appointment had represented a sharp break with the tradition of his predecessor (the Evangelical Guy Warman) without any consideration of the position of the Church in Cornwall. 'I am pressed to do what they consider is my duty to restore what was then undone.' MacDonald claimed that there was great resentment among ordinary churchgoers against the Frere regime, and that it was therefore his duty to

> restore confidence amongst those whom I might describe as pre-Frere. I recognise that those who have become Dr Frere's supporters would be opposed to an appointment which, on the whole, would definitely undo the Frere tradition. If, however, that is left in possession and the diocese was ruled essentially by that, I am doubtful if peace and co-operation would be possible.[21]

In his reply to the Prime Minister's memorandum Lang attempted to pour archiepiscopal oil on the troubled Cornish waters. If it were true, he said, that a sharp break had been made when Frere was appointed, it did not follow that a similar sharp break now would be the best way of restoring harmony. 'It would mean that the confidence of a certain section would be secured at the cost of disappointing another section particularly strong among the clergy and a considerable number of laity also.' In true Anglican style Lang suggested that the best course would be to appoint 'someone who was not closely identified with any party but would exercise a moderating and I hope a spiritual influence'. Lang knew that Hunkin was very much in the Prime Minister's mind as the right choice for Truro and said that he would raise no serious objection if he were chosen.

> At the same time I might point out that Hunkin, though I know him and like him, and though I know he has many qualifications for the post, does not only show difficulty in understanding other people's points of view but combines the Low Church attitudes with very Modernist opinions on Biblical and Doctrinal matters which would not, I fear, commend him to ordinary Evangelicals or Nonconformists in the Diocese of Truro.[22]

In other words, Hunkin combined the worst of both worlds: his Low Church views would annoy High Churchmen and his Broad Church views Low Churchmen.

But the Prime Minister had really made up his mind by now to appoint Hunkin. On 20 March he had him up for an interview, 'ostensibly' (in the words of Lang's chaplain, Alan Don) 'to discuss with him as a Cornishman what sort of a Bishop Truro needs, but really to have a look at him and to talk to him like a Father about the way a Bishop ought to behave'. Having done so, 'the P.M. spent half an hour in coming to a decision to offer Hunkin the Bishopric'. Don adds:

> Hunks will of course jump at it, for he is yearning to be a Bishop. His appointment will infuriate the *Church Times,* which will regard it as the result of a Protestant conspiracy. C[osmo] C[antuar] would have preferred someone less likely to reverse the policy of Bishop Frere, but did not feel justified in attempting to override the decision of the P.M. There is no doubt that dear old Frere has managed to arouse widespread discontent in Cornwall, which has resulted in much pressure on the P.M. to appoint a man of a different way of thinking. Whether Hunks will rise to the occasion and be a moderating and reconciling influence in a rather divided Diocese remains to be seen.[23]

A fortnight later, when Hunkin's appointment had been announced, Lang wrote a consolatory letter to Frere. He reported the interview with MacDonald in which the Prime Minister had impressed upon Hunkin the necessity of harmonizing and not further antagonizing the different elements in the church life of the diocese. Hunkin's response had been 'as satisfactory as was possible'. 'In view of all this I could not undertake the responsibility of telling the Prime Minister that I disapproved of his proposal. There is much that is very good in him [Hunkin], and I think he will do his utmost to be wise and fair.'[24]

The Archbishop had to surmount one further hurdle: a request from Truro Cathedral Chapter for 'guidance and help' on whether they should 'elect' Hunkin under the royal *congé d'élire.* It was not his Evangelicalism that troubled them so much as the 'somewhat pronounced Modernist tendency of his thought and teaching . . . Regarding the Bishop as the Guardian of the Faith, our consciences have been troubled . . . We find it quite extra-ordinarily difficult to "make up our minds" and reach a decision.'[25] Lang was happy to give Hunkin a clean bill of theological health.

Nothing I have known or heard of Dr Hunkin or of his views would have led me to believe that doubt could legitimately be entertained as to his fitness on the ground of his professed faith to be elected as a Bishop . . . It would be wrong to establish such a doubt on mere grounds of rumour or impression . . . In my opinion the Chapter would not be justified in refusing Election to Dr Hunkin on the ground of any heresy. I know of no other grounds on which such a serious step ought to be taken.[26]

Let the last word in this chapter come from C. R. Self, a former Headmaster of King's School, Cambridge, who, after summarizing in verse the Prime Minister's dilemma over Truro and picturing him tossing a coin for it ('If it's tails I will put some Anglo-Cat monk in, If heads I'll appoint little Protestant Hunkin'), ended on a suitably eirenic note:

> Nay, sirs, Mother Church is not narrow and her field
> Is wide as the gulf between Ridley and Mirfield.
> You aim at one goal: that your course may be steadier
> Shun high road and low road and take Via Media.
> Just give him fair play and all prejudice smother,
> And Hunkin will prove both a man and a brother.[27]

**Nominations to diocesan bishoprics 15 (7 first appointments, 8 translations**

*First appointments:*

(1) 1924: Ernest William Barnes to Birmingham.

(2) 1930: Mervyn George Haigh to Coventry.
(3) 1931: Alfred Walter Frank Blunt to Bradford.
(4) 1932: Geoffrey Francis Fisher to Chester.
(5) 1933: Clifford Salisbury Woodward to Bristol.
(6) 1934: Geoffrey Charles Lester Lunt to Ripon.
(7) 1935: Joseph Wellington Hunkin to Truro.

*Translations:*

(1) 1930: Martin Linton Smith to Rochester (from Hereford).
(2) 1930: Charles Lisle Carr to Hereford (from Coventry).
(3) 1931: Arthur William Thomson Perowne to Worcester (from Bradford).
(4) 1932: Cyril Forster Garbett to Winchester (from Southwark).
(5) 1932: Richard Godfrey Parsons to Southwark (from Middleton).*
(6) 1932: Frederick Cyril Nugent Hicks to Lincoln (from Gibraltar).†
(7) 1934: Bernard Oliver Francis Heywood to Ely (from Hull).*
(8) 1934: John Victor Macmillan to Guildford (from Dover).*

* Suffragan see.     † Overseas see.

# 18

# More than Munich

*Neville Chamberlain: Prime Minister*
*28 May 1937 – 10 May 1940*

*Arthur Neville Chamberlain (1869–1940) was very much more than the 'Man of Munich'. He had earlier made a name for himself as an architect of social reform. The son of Joseph Chamberlain by his second wife (and therefore the half-brother of Austen), he was educated at Rugby and Mason College, Birmingham, and from 1890 to 1897 managed a family estate in the Bahamas. He returned to Birmingham as a manufacturer, entering the City Council in 1911 and serving as Lord Mayor for a year during the war. In 1916 he appeared on a wider stage as Director of National Service, and two years later was elected Conservative MP for the Ladywood division of Birmingham. He held minor office under Bonar Law and served as Minister of Health in the second Baldwin administration, making his ministry a leading department of State and a field for the realization of many of his ideas as a social reformer. He served as Chancellor of the Exchequer in the National Government of 1931–5 and succeeded Baldwin as Premier in 1937. From then on the policy of appeasement towards Hitler with which his memory is indelibly associated led to the ill-fated Munich Agreement and to the Second World War. He survived the Phoney War phase; but, when the fighting really began, his lack of drive as a war leader soon led to his replacement by Churchill. He died a few months later.*

Neville Chamberlain's name is so inevitably linked to Munich and the pre-war policy of appeasement that it is difficult to think of him in any other context. But he, too, as Prime Minister, had to choose bishops for the Church of England; and, though his total of eight is modest compared with the thirty-two apiece named by his immediate predecessor and successor, Baldwin and Churchill, at least half his nominees achieved real distinction. Chamberlain was handicapped in the eyes of the critics by the fact that he held Unitarian views. In February 1938 Lord Hugh Cecil publicly protested against the 'impropriety' of a man holding such views being permitted to appoint bishops. But in fact Chamberlain never allowed his personal religious feelings to intrude on his official ecclesiastical duties; and his policy and practice regarding church appointments carried on the tradition of his immediate predecessors. Like them he consulted the Archbishops as a matter of course before making an appointment. Occasionally his choice differed from theirs, but his nominations never excited any real controversy.

The Prime Minister had of course to tender his names to the sovereign for approval – and by now the sovereign was George VI, who had succeeded his brother after the latter's abdication in December 1936. The new king, like his father before him, was a sincerely religious man. He had been confirmed in 1912 by Bishop Boyd-Carpenter of Ripon as Clerk of the Closet. Even then he had shown a spiritual awareness that was to grow over the years, especially towards the end of his life. He was regular in his church attendance, worshipping at both Sandringham and Balmoral as a squire attending his parish church rather than as a sovereign in his private chapel. He preferred simplicity in matters of worship, though he loved the stately prose of the Book of Common Prayer. He found himself able to talk freely and without inhibitions on many religious subjects;* he tended to be more diffident when discussing the deeper religious issues. He took a proper interest over church appointments, but, so far as is known, never attempted to overrule any of his prime ministers over a particular name.

The first vacancy Chamberlain was called upon to fill was the see of Oxford in the summer of 1937. In the choice of a successor to Tommy Strong Church and State found themselves in complete agreement. The ball was set rolling by the Bishop of Chichester, George Bell, who, as a former resident chaplain to Archbishop Davidson, felt no inhibitions about suggesting names to Davidson's successor. However, he went through the motions of kowtowing to authority; and, 'greatly daring' ('Your Grace knows that I am not lacking in "cheek"'), he suggested that the ideal man for Oxford would be Kenneth Kirk, who was then Regius Professor of Moral and Pastoral Theology at the University. Kirk, Bell pointed out, was a first-class theologian, and so would be an 'immense enrichment' to a Bench which needed strengthening on its theological side. He was also pastorally-minded and had the sympathy of the clergy.[2] Lang agreed with Bell's diagnosis, though

---

*He once asked a lady sitting next to him at dinner: 'What do you think of the Ten Commandments?' It was she who was the inhibited one on that occasion![1]

he pointed out that Kirk had already refused several offers. But he put him top of the list of four names which he submitted to the Prime Minister. Chamberlain, on his side, submitted the four names to the Chancellor of Oxford University, Lord Halifax, a political colleague and, as it happened, a devout churchman. Halifax agreed that Kirk was the pick of the bunch. He was duly named as the new Bishop of Oxford and fulfilled his sponsors' hopes in every way.

The two most important sees Chamberlain had to fill were Durham and London. They turned out to be interdependent. The Bishop of Winchester, Garbett, was still considered a possibility for London (though, because of his age, no longer a certainty). The alternative candidate was the Bishop of Chester, Fisher, who in 1938 was 51 to Garbett's 63. But he was (by Church of England standards) in the prime of life, and might, it was thought, be better fitted to cleanse the 'Augean stable' of the diocese of London after Winnington-Ingram's departure than the sexagenarian Garbett.

Durham fell vacant first, Hensley Henson announcing his intention to resign in October 1938. Henson himself wanted Haigh of Coventry to succeed him, but Haigh was never a serious runner in this particular episcopal race. Temple wrote to Lang on 11 October after receiving Henson's formal notice of resignation. He said that, if Garbett were to take on London (Winnington-Ingram's resignation was now only months away), he hoped that Fisher would be chosen for Durham. This seemed to him the best arrangement, partly because, in his view, the next tenure of London should be a shortish one after Winnington-Ingram's over-long occupancy of the see and Garbett was of course very senior to Fisher. 'If, however, it is felt better to take a younger man at the very height of his vigour for London, and Chester is chosen for this, I should like to urge, as the next best candidate for Durham, the present Dean of Christ Church [A. T. P. Williams].' Temple said that it was important to have at Durham not necessarily a great scholar but a man of practical capacity who sympathized with university standards and life. 'Apart from Fisher, I see no one among the Bishops who combines these qualities in the same degree as Williams.'[3]

Lang next discussed the matter with Garbett himself. Hedging his bets he told him (according to a memorandum he wrote subsequently) that it was 'possible, perhaps even probable, that he might be asked to undertake the charge of the Diocese of London when the present Bishop resigns', but that, contrariwise, it was possible that, 'though Ramsay MacDonald had said to him when he went to Winchester that he might be wanted for London, the authorities might now think that he was too old and be anxious to get a younger man who could give a longer time of service'.[4] Lang saw the Prime Minister on 9 November and pointed out that it would be unwise to send Fisher to Durham in case he might soon be wanted for London. Chamberlain agreed with Lang that Williams would be the best alternative; and Williams was duly appointed.

When, four months later, the see of London at last fell vacant, the discussion centred on whether Garbett or Fisher should succeed Winnington-Ingram. These were the two front-runners, though the Bishop of Derby (Rawlinson) and the Bishop of Oxford (Kirk) were two possible outsiders. The qualities of all four candidates were discussed in a letter to Lang from the Prime Minister's secretary, Jasper Rootham. 'It seems agreed on all hands', said Rootham, 'that intellectually the Bishop of Chester is quite outstanding, but it is not so certain whether he has the presence and the more rugged qualities of the Bishop of Winchester.' Then, reverting to Temple's comment about the desirability of a short rather than a long tenure of the new see ('the new holder of the post would almost certainly incur some odium in the course of his duties' – i.e. in clearing up the mess left by Winnington-Ingram), Rootham observed: 'It seems to me that, unless it is intended quite definitely that the Bishop of Chester should ultimately be raised to even higher rank, to make him Bishop of London at the age of 50 [*sic*: he was actually almost 52 by now] perhaps means another long tenure for London.' As to the two outsiders, Rawlinson's churchmanship was 'rather too High' to be suitable for that required of the new Bishop of London, and Rootham had not gained the impression that he was such a 'rock-like' character as Garbett. Of Kirk 'I do not know enough to speak with any real knowledge.'[5]

At this stage the scales appeared to be evenly balanced at Downing Street between Garbett and Fisher. But, in his reply to Rootham, Lang (did he perhaps envisage the Bishop of Chester as an eventual successor to himself?) came down definitely in favour of Fisher. He saw the Prime Minister personally on 27 March, but left it to him to make the final choice. Chamberlain still hesitated, however, before taking the plunge. His doubts now centred on the spiritual as opposed to the intellectual side of Fisher's character. Lang at once took steps to reassure the Prime Minister on this point. He was able to write to Rootham on 31 March to say that he had consulted a friend of his (the canon-missioner at Chester) and that the friend was able to give Fisher a clean bill of spiritual health. He quoted a 'summary' of the canon's argument:

The Bishop is undoubtedly a man of genuine deep personal religion. His piety is that of the best type of English layman, perhaps, rather than that of the 'religious'. His reverent demeanour in celebrating in the Cathedral is most marked. His religious life is not easily seen for two reasons. (a) He is very shy and humble about it (very English), and (b) because his other gifts of intellect and administration are vastly more obvious to the world.[6]

Chamberlain was now fully satisfied that Fisher had all the requisite qualifications for London, and he was duly nominated to succeed Winnington-Ingram – though he was *not* in the end to enjoy a long tenure of the see.

Surprisingly, in view of his later reputation for reaching quick decisions, he took some time before he could make up his mind to accept the offer – and indeed, according to his official biographer, went through a long period of self-analysis and introspection which was wholly out of character and indeed led to an 'agony and travail of spirit'. He received the Prime Minister's letter on the Wednesday of Holy Week, together with a letter from Lang urging him to accept the offer. As soon as he had read the letters, Fisher records in his diary, 'I knelt down and wept like a child'. Recovering from his immediate shock (though he cannot have been really surprised at the offer, which had been widely forecast), he wrote to both archbishops protesting his inadequacy for London and seeking reassurance – which of course was forthcoming. He even, at Temple's suggestion, sought advice from the Dean of St Paul's, who would preside at his 'election'. A few days after Easter, his doubts resolved by his friends' encouragement and his own prayers, he wrote to the Prime Minister to accept his offer.[7]

The one real difference of opinion that Chamberlain had with Lang was over the appointment of a new Bishop of Rochester in 1939. The Archbishop had set his heart on the promotion of an old friend, Neville Talbot, the son of a former Bishop of Rochester and himself a former Bishop of Pretoria who was now Vicar of Nottingham. Chamberlain, on the other hand, felt that it was time to appoint an Evangelical to the Bench – which Talbot was definitely not. At least, however, the Premier was prepared to consider the claims of Talbot, so Lang enlarged on these in a letter to Rootham. 'Though I am well aware of some of his defects', he wrote, 'they are those of manner rather than of ability and personality; and, though he might not do as well in such a place as Tunbridge Wells as he would do at Chatham, I still think that he might well be entrusted with a Diocesan Bishopric.'[8]

At a personal meeting with Chamberlain in the House of Commons on 12 July Lang again pressed the claims of Talbot, though all the time conscious that his protégé's rugged rather than suave personality might not be best suited to the polite suburban tea-parties of the diocese of Rochester. 'Though I was very well aware of all that could be said on the other side', he noted after the meeting, 'I felt that he had qualities of personality which would outweigh all these disadvantages.' But, evidently sensing that the writing was on the wall for poor Talbot and that the Prime Minister might be minded to appoint some 'rather stalwart Evangelical', he suggested the Rev. C. M. Chavasse, Principal of St Peter's Hall, Oxford, as the best available.[9] In a further memorandum two days later Lang was 'sorry to say that the Prime Minister is still disinclined to appoint Bishop Neville Talbot' and was thinking instead of choosing either Chavasse or Dr Taylor of Wycliffe Hall. 'I sent a message to say that, if Talbot must be passed over, I thought that Chavasse was a stronger and more vigorous man than Taylor.'*[11] The letter helped persuade Chamberlain to think so too, and Chavasse was appointed. The unlucky Taylor was rewarded three years later (by Churchill) with the consolation prize of Sodor and Man.

Chamberlain's final appointment was that of G. Vernon Smith, Suffragan Bishop of Willesden, to the see of Leicester. The preliminary negotiations took place during the final stages of the 'Phoney War'. On 12 April, three days after that particular phase of World War II had come to an end with the German invasion of Denmark and Norway, Chamberlain wrote to Vernon Smith with his formal offer of the see. A month later, a broken man, he resigned as Prime Minister in favour of Winston Churchill.

**Nominations to diocesan bishoprics 8 (4 first appointments, 4 translations)**

*First appointments:*

  (1) 1937:  Kenneth Escott Kirk to Oxford.
  (2) 1938:  Alwyn Terrell Petre Williams to Durham.
  (3) 1939:  Leslie Stannard Hunter to Sheffield.
  (4) 1939:  Christopher Maude Chavasse to Rochester.

---

*Chavasse had won the MC in the war. The *Manchester Evening Chronicle* commented on his appointment: 'St Helens remembers the new bishop not so much as a vigorous and manly preacher in the pulpit, but as a wing three-quarter of electrifying pace who played as an amateur for several seasons before the war.' Even the *Church Times* dubbed Chavasse 'in every sense a "man's man"'.[10]

*Translations:*

(1) 1938:  Campbell Richard Hone to Wakefield (from Pontefract).*
(2) 1939:  Geoffrey Francis Fisher to London (from Chester).
(3) 1939:  Douglas Henry Crick to Chester (from Stafford).*
(4) 1940:  Guy Vernon Smith to Leicester (from Willesden).*

* Suffragan see.

# 19

# Buttress of the Church

*Winston Churchill: Prime Minister*
*11 May 1940 – 26 July 1945*
*26 October 1951 – 5 April 1955*

Sir Winston Leonard Spencer Churchill (1874–1965), *statesman, soldier and historian, enjoyed his finest hour as Prime Minister for the greater part of the Second World War and effective saviour of the nation. Born at Blenheim Palace, he was the son of Lord Randolph Churchill and grandson of the 7th Duke of Marlborough. He was educated at Harrow and Sandhurst, entering the army in 1895 and seeing service in Cuba, India, the Sudan and South Africa. In 1900 he entered Parliament as Conservative MP for Oldham, but switched to the Liberals in 1904. He was Home Secretary under Asquith and First Lord of the Admiralty at the outbreak of the First World War, but resigned over Gallipoli. Returning to office in 1917, he served for five years in the Lloyd George coalition. In 1924 he returned to the Conservative fold and was Chancellor of the Exchequer under Baldwin. He declined to serve in MacDonald's National Government as he disapproved of its Indian policy: he remained in the political wilderness until the outbreak of World War II. He served as First Lord under Chamberlain, displacing him as Prime Minister in May 1940 and eventually leading the country to victory over the Axis powers in a sequence of events that needs no retelling. Defeated in the general election of 1945, he led the opposition for the next six years. Then followed his Indian summer as Premier from 1951 until 1955, when he retired. Churchill's published works include lives of his father and of his ancestor the 1st Duke of Marlborough; multi-volume histories of the two world wars; and a four-volume* History of the English-Speaking Peoples. *He was a brilliant orator and an amateur artist of no mean talent; but it was of course as a war leader that he stood supreme.*

Archbishop Fisher, in an after-dinner speech, once referred to the great support he had received from Winston Churchill in certain ecclesiastical matters. Churchill, in replying, observed: 'I hope that, when you call me a supporter of the Church, you do not imply that I am a *pillar* of the Church. I am not. Though I might perhaps claim to be a buttress – a flying buttress, on the outside.'[1]

Churchill's religious position was far from clear-cut. He tended not to call himself a churchman, though he had too vivid a sense of history to treat with indifference the Crown nominations to bishoprics for which he was constitutionally responsible. His beliefs were perceptively summed up after his death by Fisher himself, preaching in the Dorset village church of which he had been in charge since his retirement. The late Prime Minister, he said, had had a very real religion,

> but it was a religion of the Englishman. He had a very real belief in Providence; but it was God as the God with a special care for the values of the British people. There was nothing obscure about this; it was utterly sincere, but not really linked on to the particular beliefs which constitute the Christian faith and the life which rests on it.[2]

As a bishop-maker Churchill left much to be desired. 'Evidently he knows almost nothing of the Church and its personalities', Lang recorded in his journal on 1 August 1940, as the Battle of Britain got under way. He had called on the Prime Minister to discuss the appointment of a new Bishop of St Edmundsbury and Ipswich – 'his first introduction to his ecclesiastical duties'. Churchill had just awakened from his afternoon sleep – which, said Lang, 'he regards as the best protection of his health'. Lang found his comments entertaining. 'He said very little about the business in hand, but discoursed on things in general with immense vitality as he puffed the inevitable cigar, as inevitable as Stanley Baldwin's pipe.'[3]

A year later the Archbishop found the position much the same. 'I must admit', he complained to Anthony Bevir, Churchill's patronage secretary, 'that when I had a talk with the Prime Minister on July 23rd he was apt to talk about other things, and did not give me the impression of having a very clear grasp of the appointments he had to make and the qualifications of the various persons recommended for them.' Then, with a masterly touch of understatement, he added: 'But of course I must make allowances for his immense burden.'[4]

Lang's chaplain–secretary, Alan Don, felt the same anxiety about Churchill's lack of ecclesiastical expertise. 'The worst of it is', he confided in his diary on 8 March 1941, 'that he [Winston] has no first-hand knowledge of the personnel of the Church and is apt in consequence to have "bright ideas" – e.g. Bishop Henson in the Canonry of Westminster!'[5] (That particular 'bright idea' in fact came from Churchill's aide, Brendan Bracken.) And on 28 April Don observed (à propos of the vacant bishopric of Ely): 'Unfortunately the P.M. is hopelessly out of his depth in such matters and is consequently liable to be stampeded by bright suggestions which, on further enquiry, are found to be fantastic.'[6] Six weeks later (11 June) Don recorded that 'C.C. [i.e. Cosmo Cantuar = Lang] is rather troubled about his relations with the P.M., who does not grant such opportunities of personal discussion as his predecessors have usually done'.[7] And, even when Lang *did* have a chance to talk to the Prime Minister on his own, it proved hard to bring him to the point. In his diary entry for 24 July Don reported on a lunch which Lang had had with the Prime Minister the previous day. 'Winston gave him half an hour beforehand, but talked mainly about the war, etc., and seemed reluctant to discuss the ecclesiastical affairs about which C.C. wished to speak: e.g. the appointments to no less than five vacant Bishoprics.'[8]

Churchill's total involvement in the war effort may have left him with virtually no time for dealing with ecclesiastical affairs. But it did not prevent his patronage secretary from arguing the toss with Lang's chaplain over the proper protocol to be observed over Crown appointments. Back in February 1941 Bevir had asked Don whether it would be in accordance with custom that the Prime Minister, either personally or through his secretary, should let the Archbishop of Canterbury know if he intended to make an appointment to high ecclesiastical office 'other than that recommended by the Archbishop himself'. Don subsequently wrote to Bevir:

I mentioned this point when last I saw the Archbishop, and what he said went a little further than what I told you. I said that as a matter of courtesy it had been customary for the Prime Minister to inform the Archbishop of the decision at which he had arrived before steps had been taken to make that decision effective. The Archbishop on the other hand said that it had been customary for the Prime Minister in such a case to inform the Archbishop what he had in mind, and at the same time to ask him whether he had any objection to offer. This procedure would give the Archbishop a last chance of stating any strong objections that might exist in his mind to the appointment of a particular person whom he had not personally recommended as first choice for the post in question.[9]

Don told Bevir that it would be a satisfaction to the Archbishop if this procedure could be followed by the present Prime Minister, as it had been by his predecessors. He also claimed that it was a long-established practice that the Archbishop should have a personal consultation with the Premier whenever a see became vacant. This claim was disputed by Bevir. He told Don that he had researched into the matter and had found 'several occasions' during Archbishop Davidson's time at Lambeth in which there had been no such consultation. 'While it may have been the practice in recent years, it has not been an invariable practice.'[10] Lang felt it prudent not to press the point. 'He fully appreciates the difficulties which lie in the way of personal communication with the Prime Minister at the present time', Don reassured Bevir. But, in a postscript, he said that he would send Bevir a copy of Bell's life of Davidson, so that he could read the chapter relating to that archbishop's dealings with successive prime ministers over Crown appointments.[11] Bevir thanked him for the book, but stuck to his point that two or three of the vacancies which had occurred during Davidson's reign at Lambeth had *not* been discussed in conversation with the prime minister of the day.[12]

In spite of his preoccupation with the war, Churchill did occasionally find time to put his ecclesiastical foot down (or it could be that Bevir put it down for him). A case in point occurred in August 1941, when Churchill disregarded Lang's recommendation that the Dean of St Paul's, Walter Matthews, should be made Bishop of Worcester and instead nominated Lang's second choice, W. W. Cash, General Secretary of the Church Missionary Society. His reason for rejecting Matthews, however, had something to do with the war, for it so happened that both Primate and Premier had already agreed that the Precentor of St Paul's, Canon F. O. Cockin, should be offered the see of Southwark. Churchill defended his decision to Lang thus: 'You recommend the Dean of St Paul's for the See of Worcester, but if Canon Cockin is to leave St Paul's it would leave that great Metropolitan Church, scarred as it is by enemy action, sadly equipped if the Dean too were to be removed. His task should be to stand by his post.'[13]

Paradoxically the reason for not sending Matthews to Worcester evaporated, as the offer of Southwark was turned down by Cockin on the ground that he ought to carry on the work he was doing on the church training colleges for another year or two rather than accept a see. Lang made a frantic last-ditch attempt to change Churchill's mind and persuade him to send Matthews rather than Cash to Worcester. In a letter to Bevir he pointed out that the simultaneous appointment to bishoprics of Hudson,

Secretary of SPG, and Cash, General Secretary of CMS, would deprive the two great missionary societies of their 'very capable heads' simultaneously. Lang lamented such a possibility, though adding: 'I fear I am too late in asking for this reconsideration.'[14] He was. The die was cast and the Churchillian recommendation went forward. Matthews remained at St Paul's till his retirement twenty-three years later. Cockin, however, was appointed Bishop of Bristol by Attlee in 1946.

Churchill may have had another reason for preferring to send Cash to Worcester. Cash had won a DSO in the First World War; and, as one who had himself served on the Western Front during that war, Churchill had a natural respect for gallantry. Indeed, in a letter to Bevir commenting on a recent interview he had had with the Prime Minister on another episcopal vacancy, Lang mentions Churchill's having been 'greatly impressed by the record of Bishop Hudson's military service in the last war' (Hudson had won a DSO and bar plus an MC and bar). The net result was a much-decorated trio to adorn the Bench of Bishops. In the words of Alan Don:

> The vacant Bishoprics have at last been filled . . . then follow three D.S.O.s, viz. Noel Hudson to Newcastle, W. W. Cash to Worcester and [F. R.] Barry to Southwell. Another D.S.O., Milner White, becomes Dean of York. Thus the P.M. has not only filled the vacancies with good men, but has served to demonstrate that the ranks of the clergy include not a few stalwart warriors of the last war.[15]

Lang had to fight hard for regular consultations with the Prime Minister over episcopal vacancies that arose. The man to whom the Premier *did* always turn a ready ear was his close friend and confidant, Brendan Bracken, whom he had appointed Minister of Information in 1941. Bracken, a man of shadowy antecedents and a bit of an adventurer, had travelled from Australia to England as a teenager and had persuaded the Headmaster of Sedbergh, a minor public school in Yorkshire, to admit him as a pupil at his school. He stayed only a term – sufficient for him to acquire a rudimentary coating of English culture and to describe himself as a public school man. But it was during his term at Sedbergh that he made friends with the chaplain, Neville Gorton, who introduced him to the joys of ecclesiastical history. The two would take long walks over the Yorkshire moors deep in discussion, and in return Bracken was assiduous in his attendance at services in chapel – though his latest biographer says that he has discovered no evidence that he was ever a practising member of the Church of England.[16] He was, however, always well informed on religious matters and came to acquire an encyclopaedic knowledge of the Church establishment.

Indeed he became fascinated by the whole business of appointing bishops and soon determined to make it his own particular hobby-horse and to attempt to influence the choice of candidates. Since, in the words of another biographer, 'Churchill suffered from a characteristic allergy even to discussing episcopal appointments, he was content to underwrite the opinionated decisions of his court-favourite, Brendan'.[17] But at least the court-favourite knew his facts. Sir Kenneth Grubb, later to be president of the Church Missionary Society, conceded that Bracken was an expert on bishops. 'He took this role very seriously; and his advice, presumably given direct to the Prime Minister, was to the lay judgment perceptive and usually sound.'[18] Even the sagacious Garbett was among Bracken's admirers, and defended him against those who told him that the man was a charlatan. 'Brendan Bracken recognizes goodness', Garbett noted after an evening spent in his company. 'He always attracts me. He is first-rate company, a mass of information of all sorts and kinds, a very good brain, outspoken and courageous, and he has real ideals.' Garbett noted on another occasion: 'He has an uncanny knowledge of ecclesiastical persons and affairs . . . He belongs to none of the Churches but "takes a detached interest in all, excluding the Quakers" . . . I think it is always possible he may become an R.C..'[19]

It is still a matter of debate how genuine was Bracken's religion. Garbett was obviously convinced; and John Colville, another of Churchill's private secretaries, conceded that 'Bracken has, I think, a religious temperament beneath his blasphemous exterior'.[20] There was certainly an element of the actor in his ecclesiastical interests. Lord Francis-Williams recalled how he would 'often hear him shouting down the telephone with elaborate schemes for moving church dignitaries around in a game of political and ecclesiastical chess'.[21] And, on another occasion, Eric Whelpton came into Bracken's room one day and found him studying the latest edition of *Crockford's Clerical Directory*. 'What on earth are you doing with that?', he enquired. 'Looking up one of your imaginary relations?' 'Nothing like that, Eric', replied Bracken. 'I'm simply getting *Crockford*'s by heart. Believe it or not, I'm doing the same thing with *Who's Who*.'[22]

One of Bracken's first suggestions was that Hensley Henson, who had retired the previous year as Bishop of Durham, should be appointed to a vacant canonry of Westminster Abbey. Colville noted in his diary for 11 July 1940: 'I went to see the Dean of Westminster, who jumped at it.'[23] The appointment turned out to be a complete fiasco. Henson's poor health and failing eyesight caused him to resign the canonry within a few months of being installed. A more successful suggestion of Bracken's was for the appointment of his old friend of Sedbergh days, Neville Gorton, to succeed Mervyn Haigh as Bishop of Coventry in 1943. Gorton was by now Headmaster of Blundell's School, Tiverton, and in his mid-fifties – still young by Church of England standards. Bevir felt that a youngish man was needed to oversee the task of building a new cathedral to replace the one destroyed in the blitz of 1940. The other possible candidates were all in their sixties. Bracken mentioned Gorton's name to Bevir and sang his praises. Temple shared Bracken's enthusiasm, and Churchill was happy to go along with this chorus of approval and appoint Gorton to the vacant see.

In the summer of 1941 Archbishop Lang began to give serious thought to his own resignation. He told Garbett that he dreaded staying on after his usefulness had come to an end, and that he would rather resign at the height of his powers (he was now 77). He was, however, anxious about his successor. He felt that Temple was the only possibility, but that the Prime Minister, knowing little about the Church and being self-willed over appointments, might be frightened off him as too left-wing. Garbett agreed that, in spite of his lack of judgement, Temple was 'head and shoulders above everybody else'.[24] Afterwards he wondered if the purpose of this conversation had been not only to elicit his support for Temple but to make it plain to him that he could not expect promotion to Canterbury for himself. 'My name might easily be suggested as an alternative by those who objected to Ebor, as I am known through my attendance at the Lords. But of course it would be absurd for me at 66 to think of such an appointment.'[25] (Temple was five years his junior.) Three weeks later he discussed the matter with Fisher, who (Garbett records in his diary) agreed that Temple was the obvious successor. Fisher added, however: 'I wish *you* could have been Archbishop for a few years. William's prophetic gifts may be quenched if he has to speak for the whole Church.'[26]

Fisher himself was already beginning to be spoken of as a possible for Canterbury, his claims being pressed on Churchill by an influential section of the Conservative Party. A third alternative at one time had been Bell of Chichester; but he for various reasons was now considered out of the running. Don had recorded in his diary a few months earlier, in the course of speculating on Lang's successor: 'At one time I thought, and others thought, that George Cicestr: would run Ebor: close – but

not now, much as I admire our George's great abilities.'[27] Three
months later Don was still of the same conclusion: 'George
Cicestr: is hopelessly out of the running, though I did not think so
ten years ago.' Don thought Temple's claims to the succession
'emphatic', though he foresaw the problem: 'The P.M., prompted
by all the "Colonel Blimps" among his Conservative friends, will
probably shy at the suggestion. But what alternative can he
propose?'[28]

Temple was in truth by far the strongest candidate for
Canterbury. As his biographer puts it:

No other bishop possessed in equal measure his many
qualifications – a temperament exactly adapted to varied
human relationships, unusual stamina, immense powers of
concentration, a conveniently mediating mind which was yet
without smudges, exceptional lucidity in teaching and speaking,
a deep devotional life, a wide knowledge of the history of the
Church and State, a great reputation among the continental
and American Churches and in the Anglican Communion
overseas, and a fund of learning on which he seemed at all
times to draw with accuracy and ease.* He was the most
enlightened bishop in the National Church.[29]

Bernard Shaw remarked that, to a man of his generation, 'an
Archbishop of Temple's enlightenment was a realized impossibil-
ity'.[30] And even Churchill in the end came to the conclusion (as
he told Attlee) that Temple, for all his Socialist ideas, was the
'only half-a-crown article in a sixpenny bazaar'.[31]

By September Lang had made up his mind to announce his
resignation in January 1942, to take effect at the end of March.
'The P.M. will be annoyed with him', Don wrote in his diary, 'but
C.C. wisely feels that he cannot allow the matter to drag on
indefinitely.'†[33] It was a further two months before the
Archbishop told Churchill of his decision to resign. 'C.C.'s talk
with the P.M. passed off well', says Don. 'There seems to be little
doubt that he will consider William Ebor: favourably for the

---

*Among his many other talents Temple had a photographic memory, inherited from
his father, which enabled him to remember what a page of printed words looked
like, and never to forget it. He could quote long passages from memory without a
mistake. Peter Green once asked him whether, when he read a book, he learned it by
heart. 'Oh, no', said Temple with a laugh. 'But I can generally remember the position
on the page and can see it before me.'

†Don pays tribute to Lang's 'stern sense of duty' which had prompted his decision to
resign. 'It can be no fun to contemplate a future of obscurity and loneliness after
being in the centre of things for so many years. He has come to the conclusion that he
is doing what is right in the circumstances – and that settles the question.'[32]

succession.'[34] It was not, however, until mid-February that Temple's appointment was actually announced – to the relief of Don, 'for the delay was giving opportunity to ill-informed or prejudiced people of putting pressure on the P.M. to keep William Ebor: out owing to his "advanced" views etc.'.[35]

There remained the archbishopric of York to fill – and here Garbett was an obvious candidate. He discussed the possibility dispassionately in his diary. 'It may be thought wise to put in an older and more cautious man to balance Temple, and one who could not possibly be the third in succession to go from York to Canterbury.'[36] Don, writing in *his* diary, thought it more than a possibility. 'As to York, Cyril Winton: will probably be pressed to go there in order to give balance to the team – this would pacify those who wish to see him at Canterbury as a good safe man. But he is not really so "safe" as the advocates of the status quo suppose!'[37]

When the offer actually came, Garbett at first hesitated whether to accept. 'Poor Winton: is most reluctant to move', Don complained in his diary.[38] Garbett brooded over the matter for several days. He was not helped by an article in the left-wing *Tribune* which stated bluntly: 'Dr Garbett might have made a good Primate in the Boer War. He is an old-fashioned Liberal. He is overdue for superannuation!'[39] He consulted Lang and Temple, who both urged acceptance. Garbett bowed to the call of duty and said Yes. The announcement of the nominations to the two archbishoprics appeared in the papers on 23 February. 'Thus the P.M. has been guided', wrote Don, 'as I hope and believe, aright by C.C. and others. The Diehards and "Blimps" will not be pleased about W.E. – but the days of the advocates of "safety first" and the status quo and "back to normality" are numbered.'[40] Churchill's half-crown article was now safely installed at Lambeth – and the Church of England seemed set for a brave new era under his leadership.

A few months after his enthronement at Canterbury Temple received an embarrassing letter from the Archbishop of Perth, Henry Le Fanu, writing in his capacity of Primate of the Church of England in Australia. It concerned a fellow-archbishop, William Wand of Brisbane, a former Oxford don who had come out from England in 1934 and had now served eight years in his Australian see. The burden of Le Fanu's letter was that Wand, an Anglo-Catholic, had alienated many of his leading clergy and laity by his intolerance. 'He has no time for anyone who really differs from him – in other words, he might be a good leader of a Party, but he is not in the least suited to the conditions which must govern the behaviour of a Bishop out here.' Le Fanu asked Temple if it would be possible to tempt Wand back to Britain with an offer, probably academic, 'which he could accept without serious loss of dignity'.[41] Temple sat on the letter for weeks. When eventually he could bring himself to reply he pointed out to Le Fanu that, 'as you know quite well, one cannot create the opportunities for the kind of offer that you contemplate: but they may arise at any time, and I will promise to keep my eyes open'.[42]

As it happened, an opportunity had arisen a few weeks before he wrote his letter. The Bishop of Bath and Wells, Francis Underhill, had died in January 1943. A successor was sought, and Wand's name was being canvassed – by Brendan Bracken. Bracken of course knew nothing of Le Fanu's letter to Temple. Wand's name had been brought to his attention in a completely different context: as the author of a patriotic pamphlet, *Has Britain Let Us Down?*, in which he rebuked the growing section of Australian opinion which was belittling Britain's part in the war and blaming her for the precarious position now facing Australia. Bracken noted and approved Wand's spirited defence of the mother country, which had helped to calm down the wave of anti-British feeling in Australia following the fall of Singapore. He thought that such a splendid patriot should be rewarded with the offer of an English see, and pressed his name on Churchill.

Temple was in a dilemma. He did not know Wand well, though he had thought him, when a don at Oxford, able but narrow in sympathy and a little overbearing. He did not feel free to forward Le Fanu's highly confidential letter to the Prime Minister; but, he assured Le Fanu, 'I did press upon those responsible that they should do their utmost to investigate the extent to which he [Wand] had got across the people of his diocese and the occasion for this.'[43] He also, of course, suggested other names to Downing Street – including a number of suffragan bishops. Eventually the short-list was whittled down to the Bishop of Sherborne, H. N. Rodgers; the Dean of Winchester, E. G. Selwyn; and Wand. With Bracken lauding him to Churchill as a fire-eating patriot, Wand was an easy winner. At least, however, the authorities had done what Temple had asked and made enquiries locally. 'Archbishop Wand is a man of independence and scholarship who has made a reputation for himself in Australia by his public utterances', Bevir assured Temple. 'There were suggestions that he has been a little too outspoken, but it may well be that conditions in Australia required this.'[44]

To Wand himself the offer of an English diocese had come entirely out of the blue.

I was later to connect it with the British Minister of Information, Brendan Bracken, and the respect he was kind enough to express for *Has Britain Let Us Down?*. But at that time I had not the wit to put two and two together, and only felt glad that the pamphlet had evidently not done me so much harm with the authorities at home as I had feared.[45]

He had no hesitation in accepting the offer – 'It has been a merciful dispensation of Providence that I have never been in doubt about accepting or refusing any post offered to me.'[46] Wand returned home as speedily as wartime conditions permitted and took up his new responsibilities in rural England.

There was an initial spot of unpleasantness in that the confirmation of his election was opposed by the National Union of Protestants. The NUP's general director, P. W. Petter, lived at Yeovil, in Wand's new diocese, and had a brother who was a doctor in the diocese of Brisbane. He turned up in person at the ceremony in St Margaret's, Westminster, on 27 October 1943 to protest with other objectors before the Vicar-General, Sir Philip Baker-Wilbraham. A statement was read out alleging that Wand was a notorious Anglo-Catholic who practised and upheld the service of the Mass, the doctrine of transubstantiation and the reservation of the sacrament contrary to Articles 28 and 31. Petter received as short a shrift from Baker-Wilbraham as objectors to the election of Bishops Hampden, Frederick Temple and Henson had had from his predecessors in the past. The Vicar-General ruled that he could not entertain the objections* and went on with the main part of the ceremony.[47] Wand soon began to make a new name for himself.

On 26 October 1944, a bare two-and-a-half years after his enthronement, the death occurred both suddenly and unexpectedly of Archbishop William Temple. The nation at large was shattered by the news. 'His death just now', Bishop Haigh of Winchester wrote to his diocese, 'seems like a master-stroke of the evil one.'[48] Joseph McCulloch, then a radical young priest, said at Temple's funeral service in Canterbury: 'We are burying the hopes of the Church of England.'[49] And R. H. Hodgkin, Provost of Queen's College, Oxford, declared: 'Temple's death seemed to shake the Western world as if one of its pillars had been removed.'[50]

---

*Petter more than once referred to the King as Defender of the Faith, causing the Vicar-General to observe: 'You have several times in the course of your speech referred to the name of King Henry VIII. I do not like to think what would have happened to you, Mr Petter, if you had dared to object to one of that King's nominees.'

Geoffrey Fisher heard the news from a fellow-member at the House of Lords and spent an hour in silent prayer in the Bishops' Robing-Room. He said afterwards that he was 'trying to assimilate myself to a completely changed world and a completely changed Church'.[51]

Fisher was of course a leading candidate for the succession to Temple. His claim to succeed him was not, however, as strong as had been Temple's to succeed Lang. Once more both Garbett and Bell had their hats (or mitres) in the ring, the claims of Bell being especially convincing. A fourth possibility was Mervyn Haigh, who had been translated from Coventry to Winchester three years before and who, as a former resident chaplain at Lambeth, had an intimate knowledge of the central councils of the Church. Many years before, Davidson had assured an enquirer: 'Haigh could be Archbishop of Canterbury tomorrow.'[52] But Haigh was highly-strung by temperament; he was apt to be indecisive or negative in his decision-making; and his health was none too good. His name was seriously considered by Churchill, however, and he was invited to lunch at 10 Downing Street.

If Garbett had been a serious candidate to succeed Lang in 1942, his claims were less strong three years later. He was now 69 and contemplating retirement. He told Lang: 'What is really out of the question is a man who will be 70 next year going to Canterbury . . . it would be absurd.'[53] In the end it boiled down to a choice between Fisher and Bell. Temple had seen Fisher as his natural successor. 'I must give up in time to let Geoffrey have his whack', he remarked to his wife on one occasion.[54] As Bishop of London Fisher had shown himself a brilliant administrator in coping with the muddle left behind by his predecessor. He was a hard worker, with a businesslike approach to problems. He attracted people by his friendliness, good-humour and absence of pomposity. But he would hardly have claimed to be a prophet, of the kind which many churchmen considered essential for the post-war era. That role sat more easily on George Bell, his rival for the primacy.

Bell had certainly travelled a long way since the time nearly twenty years before when Sidney Dark, the then editor of the *Church Times*, writing anonymously about him, had described him as 'bustling, eager, almost too obviously ambitious . . . diplomatic, courteous and the inheritor of the tradition of comprehensiveness and peace at any price'.[55] He was now a marked man as far as Churchill was concerned – marked with the Prime Minister's disapproval for his wartime speeches in the House of Lords denouncing as immoral the RAF's 'obliteration bombing' offensive. Don noted in his diary: 'The Prime Minister admires courage and deplores indiscretion; and George has been both courageous and indiscreet in his speeches about the war.'[56] When Liddell Hart, the military historian, wrote to Bell to tell him that he was the man best fitted to succeed Temple he added:

> I hardly imagine that . . . the Prime Minister is a big enough man to recognise the value of such an appointment and swallow his resentment of your attitude to the war. It is a supreme tribute to you that your honesty will have cost you the chance of attaining the supreme position in the Church – but it is also a sad reflection on the nation and its leaders.[57]

Replying to Liddell Hart a few days later, Bell wrote: 'I have no illusions about Churchill's attitude to me – he is the last man to put me in any position of greater influence.'[58]

In fact Bell's opposition to aspects of the British war effort which he considered morally wrong was not the only thing that cost him the primacy. In the 1930s, speaking with all the authority of an ex-chaplain to Archbishop Davidson, he had made himself unpopular in some quarters by urging a reform of Church–State relations in England. And he sometimes offended members of the House of Lords by the manner as well as by the matter of his speaking: he gave the impression of lecturing or preaching to his audience. So, in spite of his great reputation abroad as well as at home, he paid the price of his outspokenness and stayed put at Chichester – though, as one writer put it, 'being the senior clergyman in Sussex cannot be martyrdom'.[59]

For Fisher meanwhile the day of glory was about to dawn. He too was summoned to Downing Street to lunch with the Prime Minister. 'It was a funny lunch', Fisher recalled afterwards. 'He was obviously not at all at ease; I was certainly not. But we got on very contentedly and talked about many things, including religion . . . I think probably he said to himself at the end: "Well, presumably he'll have to do!"'[60] So the ex-headmaster rather than the prophet was chosen for Canterbury; and, in the oft-quoted words of Donald MacKinnon, 'The historian of the Church of England may yet recognise that the worst misfortune to befall its leadership at the end of the war was less the premature death of William Temple than his succession by Fisher of London and not by Bell of Chichester.'[61] That must remain a matter of opinion. The burden of being an archbishop could well have lessened Bell's effectiveness on the ecumenical stage, for which his lighter work in Sussex gave him the necessary leisure. Moreover, as Fisher's *Church Times* obituary put it, 'The hand of providence can be seen in giving the Church an administrator when the work of the prophet [i.e. Temple] was done.'[62]

One of Fisher's first tasks as Primate was to guide the Prime Minister's choice of a new Bishop of London. After taking counsel with Garbett, he sent Bevir a short-list of four names to show Churchill. At the top of the list was George Bell, whom Fisher must have known had been his main rival for Canterbury. Here was an obvious chance of making amends with the offer of the third senior post in the Church – though neither archbishop was over-sanguine about the chance of Bell's being any more acceptable for London than he had been for the primacy.

Garbett wondered in fact how far Churchill personally had really made up his mind against him, or whether it was Bevir who had hesitated about mentioning his name. He told Fisher that Bell was clearly the right man for London.

> His semi-political utterances have prejudiced him. As you know, I disagree with most of them profoundly. But in two or three years, when peace has come, his less wise remarks will have been forgotten, and he will be remembered on the Continent as the man who above all others did his utmost for the refugees and the destitute, and who urged that we should show mercy to Germany.[63]

Fisher agreed. He told Bevir that, in spite of Bell's wartime utterances and a queer streak of obstinacy in his nature, 'he might well be really in the long run the best appointment'. In second place Fisher put Mervyn Haigh of Winchester and in third place the Bishop of Bristol, Clifford Woodward, who was elderly but shrewd and sagacious. Bottom of the list was William Wand, with some headmasterly criticism attached to his name: 'I doubt whether yet he has got the feel of things at home . . . he would not carry the trust nor has he quite the spiritual equipment which belongs to the other three.' In spite of having given top marks to Bell, Fisher hedged his bets by telling Bevir that he would be 'very satisfied' with either Bell or Woodward – 'I find it hard to give a final decision between them.'[64]

The list of names was sent to Bevir on 17 January 1945, a fortnight after Fisher's nomination to Canterbury. But Churchill, involved as he was in master-minding the closing stages of the war, took his time in replying. It was not until 14 March that he wrote back briefly to Fisher. He made no reference to either Bell, Haigh or Wand; pointed out that Woodward was 67, and that there must therefore be 'some doubt about his suitability for this heavy task'; and asked the Archbishop for some more names to consider.[65] Fisher assumed, rightly, that the Prime Minister had decided against Bell – and told the bishop so when they met by chance in London. Bell wrote the next day to express his dismay:

> What troubles me is that, at a time when the Church is being tested in a severe way – as well as criticised – although you as Archbishop are convinced in your own mind that a particular person is the best person from the point of view of the Church for the difficult and responsible office of Bishop of London, you should let the case go without a vigorous effort to give effect to your conviction, because of 'political' objections raised by the Prime Minister and Buckingham Palace.[66]

Fisher was hurt by Bell's implied reproach to himself. He wrote back to explain that Bell's had not been the only name on his list. 'What was greatly felt was that you were one of the two best people from the point of view of the Church: on that there was agreement. But it did not go beyond that, and my representation was in that form . . . It was the judgment of myself and of others, and for it I am prepared to press vigorously.'[67]

Matters dragged on for weeks without a decision being reached in Downing Street. It eventually came down to Woodward v. Wand. Brendan Bracken took Wand out to lunch and asked him whether, if offered London, he would accept. Wand said Yes – and assumed that the official invitation would soon follow. But more weeks went by before he was summoned to lunch with the Prime Minister. 'He was very distrait', Wand recorded in his autobiography, 'with his mind evidently on the [Cabinet] discussions he had just left.' Although the table-talk eventually got round to religion (Bracken and Bevir were also present), not a word was said about London.[68] After that there was, for Wand, another period of waiting.

On 31 May Garbett saw Bevir to discuss the position. He reported afterwards to Fisher:

> He [Bevir] said the Prime Minister was inclined to appoint Bath and Wells as the younger man [than Woodward]. I said that if he did so he would be acting against the advice we had both given . . . that, if there was widespread criticism of the appointment, it would put you in a difficult position, as people would naturally think that you approved. I thought Bevir was shaken by this.

As Garbett said good-bye to Bevir outside No. 10, Bracken arrived for a Cabinet meeting. He took the Archbishop aside and asked about London. 'I repeated what I had said to Bevir, adding that it was only right and fair that the new Archbishop of Canterbury should have at London someone who he knows he could work with. Bracken . . . said: "Yes, I think you are right. It will have to be Bristol."' There followed a curious incident – what Garbett, in his letter to Fisher, described as a 'queer story':

> As I was walking across the Guards Parade I heard hurried steps behind me. I looked round and found Bevir, who had come out by the back way to catch me up. He said to me, 'Brendan is out of favour, there has been a big row. I do not want you to think that he has influence. Whatever he says will be sure to have the opposite effect: if anything happens you must not think it has been due to his influence'!![69]

Whether or not the story about Bracken was true, the net result was that Churchill stuck to his choice of Wand for London. He justified the choice to Fisher by claiming that he would 'find it difficult to commend to the King Dr Bell of Chichester', and that a commendation of Woodward 'would be open to public criticism' (presumably on the score of his age). In preferring Wand, the Prime Minister added smugly, 'I am not without responsible advice in the Church.'[70] Bevir excused himself to Fisher afterwards by saying that he had been away when the Prime Minister had made his decision. 'I did tell him very plainly indeed what your views and what Dr Garbett's were, and that you had misgivings about it.'[71]

Wand again had a baptism of fire to undergo before he could get down to his new duties. At the ceremony for the confirmation of his election 'Mr Petter and his merry men made an even more vociferous objection than before. This time they penetrated to the service itself and shouted their dislike of me even through the prayers, barely allowing a moment's lull while I gave the blessing.' Wand had the grace to allow that the demonstration underlined one of the reasons why the ecclesiastical authorities had been so hesitant about his nomination. At his enthronement a few weeks later the protesters were out in greater force. 'When my car reached St Paul's', says Wand, 'there was a howling mob around the forecourt, with the police trying to keep open an avenue for the arriving congregation.'[72] Wand soon lived down the opposition to his appointment and developed into an able and popular Bishop of London. Even Garbett, who had opposed his nomination, told him years later: 'I know now that I made a mistake.'[73] So Churchill, with or without the prompting of Bracken, had made the right decision in preferring Wand to the more elderly Woodward.

A few weeks after Wand's appointment the Conservatives were defeated in the general election and Churchill found himself out

of office. It was over six years before he was returned to power –
and again had the opportunity to be a bishop-maker. But by this
time he was advanced in years and took even less interest than
before in this side of his duties. Bevir, by now overseeing
patronage and nothing else, was at his side to pull the necessary
strings on his master's behalf.

As Fisher put it in a memorandum he drew up in 1956:

> Winston Churchill knew nothing. I settled the whole thing
> with Bevir securing my own order of preference, knowing that
> when my letter got to Winston Bevir would support it and
> Winston accept it. Winston grumbled once or twice if I put up
> a person who appeared to be merely a scholar, but in fact he
> always accepted the name and all was well.[74]

One of the first problems with which Fisher had to deal
occurred within a few weeks of Churchill's return to Downing
Street. Mervyn Haigh had resigned as Bishop of Winchester; but
the problem concerned not so much the choice of his successor as
the right of the Dean and Chapter of Winchester to play a more
than nominal part in the process of 'electing' that successor.
Fisher's chaplain, Eric Jay, recorded a telephone conversation he
had had with Bevir concerning a request from the Dean and
Chapter to add to their petition to the King for a *congé d'élire*, a
statement about the needs of the diocese. Bevir had phoned to get
some advice from the Archbishop. His point was that, though the
formal petition for a licence was undoubtedly historical, a
representation about the needs of the diocese was something new
– and that there should therefore be no hurry to do what might be
taken as a precedent. Jay agreed with him that the addition to the
petition should be put as informally as possible.[75]

The most significant of Churchill's later appointments was
that of a new Bishop of Durham to succeed A. T. P. Williams –
the former Dean of Christ Church, Oxford, who had been
preferred to Fisher for the see in 1938 and who had now
succeeded Haigh at Winchester. Various names were discussed
in correspondence between the two Archbishops. Garbett
suggested 'without any great enthusiasm' Chavasse of Rochester,
whose translation would please the Evangelicals. Chase of Ripon
would be 'ideal in many ways', but there seemed no good reason
for moving him.[76] Six weeks later Garbett came up with some
more names, including Rawlinson of Derby and the Dean of
Winchester, E. G. Selwyn. The first mention of the future primate,
Michael Ramsey, came a week later, when Garbett reported that
both the outgoing Bishop and the Dean and Chapter of Durham
would like his name considered. He had 'won the respect and

affection of clergy of all schools of thought, and of lay people too, to a remarkable degree'. Garbett had his doubts, however. Ramsey was a very good scholar with an original mind, but he wondered whether he had the administrative gifts or 'sufficient practical common sense' (Ramsey was notorious for his absent-mindedness) for a diocese like Durham. Moreover, said Garbett, Ramsey had only recently been appointed to a professorial chair at Cambridge. Other alternatives would be Cockin of Bristol (though he was often 'apocalyptic over minor matters') and Kenneth Riches, the Principal of Cuddesdon. He suggested Riches, Cockin and Ramsey as the three names to put before the Prime Minister.[77]

It was another two months, however, before Fisher wrote to Churchill. He put *his* three names before the Prime Minister – Ramsey, Chase and Cockin – but said that 'no one of them for various reasons claims absolute precedence over the other two'. Ramsey, he told Churchill, he had known intimately ever since he had been a pupil of his at Repton. He put the pros and cons fairly enough and left it to the Premier to decide. 'He [Ramsey] is outstanding both for his theological ability and for his personal saintliness of character.' But he had been Regius Professor at Cambridge for less than two years, and Fisher could not tell how well he would do the 'purely administrative work which inevitably falls upon a Bishop'.[78] Fisher could have added that Ramsey was a definite Anglo-Catholic, though in no sense partisan, so that his appointment might offend Protestant opinion in the Church. However, Bevir had been busy at Durham taking soundings, and it seemed that Ramsey's nomination would be popular locally. In the words of his official biographer, 'Churchill, confronted by a choice between a totally safe appointment and an exciting gamble, would have no doubts.'[79] On 30 May the formal offer was made to Ramsey; and, after a few days for thought and consultation, he accepted it. 'The Lord works in mysterious ways!', he told a friend he met in the street at Cambridge. 'I am to be Bishop of Durham.'[80] The choice turned out to have been inspired.

Every so often Geoffrey Fisher reverted to being a headmaster. A case in point was over the appointment of Leonard Wilson as Bishop of Birmingham. Wilson had been a heroic figure as Bishop of Singapore during the Second World War and, while a prisoner in Japanese hands, had been an inspiration to all around him. Since 1949 he had been Dean of Manchester; but he was ripe for a move, and Fisher had no hesitation in recommending him to the Prime Minister as Barnes's successor at Birmingham.

Churchill, ever keen to recognize gallantry, needed little prompting, and the offer was duly made.

Now came the rub. Wilson, after consulting his own diocesan, W. D. L. Greer, and discovering that the Archbishop both knew and approved the offer, wrote back to accept it. But he did so without consulting Fisher direct; and the ex-headmaster was not best pleased. On 9 June he wrote to Wilson to say that he hoped that Wilson would neither decline nor accept the invitation without a reference to himself. 'The Prime Minister is, in fact, acting upon the advice which I gave to him: but the problem is one so prickly that it deserves full consideration.'[81] Alas for Fisher's hopes! By the time his letter reached Wilson, the offer had already been accepted. Wilson had now perforce to grovel. He wrote back to Fisher to confirm that he had accepted the offer on the assumption that it had been sent with the Archbishop's approval and goodwill.[82] At first Fisher stood on his dignity. He asked Greer gently to point out to Wilson that this was not a matter in which he ought to rest upon assumptions, and that it had been a 'real error of judgement' on Wilson's part to accept the offer without reference to the Archbishop. 'I do not want to rub it in myself any more than my letter by implication did', Fisher told Greer, 'but I think he ought to be told by you that it was a grave discourtesy if nothing else to one who would become his Metropolitan.'[83]

Greer duly did as instructed and hauled Wilson 'gently' over the coals. Wilson wrote again to Fisher, assuring him that very few things had distressed him so much over his new appointment as to 'hear from my bishop of your displeasure that I had not consulted you before accepting'.[84] This second grovel was sufficient to calm Fisher down. He replied to Wilson in his own handwriting, thanking him for having apologized so generously and assuring him that 'we can now most cheerfully forget the matter altogether'.[85] Wilson's biographer sums up the whole trivial but revealing episode thus: 'Those who have worked in a school know it is unwise for assistant masters to assume that they know what is in the headmaster's mind.'[86]

**Nominations to diocesan bishoprics 32 (12 first appointments, 20 translations)**

*First appointments:*

(1) 1940: Richard Brook to St Edmundsbury and Ipswich.
(2) 1941: Frank Russell Barry to Southwell.

(3) 1941: William Wilson Cash to Worcester.
(4) 1941: Harold Edward Wynn to.Ely.
(5) 1941: Wilfred Marcus Askwith to Blackburn.
(6) 1942: John Ralph Strickland Taylor to Sodor and Man.
(7) 1943: Neville Vincent Gorton to Coventry.
(8) 1944: Clifford Arthur Martin to Liverpool.

(9) 1952: Arthur Michael Ramsey to Durham.
(10) 1953: Arthur Stretton Reeve to Lichfield.
(11) 1953: Ronald Ralph Williams to Leicester.
(12) 1954: Harry James Carpenter to Oxford.

*Translations:*

(1) 1941: Richard Godfrey Parsons to Hereford (from Southwark).
(2) 1941: Noel Baring Hudson to Newcastle (formerly of Labuan and Sarawak).†
(3) 1941: Bertram Fitzgerald Simpson to Southwark (from Kensington).*
(4) 1941: William Louis Anderson to Portsmouth (from Croydon).*
(5) 1941: Percy Mark Herbert to Norwich (from Blackburn).
(6) 1942: William Temple to Canterbury (from York).
(7) 1942: Cyril Forster Garbett to York (from Winchester).
(8) 1942: Mervyn George Haigh to Winchester (from Coventry).
(9) 1942: Henry Aylmer Skelton to Lincoln (from Bedford).*
(10) 1943: John William Charles Wand to Bath and Wells (from Brisbane).†
(11) 1944: Philip Henry Loyd to St Albans (from Nasik, India).†
(12) 1945: Geoffrey Francis Fisher to Canterbury (from London).
(13) 1945: John William Charles Wand to London (from Bath and Wells).

(14) 1952: Alwyn Terrell Petre Williams to Winchester (from Durham).
(15) 1953: John Leonard Wilson to Birmingham (formerly of Singapore).†
(16) 1953: Wilfred Marcus Askwith to Gloucester (from Blackburn).
(17) 1954: Arthur Harold Morris to St Edmundsbury and Ipswich (from Pontefract).*
(18) 1954: Benjamin Pollard to Sodor and Man (from Lancaster).*
(19) 1954: Walter Hubert Baddeley to Blackburn (from Whitby).*
(20) 1954: Gerald Alexander Ellison to Chester (from Willesden).*

* Suffragan see.
† Overseas see.

# 20

# Men of Business

*Clement Attlee: Prime Minister*
*26 July 1945 – 26 October 1951*

Clement Richard Attlee, 1st Earl Attlee (1883–1969), *was the Labour Prime Minister responsible for laying the foundations of the Welfare State in Britain. The son of a London solicitor, he was educated at Haileybury and University College, Oxford. He was converted to Socialism through his experience of working in an East End social settlement. He was called to the Bar in 1905, lectured on social science at the London School of Economics and served in the army in the First World War, retiring with the rank of major. He entered Parliament in 1922 as member for the Limehouse division of Stepney and held minor office in MacDonald's two Labour ministries. He broke with MacDonald following the financial crisis of 1931 and the formation of a National Government, and in 1935 succeeded George Lansbury as leader of the Labour Party. He was a loyal member of Churchill's wartime coalition, serving as Deputy Premier from 1943 to 1945. His finest hour followed Labour's overwhelming victory in the 1945 general election, when he found himself the first Labour Prime Minister to enjoy an independent majority in the Commons. As such, besides granting independence to India, Pakistan, Burma and Ceylon, he was able to steer through Parliament the massive programme of social reform and nationalization which formed the basis of the Welfare State. After Labour's defeat in the 1951 general election he once again led the opposition in the Commons. He retired at the end of 1955, when he received an earldom. Attlee proved himself one of the greatest of Britain's peacetime prime ministers, displaying unexpected powers of leadership besides consummate administrative skill.*

Many people regarded Clement Attlee, with his perpetual pipe and his air of benign and shrewd elder-statesmanship, as a prototypical Anglican. They were wrong. Although he had gone through the motions of being confirmed at school, he never regarded himself as a professing Christian. It was social conscience, not Christianity, that had led him into politics and the Labour Party. In this respect he was the odd man out of his family. His parents, brothers and sisters were deeply convinced Christians. Not so Clem. He had to attend church regularly with the rest of the family, but was bored to tears by the services. He was good at assimilating facts, however, even religious facts, and left his prep school knowing so many of the names, dates and places to be found in the Old Testament that he was assumed by some people to be 'religious-minded' (he won top marks in a local diocesan examination). It was when he went on to Haileybury that he formally abandoned his belief in God, though he continued to share his parents' high sense of moral and social responsibility. Confirmation meant nothing to him: 'So far as I was concerned, it was mumbo-jumbo.'[1] In a revealing interview with Kenneth Harris towards the end of his life, when he might have felt disposed to modify his agnosticism, he could still affirm: 'I'm one of those people who are incapable of religious experience.' He believed in the ethics of Christianity, but not in the 'mumbo-jumbo'. When asked whether he was an agnostic, however, he replied, 'I don't know'; and, to a question whether he thought there was an after-life, 'Possibly'.[2]

In spite of being a non-believer, Attlee was passionately interested in ecclesiastical affairs – including Crown appointments and the exercise of his patronage, which he took very seriously. He had no small talk, and one friend remarked that it was very difficult to have a relaxed discussion with him on any subject except bishops or cricket. He always took a personal interest in episcopal nominations and had plenty of ideas of his own. Thus, when the name of John Groser, a well known radical priest working in the East End, was mentioned as a possibility for a bishopric, he wrote to his brother Tom: 'I know Groser and have considered him. But I am inclined to think him a bit of an advertiser and not quite the quality for a Bishop. There seems today to be a dearth of really able Socialist parsons such as we knew in our younger days.'[3] Three years later he was consulting Tom (who lived in Cornwall) about the choice of a successor to the Bishop of Truro, Hunkin, who had just died. 'The Archbishop is away in Australia, but I shall begin looking round soon. What elevation is desirable now? Something in the middle, I should think, as you have rather swung from one extreme to another recently' (i.e. from the High Church Frere to the Low Church Hunkin). A few weeks later he wrote to Tom: 'I've been looking over the runners for the Truro stakes. I can't do anything until the Archbishop returns.'[4]

Fisher found Attlee an admirable person with whom to do business. Both were eminently practical men and not accustomed to beating ineffectually about the bush. 'I generally settled matters on an agreed short-list in a personal conversation with Attlee', the Archbishop wrote in 1956 in a private memorandum.[5] There were occasional 'tangles' resulting in long delays over particular appointments, but these were as often as not the fault of Anthony Bevir, Attlee's appointments secretary, and not of the Prime Minister himself. Bevir's position in the Downing Street secretarial hierarchy was now much more assured. He had joined the team at No. 10 in 1940, beginning as one of Chamberlain's private secretaries and continuing in that capacity under Churchill and Attlee. In the early days there was no clear allocation of duties, but over the years Bevir found himself concentrating more and more on ecclesiastical work. In 1947 it was thought desirable that a single secretary should advise on all appointments which lay within the prime minister's prerogative; and Bevir was given this particular portfolio. Part of his duties consisted in going round the country to see people and collect opinions – and in the process to compile a useful dossier of men deserving consideration for appointment as bishops. He became a storehouse of facts, figures and judgements about the clergy (Attlee called him a 'walking *Crockford*'). Indeed, so thorough were his methods and so massive his intelligence system that he caused some minor misgivings among leading churchmen. Gerald Ellison, who rose to be Bishop of London but was once chaplain to Cyril Garbett at both Winchester and York, recalled many years afterwards that Garbett, 'while recognizing the debt which the Church owed to Bevir's skill and sense of duty and admiring his devotion, at the same time expressed some fear lest he should become a kingmaker, and the Church would have less authority than it should have in deciding who should be appointed to positions of leadership'.[6] In Ellison's view these dangers never materialized, and the foundations laid by Bevir were built up by his successors. It is significant that so shrewd a man as Garbett should be talking about the Church having 'authority' in the sphere of bishop-making, which was still nominally the sole prerogative of the prime minister. There was now less and less pretence that the consultations with the archbishops were a matter of courtesy rather than of right.

Fisher, in his 1956 memorandum, says that his discussions with Bevir were very full. 'He was terribly long-winded – but it did mean that the whole ground was covered. Bevir never revealed any opinions of his own to the people he consulted, but was merely a receiver of impressions.' The Archbishop goes on:

With the Archbishop of York and myself he was tactful, though it took a long time for him to say what he wanted to say: but he was always very anxious not to force a name on us, and, though we were always perfectly aware when he had a particular name he favoured, we could ignore it without resistance. He was always very careful to say that he could not commit the Prime Minister. What we did know was that, when we did finally write to the P.M., Bevir would have known all that had gone before, would not attempt to go outside the names put forward by the Archbishops, and would loyally represent the reasons for accepting the Archbishops' order of preference in the two or three names submitted.[7]

Fisher adds that 'I do not remember any occasion when the first name was not taken', but his memory here could have been playing him up. Even as early as May 1946 he was complaining to Garbett of his 'irritation' with Bevir. 'Quite frankly I dislike it when Bevir puts up a suggestion and I turn it down, and a fortnight later he gets the Prime Minister to put up the same suggestion.'[8]

A feature of the Downing Street apparatus that Fisher found himself envying was the dossier of men considered *episcopabile*. He decided to compile his own list, and with this end in mind sent a circular letter to all the English diocesans asking for their assistance. He told them that the absence of such a list of men deserving consideration for appointment as bishops was a 'disadvantage and weakness'.

The Archbishops ought not to have to rely just upon such men as they happen to know, which cannot cover the whole field, or on casual suggestions. We think that there ought to be at Lambeth a list to which all Diocesan Bishops have contributed their suggestions and which from time to time can be brought up to date.[9]

Fisher's fellow-diocesans were exhorted to send in the names and brief particulars of suitable candidates for bishoprics. The response was sufficient to ensure the compilation of a dossier on a par with Bevir's, and the exercise was repeated from time to time.

Fisher also had an 'inner cabinet' of senior diocesans whom he consulted when Garbett and he were unable to make up their minds on a particular appointment, or when a number of sees had fallen vacant at the same time. Thus, at the beginning of 1949, he wrote to Bell, Haigh and Wand as well as to Garbett to sift their brains about the right bishops for five dioceses which were simultaneously vacant.[10] A further 'democratization' of the system was Fisher's decision always to consult the dean and chapter of a vacant diocese before suggesting a name to the prime minister, 'so that in this way the diocese may have some voice in the matter'. Writing to the Dean of Exeter in October 1948, he said: 'I should be very grateful if you would consult with your Chapter and let me have any observations or suggested names which they would wish to be in my mind.'[11] The Winchester request in 1951 to be allowed to address such observations direct to the prime minister (see previous chapter) was a logical sequel to this development.

Attlee's close personal interest in episcopal appointments was reflected in his habit of dealing with Fisher direct. Quite apart from his personal conversations with the Archbishop at which individual appointments were discussed, the Prime Minister often preferred to write to Fisher himself rather than get Bevir to do so. The most significant of his letters is one which he penned within a few weeks of his becoming Premier and in which he put forward some ideas of his own on the type of candidate he preferred.

The letter was written in response to one from Fisher enclosing a list of recommendations for various vacant bishoprics. 'I am not very expert in these matters', Attlee began – before laying down the law (as he saw it) to the Archbishop. His main grouse was that the men recommended were all 'elderly'. 'They are obviously men of considerable qualities and attainments. They would appear to be suitable for routine appointments, but no one appears to me to have outstanding qualities of leadership with the ability to arouse enthusiasm.' To use a military analogy, said Attlee, they seemed to be suitable for holding a quiet sector of the front line but not to be in any sense shock troops. 'Some, indeed, are rather good staff officers and technicians rather than commanders in the field.' Attlee suggested that, in the aftermath of a devastating world war, 'something more was needed on the Bench than average personalities'. The first post-war appointments to the Bench would be regarded as something of a test by many of the younger generation. 'Unless there is a real touch of imagination, I think they will be disappointed. I do not mean by imagination theatricality or sensation but some boldness, some readiness to take risks, and some appreciation of the need for youthful drive rather than for elderly safety-first.' Attlee ended: 'The times we live in seem to me to call for boldness and the crusading spirit. I should like to see this exhibited in further appointments to the Bench.'[12]

Fisher was horrified at the thought of a series of brash young bishops arriving to challenge his headmasterly rule over the Church of England, and did his best to dissuade the Prime Minister by counter-arguments of his own. *If* there were younger men available with outstanding qualities of leadership and the ability to arouse enthusiasm, he assured Attlee, they ought certainly to be appointed 'rather than senior men of less dynamic power'. There were, however, dangers in the Prime Minister's military analogy. The right analogy, in his view, was neither a commander in the field nor a commander suitable for a quiet sector of the front line so much as a chief of staff. The analogy was also misleading in that a commander in the field did his job and then disappeared from the scene. A bishop, however, was not so easily placed on the retired list. 'If made a Bishop young, he must have the qualities which will make him still a good Bishop perhaps twenty years later.' Fisher claimed that the two clerics most capable of arousing enthusiasm after World War I had been Studdert Kennedy and Dick Sheppard, but that it would have been 'disastrous to make either of them bishops'. He doubted whether there were any people now in sight comparable to those two in popular appeal, the best of the younger clergy being more like good chiefs of staff. 'I incline still to think that . . . for the present we must be content with older men whose qualities will be a real addition to the Bench until some of the younger men . . . have had a little more time to mature.'[13]

Older rather than younger men continued to be recommended for the Bench, and Attlee occasionally protested. Thus, when Fisher proposed F. A. Cockin for Bristol in March 1946, Attlee complained that at 57 he was too old – 'I would sooner have a younger man.'[14] Fisher was at once up in arms. 'I should not find it easy to accept as a principle', he wrote back, 'that a man of 57 is too old to be a Bishop, even of a small diocese' [Fisher himself was then 58].

Indeed, such a principle would, I think, be quite disastrous . . . I should wish to press most strongly that he [Cockin] should be appointed to Bristol now while he is only 57. It disturbs me that you say nothing at all about his merits, which are very considerable, but simply dismiss him on grounds of age. It is surely evident in other professions as well as in the Church that an age-rule of this kind is really not applicable.[15]

Attlee bowed to Fisher's argument and agreed to appoint Cockin.

On another occasion he crossed swords with Fisher over the Archbishop's insistence that the Bench needed people with specialist knowledge of certain aspects of theological or ecclesiastical learning. The difficulty was, he said, that a diocese might require 'other more positive qualities' than specialist learning. 'It should not be necessary to have amongst them [the bishops] specialists in all the main branches of theological or canonical learning; and the practice of referring technical questions to experts for advice might be developed, as well as taking them into closer consultation.'[16]

Occasionally Attlee dug in his heels over an appointment and refused to play ball with Fisher. A case in point was that of E. G. Selwyn, a scholar of distinction who had been Dean of Winchester since 1931. Selwyn was an expert canonist and Fisher thought that, with canon-law revision very much in the air, he would be an invaluable recruit to the Bench.* He urged Selwyn's name on the Prime Minister in late 1945 for the see of Bath and Wells, vacant by the translation of Wand to London. Attlee was unenthusiastic. 'Dr Selwyn, with all his qualities, has a certain rigidity which has not always made for harmony in the posts which he has held.'[17] Early in the new year Fisher again urged Selwyn's nomination. 'You are perfectly right', he told Attlee, 'in saying that there has not always been harmony in the posts which he has held, but he really is a person of outstanding ability in the Church and a certain risk of some friction ought to be taken.'[18] But this was a risk that the Prime Minister was not prepared to run; and he stuck to his guns when Selwyn's name was mentioned as a possibility for two other sees, Lincoln and Salisbury. In a letter to Fisher he said that evidence which he had received from 'many responsible quarters' confirmed his doubts as to how Selwyn would manage a diocese. 'This, capped by a strong indication from both Lincoln and Salisbury that he was not *persona grata*, made it very difficult for me to follow your advice.'[19]

Attlee ended his letter by saying that he was sorry for Selwyn, but that the Archbishop of York had seen him and hoped that 'he is now ready to accept the position'. Such an approach to an unsuccessful candidate was so unusual that it deserves a word of explanation. Garbett's visit to pacify Selwyn had been sparked off by an attempt to enlist Buckingham Palace's aid on the Dean's behalf. Garbett described his interview in a letter to Fisher of 13 May 1946.

---

*Eventually Fisher got his episcopal canonist in the person of Professor R. C. Mortimer of Oxford, who was appointed Bishop of Exeter in 1949 – on the poacher-turned-gamekeeper principle, critics said, that he would cease to attack the canon-law proposals if he had had a hand in formulating them.

Selwyn, who is obviously in great mental distress, told me that early in the year Mervyn Haigh had very deliberately said to him that he [i.e. Selwyn] would not be much longer in the diocese of Winchester and that to his regret he would soon be moving. Selwyn took this as a definite hint that he was to be offered a bishopric in the near future.

When nothing happened Selwyn had asked Haigh if he had given him a deliberate hint to that effect.

Mervyn replied that the Archbishop of Canterbury and some senior bishops had recently met and had decided that Selwyn's name should go forward for Bath and Wells . . . Selwyn thereupon began to adjust his mind to this move, began to prepare himself for consecration, and, apparently, discussed the matter confidentially with various friends.

Then, said Garbett, Selwyn had had Fisher's letter 'as a thunder bolt' saying that it was not to be. He had approached Lascelles [the King's secretary] and had found out from him that during the past few months his name had *not* been sent forward to His Majesty in connection with a bishopric. 'Selwyn then went on to say that not only was he himself greatly distressed and disappointed at the way in which he had been deliberately passed over, but he felt a grave constitutional issue had been raised if the Prime Minister refused to pass on to the King a name recommended by the Archbishop and Bishops!'[20]

So Haigh's indiscretion and Selwyn's curious idea of the constitutional position between them led to an embarrassing misunderstanding; and it took all Garbett's diplomatic skills to smooth down the Dean's ruffled feathers. Three years later, in a letter to Attlee, Fisher made yet another attempt on his behalf, this time for the see of Hereford. 'It is widely felt that it is really a scandal that his very great abilities and scholarship should not be available on the Episcopal Bench.'[21] It was all to no avail. Selwyn ended his distinguished ministerial career as Dean of Winchester.

One of the sees for which his name had come up, Salisbury, proved unusually difficult to fill. Fisher began by making yet another attempt to persuade the Prime Minister to move George Bell from Chichester.

He is in all ways an outstanding person and knows more of the internal affairs of the Church perhaps than any other single person. But, as you know, he has incurred a certain degree of odium due not really to his opinions so much as to his persistence in urging them on certain particular matters. As a result he has been passed over for Winchester and for London.[22]

Salisbury, Fisher added, was one of the 'great Sees' to which Bell could properly move from Chichester. But nothing came of the suggestion, and instead Geoffrey Lunt* was translated from Ripon. There was to be one more attempt to shift poor Bell, but by then Attlee had ceased to be Prime Minister.

**Nominations to diocesan bishoprics 20 (12 first appointments, 8 translations)**

*First appointments:*

(1) 1945:  Henry McGowan to Wakefield.
(2) 1946:  Harold William Bradfield to Bath and Wells.
(3) 1946:  Frederick Arthur Cockin to Bristol.
(4) 1946:  George Armitage Chase to Ripon.
(5) 1946:  Thomas Bloomer to Carlisle.
(6) 1947:  William Derrick Lindsay Greer to Manchester.
(7) 1949:  Robert Cecil Mortimer to Exeter.
(8) 1949:  Roger Plumpton Wilson to Wakefield.
(9) 1949:  Tom Longworth to Hereford.
(10) 1949:  Spencer Stottisbury Gwatkin Leeson to Peterborough.
(11) 1949:  William Launcelot Scott Fleming to Portsmouth.
(12) 1950:  Sherard Falkner Allison to Chelmsford.

*Translations:*

(1) 1945:  Clifford Salisbury Woodward to Gloucester (from Bristol).
(2) 1946:  Leslie Owen to Lincoln (from Maidstone).*
(3) 1946:  Geoffrey Charles Lester Lunt to Salisbury (from Ripon).
(4) 1947:  Maurice Henry Harland to Lincoln (from Croydon).*
(5) 1949:  Henry Colville Montgomery-Campbell to Guildford (from Kensington).*
(6) 1949:  William Louis Anderson to Salisbury (from Portsmouth).
(7) 1950:  Edward Michael Gresford Jones to St Albans (from Willesden).*
(8) 1951:  Edmund Robert Morgan to Truro (from Southampton).*

* Suffragan see.

*He died three years later, and the see was then offered to W. M. Askwith of Blackburn, on the ground that his poor health dictated a move to a warmer climate. Askwith preferred the bracing air of the North, however, to the prospect of the 'damp climate' of Salisbury and declined the offer. He was eventually translated to Gloucester in 1954.

# 21

# Breaking the Rules

*Anthony Eden: Prime Minister*
*6 April 1955 – 9 January 1957*

(Robert) Anthony Eden, 1st Earl of Avon (1897–1977), *the Prime Minister whose name is inevitably associated with the Suez débâcle of 1956, was the second son of Sir William Eden, a Durham landowner. Educated at Eton, he won an MC in the First World War and went on to take a first in Oriental languages at Christ Church, Oxford. He entered Parliament in 1923 as Conservative MP for Warwick and Leamington, retaining the seat till his retirement in 1957. He chose foreign affairs as his speciality, serving as parliamentary private secretary to Sir Austen Chamberlain from 1926 to 1929 and winning international recognition for his diplomatic skill as minister in the National Government responsible for League of Nations affairs. In 1935 he succeeded Sir Samuel Hoare as Foreign Secretary, but resigned three years later over Chamberlain's attempt to secure an Anglo-Italian pact. He rejoined the government at the outbreak of war and served as Foreign Secretary from 1940 to 1945 and again, following a six-year period in opposition, from 1951 to 1955. He was Churchill's natural successor as Prime Minister, but his premiership reached a disastrous climax in the autumn of 1956 with his sanctioning of Anglo-French armed intervention in Egypt following Nasser's seizure of the Suez Canal – an episode which still provokes controversy. A breakdown in health caused Eden to resign in January 1957. He was granted an earldom in 1961. The Suez affair sadly overshadowed his earlier achievements in the realm of foreign affairs as a statesman of no mean diplomatic skill.*

Eden, as bishop-maker, suffered from a potential handicap in the eyes of some churchgoers. It was not that he was a Free Churchman or even an agnostic: on the surface he was a perfectly good Anglican. It was simply that he had remarried after divorce. His second marriage in 1951 had excited criticism in some sections of the Church of England, and not only among Anglo-

Catholics. This admittedly minority opinion was reflected in the *Church Times*, which commented in its issue of 15 August: 'It is now apparently to be accepted as a matter of course that those who occupy the highest positions in political and public life may break the Church's law without embarrassment or reproach . . . The world has now openly rejected the law of Christ in this, as in so much else.' Such blunt words attracted much hostile comment in the national press – and perhaps scared the paper off renewing its attack in 1955, when Eden became Prime Minister and, because of his breach of church law, might have been considered an unsuitable person to nominate the Church's bishops. Many years later the then editor of the *Church Times*, Rosamund Essex, explained her decision to keep silent thus: 'We wanted to preserve a principle, but we did not want to hound a person who, when he became Prime Minister, would, most likely, especially because of his unhappy divorce, be super-solicitous to see that the names of future bishops should be good ones.'[1]

The paper's confidence was justified. Eden's nominations during his brief premiership included those of Cuthbert Bardsley to Coventry, Donald Coggan to Bradford, Kenneth Riches to Lincoln, Robert Stopford to Peterborough and, most significantly, Michael Ramsey to York. The first see he had to fill was Bradford, vacant at long last by the retirement of 'Abdication' Blunt after an occupancy of twenty-four years. The diocese at that time enjoyed a peculiar sort of reputation. As Garbett put it in commending Coggan: 'He would attract to Bradford a higher standard of ordinand – at present it is a kind of Cave of Adullam in which those rejected by other bishops find refuge.'[2] The future archbishop was also commended by Fisher as a scholar with administrative skills who was 'well respected for his judgement, leadership and spiritual power':[3] and by Wand as a 'very sound, steady and industrious person' (though a trifle dull).[4] But for some time it was touch and go whether the see would go to Coggan or to the Suffragan Bishop of Jarrow, J. A. Ramsbotham. Garbett considered that Coggan would contribute more to the province ('It would be an advantage to have a scholarly Evangelical in our Upper House') but that Ramsbotham would be more suitable for the diocese. He thought that 'on the whole I should come down on the side of the Bishop of Jarrow' and that Bevir was of the same opinion.[5] Fisher was on the point of seeing Eden on the afternoon of Michaelmas Day to discuss the matter further, but his visit had to be put off at the last minute for an odd reason. As Eden explained: 'It has been represented to me that your visit . . . might possibly be represented as having something to do with the Princess Margaret [and her possible marriage to Group-Capt. Peter Townsend]. This I feel would be embarrassing to both of us and might merely give encouragement to unfortunate rumours.'[6] Their discussion had to be continued by correspondence, and a week later Fisher was able to write: 'I am well content that Dr Coggan should be chosen.'[7] Evidently Bevir had changed his mind – or Eden had overruled him. But Ramsbotham was translated to Wakefield two years later, so all was well.

In the autumn of 1955 Eden found himself with two key sees to fill: York and London, soon to be vacated by the retirement of Garbett (aged 80 and failing fast) and of Wand (70 and still in vigorous health). The argument went on for months – and much of it centred on which of the two sees should be given to Michael Ramsey. Although York was an archbishopric, it had often been considered in the past as less important than London because of the latter's location in the capital city and near to Lambeth. Fisher first suggested to the Prime Minister that Wand himself should move to York 'as a public service, while younger men have time to develop'.[8] Nothing came of this suggestion, however, and Ramsey's name began to be canvassed as a likely candidate for either York or London. While the two archbishops were arguing about whether he would be acceptable to Downing Street, Garbett had what he described to Fisher as a 'brainwave' ('though possibly you may think it a weakening of the brain due to age and illness'): the translation of George Bell, now 72, from Chichester to London.[9] But there was yet another possibility. Fisher wrote to Eden to propose that Bell should be translated not to London but to York, and that Ramsey should be invited to move to London. Bell, Fisher assured the Prime Minister, might tide them over for five or six years. He would be in no sense a stop-gap because of the 'quite exceptional prestige' which he enjoyed in the Church at home and all over the world. London, on the other hand, would respond to Ramsey's 'commanding ability'.[10] Eden, however, was no more enthusiastic about Bell than Churchill had been and declined to consider offering him York.

On 14 December Fisher wrote a letter to the Prime Minister on the current state of play. He had had a long talk with Ramsey, he said, and there was no personal reason of health, either his own or his wife's, which would prevent him accepting London if asked to do so. On that supposition, who would go to York? The best candidate would be Chase of Ripon ('He has no enemies and would be utterly safe'). There was also the Bishop of Edinburgh, Kenneth Warner ('a good, saintly man, but light-weight'), and of course Bell. If, on the other hand, Ramsey went to York, who would go to London? Allison of Chelmsford might 'emerge', but he had not emerged yet. Mortimer of Exeter was out of the question, since 'there is a real lack of something in him which would be still more evident in London'. Bardsley of Croydon had 'two-thirds or even three-quarters of what is needed, but could he stay the course?' There would therefore (assuming Ramsey went to York) have to be a stop-gap, and of the stop-gaps Montgomery-Campbell of Guildford would be far the best ('He knows the whole Diocese and is trusted there').

As to whether Ramsey should go to York or to London, there was an objective factor, Fisher told Eden, which Ramsey himself had mentioned. 'The whole Northern Province would be alarmed if it was badly stripped. If there was to be a stop-gap or a mere pedestrian at Durham and a stop-gap at York, the Northern Province would feel very badly injured.'[11] The Prime Minister found this argument of Ramsey's convincing. 'I was born in Durham and spent all my early life there', he told Fisher, 'and I am sure that the Bishop is right at the dismay which would be felt if the Northern Province were "badly stripped".'[12] He agreed to Ramsey's translation to York.*

There remained London. In his letter to the Prime Minister of 14 December Fisher had ruled out Eden's own suggestions of the Bishop of Edinburgh and of Archbishop Moline of Perth and considered that the choice should lie between the Bishop of Guildford (Ramsey's own preference) and the Bishop of Croydon. He himself would be well content with the former. 'He is my best friend on the Episcopal Bench, and I should like to work with him now as I used to when I was Bishop of London [and Montgomery-Campbell had been one of his suffragans]. I should probably feel that it was the wisest choice.' Fisher was fair to Cuthbert Bardsley, however. He told Eden that it *might* be better to take the 'rasher' course: to

> run the risks and let the Bishop of Croydon do the things which he can do superbly well. For a very great number of people he would set the Christian faith alight as the Bishop of Guildford could not begin to do; but able people would see through him and find goodness but not intellectual ability, and that kind of prophetic fire gets easily damped down by administration.[14]

---

*Ramsey went to see Eden soon after his appointment, but the meeting was apparently a failure. He discovered that Eden had left Durham while still a boy and showed no interest in it now. He was also put off by the Prime Minister's excessively upper-class voice. 'I did not see him again and I did not want to.'[13]

Eden was of the same mind. While blandly assuring Fisher that he personally would not be 'averse to taking a certain risk of this kind', he felt that to do so might be 'unfair' to Bardsley.[15] So Montgomery-Campbell was duly promoted to London – to the general astonishment of many in the Church. In a letter written twelve days before his death, however, Garbett had told Fisher: 'Though many would smile at the appointment of Guildford, yet all those who would have to work with him most closely learned while he was at Kensington to admire and trust him.'[16] As for Bardsley, he was nominated a few months later to be Bishop of Coventry – and won golden opinions both for his work as a diocesan and, on a wider stage, for his eloquent chairmanship of the Church of England Men's Society.

Although Fisher convinced himself (and assured the Prime Minister) that the appointments to York and London had been 'extremely well received', that was not universally true in the case of York. The *Church of England Newspaper* claimed (in what Fisher dubbed a 'vitriolic outburst') that Ramsey's friends had inflated his reputation beyond what his record would endorse. And the ceremony in March 1956 to confirm his election was again the scene of a public protest, this time by Alfred Latimer Kensit on behalf of the Protestant Truth Society. Kensit objected to Ramsey's nomination on two grounds: that he had failed to discipline the Ritualists in the parish of St Mary, Tyne Dock; and that he had written an article in his diocesan magazine criticizing the evangelistic work of Billy Graham. On this occasion the objections were ruled out of order by Fisher himself, acting in his capacity of the Queen's commissioner. The only questions under discussion, he said, were whether Ramsey was Ramsey and whether he had been legally elected. As Ramsey's biographer neatly puts it: 'Since no one could imagine that . . . anyone could successfully impersonate Ramsey, the ritual was a piece of legal nothing which allowed a Protestant agitator the chance of publicity which might help his own cause but must also help Ramsey. If a man is worth protesting against, he must be somebody.'[17]

Fisher incurred a certain amount of criticism over what some considered the over-hasty promotion of Robert Stopford to the see of Peterborough a bare year after his appointment as Suffragan Bishop of Fulham, with oversight of the Anglican chaplaincies in North and Central Europe. Stopford had originally turned down Fulham, and had only accepted it under strong pressure from Bevir, who had told him that it 'would not be for long'. And now his was one of two names which Fisher sent to the Prime Minister (in a final short-list) as possibles for Peterborough, vacant by the sadly premature death of Spencer Leeson. Stopford's rival was the Suffragan Bishop of Middleton, Frank Woods. 'Undoubtedly', Fisher told Eden, 'the Bishop of Fulham is the better equipped and qualified man, though (one must in fairness add) lacking the freshness and youthfulness and infectious enthusiasm of the Bishop of Middleton.'[18]

Eden agreed to appoint Stopford – who would replace Leeson as a much-needed educationalist on the Bishops' Bench. 'It is hard on the Chaplaincies and Embassies which he is just getting to know to take him away after only a year in office', he told Fisher. 'But I think the claims of the Peterborough diocese must be preferred.'[19] Not everyone was of the same opinion. George Bell, who knew the Continent well, thought the proposed move a 'major blunder' on the part of the authorities and advised Stopford not to accept it. Bell thought that a transfer after only a year in office would be 'most unsettling for the chaplains and their congregations, a cause of surprise to all and of consternation for some of the British legations and embassies'. Bishop Cockin of Bristol also thought the authorities misguided and, in a letter to Stopford, criticized Fisher's 'hand-to-mouth policy' over recent episcopal appointments. Even the Old Catholic Archbishop of Utrecht, Andreas Rinkel, wrote in perplexity to Stopford: 'I really did not know that you were not following the long way of darwinistic evolution, but the most rapid spring – mutation.'[20] Fisher, however, was smugly unrepentant. 'I wanted to keep you at Fulham a bit longer', he told Stopford (as if the decision had been his alone!),

> *only* because you had just gone there. When you went I hinted as plainly as I dared that [there would be] a diocese very soon. The need now is insistent . . . In my opinion the Church must have you at Peterborough . . . It is really the fact that you must go there for the good of the Church . . . The Bishop of London . . . meekly accepted the unwelcome fact.[21]

The headmaster had spoken, and staff and pupils must obey!

Fisher may have got his way over the appointment to Peterborough. Later that year, however, he came a bit of a cropper over the nomination of a new Bishop of Ely and saw his wishes flouted not so much by the Prime Minister (or even by the preferred candidate) as by the Prime Minister's new secretary for appointments, David Stephens.* So angry was he at what he

---

* There have been (up till the end of 1991) only five holders of the office: Sir Anthony Bevir (1947–56), Sir David Stephens (1956–61), Sir John Hewitt (1961–73), Colin Peterson (1974–82) and Robin Catford (1982– ).

regarded as a clear breach of the rules by Stephens that he poured forth his feelings in a lengthy memorandum dated 5 October 1956.[22] Stephens had stepped into Bevir's shoes at the beginning of that year, but, said Fisher, had early shown a 'certain independence of thought' which posed an obvious threat to Fisher's own position in the appointments process. Matters had come to a head with the need to choose a new Bishop of Ely. Fisher had put at the top of his list for the vacant see the name of John Moorman, Principal of Chichester Theological College. What was his annoyance therefore to be told by Stephens on 4 October that he had been 'running round a great deal' and discovering that the popular choice would be not so much Moorman as the Bishop of Newcastle, Noel Hudson, who would be welcomed by (a) the Dean of Ely, (b) Cambridge in general, (c) Michael Ramsey, now safely installed as Archbishop of York, and, last but not least, (d) the Prime Minister himself. 'He [Stephens] ended up by saying that, if I would write to the P.M. putting forward Newcastle's name, the thing could go forward quickly.'

The delicious irony was that Fisher was hoist with his own petard, since he had himself put Hudson top of the list on two previous occasions recently 'knowing that the P.M. would dislike it and privately very willing that he should pass him over for the second name [as in fact he had done]. Stephens understood all this, and I rather thought that the resistance was entirely from the Prime Minister.' And now 'a certain gulf yawned at my feet'. Fisher saw himself having to bite the bullet and accept Hudson; but 'in some way or other I must make it clear to Stephens that this is a complete rupture of the whole system.'

> I have always maintained in public that the system worked well because there was complete freedom of discussion between the P.M. and the Archbishop of Canterbury, and over York with the Archbishop of York, and that whatever faults there might be in the system the position of the Church was thereby safeguarded. That obviously means the Archbishop and the P.M. must be in a position to consider each other's points of view without prejudice.

The duty of Stephens, said Fisher, was to advise the Prime Minister out of his own researches. But, if he wished to continue in this confidential relation with the Archbishop, he must never advise the PM on a particular appointment until after he had consulted the Archbishop and knew what was in his mind; and *only* after the Archbishop had authorized him should he convey his views to the PM or after the Archbishop had himself written to the PM. Then came the nub of Fisher's grievance:

I am perfectly sure that Stephens has erred purely from enthusiasm and lack of experience, but the result is that he presented me with a *fait accompli* and asked me to sign on the dotted line, and that about a Diocese in my own Province. This is really in fact appointing without reference to the Archbishop of Canterbury, and, even worse, appointment not by the P.M. but by Stephens.

The next step was a decision to summon the erring pupil to the headmaster's study. 'I am certain I can put this right easily with Stephens', said Fisher in his memorandum. 'He may indeed have spotted that he had put a foot wrong somewhere, since, in answer to his request that I should write to the P.M. forthwith, I developed on the spot a series of admirable reasons why Newcastle would not do for Ely, or at any rate that the matter must be thought about very carefully.' Neither admirable reasons nor careful thoughts, however, were sufficient to keep Hudson out of Ely; and he was duly nominated to the see with or without the Archbishop's concurrence. Fisher ended his memorandum with a piece of advice for Stephens: 'When he goes round and sees Deans and others he must not discuss any preferences of his own at all. He can always mention names when they come up, but he must be only a piece of blotting-paper taking impressions.'

There was a complacent postscript by Fisher to the memorandum: 'I saw Stephens again on 19th October, and we talked of the above situation with complete equanimity and satisfaction on both sides.'

**Nominations to diocesan bishoprics 10 (2 first appointments, 8 translations)**

*First appointments:*

(1) 1955:  Frederick Donald Coggan to Bradford.
(2) 1955:  Lewis Mervyn Charles-Edwards to Worcester.

*Translations:*

(1) 1955:  Arthur Michael Ramsey to York (from Durham).
(2) 1955:  Henry Colville Montgomery-Campbell to London (from Guildford).
(3) 1956:  Cuthbert Killick Norman Bardsley to Coventry (from Croydon).*
(4) 1956:  Maurice Henry Harland to Durham (from Lincoln).

(5) 1956: Ivor Stanley Watkins to Guildford (from Malmesbury).*
(6) 1956: Robert Wright Stopford to Peterborough (from Fulham).*
(7) 1956: Kenneth Riches to Lincoln (from Dorchester).*
(8) 1956: Noel Baring Hudson to Ely (from Newcastle).

* Suffragan see.

# 22

# Trollopian Echoes

*Harold Macmillan: Prime Minister*
*13 January 1957 – 19 October 1963*

(Maurice) Harold Macmillan, 1st Earl of Stockton (1894–1986), *enjoys a mixed reputation, his successes abroad during his premiership being weighed against his reputation for having sacrificed principle in domestic affairs to expediency. A member of the famous publishing family, he was educated at Eton and Balliol College, Oxford, and served with distinction in the First World War. In 1924 he entered Parliament as a Conservative, combining politics with publishing and remaining an MP (apart from two short intervals) until his retirement in 1964. As an MP he soon showed independence of mind, both as a critic of his party's foreign policy and as a would-be social reformer in advance of his times. He held various minor offices during the war, notably that of Minister-resident in North Africa from 1942 to 1945. For the next six years he was a leading member of the Opposition and, when the Conservatives returned to power in 1951, an outstanding Minister of Housing. He was briefly Foreign Secretary under Eden and then served as Chancellor of the Exchequer (he was responsible for introducing premium bonds) until he succeeded Eden as Premier in January 1957. He began well, restoring Conservative unity in the wake of Suez and ushering in the affluent society with its 'never had it so good' image. Abroad he achieved diplomatic success, not least in accepting the 'winds of change' in Africa and the need to shed Britain's remaining colonial possessions. But, over the years, his 'Supermac' image became dented and by 1963, in the aftermath of the Profumo affair, was sadly tarnished. A sudden severe illness in October of that year led to his almost immediate decision to resign as Premier. He enjoyed a long Indian summer, however, as elder statesman and publisher – and a new incarnation as Chancellor of Oxford University. He was awarded the Order of Merit in 1976, and experienced some moments of final glory in the House of Lords as the newly-ennobled Earl of Stockton.*

'I rather enjoy patronage', Harold Macmillan once remarked. 'At least it makes all those years of reading Trollope worthwhile.'[1] He certainly relished the ecclesiastical side of his duties – more so than any of his recent predecessors. As an informed member of the Church of England he particularly enjoyed his Tuesday evening audiences with the Church's Supreme Governor – audiences at which, from time to time, the choice of new bishops might be discussed. He found the Queen even better informed than himself on the subject. On one occasion he reminded her of how a former monarch, Elizabeth I, had put in his place a bishop who had protested at her evicting him from his palace. 'Proud Prelate', the Tudor sovereign had declared, 'you know what you were before I made you what you are. If you do not immediately comply with my request I will unfrock you, by God!' 'I feel sure', Macmillan told the Queen, 'that Your Majesty is conscious that I have never advised you, as yet, to take any such drastic action in Your capacity as Head of the Church.'[2]

Macmillan was not merely a well-informed Anglican: he was a practising one, with strong religious beliefs. Towards the end of his life he told his biographer, Alistair Horne: 'I still find religion a great help. I go to Communion as long as I can. At home in the house, I reach for the Bible whenever I can.' And he once declared in a television interview: 'If you don't believe in God, all you have to believe in is decency . . . Decency is very good. Better decent than indecent. But I don't think it's enough.'[3]

He was prepared to tackle serious works of theology. When he was having to decide whether to nominate Michael Ramsey to succeed Geoffrey Fisher as Archbishop of Canterbury he took the trouble to read a new book of Ramsey's, *From Gore to Temple*, a study of liberal Catholic thought in recent English religion, and is said to have enjoyed it. He told Ramsey not long afterwards that his own sympathies were with the High Church wing of the Church of England, but that it was necessary, in appointing bishops, to hold the High and the Low together. 'He added that, while the Evangelicals had their part in the Church, he did not think that on the whole they had the qualities suitable for being bishops.'[4]

Ramsey was far more on the Prime Minister's wavelength than Fisher had ever been. In fact Macmillan found his occasional interviews with the latter a duty rather than a pleasure. 'I try to talk to him about religion', he once declared. 'But he seems quite uninterested and reverts all the time to politics.'[5] Fisher's politics, moreover, were not always Macmillan's. The Archbishop made a fierce attack in the House of Lords on premium bonds when they

were first introduced, denouncing them as 'this squalid enterprise'. And he criticized Macmillan's 'You've never had it so good'
slogan. Ramsey, on the other hand, though he too criticized
government policy from time to time, proved an altogether more
congenial companion. He and Macmillan had intellectual interests
in common and they became firm friends. But even Fisher could
occasionally unbend. A handwritten postscript to a long letter
about a vacant bishopric ends with a reference to the Prime
Minister's forthcoming visit to Moscow: 'God go with you and
uphold you in that den of thieves!'[6]

Macmillan took a great deal of trouble over ecclesiastical
nominations. A good example is his response to a plea by Lord
Brentford for the appointment of more Evangelicals to diocesan
bishoprics. David Stephens, still the patronage secretary at
Number 10, wrote to Fisher's chaplain, Freddy Temple, on the
Prime Minister's behalf, to test his reactions. 'One way of
replying', he said, 'would be to send a bare acknowledgement
which would give nothing away, on the following lines: "Thank
you for your letter about the selection of Diocesan Bishops. I will
bear your views in mind." On the other hand it might be worth
while to be rather more forthcoming.'[7] Stephens enclosed a draft
which, after discussion with Temple, emerged in the following
form for the Prime Minister's signature:

> Thank you for your letter about the selection of Diocesan
> Bishops. The point that you make about the importance of
> preserving a balance of churchmanship on the Bishops' Bench
> is very much in my mind. At the same time I feel – and I am
> glad to see that you agree – that it would be wrong to lay too
> much emphasis on the representation of particular interests or
> parties as a factor in the process of selection. I am sure the
> right course is to consider carefully the needs of the particular
> Diocese as each vacancy arises and to pick the best man
> available for the job, taking everything, including churchman-
> ship, into account. I am not conscious that the appointments
> which I have been responsible for recommending to The Queen
> have shown a marked trend in respect of churchmanship in
> any particular direction; and I rejoice at the signs that the
> Church is coming to a more united mind.[8]

It was part of the established convention that, at the final stage
of the procedure for nominating a new bishop, the archbishop of
the province concerned should give the prime minister the names
of two or three persons, indicating that the choice of any one
would have his approval. But Macmillan expected the Church to
play fair and to present him with a genuine choice. So he was not

best pleased when, in July 1960, the so-called 'choice' of a new bishop for Rochester was 'in effect limited to one man'. Fisher, in an admittedly devious way, had contrived to hedge four of his five alternative names with caveats that were intended effectively to rule them out of court – one 'should be moved to a lighter diocese, but I do not think that Rochester would be the right move for him'; the second was 'too pronounced an Evangelical'; the third 'should be left at Cambridge a while longer'; the fourth was a 'quite definite High Churchman: the change of tradition would be too abrupt'. So Macmillan could justifiably complain, in agreeing to nominate to the vacant see the only blemish-free candidate, R. D. Say (fortunately, it was to turn out, the perfect choice): 'I know your difficulties, but I very much hope that for future vacancies you will generally be able to give me at least two or three names to choose from.'[9] The alleged difficulty was finding people who had the qualities needed for episcopal office. Fisher complained to Stephens about this time: 'We have drained the reservoir dry at the moment.'[10]

Stephens was again giving trouble by (in the opinion of both Fisher and Ramsey) getting too personally involved in the appointments process. Ramsey had complained that his activities in the dioceses were becoming too open and thought that he ought to conceal them more cleverly. Fisher agreed. He wrote to Ramsey in May 1958 to say that Stephens tended to meet 'the Dean and Chapter' as such. 'I said that every Dean and Chapter . . . had the fullest right to send a memorandum to the Prime Minister: they could not as a corporate body present a verbal memorandum to Stephens: that was putting the man himself into a false position.' Fisher reminded Ramsey about his warning to Stephens that it was his duty to be a piece of blotting-paper and not an originator of ideas (see previous chapter).

> I now had to tell him that, inevitably, he was a bit of 'under-the-counter' machinery. He had every right, and indeed it was his duty, to pick up suggestions and ideas from as many people as he could, as individuals . . . in order that he might be in a position to advise the Prime Minister wisely; but, once he met a Board or a corporate body, he was in great danger of becoming a negotiator; and outside people, hearing of it, might begin to say that the corporate body had rigged the appointment.

The dutiful Stephens, Fisher added, 'took all this in very good part'.[11] But his temptation to exceed his brief was a symptom of the still-evolving procedure over episcopal nominations and of the increasingly important part that the Prime Minister's secretary for appointments had to play in it. Stephens's successor, John

Hewitt, who took over in 1961, was to display a very definite mind of his own and to develop into something much more than prime ministerial blotting-paper.

Fisher never ruled out a candidate on the ground that he was unlikely to see eye to eye with him once he had become a bishop. A case in point was that of Mervyn Stockwood, the radical Vicar of Great St Mary's, Cambridge, who was nominated at the end of 1958 to succeed Bertram Simpson as Bishop of Southwark. Fisher had suggested him to Stephens as early as April as 'really the best person'. 'If he makes his mistakes, it [i.e. Southwark!] is a very good place for him to make them in, while he will really bring great strength and vigour.'[12] As a committed Socialist, however, Stockwood might not have been to Macmillan's political taste; so, when the time came in November to present the Prime Minister with a definitive short-list of candidates for the vacant see, Fisher was prepared to pull out all the stops on Stockwood's behalf. After a few conventional phrases ('a man of undoubted strength of personality, strength of conviction and proved powers of leadership') he came to more delicate ground.

> I am not required to say that he has never said or done anything unwise . . . What I *can* say is that he has never been a propagandist for any political or ecclesiastical view, but merely a propagandist for religious realism . . . I hope that I have shown that any supposed tinge of political partisanship can be completely ignored.

Stockwood, Fisher assured Macmillan, was, of all the possible candidates (and there were six others on his list), 'the one who could be recommended with the most conviction'.[13] Macmillan agreed to nominate Stockwood.*

A see that proved more difficult to fill was Norwich in 1959. At first, however, Fisher was optimistic. The diocese had, of course, a particular connection with the Royal Family because of Sandringham. So, when Fisher sent in a short-list of three names to Macmillan, he wrote to the Queen in his own hand to tell her that he had done so – and that his first choice had been Bishop Gresford Jones of St Albans ('splendid where is, but he has carried that heavy load for nine years and would have to be moved before long . . . just the right kind of person for

---

*Among the many people whose advice Stockwood sought before deciding to accept Macmillan's offer was Michael Ramsey, who replied: '*If* you decide to become a bishop I shall be glad to welcome to the bench a man who, when all of us, like sheep, are saying "Yes, yes, yes", will have the courage to say "No, no, no, no, no".'[14]

Norwich').[15] The see was duly offered to Gresford Jones, but he preferred to soldier on with his 'heavy load' and declined it. So Fisher had to think again, and was reduced to writing round to a dozen or so senior bishops for suggestions. 'What is needed is a Bishop able to lead the rather feudal and slow-going people of Norfolk, with a wife who understands that kind of life . . . the churchmanship must be as unobtrusive as possible.'[16] All sorts of names were cast up in the Archbishop's net – including Harland of Durham, to whom Fisher wrote that he had heard that 'you and the mining population have not clicked and that you are feeling your work there as a burden hard to be endured'. Harland assured his superior that, on the contrary, he was 'entirely happy with the challenge which Durham provides';[17] and in the end Macmillan agreed to appoint the number two on Fisher's original short-list, Fleming of Portsmouth. Fleming happened to be a bachelor, and so lacked a 'wife who understands that kind of [feudal and slow-going] life', but in other respects came up to scratch and, as a geologist who had served as chaplain to the British Graham Land Expedition in the 1930s, certainly had an unusual background. He was a great success in his new diocese, and ended his ministerial career as Dean of Windsor.

Another example of Fisher's fairness in stressing a candidate's strong points while seeking to underplay what might be regarded as his weak ones was the case of George Reindorp, who had been since 1957 Provost of Southwark. Reindorp, in Fisher's words, was 'lively, imaginative and progressive' and had been an exceptionally able Vicar of St Stephen's, Rochester Row, in Westminster. He had been sent to Southwark, Fisher told the Prime Minister, to try him out under sterner conditions and had stood the test well. Now came the nub of the argument:

> He has been regarded in the past as a bit of a 'showman': in fact he has always had very solid results of great value to show for his work. He always breeds enthusiasm – it may do him a great injustice if the idea continues that he succeeds only by his charm, his lively wit and his quickness of invention. I have come to think that he has reached the point when he could be safely entrusted with diocesan responsibility.[18]

Macmillan was persuaded – and chose Reindorp, in preference to the five others on the short-list, to succeed Ivor Watkins as Bishop of Guildford. The new diocesan had an early baptism of fire as, shortly after his enthronement, a row broke out over Macmillan's nomination of the first Dean of Guildford – or, rather, over his declining to nominate for the post Walter Boulton, who had served as Provost of the Cathedral for the previous nine years. Boulton himself and many people in the diocese had confidently expected that his nomination to the deanery (whose duties were much the same as his existing ones) would be a mere formality; and his failure to secure it kept the correspondence columns of the papers buzzing for many weeks. The controversy was too complex to discuss at length in a book concerned primarily with bishops, though the bitterness it engendered helped to fuel the rising clamour for a reform in the whole system of Crown appointments.

The only case during Macmillan's premiership in which politics affected the outcome was that of Ambrose Reeves and his failure to be appointed to the charge of a diocese in England. Reeves had, since 1949, been Bishop of Johannesburg and had emerged as a leading champion of the blacks in South Africa against the iniquities of apartheid. As such he was very much a political figure. So, when his name came up as a possible for the bishopric of Blackburn in April 1960, it was unlikely that it would get by on the nod. It had been among the four submitted by Ramsey. Fisher, however, had his doubts. He agreed that Reeves was in a class by himself, but suggested to the Prime Minister that he must decide 'whether it is politic to put in an English diocese a Bishop around whom so many storms had arisen through his championing the cause of the indigenous African population'. He believed that Reeves was genuinely concerned to promote reconciliation between black and white, but pointed out that he was also the subject of strong criticism.[19] Whether or not the cold water poured on Reeves by Fisher influenced Macmillan's decision in any way, he declined to appoint him to Blackburn. He wrote to Fisher: 'I have considered all you say about the Bishop of Johannesburg, but I do not think his appointment to an English Diocese would be appropriate at this time. I therefore choose the Bishop of Warrington [C. R. Claxton], whose churchmanship seems to meet the needs of the See of Blackburn rather better than the churchmanship of the Bishop of Johannesburg.'[20] The churchmanship issue (Reeves was Higher than Claxton) was a transparent excuse to gloss over the political element in the choice.

Three months after this letter was written Reeves was expelled from his diocese by the South African government and returned to England. The need to promote him to an English see was now much more immediate; but, while Fisher remained at Canterbury, nothing was done. In June 1961 Ramsey took over as Primate. He thought that, as a sign to the Anglican Church in South Africa and its witness against apartheid, Reeves should be offered an English diocese. He suggested as much to Macmillan, but the Prime Minister declined to oblige him. He told Ramsey that Britain's relations with South Africa were difficult enough without adding to the friction an appointment which it was not necessary to make and for which plenty of other good people were equally qualified.[21] Ramsey was unable to let Reeves (or his friends) into the reasons for the absence of suitable work for him in England; and indeed, to begin with, he lived in hopes that the Prime Minister would eventually relent. On 2 October 1961 he saw Reeves at Lambeth – and advised him to continue to wait, as (says Reeves) 'he hoped that in a month or two I would be offered a sphere of work in which I could best serve the Church'. Nothing happened, however, and it was not until 9 January 1962 that Reeves was again summoned to Lambeth, by when Ramsey had received a definite 'thumbs down' from Macmillan. 'At this meeting', says Reeves, 'the Archbishop, contrary to his previous counsel, advised me not to wait any longer for any possible appointment to a diocese, but to take a living.'[22] Eventually Reeves was offered the general secretaryship of the Student Christian Movement; but SCM was then in decline and Reeves's three-year spell there was not a happy one. He ended his career as a parish priest in Sussex.

Macmillan's key appointment was that of a new Archbishop of Canterbury in succession to Geoffrey Fisher. It was in the late autumn of 1960 that Fisher, then 73, told him of his wish to resign the following year. The most obvious successor was Michael Ramsey, but there were a number of other possible candidates. Fisher organized a 'straw vote' among his fellow-diocesans, the results of which he passed on to Stephens. The bishops came up with three names: Ramsey, Coggan of Bradford and Allison of Chelmsford. Ramsey had his own private short-list: Coggan, Stopford of Peterborough and himself.

In January 1961 Fisher went to Downing Street to discuss the succession. The meeting was not a success, partly because Macmillan had never warmed to Fisher but mainly because they backed rival candidates. The Prime Minister wanted to see Ramsey installed at Lambeth, while Fisher would much have preferred Coggan. Fisher's own version of the meeting is given by his official biographer:

I sat beside him, and he talked in the kind of impersonal way that he could sometimes, not really paying any attention to me but asking the necessary questions and taking the answers I gave with hardly a comment. It was a truly frigid proceeding. All the right things were said . . . I did say that, while Michael's claims as a theologian were far better than anybody else's on the Episcopal Bench, he had some very odd traits which might cause difficulty – more than that I couldn't obviously say. There I left it.[23]

As Fisher was leaving Macmillan let the cat out of the bag by observing: 'Of course this will mean a lot of changes when you go; there will be York to be filled.' Then, realizing his gaffe, he added: 'That is to say, if Ramsey is appointed.'[24] Fisher left Downing Street with a strong feeling that the matter was already settled in Macmillan's mind. He felt definitely uneasy at the thought of Ramsey as his successor, though he had been perfectly happy to see him following Garbett at York. In recent years, however, he had come to feel that Ramsey, as a convinced Anglo-Catholic, was suspicious of reunion schemes and would not therefore play a leading part in the Ecumenical Movement. He also doubted his ability to cope with the Lambeth workload – he was more interested in 'theologizing' than in administration. Macmillan, on the other hand, felt more of a *rapport* with Ramsey than with any other of the potential candidates. He admired his capacious intellect and deep spirituality. For the Prime Minister Ramsey stood head and shoulders above his fellows. But he went dutifully through the due processes of consultation. He interviewed all the other candidates, but ended up with the same conclusion: that Ramsey was the right man for the job. In his own words: 'I thought we had had enough of Martha and it was time for some Mary.'[25]

Fisher announced his resignation on the morning of 17 January 1961. The same evening Macmillan telephoned Ramsey with the offer of the succession. He asked him to ring through his answer next morning. He apologized for the haste, but explained that the Queen was about to go abroad for several weeks and the matter had to be settled before she left. He added that, if Ramsey accepted, he had it in mind to recommend Coggan for the archbishopric of York. Ramsey phoned next morning with his acceptance, and both appointments were announced a day or two later. The speed of the announcement, coming so soon after the news of Fisher's resignation, took people by surprise. Ramsey and Coggan might have come as the answer to their prayers; but the Prime Minister had hardly given them time to get on their knees. He had also committed an error of protocol by not consulting Fisher about the appointment of the new Archbishop of York. 'Is this not unfair to me and to the Church?', Fisher asked Ramsey. 'Appointment to York is a question on which I have a right to be heard.'[26]

Ramsey had a memorable conversation with the Prime Minister a few days after his appointment had been announced. 'Fisher seems to disapprove of you', Macmillan began. 'Yes', said Ramsey, 'he was my headmaster and headmasters often know the worst.' To which Macmillan retorted: 'He may be *your* headmaster, but he is not going to be mine!'[27] *The Times*, in an editorial, said that the Prime Minister, in providing a High Churchman for one archbishopric and a Low Churchman for the other, had shown a sensitivity worthy of Trollope.

Two of the outsiders in the Canterbury Stakes won consolation prizes soon afterwards, Stopford going to London and Allison to Winchester. Stopford's appointment was enlivened by a protest at his election: not on theological but on political grounds. Canon John Collins, a member of the St Paul's Cathedral Chapter, registered an objection to the Crown's nominee on the grounds of a speech made in 1958 in which he was alleged to have expressed support for nuclear weapons. Stopford replied that he had been quoted out of context.[28] He was duly elected.

Macmillan's final appointment was an odd one: that of Joe Fison, Mervyn Stockwood's successor as Vicar of Great St Mary's, Cambridge, to be Bishop of Salisbury. It was odd because a rural diocese with hundreds of villages hardly seemed the right milieu for a man whom his friend Max Warren described after his death as 'perhaps the most truly prophetic person I have ever had the privilege to know'.[29] Indeed, when his name had come up five years earlier as a possibility for the see of Bristol, Fisher had dismissed him to Ramsey as 'too much of a prophet'.[30] But it was now Ramsey rather than Fisher who was producing the lists for the Prime Minister; and maybe Fison's radiant if explosive personality (he was known irreverently as 'Nuclear Fison') helped recommend him to the new Primate. But Fison's administration of his diocese was not an unqualified success. 'I think the strain of this unnatural occupation killed him,' said Warren. Or, in the words of his obituary in *The Times*: 'When his appointment to the see of Salisbury was announced, many of his friends thought that a race-horse was being harnessed to the shafts of a farm-wagon.'[31]

Nominations to diocesan bishoprics 25 (10 first appointments, 15 translations)

*First appointments:*

   (1) 1957:  Hugh Edward Ashdown to Newcastle.
   (2) 1958:  Oliver Stratford Tomkins to Bristol.
   (3) 1958:  Arthur Mervyn Stockwood to Southwark.
   (4) 1959:  John Richard Humpidge Moorman to Ripon.
   (5) 1959:  John Henry Lawrence Phillips to Portsmouth.
   (6) 1960:  Richard David Say to Rochester.
   (7) 1961:  George Edmund Reindorp to Guildford.
   (8) 1962:  John Gerhard Tiarks to Chelmsford.
   (9) 1962:  Francis John Taylor to Sheffield.
 (10) 1963:  Joseph Edward Fison to Salisbury.

*Translations:*

   (1) 1957:  Roger Plumpton Wilson to Chichester (from Wakefield).
   (2) 1958:  John Alexander Ramsbotham to Wakefield (from Jarrow).*
   (3) 1959:  Geoffrey Francis Allen to Derby (formerly of Egypt).†
   (4) 1959:  William Launcelot Scott Fleming to Norwich (from Portsmouth).
   (5) 1959:  John Maurice Key to Truro (from Sherborne).*
   (6) 1960:  Charles Robert Claxton to Blackburn (from Warrington).*
   (7) 1960:  Edward Barry Henderson to Bath and Wells (from Tewkesbury).*
   (8) 1961:  Arthur Michael Ramsey to Canterbury (from York).
   (9) 1961:  Frederick Donald Coggan to York (from Bradford).
 (10) 1961:  Robert Wright Stopford to London (from Peterborough).
 (11) 1961:  Sherard Falkner Allison to Winchester (from Chelmsford).
 (12) 1961:  Mark Allin Hodson to Hereford (from Taunton).*
 (13) 1961:  Cyril Eastaugh to Peterborough (from Kensington).*
 (14) 1961:  Clement George St Michael Parker to Bradford (from Aston).*
 (15) 1962:  Basil Tudor Guy to Gloucester (from Bedford).*

* Suffragan see.
† Overseas see.

# 23

# From Right to Left

*Sir Alec Douglas-Home: Prime Minister*
*19 October 1963 – 16 October 1964*

*J. Harold Wilson: Prime Minister*
*16 October 1964 – 19 June 1970*
*4 March 1974 – 5 April 1976*

*Edward Heath: Prime Minister*
*19 June 1970 – 4 March 1974*

*James Callaghan: Prime Minister*
*5 April 1976 – 4 May 1979*

Alexander (Alec) Frederick Douglas-Home, formerly 14th Earl of Home and later Baron Home of the Hirsel (1903–    ), *was the little-known Conservative politician who was unexpectedly called upon to succeed Harold Macmillan as Prime Minister in 1963. Educated at Eton and Christ Church, Oxford, he was MP for S. Lanark (as Viscount Dunglass) from 1931 to 1945 and parliamentary private secretary to Neville Chamberlain at the time of Munich. In 1951 he succeeded his father as Earl of Home. He served under Eden and Macmillan, first as Commonwealth Secretary and then as Foreign Secretary; and, when illness caused Macmillan's sudden resignation in 1963, he was the compromise candidate – respected on all sides for his integrity – chosen to succeed him. He renounced his peerage and re-entered the Commons as Sir Alec Douglas-Home; but he was Premier for only a year, being narowly defeated in the 1964 general election. In July 1965 he resigned as party leader and was succeeded by Edward Heath. He returned to the Lords with a life peerage in 1974.*

(James) Harold Wilson, Baron Wilson of Rievaulx (1916–    ), *was elected leader of the Labour Party following the sudden death of Hugh Gaitskell in 1963. Born at Milnsbridge, Yorkshire, and educated at Royds Hall and Wirral Grammar Schools and Jesus College, Oxford, he became a lecturer on economics at New*

*College in 1937. During the war he served in the Ministry of Fuel and Power, and in 1945 entered Parliament as Labour MP for Ormskirk. He was President of the Board of Trade under Attlee, but resigned in 1951 in protest against the government's proposed prescription charges and defence expenditure. During Labour's long period in opposition he became a leader of its left-wing faction, but, after being chosen to succeed Gaitskell, rallied the Party and steered it to its narrow victory in the 1964 election. His forceful personality and political skill ensured Labour a greatly increased majority in the 1966 election. He was defeated by the Conservatives in 1970, but turned the tables on them in 1974 and was again Prime Minister until his resignation in 1976. He was made a life peer in 1983.*

Sir Edward Richard George Heath (1916–    ) *was the Tory leader responsible for taking Britain into Europe. Born at Broadstairs, Kent, and educated at Chatham House School, Ramsgate, and Balliol College, Oxford, he served in the army during the Second World War. After a brief spell as news editor of the* Church Times *(1948–9) he was elected in 1950 as Conservative MP for Bexley. He soon made his mark and was successively Government Chief Whip, Minister of Labour, Lord Privy Seal and President of the Board of Trade. He masterminded Britain's first bid to enter the EEC; and, though it was unsuccessful, it established Heath's reputation on the Continent as an ardent pro-European. He was elected to succeed Douglas-Home as Party leader in 1965 and became Prime Minister five years later. His great achievement was to secure Britain's entry into the EEC on 1 January 1973, but he was defeated in the general election of 1974 and the following year was replaced as Party leader by Margaret Thatcher. A man of many parts, Heath is a talented organist, conductor and yachtsman.*

(Leonard) James Callaghan, Baron Callaghan of Cardiff (1912– ), *succeeded Harold Wilson as Labour Prime Minister in 1976. Educated at state schools in Portsmouth, he worked as a tax officer for the Inland Revenue. After service in the navy during World War II he entered the Commons in 1945 as MP for Cardiff South and held junior office under Attlee. During Labour's long spell in opposition he became its chief spokesman on financial affairs. He served in Wilson's 1964–70 administration first as Chancellor of the Exchequer and then as Home Secretary, and in his second administration as Foreign and Commonwealth Secretary. When Wilson retired Callaghan was elected leader of*

*the Labour Party, serving as Prime Minister until his defeat in
the 1979 general election. He was given a life peerage in 1987.*

From now on the student of bishop-making must walk
circumspectly. The thirty-year rule relating to official documents
precludes the examination of many sets of archives, and published
material is at present thin on the ground. A lot of what passes for
established fact is little more than intelligent speculation. In the
absence of much source material it seems best to deal in a single
chapter with the four (at the time of writing) surviving prime
ministers to have worked the traditional system.

The year 1965 saw two significant developments in the
evolution of that system: the setting up of vacancy-in-see
committees in dioceses whenever a new diocesan bishop was
required, and the provision of a 'Secretary for Appointments' to
the Archbishops of Canterbury and York. The committees were
established by a resolution of the Church Assembly dated 10
November 1965. They had a purely advisory role. Their function
was to prepare a statement of the needs of the diocese and to
transmit it for the consideration of the archbishops, with a
request that they forward a copy of it to the prime minister. The
discussion of names of potential diocesans was not precluded.
But, if a committee exercised its discretion to discuss names and
submit them to the archbishops, this was done in a confidential
document separate from the statement of needs. During the first
seven years that the committees were in operation twenty-six
vacancies occurred, but names were discussed in only ten of
these. The proceedings of the committees were intended to be
totally confidential, though in fact a number of 'leaks' occurred.
The committees normally met under the chairmanship of one of
the suffragan bishops in the vacant diocese; its membership was
made up of representatives of the clergy and laity of the diocese.

Vacancy-in-see committees were one of the few proposals of
the Howick Commission on Crown Appointments to be accepted
by the Church Assembly. The fate of the Commission's report
will be discussed further in the next chapter, but one other of its
suggestions to be adopted was that the two archbishops should
be provided with a secretary specially concerned with appointments. The secretary's function was to maintain records of
potential candidates for episcopal office and to liaise with the
prime minister's secretary for appointments. The first holder of
the new post was W. H. Saumarez Smith, a former Indian civil
servant. A natural result of the new form of liaison between

Downing Street and Lambeth/Bishopthorpe was to gather more power into the hands of the two officials responsible for operating it. This was especially so in the case of the prime minister's secretary for appointments. As a civil servant he was of course technically impartial. But he ceased to be the pure blotting-paper beloved of Archbishop Fisher and developed a mind of his own. This led to exaggerated ideas of his importance in the scheme of things. Thus the Rev. Christopher Wansey, a leading opponent of the system of Crown appointments, sent an open letter in 1974 to the PM's then secretary for appointments, Colin Peterson, concerning the choice of a new Archbishop of Canterbury. 'The apostolic succession', Wansey claimed,

> goes through a filing-Cabinet presided over by the Secretary for Appointments, for no one who is not filed there has the remotest chance of becoming a bishop. So, in this episcopal garden, it is not the royal gardener who does the planting and transplanting, nor even the gardener's boy – the Prime Minister. No, it is the gardener's boy's boy – your own good self. You are the one and only bishop-maker in the Church of England today. I respectfully ask: 'Who are you to choose the successor to St Augustine?'[1]

Beneath the colourful language there was an element of truth. In his life of Michael Ramsey Owen Chadwick suggests that Sir John Hewitt, who served as the prime minister's appointments secretary from 1961 till the end of 1973, was so conservative on the subject of Church–State relations that he refused to countenance the nomination of Eric Kemp as a diocesan on the grounds of his radicalism. The thought of anyone considering Kemp a radical seems droll today. But, says Chadwick, Kemp 'could be radical in what he wished to happen over the relation between Church and State. Ramsey wanted him on the bench. It was impossible for Ramsey to get Kemp made a bishop until after John Hewitt retired.'[2] Kemp was certainly made Bishop of Chichester a few months after Hewitt's retirement. So, if Hewitt was indeed responsible for laying down a secretarial veto, Wansey's quip about the gardener's boy's boy may not have been so wide of the mark after all. But it is always possible that the gardener's boy at the time needed no prompting from his assistant.

Macmillan's immediate successor as Prime Minister was Sir Alec Douglas-Home. A staunch Anglican, he was married to a daughter of Cyril Alington, for many years Dean of Durham, and was an old friend of Michael Ramsey. But he was in office for barely a year, and in that time appointed only two diocesans. The first of these, E. J. K. Roberts, established some sort of a record in that he straddled, as it were, two prime ministerial reigns. Macmillan wrote to him at the beginning of October 1963, offering him the bishopric of Ely. Macmillan was then taken suddenly ill and, before Roberts could answer the letter, had resigned. Roberts had perforce to wait until the new Prime Minister had divested himself of his earldom and returned to the Commons as plain Sir Alec Douglas-Home before he could write to accept the proposal made to him by the former Premier. It was Sir Alec who made the formal submission to the Queen and thus ensured Roberts's status as a Douglas-Home rather than a Macmillan bishop.

Harold Wilson's two premierships covered a total period of seven years and nine months, during which he was responsible for appointing twenty-five diocesan bishops. Fourteen of these – including new Archbishops of Canterbury and York – were nominated during his shorter period in office in 1974–6. Like Asquith, Wilson greatly enjoyed the ecclesiastical side of his duties. In his book, *The Governance of Britain*, he remarks, à propos of church appointments: 'This was always a matter to which I gave the most careful consideration. But that was not all: I came to look forward, when ploughing through a succession of weekend boxes, to identifying the modest files from the No. 10 appointments secretary. For an hour or more, work on this was an oasis of peace.'[3]

Wilson, in spite of his Nonconformist background, got on well with Ramsey. Apart from church appointments they had other points of contact, such as Africa and race relations in Britain. Ramsey appreciated the care Wilson took over appointments and thought him, on the whole, impartial and understanding. Wilson kept an eye on likely figures in the Anglican Communion overseas as well as in the Church of England. He admired Leslie Brown for his reconciling work as Archbishop of Uganda and brought him home in 1966 to be Bishop of St Edmundsbury and Ipswich. He also admired Kenneth Skelton for standing up to Ian Smith in Rhodesia while Bishop of Matabeleland – and in 1974 nominated him to be Bishop of Lichfield.[4]

Wilson's first premiership of 1964–70 saw a number of significant nominations: Stuart Blanch to Liverpool, Ian Ramsey to Durham, Robert Runcie to St Albans and Patrick Rodger to Manchester. Blanch, Runcie and Rodger were to go on in due course to higher things – as would, in all probability, Ian Ramsey had he not died prematurely in 1972 at the age of 57 and only six years after his consecration.

It is part of the conventional wisdom to say that Ramsey would have succeeded his namesake at Canterbury had he lived longer, but that must remain one of the great 'ifs' of church history. At the time of his appointment to Durham Ramsey was Nolloth Professor of the Philosophy of the Christian Religion in the University of Oxford. He was a diminutive figure who spoke with a Lancashire accent and, in the words of Trevor Beeson, 'gave an initial impression of an affable North-country rural dean'. But the impression was short-lived:

> As soon as he moved into action it became apparent that a mind of outstanding quality was at work – a mind able to engage the attention of distinguished scientists, physicians, philosophers and politicians and of relating theological insights to their areas of concern. Yet Ian Ramsey moved with equal ease at a party following a village confirmation.[5]

Such a combination of academic brilliance and down-to-earth friendliness had a rare appeal. But Ian Ramsey was also a compulsive workaholic who could never say No when requested to take on a new task. He suffered a heart attack in April 1972, and a second one six months later which proved fatal. As Beeson put it: 'This was a devastating blow to the Church of England, for not only had it lost its most able bishop; it had also been deprived of the only serious contender for the Archbishopric of Canterbury when Michael Ramsey offered his resignation.'[6] It is, however, far from certain that, had Ian Ramsey lived, he would have been nominated to the primacy. David L. Edwards suggests that a proposal to appoint him would certainly have been resisted behind the scenes by some on theological and by others on political grounds. 'Although his temperament was eirenic, his integrity was such that he never hid his rejection of religious or political conservatism. On most of the topics of the day he had views to offer, and most of his views were liberal.' Edwards adds that Ramsey's temperamental suitability to be Archbishop of Canterbury would not have seemed obvious to every conscience, and that 'an issue also in doubt for theological or political reasons might have been settled by a lack of confidence about the personal element'.[7]

In March 1974 Michael Ramsey announced his intention to retire at the end of the year. With his namesake out of the running, the field remained open. There was a front-runner of sound pedigree in the person of the Archbishop of York, Donald Coggan. But Coggan was now 65, and his appointment would necessarily be a stop-gap one. In the fashionable phrase he would, if nominated, be considered a caretaker-archbishop until one of the more promising outsiders, such as Kenneth Woollcombe of Oxford or Robert Runcie of St Albans, had had a bit more experience.

Racing metaphors are appropriate on this occasion. Following the official announcement of Ramsey's resignation on 11 March, Ladbroke's opened a 'religious book' on the race to succeed him. They had received so many enquiries about the odds for the Canterbury Stakes that they had, they said, decided to bow to popular demand and open a book. Coggan led the field from the start at 3–1. He was closely followed by Bishop John Howe, Secretary-General of the Anglican Consultative Council; by Woollcombe of Oxford; and by Owen and Henry Chadwick, Oxbridge professors and college heads much fancied at one time for bishoprics. Among the other runners Blanch of Liverpool and Say of Rochester opened at 10–1, and Williams of Leicester at 9–1. The Churches' Council on Gambling took a light-hearted view. 'Ladbroke's will not take bets where life and limb are at stake', a spokesman commented, 'and I don't think even the Archbishopric comes into that category.'[8]

In the event Ladbroke's had done their sums correctly; and Coggan romped home an easy winner. After the news had been announced on 14 May David L. Edwards likened his succession to Ramsey to that of Attlee after Churchill.[9] Coggan was not a man who struck the imagination or was the subject of anecdotes or mimicry, nor did he say the sort of things that a bishop was not expected to say or deliver himself of quotable remarks to journalists. On the other hand he was a model overseer of the Church, conscientious and with a tidy mind that took trouble over people and details. Above all he was a hard worker whom Fisher had once likened to a man with a wheelbarrow: 'However much you pile on him, he goes on pushing.'[10] But he managed his increasing load without any seeming strain. When taunted gently in a TV interview about his 'caretaker' image he replied that he thought it a 'very high privilege to take care of Christ's Church'.

The choice of a successor to Coggan as Archbishop of York proved more difficult. The see was politely declined in turn by Bishop Howe, by Rodger of Manchester and by Runcie of St Albans. Although Runcie would have liked to return to the North, where he had begun his ministry, he felt that this was not the time to do so. After five years at St Albans his plans were just beginning to come to the boil; and his wife had settled down happily in Hertfordshire after ten years in the Principal's house at Cuddesdon and was building up her life anew. Runcie had no real doubts about saying 'No' to York.[11] Fortunately the fourth

"... Yes, he'd be delighted to see the Archbishop tomorrow—and would it be possible to remove the spell now?"

*Cartoonist **JAK**'s reaction to the news that Archbishop Coggan had asked Prime Minister Callaghan for an interview on some weighty matter and had been told that the Premier was too busy to see him.*

candidate to be offered the see, Blanch of Liverpool, was happy to accept. An engagingly modest man, he assured the media that he had been 'stunned' by the offer from Downing Street.

In his eight years at Liverpool Blanch had made a name for himself as a new-style, no-nonsense bishop. He would park his car on the outskirts of the city and ride to diocesan headquarters on the folding bicycle which had been given to him as a parting gift by the students of Rochester Theological College, whose first warden he had been. Blanch, like Coggan, was an avowed Evangelical; but he was a traditionalist rather than a radical in matters of faith, and his churchmanship was never held against him.

The four-year gap between Wilson's two premierships was spanned by the Conservative administration of Edward Heath. Heath was a devout and knowledgeable Anglican; his stint as news editor of the *Church Times* had given him much background information about the Church of England which he doubtless found useful when faced with the duty of choosing the Church's chief officers. A number of the bishops he appointed proved exceptionally able. Among others he nominated Kenneth Wooll-combe to Oxford, Maurice Wood to Norwich and John Habgood to Durham, all first appointments; and he translated George Reindorp from Guildford to Salisbury, Gerald Ellison from Chester to London and Graham Leonard from Willesden to Truro. He had told Ramsey when he assumed office in June 1970 that he meant to do what he could for the Church. Although the Archbishop's politics were not those of the Prime Minister, Ramsey warmed to him over the years. 'I felt him to be a man of integrity', he remarked, 'an impression which I repeatedly got.'[12] Heath discussed with Ramsey the type of bishop he thought the Church needed. He liked outgoing personalities like George Reindorp (though Reindorp was also chosen to sort out the administrative muddle left behind at Salisbury by the saintly but disorganized Joe Fison) and Robin Woods, who was made Bishop of Worcester.

Heath always took the closest possible interest in the process of bishop-making. John Hewitt was never allowed to rule the roost where Heath was concerned or to be the tail that wagged the dog. Throughout the run-up to each appointment Heath always considered both the requirements of the diocese and the need to preserve a balance on the episcopal bench. From 1972 onwards, he has informed the author, the authorities of a vacant diocese were required to fill in a pro forma setting out their requirements (a development of the vacancy-in-see procedure). Heath told me that the completed pro formas always showed a remarkable similarity. Every diocese wanted a man aged between 44 and 48, married with four children (preferably two at university and two still at school), and with a knowledge both of agriculture and of industry. The only difference that ever arose was that the diocese which had had a High Church bishop usually wanted his replacement to be a little Lower, while a diocese with a Low Church bishop asked for one a little Higher.

The Prime Minister also felt that he wanted to get to know the bishops more, so he instituted a series of dinners at 10 Downing Street to which the bishops and their wives were invited. He worked his way along the bench: first the province of Canterbury and then that of York. The dinners proved such a success that Heath thought it would be a good idea to throw one for the Roman Catholic bishops (no wives there, so they could be got through in one go). Hewitt was less enthusiastic, and kept on reminding Heath that the Queen was Supreme Governor of the Church of England and that he was the Queen's first minister. But Heath insisted, and eventually the reluctant Hewitt booked a firm date in the prime ministerial diary. Then came the first problem: whether to invite the Archbishop of Canterbury to the feast. Hewitt was sent to Lambeth to enquire whether such an invitation would prove acceptable – and was told that it would be. The second problem was who should sit on the Prime Minister's right hand: the Archbishop of Canterbury as leader of the Established Church or the Cardinal-Archbishop of West-minster as guest of honour. Hewitt thought that Ramsey should be in the position of honour. Heath was more doubtful – and sent Hewitt back to Lambeth to take fresh soundings. Ramsey said he would be perfectly happy to sit on the Prime Minister's *left* hand. The final problem concerned who should say Grace: Ramsey or the Cardinal. Heath solved this one by deciding to say Grace himself![13]

On two occasions Heath nominations came under fire. The first was in 1971, when Prebendary Maurice Wood was appointed to be Bishop of Norwich. Wood had won a DSC as a naval chaplain in the war and had distinguished himself subsequently as a go-ahead vicar in Oxford and Islington and as Principal of Oak Hill Theological College. For over a decade he had been among the two or three leading Conservative Evangelicals in the Church of England, and his eirenic approach to many controversial issues had led to their wider participation in general church life. Nevertheless, to some critics, he was indelibly tarred with the Evangelical brush, and, in their eyes, he hardly squared up to the 'specifications' of the Norwich vacancy-in-see committee, which had asked for a man who would be acceptable in parishes of varying shades of theological opinion. Moreover, all his pastoral experience had been in urban areas, whereas the committee had wanted someone who would be able to discern the changing role of the Church in a changing rural society. Wood thus seemed to the committee (or at least to some members of it) to fail on two counts. In this case, however, the Prime Minister's eye was on the wider church horizon. He was concerned to maintain the episcopal balance of churchmanship and with the need for the Evangelical voice to be represented on the bench.[14] Wood was a leading Evangelical as well as an outgoing personality, and his claims seemed strong to Heath. And the Queen, with her traditional claim to a say in respect of this particular diocese, was happy to go along with his choice – even though, according to Archbishop Ramsey, the expression 'Conservative Evangelical' was new to her and she had to have it explained.[15]

Much more controversial was Heath's decision two years later to nominate to the see of London the Bishop of Chester, Gerald Ellison, rather than the Suffragan Bishop of Willesden, Graham

Leonard. Ellison was 62 and, as a former domestic chaplain to Archbishop Garbett, a prototypical 'Establishment' figure. He had been a rowing blue at Oxford – which led George Reindorp to observe, à propos of Ellison's opposition to attempts to end the parson's freehold: 'The Bishop of Chester, like most oarsmen, believes that he can only move forward by looking backward.'[16] Ellison was certainly conservative – but not quite so conservative as the critics alleged: his occasional interventions on behalf of radical causes were the more effective as coming from a normally conservative quarter. He had, incidentally, himself been Suffragan Bishop of Willesden for five years before moving to Chester, so (like Leonard) was familiar with the diocese of London. Leonard was ten years younger than Ellison and a leading Anglo-Catholic. He was also a prominent opponent of the Anglican–Methodist reunion scheme. When the London vacancy-in-see committee submitted its views to the Archbishop, Leonard's name, but not Ellison's, was among the three put forward. Leonard was also on the list of three names which Ramsey himself sent to the Prime Minister, but came well below Ellison. The Archbishop suggested that Ellison's experience of the House of Lords would make him the better Bishop of London, but that Leonard might well be translated to Truro, a see which would shortly be vacant.[17] Heath agreed. Both offers were accepted during April and a joint announcement was made on 15 May.

Ellison's nomination at once became the target of criticism. It was alleged that the diocese as a whole had wanted Leonard. A lay member of the vacancy-in-see committee breached the seal of confidentiality enjoined on members of the committee and wrote to *The Times* to complain that the committee's advice had been ignored. A deluge of other angry letters rained down on the press. The opposition reached its climax on 25 June, when eight prebendaries of St Paul's Cathedral issued a formal protest at the meeting of the greater chapter held to elect Ellison as the new Bishop of London. Although they stopped short of actually voting against his nomination and merely abstained, their statement expressed 'deep dissatisfaction' about the method of his election. 'We are called upon to take part in an election the issue of which is already decided. The unreality of the whole process is manifest.'[18]

The cathedral dissentients were themselves assailed three months later in a hard-hitting article by Eric James appearing in the radical quarterly, *New Outlook*. James, at that time diocesan missioner for St Albans, claimed that Ellison's appointment had 'scandalized many', but for a variety of reasons. He dismissed the St Paul's protest as 'pretty in-group ecclesiastical stuff', for the

Crown could enforce its choice by letters patent. In any case, said James, most of the electing body held senior positions in the Church 'which to arrive at, and maintain, requires some skill in the gentle art of enduring formality and in the craft of compromise. It was somewhat odd that these ecclesiastical high-ups should refuse this particular fence of meaningless formality, having jumped so many others in their time.' But James, in his article, had even harder things to say about the vacancy-in-see committee itself, which he stigmatized as a 'self-important little caucus':

> They were for the most part a group of dyed-in-the-wool ecclesiastics, of differing ecclesiastical preoccupations – Herod and Pilate had been made friends from the hour of the Anglican–Methodist unity debate – who were known to be hell-bent on causing maximum trouble if their man, the Bishop of Willesden, was not given the job. The rejection of their advice was bound to be treated by them as scandalous.

James went on to suggest that 'the London scandal has produced the Truro scandal'. No one could seriously believe, he suggested, that the Bishop of Willesden (the rallying-point for those against Anglican–Methodist unity) would have been first choice for Truro (where there were more Methodists per head of population than anywhere else in England) had not the Crown been 'desperate to dispose of his body before the Vacancy-in-See Committee of London were in full cry against Chester and for their man, Willesden'.

> It cannot be doubted that the simultaneous announcement of this appointment . . . was made by a Crown Patronage Office supremely confident in its skill at the Establishment game. 'Shout now if you dare', it seemed to be saying to the Vacancy-in-See Committee of London, 'now that Willesden's been bought off and silenced with Truro'.[19]

To which the only appropriate retort (as so often before in this book) would seem to be: 'See how these Christians love one another!' And, in subsequent letters to the press, outraged readers of James's comments rallied to the defence of the various targets of his attack.

James Callaghan succeeded Harold Wilson as Prime Minister in April 1976, and so had a bare fourteen months in which to operate the traditional system of appointing bishops before this gave way to the Crown Appointments Commission. Callaghan, as a Baptist, naturally knew rather less about the Church of

England than did Colin Peterson, who had succeeded John Hewitt as secretary for appointments at the beginning of 1974. In a personal letter to the author the former Prime Minister described his practice thus:

> He [Peterson] would do all the preliminary sifting of candidates and would consult widely. When he had completed this he would produce some names, and he and I would have a discussion in which he would give me his opinions. We would seek to relate the candidates to the nature of the diocese – urban, rural, industrial, north or south, etc. I also sought for a balance between what I (perhaps improperly) called high or low church. An approach would then be made to a selected candidate, and either Colin Peterson or I would see him.

Lord Callaghan added in his letter that the appointment on which he had spent most time personally had been that of a new Dean of St Paul's to succeed Martin Sullivan, and that the man chosen, Alan Webster (at that time Dean of Norwich), had been his own personal choice. 'He was reluctant to accept, and I had a hard time persuading him to undertake the task. I am glad to say he has forgiven me and we remain friends.'

The Church–State discussions about changing the system had been initiated during Harold Wilson's premiership; and, said Lord Callaghan, he would have been entitled to reverse them. 'I decided, after discussion, to let them continue – especially as democratic decisions had been arrived at by the Synod.' He had had a full discussion on the matter with the Queen, who took her responsibilities and duties as the Church's Supreme Governor very seriously.

> I found no real opposition from her for a step which involved her personally, and as a Free Churchman I felt I should not stand in the way of the Church's desires, even if my opinion had been different. Of course important powers (i.e. the right of the Prime Minister to submit either No. 1 or No. 2 of the candidates to H.M., or indeed to call for other names) still reside with the Prime Minister, and that is in itself a safeguard of the Queen's position.[20]

The Crown Appointments Commission formally came into being on 1 June 1977, a few days before the announcement of the names of the last two diocesans to be appointed under the old system. The two final old-style nominees were the Suffragan Bishop of Dorchester, Peter Walker, appointed to Ely; and the Archdeacon of Huntingdon, David Young, appointed to Ripon. On 11 October the name of the Commission's first nominee was announced: the Suffragan Bishop of Kingston, Hugh Montefiore, to be Bishop of Birmingham. Speculation that he might be the successful candidate had begun several weeks before the official announcement and had provoked much controversy in the media. The criticisms centred on two completely different issues: a suggestion that he had made ten years before that Christ might have been a homosexual; and a claim that his progressive views on the environment might damage Birmingham's industrial interests.

The Bishop defended himself stoutly on both counts. He had said in his original 1967 lecture, he explained, that the fact that Jesus was still celibate at the time of his baptism, when his male contemporaries would have been married at 17 or 18, suggested that he might have been homosexual in nature. 'I thought that he could be homosexual in nature because he was celibate – and celibacy precludes the practice of homosexuality'. And the Bishop denied that he was opposed to the motor-car: he thought the car a 'marvellous convenience' which people should be free to buy – but not to use indiscriminately.[21] Bishop Montefiore had no difficulty in living down the initial hostility to his appointment, though, as press comment had grown more and more intense in the weeks leading up to its announcement, Lord Callaghan may have found himself hankering after the calmer waters of the old appointments system. The new system had certainly got off to a stormy start. How it had come into being will be the subject of our next chapter.

### Sir Alec Douglas-Home

### Nominations to diocesan bishoprics 2 (both translations)

(1) 1963:  Edward James Keymer Roberts to Ely (from Kensington).*
(2) 1963:  Gordon David Savage to Southwell (from Buckingham).*

### Harold Wilson

### Nominations to diocesan bishoprics 25 (12 first appointments, 13 translations)

*First appointments:*

(1) 1965:  Stuart Yarworth Blanch to Liverpool.
(2) 1966: George Eric Gordon to Sodor and Man.
(3) 1966: Ian Thomas Ramsey to Durham.

(4) 1969: Cyril William Johnston Bowles to Derby.
(5) 1969: Robert Alexander Kennedy Runcie to St Albans.
(6) 1970: Patrick Campbell Rodger to Manchester.
(7) 1970: John Denis Wakeling to Southwell.

(8) 1974: Vernon Sampson Nicholls to Sodor and Man.
(9) 1974: Eric Waldram Kemp to Chichester.
(10) 1974: John Vernon Taylor to Winchester.
(11) 1975: Archibald Ronald McDonald Gordon to Portsmouth.
(12) 1975: Ernest John Tinsley to Bristol.

*Translations:*

(1) 1966: Leslie Wilfred Brown to St Edmundsbury and Ipswich
(from Namirembe, Uganda).†
(2) 1966: Sydney Cyril Bulley to Carlisle (from Penrith).*
(3) 1968: Eric Treacy to Wakefield (from Pontefract).*
(4) 1969: Laurence Ambrose Brown to Birmingham (from
Warrington).*

(5) 1974: Frederick Donald Coggan to Canterbury (from York).
(6) 1974: Simon Wilton Phipps to Lincoln (from Horsham).*
(7) 1974: Stuart Yarworth Blanch to York (from Liverpool).
(8) 1974: Kenneth John Fraser Skelton to Lichfield (formerly of
Matabeleland, Rhodesia).†
(9) 1975: David Stuart Sheppard to Liverpool (from Woolwich).*
(10) 1975: John Monier Bickersteth to Bath and Wells (from
Warrington).*
(11) 1975: John Yates to Gloucester (from Whitby).*
(12) 1975: Stuart Hetley Price to Ripon (from Doncaster).*
(13) 1976: John Gibbs to Coventry (from Bradwell).*

## Edward Heath

**Nominations to diocesan bishoprics 18 (8 first appointments,
10 translations)**

*First appointments:*

(1) 1970: Kenneth John Woollcombe to Oxford.
(2) 1970: Robert Wylmer Woods to Worcester.
(3) 1971: Maurice Arthur Ponsonby Wood to Norwich.
(4) 1972: Douglas Russell Feaver to Peterborough.
(5) 1972: Ronald Oliver Bowlby to Newcastle.
(6) 1973: John Stapylton Habgood to Durham.
(7) 1973: David Alan Brown to Guildford.
(8) 1973: John Richard Gordon Eastaugh to Hereford.

*Translations:*

   (1) 1971: William Gordon Fallows to Sheffield (from Pontefract).*
   (2) 1971: Albert John Trillo to Chelmsford (from Hertford).*
   (3) 1971: Robert Arthur Schurhoff Martineau to Blackburn (from Huntingdon).*
   (4) 1972: Ross Sydney Hook to Bradford (from Grantham).*
   (5) 1972: Henry David Halsey to Carlisle (from Tonbridge).*
   (6) 1972: George Edmund Reindorp to Salisbury (from Guildford).
   (7) 1973: Gerald Alexander Ellison to London (from Chester).
   (8) 1973: Graham Douglas Leonard to Truro (from Willesden).*
   (9) 1973: Eric Arthur John Mercer to Exeter (from Birkenhead).*
(10) 1973: Hubert Victor Whitsey to Chester (from Hertford).*

**James Callaghan (up to 31 May 1977)**

**Nominations to diocesan bishoprics 3 (1 first appointment, 2 translations)**

*First appointment:*

   (1) 1977: David Nigel de Lorentz Young to Ripon.

*Translations:*

   (1) 1976: Colin Clement Walter James to Wakefield (from Basingstoke).*
   (2) 1977: Peter Knight Walker to Ely (from Dorchester).*

\* Suffragan see.
† Overseas see.

# 24

# Recipe for Change

James Callaghan was the last prime minister to appoint bishops by the traditional method. But in fact the method had been so refined and improved over the previous seventy-odd years (as this book has made plain) that it now differed substantially from that which had been operated by Queen Victoria's premiers. While the Queen reigned she took an active voice in the appointments process, and sometimes persuaded the prime minister to think again. The Archbishop of Canterbury was often consulted, but not necessarily heeded. His role in the process was much less important than it was to become under Randall Davidson and his successors. To Davidson belongs the credit for vastly increasing the importance of the archbishop's role in the consultative process. Under Geoffrey Fisher the Church's influence in helping the prime minister in his choice became even greater. But the Church's role was still only an advisory one. The prime minister still had the last word – and occasionally, even late into the twentieth century, was still prepared to utter it. So, throughout the first three-quarters of this century, there was a constant barrage of complaints over the alleged iniquities of the system and repeated calls for its reform.

Defenders of the system could stress its good points. The prime minister had a wider field of choice than would be available to a body of local electors; there might be wire-pulling on behalf of rival candidates or an open struggle between ecclesiastical parties, possibly resulting in a weak compromise candidate when the two sides had reached a deadlock. Such arguments failed to persuade opponents of the system, as did the pragmatic argument that the system for the most part worked well enough and that most of the men appointed under it would have been voted into office under an electoral system. It was the principle that offended the opposition: the principle that the chief officers of a spiritual society should be chosen by a layman who need neither belong to it nor sympathize with its aims. However strong the safeguards against abuse of the system by an unfriendly or unscrupulous premier, in the last resort he could always insist on getting his way.

An abortive attempt by the Church to change the system took place in the 1930s. Dissatisfaction with the Church–State set-up following the Commons' rejection of the revised Prayer Book in 1927–8 led to the appointment by the archbishops in 1930 of a commission to consider the relations between Church and State. The commission met under the chairmanship of Lord Robert Cecil, and took five years to produce its report. In respect of appointments to bishoprics the five years' labour brought forth an insignificant mouse: a suggestion that cathedral chapters should be freed from the penalties of *praemunire* if they declined to elect the Crown's nominee, and that the archbishop of the province should be similarly immune if he failed to consecrate that nominee. As those penalties had not been enforced for centuries, their proposed repeal was hardly revolutionary – though a Free Church commentator on a sentence in the report, 'It is not the selection [of bishops] but their consecration which gives them spiritual authority', was led to remark: 'Is it really maintained that it does not matter who is chosen, or how, so long as he is duly consecrated?'[1] This particular proposal sank without trace, and recalcitrant archbishops and chapters remained theoretically subject to outlawry and the confiscation of all their goods.

The war came while the Church was still digesting the last crumbs from the Cecil Report. It was not till 1946 that the appointments system again came under review: by an informal group meeting under the chairmanship of Mr Justice Vaisey and including among its members the Dean of Winchester, E. G. Selwyn, and the future Bishop of Exeter, R. C. Mortimer, then a professor at Oxford. They reported direct to Archbishop Fisher in November 1946. Their key proposal required the Crown to put its nominee before the dean and chapter of the relevant diocese, which would then be free either to accept or to reject him. In the case of rejection the prime minister would have to think again and come back with a further name or names. After showing the report to Archbishop Garbett, Fisher pointed out to the group that the chapter's proposed power of veto would encroach on the Crown's prerogative and would therefore be unacceptable. Nothing more was heard from the Vaisey group.[2]

Six years after the Vaisey Report came the Moberly Report – the work of a commission set up by the Church Assembly in 1949 under the chairmanship of Sir Walter Moberly to review once again the whole field of Church–State relations. Its key proposal on episcopal appointments was far less radical, and therefore far more realistic, than that of Vaisey and his colleagues. The Moberly Report suggested that there should be set up a consultative body with which the two archbishops should take counsel over each see that fell vacant. The archbishops would then give their advice to the prime minister, buttressed by the advice *they* had received from the consultative body. As Lord Quickswood (the former Lord Hugh Cecil) put it in a comment on the proposal: 'It is the essence of the Commission's proposal that they do not wish to make a fundamental change, but only to emphasise and formally to establish a plan of appointment which they suppose to be already in existence.'[3] But of course, as critics pointed out, if a prime minister really wanted to appoint someone anathema to the Church authorities, the existence of a toothless 'consultative body' of church worthies was hardly likely to dissuade him. Alternatively, Parliament might take the view that the proposal was an ingenious attempt to transfer the power of appointment from the State to the Church and would decline to countenance it. The idea never got off the ground – and the existing system continued as before.

It was a general sense of dissatisfaction over two particular events in 1961 that sparked off yet another Church commission to mull over Crown appointments. The two events were, first, the unseemly haste with which the announcement of Geoffrey Fisher's resignation as Archbishop of Canterbury had been followed by the news of his successor's nomination; and, secondly, the prolonged controversy over the Prime Minister's failure to appoint Walter Boulton, Provost of Guildford since 1952, as first dean of the new cathedral. Brief reference has already been made to the Boulton affair; and it was above all the sense of outrage engendered by the apparent slighting of the Provost that led to an impassioned debate in the Church Assembly on 7 November 1961. By a large majority the Assembly requested the archbishops to set up a commission to consider the method of Crown appointments to ecclesiastical offices. The commission was duly established early in 1962 under the chairmanship of Lord Howick of Glendale and reported in December 1964.

Once again it was a mountain which produced a very small mouse. The commission firmly rejected proposals that nominations to the Crown should be made by the Archbishop of Canterbury or by an exclusively church body, or that bishops should be genuinely elected. 'There is, we consider, no evidence that elections would produce better bishops or that they would in some way have more authority.' But, although proposing that the existing system should be retained, the commission suggested that it should be reformed in certain particulars. They also included a useful documentary account of how the system operated in the post-Davidson, post-Fisher era:

> As soon as it is known that a see is vacant or will shortly become vacant, the Prime Minister's Secretary for Appointments undertakes a series of consultations with the laity as well as with bishops and other clergy both within and outside the diocese. The widest possible information is sought and obtained in regard to the needs of the diocese as well as of the Church as a whole. This enquiry is made against the background of a continuous process of consultation and collation. Only thus can the Prime Minister exercise properly his personal responsibility for the nomination he makes to the Sovereign. Both at an early and at a late stage the respective Archbishop is consulted . . . At the final stage the respective Archbishop gives the Prime Minister the names of two or three persons, indicating that the choice of any one of them would have his approval . . . The Prime Minister, who has at his disposal all the information afforded by the process of consultation, is then in a position to consider his recommendation to the Sovereign for election by the dean and chapter.[4]

Both Church and State had travelled a long way in the century that had elapsed since Disraeli sent his frantic appeal from Balmoral to his secretary in London urgently requesting the dispatch of a copy of *Crockford*.

Among the reforms suggested by the Howick Commission was that each diocese should establish a 'vacancy-in-see committee' with the task, when a vacancy occurred, of drawing up a statement of the needs of the diocese which would then be sent to the archbishop, thereby involving the dioceses more closely in the consultative process; and that the archbishops should have a secretary specially concerned with appointments. Even Fisher, now officially retired but still very much in touch with affairs, welcomed this latter proposal. 'The greatest weakness in the present system', he observed, 'is that the Archbishop has to rely too much upon his own rather casually gathered information as to the needs of the Church and the persons available for high office.'[5] The commission also proposed that the ceremony of a new bishop's election by the dean and chapter should be abolished and that he should be appointed by letters patent.

The Church Assembly was unenthusiastic about the Howick Report. 'Throughout the debate', says Paul Welsby in his history of the post-war Church of England, 'there was a clear note of dissatisfaction and there was great reluctance to make minor changes in the existing system lest this should postpone a more thorough consideration of constitutional change.' In the Church as a whole, says Welsby, the report was received 'with disappointment because of its timidity, its theological inadequacy, its refusal even to give consideration to any radical reform of the present system, and its cavalier dismissal of possible alternatives. It was felt that its proposals would give the archbishops too much power and that there was too much bland talk about agreements being reached by goodwill on both sides.'[6]

In spite of its reluctance to make 'minor changes' in the existing system the Assembly did bring itself to approve the proposals for vacancy-in-see committees and for an archbishops' secretary for appointments. But it declined to countenance the abolition of the election ceremony; and it expressed its general dissatisfaction by asking the archbishops on 10 November 1965 for yet another commission to examine the constitutional relationship of Church and State and to suggest possible modifications – bearing in mind the effect of that relationship on inter-Church unity. The result was the setting up in the autumn of 1966 of a commission under the chairmanship of Professor Owen Chadwick. After four years' discussion the new commission produced in 1970 a report which really did go beyond a desire to maintain the status quo – and which included the proposals that eventually bore fruit in the Church–State concordat of 1976.

While the Chadwick Commission was sitting, however, the State offered a tiny gesture of its own – the abolition of almost all offences committed under the fourteenth-century statutes of *praemunire* and subsequent related Acts of Parliament. Recalcitrant deans and chapters who declined to elect, or archbishops to consecrate, the royal nominees were no longer to be liable to the forfeiture of their property, outlawry and even life imprisonment. The abolition of the *praemunire* penalties in relation to the Church was recommended by the Law Commission and incorporated in a Criminal Law Bill which came before Parliament towards the end of 1966. Archbishop Ramsey declared in the House of Lords on 16 November that he personally would have preferred the penalty of execution, which had been the fate of several of his predecessors – a penalty which had at least the possibility of a martyr's crown. But, on behalf of the Church, he welcomed the ending of the 'terrible' penalties of *praemunire*.

When the Chadwick Commission at last produced its report on 10 December 1970 it revealed that, on the subject of appointments to bishoprics, the commissioners were of two minds. They agreed that a committee or electoral board, representing both the diocese and the Church at large, should be formed to present the Church's view when a diocesan bishop was nominated for election. They disagreed, however, on how such a committee or board should take its place in the constitution of the Church. Eight members recommended that it should advise the Crown on the names of bishops through the prime minister. Five members recommended that the prime minister should cease to play any part in the process, and that the committee or board should itself elect the bishop and present his name directly to the sovereign. It was in fact the first alternative which was eventually to win the day. The prime minister, in other words, was to be left with at least a nominal role in choosing one of the names put up to him by a church advisory committee, even if that role was to act as an exalted postman bearing the chosen name to the sovereign.

But it took several years before this very substantial reform could be implemented. The Church played it cool to begin with. When its General Synod (the body which had replaced the Church Assembly in 1970) debated the issue on 17 February 1971 it voted unanimously in favour of 'receiving' the Chadwick Report (a neutral term) and commending it to the dioceses for study. This was then (as it is still) the classic Church of England remedy for dealing with potatoes too hot for immediate consumption – though of course the report dealt with other vital issues such as worship and doctrine as well as with Crown appointments. The cooling-off period lasted a couple of years. When the report again came before the Synod in February 1973 the Synod grasped the nettle firmly. It instructed its Standing Committee (a kind of unofficial church cabinet) to bring forward proposals to secure for the Church a more effective share in the making of bishops and other senior ecclesiastical appointments; and to enable the Synod to decide whether or not, in any new system of appointments, the final choice should in its view lie with the Church itself.

The following year the process of gestation by the Standing Committee resulted in a three-part motion which the Synod approved on 5 July 1974 by 270 votes to 70. First, and most significantly, the Synod affirmed its belief that 'the decisive voice in the appointment of diocesan bishops should be that of the Church'. Secondly, it suggested that, when a vacancy in a see arose, a 'small body representative of the diocese and of the wider Church' should choose a suitable person for appointment to that diocese and that the name should be submitted to the sovereign. Thirdly, the Synod instructed its Standing Committee to arrange for further consideration of these matters, 'including the administrative, legal and constitutional implications', and to report the results to the Synod at an early date. There was nothing in the least surprising in the Synod's decision. Any assembly invited to take more power to itself is inclined to accept the invitation. The Synod was, however, nailing its colours to the fence rather than to the mast, in that, though a principle was affirmed, it was left studiously vague as to how that principle was to be put into practice. The result in the end was a compromise, though it was the Church that obtained the substance of power over appointments and the State the shadow. And the prophets of doom who foresaw disestablishment as the logical outcome of the Synod's insistence on change were proved completely wrong.

The next stage in the process was a series of negotiations conducted by Archbishop Coggan and Sir Norman Anderson, chairman of the House of Laity, on behalf of the Church and by the Prime Minister (first Harold Wilson and then Jim Callaghan) and leaders of the other main political parties on behalf of the State. And the first crucial fact to be revealed was that, as the matter concerned the royal prerogative, there would be no need for legislation – which immensely simplified matters, ensured a much easier timetable and paved the way for a classic 'gentlemen's agreement'.

The fruits of the negotiations were revealed in the House of Commons by Callaghan on 8 June 1976: in a written reply to a pre-arranged request from the then Leader of the Opposition, Margaret Thatcher, for a statement about the appointments procedure. After reminding the House of the Synod motion of 1974 affirming the principle that the decisive voice in the appointment of diocesan bishops should be that of the Church, the Prime Minister insisted that there were in his view 'cogent reasons why the State cannot divest itself from a concern with these appointments'. The sovereign, said Callaghan, must be able to look for advice on a matter of this kind – 'and that must mean, for a constitutional Sovereign, advice from Ministers'. Moreover, the archbishops and some of the bishops sat by right in the House of Lords, and their nomination must therefore remain a matter for the prime minister's concern.

Callaghan then came to the nub of the issue. He conceded that there was a case for making *some* changes in the present arrangements, so that the Church should have, and be seen to have, a greater say in the process of choosing its leaders. Under the suggested new procedure archbishops and bishops would continue to be appointed by the Queen – who would continue to receive, as now, final advice from the prime minister on these appointments. In giving that final advice the prime minister would retain a 'real element of choice'. To assess a vacancy and possible candidates for it, a small standing committee would be set up by the Church. The committee would draw up a short-list of two names which could be in order of preference. But (and here came the crux of the matter) the prime minister would retain the right to recommend the second name, or to ask the committee for a further name or names. Such arrangements as these, which did not require legislation to put them into effect, would, said Callaghan, give the Church a greater say in the choice of its leaders and at the same time 'preserve the constitutional essentials of an established Church'.[7]

When one came to analyse the Prime Minister's statement, its proposals could be interpreted (according to one's point of view) either as a judicious compromise nicely typical of the spirit of Anglicanism or as a dusty answer which left the Church with an unsatisfactory half-loaf. The scheme put forward was uncompromising in its insistence that, if the Church of England was to remain established, its unique links with the State unimpaired and its bishops sitting by right in Parliament, then those bishops must continue to be appointed by the sovereign, constitutionally advised by her prime minister. The PM would be left with the real (if negative) power to reject the Church's nominees; but the fact that he would be limited to considering only those names put forward by a church committee would give to the Church an equally real positive power which at present it did not possess. What the State now offered was certainly a lot less than the Church had demanded – but it was much more than the Church currently enjoyed. It could almost certainly be taken as representing the most that the Church could expect so long as it wished to remain the Established Church of the land. The alleged parallel with the Church of Scotland, established yet free, had often been quoted in aid of complete freedom of choice for the Church of England. Yet the two cases were not really parallel, if only because no Scottish cleric sat by right in the House of Lords. The half-loaf offered by the State was a substantial half, in that the positive initiative in the choice of bishops would rest with the Church and only negative powers with the State. To demand more would be unrealistic except at the price of disestablishment.

At the end of his Commons reply to Mrs Thatcher's request the Prime Minister had expressed the hope that his proposals would 'commend themselves as settling this issue in a satisfactory way for the foreseeable future'. This hope was speedily realized. When the General Synod debated the proposals on 13 July it gave them an emphatic welcome. Following a powerful appeal from

Archbishop Coggan to stop dithering and to have the courage to make up their minds on the long-drawn-out issue, Synod members rejected a series of amendments designed to keep the matter open so that the Church could continue to press for an absolutely decisive voice in choosing its bishops. They went on to approve the official motion welcoming the Prime Minister's statement by 390 votes to 29 – an overwhelming majority. Coggan had warned the Synod that to reject the motion would be to retreat into denominationalism. The Callaghan proposals, he pointed out, were not so much a sop given by the Government to the Church as an invitation to continue a relationship of many centuries' duration on new terms which gave the Church practically everything for which it had asked.

The next stage in the projected change-over was the need to decide on the composition of the body which was to present the names of potential bishops to the prime minister. Within three months the Synod's Standing Committee had come up with its solution. This was for a sixteen-member Crown Appointments Commission, including nine permanent or 'central' members representative of the wider Church and five members representative of the vacant diocese under consideration. Both the prime minister's and the archbishops' appointments secretaries would be non-voting members of the commission. The Standing Committee proposed that the two archbishops should be ex-officio members, while the seven other permanent members should be elected – three clerics by the General Synod's House of Clergy, three laypeople by the House of Laity and one non-Synod layperson by the Standing Committee itself. It was proposed that the five representatives of the vacant diocese should be elected by the diocesan vacancy-in-see committee.

In arriving at this composition the Standing Committee set itself to reconcile the principle that the commission should be small in the interests of proper confidentiality, and yet also sufficiently 'open', with a strong elective element, to avoid the risk of becoming a mere cabal. The Committee rejected suggestions that there should be separate commissions for the provinces of Canterbury and York, but considered it vital that there should be a proper balance between the two provinces in the membership of the commission. They also proposed that, when a bishopric was under consideration, the chair at meetings of the commission should be taken by the archbishop of the province concerned. The Standing Committee's report to the Synod (though it was signed by Coggan as chairman) also noted that the two archbishops had strong reservations about the size of the proposed commission and would like to have seen it much smaller: they feared that a commission as large as this would be more likely to be subject to 'leaks'* and to be generally less manageable than a smaller body.

It was this disagreement between the archbishops and the other members of the Standing Committee which helped persuade the General Synod, when it met on 12 November 1976, to reduce by two the proposed membership of the commission. The two people eliminated were the non-synodical member and one of the five diocesan members. The Synod also voted to increase the term of office for the central elected representatives from four years, as recommended by the Standing Committee, to five years, as suggested by Coggan. With these two minor amendments the Synod was happy generally to approve the proposals and to issue instructions for the necessary action to be taken for bringing the Crown Appointments Commission into being on 1 June 1977. After a further brief debate on 15 February to tie up a few loose ends, all was now accomplished and the stage set for the beginning of the Church's new deal. The period covered by this book formally ends here; but a final chapter will take a brief look at the first dozen years of the new regime.

---

*One obvious source of leaks was mentioned during the General Synod debate on the proposals and led a member, R. R. Feilden of Bath and Wells, to remark that he had been shocked to hear 'pillow talk' described as a danger to confidentiality. 'It is an essential element of connubial bliss', Feilden declared.

# 25

# Postscript – The Thatcher Years

As she stood on the doorstep of No. 10 Downing Street after her election victory in May 1979 Mrs Margaret Thatcher repeated the words of the well-known prayer beginning 'Lord, make me an instrument of thy peace', which she wrongly attributed to St Francis of Assisi.* Her rumbustious premiership was to span three Parliaments and last for eleven and a half years; though it may have had its moments of peace, it was in fact to be the instrument of a great deal of domestic strife. And even her role as bishop-maker, rendered largely nominal by the Church–State concordat of 1976, was to produce its moments of controversy when she occasionally chose a name, out of the two presented to her by the Crown Appointments Commission, not to everyone's liking.

Appropriately enough, her first diocesan nomination was that of a new Archbishop of Canterbury to succeed Donald Coggan, who announced his resignation only a month after she had become Premier. But of course she had taken no initiative in the matter. For the first time the Church itself (or at least those empowered to act on its behalf) was to be responsible for the selection of its leader. And, for the first time since the Reformation, men from outside England could be considered. The field was a wide one, though only two overseas candidates were serious runners: Archbishop Ted Scott, Primate of the Anglican Church of Canada, and Bishop John Howe, Secretary-General of the Anglican Consultative Council and a former Bishop of St Andrews in Scotland. Among the likely English diocesans

*According to the late Bishop John Moorman, the great authority on St Francis, the prayer was first published in a French periodical in January 1913, but no one knows who wrote it. In 1916 it appeared in the Vatican newspaper *Osservatore Romano* among several prayers for peace, but with no suggestion that it had anything to do with St Francis. The first English versions appeared in or about 1936, a version published as a 'Challenge Card' by Mowbray's being headed 'A Prayer of St Francis'. 'It looks', said the Bishop in a letter published in the *Church Times* of 15 June 1979, 'as if it must have been someone at Mowbray's in 1936 who first attributed it to St Francis.'

considered ripe for translation were Leonard of Truro, Runcie of St Albans, Habgood of Durham, Bowlby of Newcastle, Sheppard of Liverpool and, not least, the Archbishop of York, Stuart Blanch. There were also, once again, the eminent and learned brothers Owen and Henry Chadwick, though they were both considered too well dug into academic groves to wish to move higher. Leonard's stature had increased during his years at Truro, but he was a strong Anglo-Catholic and a definite 'party' man. Habgood was a fine scholar and an outstanding preacher, but aloof in manner. Bowlby was too fervent an advocate of the ordination of women to appeal to the Church's Catholic wing. Sheppard at 50 was a bit on the young side and was thought to lack *gravitas*. Lack of *gravitas* was also, surprisingly, held against Blanch, though his warm personality and abundance of humour combined to make him universally liked. Runcie was a moderate Catholic with radical leanings. On the ordination of women he was conservative but not dogmatic. He too had charm and a great sense of humour. He had had a distinguished war record and had shown himself a skilful negotiator in his official dealings with both Roman Catholics and Orthodox. It was therefore no surprise when his name emerged out of Mrs Thatcher's hat as the winner of the 1979 Canterbury Stakes – and her choice was a popular one.[1]

Less widely acclaimed was her selection of Leonard two years later to succeed Ellison as Bishop of London. As soon as the appointment was announced a storm of controversy broke out – based on the claim that Leonard had received fewer votes than the other alleged name on the list, Habgood of Durham. Habgood, according to Leonard's biographer, received seven votes to Leonard's five – less than a two-thirds majority. He might not have been passed over had it not been for intensive eleventh-hour political lobbying by Leonard's Anglo-Catholic supporters. This followed a powerful and persistent lobby for Leonard's nomination throughout the consultative process – and particularly within the vacancy-in-see committee and the Commission itself. There was also dogged opposition to Leonard, though on a much less organized and less politically active basis than the pro-Leonard lobby. Many of the diocese's senior staff (including the area bishops) were said to be opposed to his nomination; and, after a long period of discussion and deadlock, his opponents carried the day – in the sense that marginally more votes were cast for Habgood than for his rival at the final meeting of the Crown Appointments Commission. But then somehow the Anglo-Catholics got wind of the fact that the names of both Leonard and Habgood were going to the Prime Minister – and that their man did not have the majority vote. Immediately they swung into a burst of last-minute lobbying among MPs – including direct approaches both to the Prime Minister herself and to the then Leader of the Opposition, Michael Foot. Shortly afterwards Mrs Thatcher cast her vote for Leonard. It was alleged that the Queen was dismayed at the Prime Minister's choice and contacted Archbishop Runcie to see if it could be reconsidered – to be told politely, 'No'.

In the light of the protests both the Prime Minister and the Archbishop issued statements stressing that the procedures agreed between Church and State had been meticulously followed and that 'any suggestion to the contrary is wholly without foundation'. Bob Edwards, a leader of the Anglo-Catholic lobby and vice-chairman of the vacancy-in-see committee, launched a vigorous counter-attack on the critics. He said he felt that the Catholic action had been justified since, he claimed, Leonard had been wanted by a 'very large majority' on the committee. The representations to MPs had been intended to make it plain that the Bishop of Durham would be 'quite unacceptable' to the diocese of London – 'which is not quite the same thing as asking for the Bishop of Truro'. Commenting on the belief widely held in the Church that the Prime Minister would pick the second name on a list only in extraordinary circumstances, Edwards maintained that this *had* been an extraordinary circumstance because of the great tension surrounding this particular appointment. He thought that the Anglo-Catholics were entitled to have at least one diocesan in the Church's five senior dioceses. Runcie was not so much a Catholic as a 'High Church liberal'.[2]

In Parliament a number of MPs came out in support of Leonard's appointment. But the opposition was crystallized in a strongly-worded editorial in the *Church Times* which, while wishing Leonard well in his new post, suggested (wrongly, as it happened) that the controversy over his nomination was likely to prove 'much more than a storm in an ecclesiastical tea-cup'. On the contrary, it raised constitutional issues of the gravest significance for both Church and State.

> Without of course questioning the constitutional propriety of Mrs Thatcher's action on this occasion we cannot but regret it, since it throws into the melting-pot the careful compromise system of checks and balances which has been in operation for the past few years. The Prime Minister may have observed the letter of this particular law, but she has surely defied its spirit.

The paper warned the Prime Minister that the 1976 settlement between Church and State provided the basis for an 'honourable partnership' in the making of higher appointments in the Church. This partnership had now been put at risk by her action – 'not, by all accounts, for the first time' – in not accepting the man favoured by a majority of members of the Crown Appointments Commission. 'She must not be surprised if her action results in demands for a modification of the 1976 settlement.'[3]

No such modification was demanded at synodical level – though it might well have been if a certain notorious nomination in 1984 had been the choice of a *minority* of members of the Commission rather than of the majority. The nominee was David Jenkins, whose appointment to be Bishop of Durham aroused achoes of the Henson controversy. The difference was that Jenkins was the Church's choice, and not that of a Nonconformist premier. And in fact it was not until several weeks after the appointment had been announced that anyone realized that there was going to *be* a controversy. Then, in a television programme, the bishop-designate appeared to cast doubts on the Virgin Birth and the Resurrection, and the flood-gates were opened. Archbishop Habgood, like Archbishop Davidson in the Henson case, was urged to refuse the alleged heretic consecration; and, like Davidson, he declined to oblige the critics and the consecration went ahead. York Minster was struck by lightning two days later – a sign, so the critics claimed, of the divine displeasure. But Jenkins soon lived down the initial hostility and proved a highly popular diocesan. And, even if he had not won popularity, the Prime Minister could hardly have been blamed for having merely endorsed the Church's choice.

The controversy following the Jenkins nomination was, however, instrumental in causing the defeat of a minor piece of church legislation in Parliament. This was the Appointment of Bishops Measure, which would have abolished the formal election of a bishop by the dean and chapter and the legal ceremony of confirmation of the election. The purpose of the measure was partly the wish to dispense with two outmoded procedures and partly to economize on the fees payable to the lawyers involved in the ceremonies. The measure went through its various processes in the General Synod without much argument and, at its final-approval stage in July 1983, was overwhelmingly endorsed by 233 votes to eighteen. When it reached the Commons, however, it was less lucky. Early on the morning of 17 July 1984, in a thinly attended House, it was thrown out by thirty-two votes to seventeen. At first some observers were forecasting a major crisis in Church–State relations. In the event the reverse represented only a minor hiccup. Although the Synod's Standing Committee recommended that the measure should be resubmitted to

Parliament, the Synod itself showed greater prudence (or pusillanimity) and, on 14 February 1985, rejected the Committee's proposal by 214 votes to 181. Nearly seven years later, on 13 November 1991, the Synod, by a large majority, approved a private member's motion and voted to 'agree with the view that the confirmation of the election of a bishop is an expensive farrago of legal gobbledegook ... and would welcome modifications of the ceremony'. But, at the time that the text of this book was finalized, it was impossible to forecast what would come of the Synod's fresh attempt to grasp this particular nettle.

The next major controversy over a nomination by Mrs Thatcher occurred in April 1987, a few weeks before her third successive victory in a general election. The diocese was Birmingham, which had been the scene of the controversy nearly ten years before over James Callaghan's nomination of Hugh Montefiore, the man recommended for the post by the newly-formed Crown Appointments Commission. On this occasion, however, Mrs Thatcher (it was alleged) had passed over the first choice for the second on wholly political rather than on partly theological grounds. The two candidates were both London area bishops: Jim Thompson of Stepney and Mark Santer of Kensington. Thompson, said to have been the Commission's first choice, was at that time regarded as further to the left than Santer politically (though some people subsequently found Santer much more of a left-wing ideologue than Thompson). It was reported that a group of Tory MPs had lobbied against Thompson for that very reason, thereby provoking calls from churchpeople (Santer among them) for the prime minister to be eliminated from the selection process for the future. Both the then Labour leader, Neil Kinnock, and the then Liberal leader, David Steel, called for parliamentary debates on the selection of bishops in the wake of the Birmingham appointment.

The controversy was even aired during Question Time in the House of Commons. Mrs Thatcher, while giving nothing away about the particular case of Birmingham, stressed that the agreed procedure had been 'scrupulously honoured' since she had first come to office in 1979 – just as she was sure that it had been honoured before then. Once again, however, it was felt that, if indeed she had chosen the second of the two names presented to her by the Crown Appointments Commission, she had broken the spirit of the Church–State concordat even though she might have observed its letter. She had set up a precedent for selecting bishops on political grounds which other governments of other party-political persuasions might be tempted to follow. The critics maintained that, while the Prime Minister had the right to choose the second name on a list rather than the first, few people had seriously thought, at the time the new proposals were being debated, that any PM would ever avail himself or herself of that right. When the new procedure had been agreed upon, it was suggested, it had been widely understood, however mistakenly, that the Church had, in effect, secured the decisive voice in the appointment of its bishops. Churchpeople therefore had every right to feel both surprised and affronted at the Prime Minister's action in not observing the 'hidden conventions'. But the critics had little hope that any call for the General Synod to debate the new system and maybe urge its modification would be heeded. It was only recently that the group chaired by Lord Blanch of Bishopthorpe, the former Archbishop of York, had reviewed the present system after its first ten years of operation and pronounced it to be working in a generally satisfactory manner. With the Church officially satisfied and the State only too anxious to let this particular sleeping dog lie, no further action was taken.[4]

The first diocesan Mrs Thatcher had been called upon to name shortly after assuming office had been Robert Runcie for Canterbury. The wheel had now come full circle; and almost her last ecclesiastical function was to appoint a new Archbishop of Canterbury to succeed Runcie. At least both she and the Crown Appointments Commission managed to spring a surprise on almost everyone by choosing the Bishop of Bath and Wells, George Carey. He was not a complete outsider, however. Ladbroke's fancied his chances at 12–1; and two writers in *The Independent on Sunday*, Peter Stanford and Simon Lee, suggested that, though he stood no real hope of success, he was one of the two most able Evangelical candidates. But then none of the twelve apostles, the two writers remarked, might have been chosen to be a bishop today. 'They did not go to the right universities; they would not have been impressive on television; they were ordinary men.'[5] George Carey was certainly an ordinary man; he was not an Oxbridge graduate like almost all his contemporaries; but he was chosen by Margaret Thatcher to step into the shoes of Robert Runcie. Even if she was merely following the wishes of the Crown Appointments Commission, it was a notable final service to the Church of England.

Mrs Thatcher's role as bishop-maker, though occasionally controversial, was but the pale shadow of a shade compared to that enjoyed by her Victorian predecessors. And no better illustration can be given of how that role had changed even before the 1976 settlement than to compare the general approach to bishop-making of nineteenth-century prime ministers to that of their modern counterparts. 'Damn it, another bishop dead!' was how Melbourne greeted the announcement of a new episcopal vacancy he was called upon to fill – whereas, to Harold Wilson, work on the modest files forwarded by the appointments secretary at No. 10 came as an 'oasis of peace'. This would have seemed strange to Lord Salisbury, who found anything to do with bishop-making especially worrying and tiring; and to Lord Rosebery, who dubbed all patronage odious and ecclesiastical patronage distressing. A generation later, however, Asquith found that such patronage interested him far more than any other branch of his prime ministerial activities; and to Macmillan its exercise made all those years of reading Trollope seem worthwhile. By then of course almost all the work of filling vacant bishoprics fell on the shoulders of the prime minister's secretary for appointments, though his masters could (and occasionally did) throw a spanner in the works.

Any attempt to generalize about the prime minister's role as bishop-maker soon founders, as it usually boiled down to how an individual would react to a particular set of circumstances. In the 140-year period under review (1837–1977) there were a mere 374 appointments to diocesan bishoprics in the Church of England, which works out at an average of less than three a year – far too few for most prime ministers to deal with on anything other than an *ad hoc* basis. What *can* be said is that it made little difference in practice as to whether a particular premier was an Anglican or not. Of the twenty-six prime ministers of the period (Melbourne to Callaghan) sixteen were at least nominally members of the Church of England; one (Balfour) regarded himself as belonging to both the Church of England *and* the Church of Scotland; four others were Presbyterians; and the remainder came from various Nonconformist backgrounds. But in their attitude to bishop-making the non-Anglicans refrained from, for example, appointing only extreme Evangelicals to vacant sees. They acted on the whole impeccably in their regard to nuances of churchmanship – or at least no more peccably than their Anglican counterparts. The Anglican Palmerston, under the influence of Shaftesbury, appointed many Evangelicals to the bench, but later prime ministers, whatever their religious affiliation, endeavoured to aim at some sort of balance of churchmanship. The earlier Victorian premiers were united only in their dislike of Tractarians. Melbourne found them hard to fathom; Peel was out of sympathy with them; Russell distrusted them as a divisive influence in the Church; Derby viewed them with extreme suspicion. Aberdeen, though a Presbyterian, was more sympathetic towards them, and of course both Gladstone and Salisbury were out-and-out supporters. It was Salisbury who appointed the High Church Gore to a bishopric in the first place, but the half-Presbyterian Balfour and the staunchly Protestant Asquith who moved him higher up in the hierarchy. It was the nominally Presbyterian Bonar Law who placed Headlam, a hobnobber with the Eastern Orthodox, on the Bench. It was Baldwin, a middle-of-the-road Anglican, who (admittedly at Archbishop Davidson's suggestion) appointed a monk, Frere, to a see. It was MacDonald, another nominal Presbyterian, who, according to Lang, took more trouble over church appointments than any other prime minister he had known. It was Attlee, a very nominal Anglican, who had more ideas of his own about the general principles of bishop-making (sensible ones too) than most other prime ministers before or since. Occasionally there was a maverick premier like Disraeli or Lloyd George who knew little and seemingly cared less about the process of bishop-making and who might therefore occasionally go off the rails. But Disraeli had Queen Victoria and Lloyd George had Archbishop Davidson to endeavour (unsuccessfully in the case of Henson) to restrain him; and, in the Davidson and post-Davidson years, an increasingly elaborate system of checks and balances was built up to dissuade prime ministers from doing their own thing.

The fact that in only three cases (Hampden in 1847, Frederick Temple in 1869 and Henson in 1917) did a nomination really lead to a prolonged public outcry is a tribute to the success of the system. (The cases of Gore in 1901 and Wand in 1943 and 1945 hardly come in the same category.) But the fact that a system works, or even works well, may not allow it to stand up for ever to the assaults of the critics, even in a nation as pragmatic as the English. Assiduous sniping over a period of fifty years or so produced a climate in which the Chadwick Report could bear fruit; and from that report it was but a short step to the Callaghan–Coggan concordat of 1976. It is too soon to be able to judge whether the new system is a real improvement on the old, or whether a better type of bishop is emerging from the deliberations of the Crown Appointments Commission than would have issued unaided (except by numerous advisers) from Downing Street. But at least this survey of the final 140 years of the old system will have shown that, though in the first part of Victoria's reign it may have left much to be desired, from Gladstone's time onwards it was not nearly so bad a system as its critics alleged. Almost without exception prime ministers took trouble to secure the right man, or at least not a hopelessly wrong man, for a vacant see. And one has only to survey the many talented men who graced the Episcopal Bench during those 140 years to realize that, though some of the premiers' swans may have turned out to be geese, their efforts by and large are deserving of praise rather than blame. If the system was eventually judged to be a failure, it was at any rate an honest failure.

# Notes

## Notes to Chapter 1

For many of the basic facts in this chapter I am indebted to two books in particular: Cyril Garbett, *Church and State in England* (Hodder & Stoughton 1950), and R. H. Malden, *The English Church and Nation* (SPCK 1952).

1. Report in *Church Times* for 5 April 1991.
2. Report of Joint Committee, p. 4.
3. ibid., p. 14.
4. ibid., p. 17.
5. *The Greville Diary*, i, p. 111; quoted by Garbett, p. 190.
6. A. Trollope, *Barchester Towers*, Chapter 1.

## Notes to Chapter 2

1. Lloyd C. Sanders, ed., *Lord Melbourne's Papers*, p. 495.
2. J. C. Thirlwall, *Connop Thirlwall, Historian and Theologian*, p. 114.
3. Sanders, p. 507.
4. Quoted by Lord David Cecil in *Lord M*, p. 140.
5. Owen Chadwick, *The Victorian Church*, i, p. 114.
6. J. H. Newman, *Apologia*, pp. 61-2.
7. Sanders, pp. 506-7.
8. J. A. Froude, *Carlyle in London*, i, p. 159.
9. Mrs Brookfield, *The Cambridge Apostles*, p. 177.
10. Thirlwall, p. 114.
11. Harriet Martineau, *Autobiography*, i, p. 256.
12. Melbourne to Russell, 27 August 1840: Chadwick i, p. 124.
13. H. P. Liddon, *Life of E. B. Pusey*, ii, p. 294.
14. W. T. M. Torrens, *Memoirs of Lord Melbourne*, ii, p. 181.
15. Sanders, p. 507.
16. *Hansard*, xxxv, p. 33: quoted by Chadwick, i, p. 121.
17. Melbourne to Longley, 11 March 1837: Chadwick i, p. 121.
18. Cecil, p. 141.
19. Melbourne to Russell, 9 January 1839: Sanders, p. 496.

## Notes to Chapter 3

1. Donald Read, *Peel and the Victorians*, p. 132.
2. E. Hodder, *The Life and Work of the Seventh Earl of Shaftesbury*, p. 197.
3. ibid., i, p. 342.
4. Read, pp. 134-5.
5. Standish Meacham, *Lord Bishop: The Life of Samuel Wilberforce, 1805–1873*, p. 42.
6. George I. T. Machin, *Politics and the Churches in Great Britain 1832–1868*, p. 48.
7. Lord Mahon and E. Cardwell, eds, *Memoirs by the Rt Hon Sir Robert Peel*, ii, p. 81.
8. Read, pp. 133-4.

9. Charles Stuart Parker, ed., *Sir Robert Peel: From his Private Papers*, p. 419.
10. ibid., p. 421.
11. Owen Chadwick, *The Victorian Church*, i, p. 226.
12. Geoffrey B. A. M. Finlayson, *The Seventh Earl of Shaftesbury, 1801–1885*, p. 165.
13. Machin, p. 149.
14. Chadwick, i, p. 228.
15. Parker, p. 419.
16. A. Blomfield, *A Memoir of Bishop Blomfield*, p. 219.
17. A. R. Ashwell and R. G. Wilberforce, *The Life of the Right Reverend Samuel Wilberforce, D.D.*, ii, pp. 184-5.
18. P. J. Welch, 'Blomfield and Peel: A Study in Co-operation between Church and State, 1841–1846', *Journal of Ecclesiastical History*, xii, p. 75 (1961).
19. Meacham, p. 46.
20. Parker, p. 416.
21. Meacham, p. 47.
22. Parker, p. 417.
23. Chadwick, p. 229.
24. A. C. Benson and Viscount Esher, eds, *The Letters of Queen Victoria*, First Series, ii, p. 40.
25. Meacham, p. 47.
26. Ashwell–Wilberforce, i, p. 275.
27. Meacham, p. 48.
28. Parker, p. 420.
29. ibid.

## Notes to Chapter 4

1. G. P. Gooch, ed., *The Later Correspondence of Lord John Russell, 1840–1878*, i, p. 184.
2. George I. T. Machin, *Politics and the Churches in Great Britain 1832–1868*, p. 182.
3. Spencer Walpole, *The Life of Lord John Russell*, ii, p. 486.
4. Machin, p. 196.
5. Owen Chadwick, *The Victorian Church*, i, p. 237.
6. A. C. Benson and Viscount Esher, eds, *The Letters of Queen Victoria*, First Series, ii, p. 159.
7. Walpole, i, p. 476.
8. ibid., i, p. 477.
9. Henry Christmas, *A Concise History of the Hampden Controversy*, pp. 50-1.
10. ibid., p. 57.
11. *Letters of Queen Victoria*, I, ii, p. 165.
12. Standish Meacham, *Lord Bishop: The Life of Samuel Wilberforce, 1805–1873*, p. 151.
13. Gooch, p. 184.
14. Edwin Hodder, *The Life and Work of the Seventh Earl of Shaftesbury*, p. 388.
15. R. T. Davidson and W. Benham, *The Life of Archbishop Tait*, i, p. 132.
16. *Letters of Queen Victoria*, II, ii, p. 264.
17. Meacham, p. 151.
18. ibid., p. 156.
19. ibid., p. 161.
20. *Letters of Queen Victoria*, II, ii, p. 264.
21. Joyce Coombs, *George and Mary Sumner: Their Life and Times*, p. 9.
22. Chadwick, i, p. 242.

23. Christmas, p. 133.
24. Machin, p. 198.
25. ibid., p. 183.
26. Gooch, pp. 216-17.
27. Chadwick, i, p. 234.
28. Walpole, ii, p. 121.
29. Coombs, p. 9.
30. ibid., p. 11.
31. Machin, pp. 198-9.
32. Walpole, ii, p. 117.
33. Chadwick, i, p. 236.

## Notes to Chapter 5

1. Frank Hardie, *The Political Influence of Queen Victoria*, p. 136.
2. ibid.
3. George I.T. Machin, *Politics and the Churches in Great Britain 1832–1868*, p. 261.
4. ibid.
5. A. R. Ashwell and R. G. Wilberforce, *The Life of the Right Reverend Samuel Wilberforce, D.D.*, ii, pp. 270-1.
6. Lady Frances Balfour, *The Life of George, Fourth Earl of Aberdeen, K.G., K.T.*, pp. 199-200.
7. Ashwell–Wilberforce, ii, p. 179.
8. ibid., ii, p. 240.
9. Dudley W. R. Bahlman, ed., *The Diary of Sir Edward Walter Hamilton, 1880–1885*, I, p. xiv.
10. ibid., I, p. xiii.

## Notes to Chapter 6

1. Edwin Hodder, *The Life and Work of the Seventh Earl of Shaftesbury, K.G.*, p. 507.
2. Standish Meacham, *Lord Bishop: The Life of Samuel Wilberforce 1805–1873*, p. 275.
3. Hodder, p. 500.
4. Geoffrey B. A. M. Finlayson, *The Seventh Earl of Shaftesbury, 1801–1885*, p. 385.
5. Evelyn Ashley, *The Life of Henry John Temple, Viscount Palmerston*, ii, pp. 226-7.
6. Ashley, ii, p. 319.
7. Hodder, pp. 608-9.
8. Finlayson, p. 377.
9. Hodder, p. 610.
10. Finlayson, pp. 379-80.
11. ibid., p. 380.
12. *Letters of Queen Victoria*, I, iii, p. 529.
13. ibid., p. 530.
14. Dudley W. R. Bahlman, 'Politics and Church Patronage in the Victorian Age', *Victorian Studies* xxii, p. 254.
15. Hodder, p. 609.
16. Owen Chadwick, *The Victorian Church*, i, p. 471.
17. Finlayson, p. 379.
18. Bahlman, p. 268.
19. ibid., p. 269.

20. Chadwick, i, p. 472.
21. Bahlman, p. 270.
22. ibid., p. 292.
23. R. T. Davidson and W. Benham, *The Life of Archibald Campbell Tait*, i, pp. 206-7.
24. David L. Edwards, *Leaders of the Church of England 1828-1944*, p. 104.
25. Davidson-Benham, i, p. 192.
26. George I. T. Machin, *Politics and the Churches in Great Britain 1832-1868*, p. 272.
27. Hodder, p. 606.
28. ibid., p. 609.
29. *Letters of Queen Victoria*, I, iii, p. 531.
30. Hodder, p. 609.
31. Bahlman, p. 272.
32. ibid.
33. Machin, p. 300.
34. Philip Guedalla, ed., *Gladstone and Palmerston*, p. 137.
35. Hodder, p. 610.
36. Phyllis Grosskurth, *John Addington Symonds*, pp. 35-7.
37. Chadwick, i, p. 476.
38. Guedalla, p. 232.
39. Joyce Coombs, *George and Mary Sumner*, p. 73.
40. Meacham, p. 278.
41. Guedalla, pp. 236-8.
42. Davidson-Benham, i, pp. 271-2.
43. ibid., p. 272.
44. H. Kirk-Smith, *William Thomson, Archbishop of York: His Life and Times*, p. 15.
45. ibid.
46. ibid.
47. ibid., p. 16.
48. Meacham, p. 281.
49. ibid., p. 282.
50. G. W. Kitchin, *Edward Harold Browne, D.D., Lord Bishop of Winchester: A Memoir*, p. 250.
51. *Letters of Queen Victoria*, II, i, p. 177.
52. ibid., pp. 177-8.
53. Finlayson, p. 385.
54. *Letters of Queen Victoria*, II, i, p. 179.
55. Chadwick, ii, p. 330.
56. Guedalla, pp. 338-9.
57. Finlayson, pp. 384-5.
58. Hodder, p. 611.
59. J. C. Thirlwall, *Connop Thirlwall: Historian and Theologian*, p. 161.
60. Chadwick, i, p. 476.

## Notes to Chapter 7

1. Edward Bulwer-Lytton, *The New Timon*, i, p. 6.
2. Wilbur Devereux Jones, *Lord Derby and Victorian Conservatism*, pp. 188-9.
3. George Saintsbury, *The Earl of Derby*, p. 214.
4. Dudley W. R. Bahlman, 'Politics and Church Patronage in the Victorian Age', *Victorian Studies* xxii, p. 274.
5. J. H. Evans, *Churchman Militant: George Augustus Selwyn, Bishop of New Zealand and Lichfield*, p. 60.

6. ibid., p. 61.
7. ibid., p. 235.
8. *Letters of Queen Victoria*, II, i, p. 471.
9. J. R. Vincent, ed., *Disraeli, Derby and the Conservative Party: the Political Journals of Lord Stanley, 1849–69*, 27 Feb. – 1 March 1868: quoted in Paul Johnson, ed., *The Oxford Book of Political Anecdotes*, p. 143.

## Notes to Chapter 8

1. W. F. Monypenny and G. E. Buckle, *The Life of Benjamin Disraeli, Earl of Beaconsfield*, v, p. 58.
2. Robert Blake, *Disraeli*, p. 504.
3. Standish Meacham, *Lord Bishop, The Life of Samuel Wilberforce 1805–1873*, p. 283.
4. R. E. Prothero and G. G. Bradley, *The Life and Correspondence of Arthur Penrhyn Stanley*, ii, p. 447.
5. Monypenny–Buckle, v, p. 58.
6. Dudley W. R. Bahlman, 'Politics and Church Patronage in the Victorian Age', *Victorian Studies* xxii, p. 279.
7. A. R. Ashwell and R. G. Wilberforce, *The Life of the Right Reverend Samuel Wilberforce, D.D.*, iii, p. 279.
8. Blake, p. 507.
9. Owen Chadwick, *The Victorian Church*, ii, p. 332.
10. Monypenny–Buckle, v, p. 73.
11. *Letters of Queen Victoria*, II, ii, p. 342.
12. Monypenny–Buckle, v, p. 60.
13. ibid., p. 61.
14. ibid., p. 62.
15. Bahlman, p. 288.
16. *Letters of Queen Victoria*, II, i, p. 537.
17. Elizabeth Longford, *Victoria R.I.,* p. 401.
18. Ashwell–Wilberforce, iii, p. 268.
19. Monypenny–Buckle, v, p. 72.
20. William Plomer, ed., *Kilvert's Diary*, i, pp. 73-4.
21. Monypenny–Buckle, v, p. 63.
22. Bahlman, p. 279.
23. ibid.
24. Monypenny–Buckle, v, pp. 59-60.
25. Bahlman, p. 281.
26. Monypenny–Buckle, v, p. 62.
27. Bahlman, p. 280.
28. Monypenny–Buckle, v, p. 65.
29. ibid., p. 61.
30. ibid., p. 64.
31. ibid.
32. ibid., p. 66.
33. J. C. Macdonnell, *The Life and Correspondence of William Connor Magee*, i, pp. 197-8.
34. R. T. Davidson and W. Benham, *The Life of Archibald Campbell Tait*, i, p. 535.
35. G. W. Kitchin, *Edward Harold Browne*, p. 451.
36. *Letters of Queen Victoria*, II, i, p. 545.
37. Monypenny–Buckle, v, p. 68.
38. *Letters of Queen Victoria*, II, i, pp. 545-7.

39. ibid., p. 548.
40. Monypenny–Buckle, v, p. 69.
41. *Letters of Queen Victoria*, II, i, pp. 549-50.
42. ibid., pp. 551-2.
43. Ashwell–Wilberforce, iii, p. 267.
44. Monypenny–Buckle, v, p. 71.
45. Ashwell–Wilberforce, iii, pp. 267–9.
46. ibid., p. 270.
47. A. C. Benson, *The Life of Edward White Benson*, i, p. 413.
48. Monypenny–Buckle, vi, p. 303.
49. ibid., p. 97.
50. David L. Edwards, *Leaders of the Church of England 1828–1944*, p. 195.
51. Monypenny–Buckle, vi, p. 407.
52. G. R. Balleine, *A History of the Evangelical Party in the Church of England*, p. 279.
53. *Letters of Queen Victoria*, II, iii, p. 78.

## Notes to Chapter 9

1. Dudley W. R. Bahlman, ed., *The Diary of Sir Edward Walter Hamilton, 1880–1885*, ii, p. 539.
2. Dudley W. R. Bahlman, 'The Queen, Mr Gladstone, and Church Patronage', *Victorian Studies* iii, p. 355.
3. David L. Edwards, *Leaders of the Church of England 1828–1944*, pp. 166-7.
4. Bahlman, *Gladstone*, p. 355.
5. James Bentley, *Ritualism and Politics in Victorian Britain*, p. 6.
6. Edwards, p. 166.
7. *Hamilton Diary*, i, p. 282.
8. Sir George Leveson Gower, *Years of Content 1858–1886*, pp. 164-5.
9. John Morley, *The Life of William Ewart Gladstone*, ii, pp. 430-1.
10. Morley, ii, p. 431.
11. Leveson Gower, p. 165.
12. Dudley W. R. Bahlman, 'Politics and Church Patronage in the Victorian Age', *Victorian Studies* xxii, p. 257.
13. ibid., p. 263.
14. *Hamilton Diary*, ii, p. 668.
15. Bahlman, *Gladstone*, p. 358.
16. *Hamilton Diary*, ii, p. 539.
17. Morley, ii, pp. 432-3.
18. Bahlman, *Gladstone*, p. 360.
19. *Hamilton Diary*, ii, p. 410.
20. ibid., pp. 486-7.
21. Leveson Gower, p. 166.
22. G. K. A. Bell, *Randall Davidson*, p. 164.
23. *Letters of Queen Victoria*, II, i, p. 627.
24. Edwards, p. 292.
25. Morley, ii, p. 431.
26. R. T. Davidson and W. Benham, *Life of Archbishop Tait*, ii, p. 58.
27. *Letters of Queen Victoria*, II, i, p. 629.
28. Edwin Hodder, *The Life and Work of the Seventh Earl of Shaftesbury, K.G.*, p. 639.
29. Geoffrey B. A. M. Finlayson, *The Seventh Earl of Shaftesbury*, pp. 516–17.
30. Davidson–Benham, ii, p. 59.

31. Morley, ii, p. 432.
32. Davidson–Benham, ii, pp. 59-60.
33. P. T. Marsh, *The Victorian Church in Decline*, p. 151.
34. Standish Meacham, *Lord Bishop: The Life of Samuel Wilberforce*, p. 295.
35. Marsh, p. 152.
36. Bahlman, *Politics*, p. 286.
37. Meacham, p. 291.
38. ibid., p. 292.
39. ibid., p. 296.
40. *Letters of Queen Victoria*, II, ii, p. 268.
41. Bahlman, *Gladstone*, p. 364.
42. ibid., pp. 364-5.
43. ibid., pp. 367-8.
44. *Hamilton Diary*, ii, p. 386.
45. *Letters of Queen Victoria*, II, iii, p. 398; *Hamilton Diary*, ii, p. 428.
46. Bahlman, *Gladstone*, p. 372.
47. ibid.
48. *Hamilton Diary*, ii, p. 428.
49. Bahlman, *Gladstone*, p. 373.
50. ibid., p. 374.
51. *Letters of Queen Victoria*, II, iii, pp. 331-2.
52. Bell, pp. 52-3.
53. ibid., p. 57.
54. Morley, iii, p. 96.
55. Bell, pp. 57-8.
56. ibid., pp. 59-60.
57. Bahlman, *Gladstone*, p. 377.
58. Morley, iii, p. 96.
59. G. W. Kitchin, *Edward Harold Browne*, p. 455.
60. *Hamilton Diary*, ii, p. 375.
61. Mary C. Church, ed., *Life and Letters of Dean Church*, p. 307.
62. *Letters of Queen Victoria*, II, iii, p. 475.
63. *Hamilton Diary*, ii, p. 544.
64. *Letters of Queen Victoria*, II, iii, p. 475.
65. Bell, p. 166.
66. *Hamilton Diary*, ii, p. 613.
67. ibid., p. 558.
68. Bahlman, *Politics*, p. 291.
69. Bell, p. 168.
70. ibid., pp. 169-70.
71. *Hamilton Diary*, ii, p. 765.
72. ibid., p. 768.
73. ibid., p. 766.
74. ibid., p. 778.
75. ibid., p. 787.
76. Bell, p. 175.
77. ibid., p. 176.
78. *Hamilton Diary*, ii, p. 785.
79. A. R. Vidler, *The Orb and the Cross*, p. 157.

## Notes to Chapter 10

1. G. K. A. Bell, *Randall Davidson*, p. 180.
2. Paul Smith, ed., *Lord Salisbury on Politics*, p. 16.

3. Dudley W. R. Bahlman, 'Politics and Church Patronage in the Victorian Age', *Victorian Studies* xxii, p. 293.
4. Bell, p. 180.
5. Bahlman, p. 294.
6. Lady Gwendolen Cecil, *Life of Robert, Marquis of Salisbury*, iv, p. 210.
7. *Letters of Queen Victoria*, III, i, pp. 644-5.
8. ibid., p. 647.
9. Bell, p. 178.
10. ibid.
11. *Letters of Queen Victoria*, III, i, p. 554.
12. ibid., p. 649.
13. ibid., p. 633.
14. Cecil, pp. 212-13.
15. Bell, p. 177.
16. ibid.
17. David L. Edwards, *Leaders of the Church of England 1828–1944*, p. 207.
18. *Letters of Queen Victoria*, III, i, p. 426.
19. ibid., p. 427.
20. ibid., pp. 427-8.
21. ibid., p. 560.
22. ibid., p. 558.
23. ibid., p. 559.
24. Bell, p. 181.
25. ibid.
26. Cecil, p. 211.
27. *Letters of Queen Victoria*, III, i, p. 543.
28. ibid., pp. 544-5.
29. ibid., p. 554.
30. ibid., p. 556.
31. ibid., pp. 631-2.
32. ibid., pp. 632-3.
33. A. V. Baillie, *My First Eighty Years*, p. 91.
34. *Letters of Queen Victoria*, III, i, pp. 639-40.
35. ibid., p. 645.
36. ibid., p. 647.
37. ibid., pp. 666-7.
38. ibid., ii, pp. 4-5.
39. Louise Creighton, *Life and Letters of Mandell Creighton*, i, pp. 398-9.
40. Edwards, p. 223.
41. David Williams, *Genesis and Exodus: A Portrait of the Benson Family*, p. 107.
42. *Letters of Queen Victoria*, III, iii, pp. 94-5.
43. ibid., pp. 95-7.
44. ibid., p. 99.
45. ibid., pp. 100-1.
46. Bell, p. 285.
47. ibid.
48. ibid., p. 361.
49. G. L. Prestige, *The Life of Charles Gore*, p. 228.
50. ibid., p. 229.
51. ibid., p. 227.

*Notes to Chapter 11*

1. Marquess of Crewe, *Lord Rosebery*, i, p. 17.
2. Winston S. Churchill, *Great Contemporaries*, p. 16.
3. Crewe, i, pp. 15-16.
4. Robert Rhodes James, *Rosebery*, p. 218.
5. ibid.
6. Dudley W. R. Bahlman, 'Politics and Church Patronage in the Victorian Age', *Victorian Studies* xxii, p. 253.
7. G. K. A. Bell, *Randall Davidson*, p. 242.
8. Bahlman, p. 294.
9. ibid., pp. 294-5.
10. *Letters of Queen Victoria*, III, ii, p. 498.
11. Crewe, i, p. 180.
12. Rhodes James, p. 354.
13. *Letters of Queen Victoria*, III, ii, p. 468.
14. ibid., pp. 469-70.
15. ibid., pp. 470-1.
16. ibid., p. 472.
17. William Temple, *Life of Bishop Percival*, p. 130.
18. Churchill, p. 27.

*Notes to Chapter 12*

1. Philip Magnus, *King Edward the Seventh*, p. 10.
2. Giles St Aubyn, *Edward VII: Prince and King*, p. 39.
3. Magnus, p. 24.
4. St Aubyn, p. 39.
5. ibid., p. 405.
6. Magnus, pp. 292-3.
7. ibid., p. 402.
8. ibid., p. 442.
9. Sidney Lee, *King Edward VII*, ii, p. 13.
10. ibid., pp. 51-3.
11. St Aubyn, pp. 372-3.
12. Lee, ii, p. 399.
13. St Aubyn, p. 386.
14. Winston Churchill, *Great Contemporaries*, pp. 191-2.
15. Blanche E. C. Dugdale, *Arthur James Balfour*, i, pp. 51-2.
16. Kenneth Young, *Arthur James Balfour*, pp. 179-80.
17. Dugdale, i, pp. 284-5.
18. G. K. A. Bell, *Randall Davidson*, p. 384.
19. Bell, p. 1237.
20. *George Bell Papers*, cxix, p. 76.
21. ibid., p. 77.
22. Bell, p. 1238.
23. *Davidson Papers*, x, p. 17.
24. Bell, pp. 1238-9.
25. *Davidson Papers*, x, p. 5.
26. E. A. Knox, *Reminiscences of an Octogenarian*, pp. 207-8.
27. G. L. Prestige, *The Life of Charles Gore*, pp. 251-4.

*Notes to Chapter 13*

1. John Wilson, *CB: A Life of Sir Henry Campbell-Bannerman*, pp. 130-3.

2. ibid., p. 574.
3. ibid., p. 573.
4. J. A. Spender, *The Life of the Right Hon. Sir Henry Campbell-Bannerman*, ii, p. 57.
5. Wilson, p. 578.
6. ibid., pp. 575-6.
7. ibid., p. 577.
8. *Davidson Papers*, x, p. 33.
9. G. K. A. Bell, *Randall Davidson*, p. 1240.
10. *Davidson Papers*, x, p. 35.
11. ibid., p. 23.
12. ibid., p. 25.
13. Wilson, p. 577.
14. *Davidson Papers*, x, p. 26.
15. ibid., p. 28.
16. ibid., p. 26.
17. ibid., p. 32.
18. ibid., p. 33.
19. ibid., p. 34.
20. Wilson, p. 578.
21. *Davidson Papers*, x, p. 33.
22. ibid., p. 37.
23. Spender, ii, p. 375.

## Notes to Chapter 14

1. Winston S. Churchill, *Great Contemporaries*, p. 111.
2. J. A. Spender and Cyril Asquith, *Life of Herbert Henry Asquith*, ii, p. 378.
3. ibid.
4. ibid.
5. G. K. A. Bell, *Randall Davidson*, pp. 1240-1.
6. *Davidson Papers*, x, p. 26.
7. ibid., p. 44.
8. William Temple, *Life of Bishop Percival*, p. 303.
9. J. G. Lockhart, *Cosmo Gordon Lang*, pp. 178-9.
10. Bell, p. 1156.
11. Bertram Pollock, *A Twentieth-Century Bishop*, p. 36.
12. *Davidson Papers*, x, p. 59.
13. ibid., p. 60.
14. ibid., p. 61.
15. ibid., p. 66.
16. ibid., p. 124.
17. Harold Nicolson, *King George the Fifth*, p. 31.
18. Kenneth Rose, *King George V*, pp. 363-4.
19. Rose, p. 365.
20. *Davidson Papers*, x, p. 113.
21. Rose, p. 364.
22. ibid.
23. Nicolson, pp. 162-3.
24. Rose, p. 287.
25. Bell, p. 1241.
26. *Davidson Papers*, x, p. 98.
27. ibid., p. 101.
28. ibid., p. 107.

29. ibid., p. 104.
30. ibid., p. 92.
31. G. L. Prestige, *The Life of Charles Gore*, p. 316.
32. ibid., pp. 317-18.
33. *Davidson Papers*, x, p. 111.
34. ibid., p. 67.

## Notes to Chapter 15

1. Owen Chadwick, *Hensley Henson*, p. 133.
2. G. K. A. Bell, *Randall Davidson*, p. 851.
3. Chadwick, p. 130.
4. ibid., p. 131.
5. Bell, p. 853.
6. ibid.
7. Chadwick, p. 132.
8. Bell, p. 853.
9. ibid., pp. 854-5.
10. ibid., p. 855.
11. H. H. Henson, *Retrospect of an Unimportant Life*, i, pp. 215-16.
12. Bell, p. 856.
13. ibid., pp. 859-62.
14. ibid., pp. 872-9; *see also* Chadwick, pp. 140-2.
15. Bell, p. 880.
16. Henson, i, p. 252.
17. ibid., p. 257.
18. Chadwick, pp. 145-6.
19. ibid., p. 147.
20. Bell, p. 1244.
21. ibid., p. 1243.
22. ibid., pp. 1243-4.
23. ibid., p. 1244.
24. ibid., p. 1245.
25. ibid., pp. 1246-7.
26. *Davidson Papers*, xi, p. 26.
27. ibid., p. 27.
28. ibid., p. 29.
29. ibid., p. 30.
30. ibid., p. 31.
31. Bell, p. 1242n.
32. Dom Anselm Hughes, *The Rivers of the Flood*, pp. 57-8.
33. Charles Smyth, *Cyril Forster Garbett*, p. 139.
34. *Davidson Papers*, xi, p. 39.
35. ibid., p. 40.
36. Bell, pp. 1248-50.
37. ibid., p. 990.

## Notes to Chapter 16

1. Roy Jenkins, *Baldwin*, p. 14.
2. R. C. D. Jasper, *Arthur Cayley Headlam*, p. 137.
3. G. K. A. Bell, *Randall Davidson*, p. 1250.
4. *Lang Papers*, cxlii, p. 213.
5. *Diary of A. C. Don 1935*, p. 86.
6. *Davidson Papers*, xi, p. 125.

7. ibid., p. 138.
8. ibid., p. 71.
9. ibid., p. 67.
10. ibid., p. 79.
11. R. C. D. Jasper, *George Bell*, p. 53.
12. Bell, p. 1365.
13. J. G. Lockhart, *Cosmo Gordon Lang*, p. 311.
14. ibid., pp. 310-11.
15. F. A. Iremonger, *William Temple*, pp. 359-60.
16. Lockhart, p. 311.
17. Owen Chadwick, *Hensley Henson*, p. 201.
18. H. H. Henson, *Retrospect*, ii, pp. 210-11.
19. *Lang Papers*, xcv, p. 299.
20. Jasper, *Bell*, p. 54.
21. *George Bell Papers*, cxix, p. 23.
22. *Lang Papers*, cxlviii, p. 267.
23. G. M. Young, *Stanley Baldwin*, p. 206.

## Notes to Chapter 17

1. Lord Elton, *The Life of James Ramsay MacDonald*, p. 38.
2. David Marquand, *Ramsay MacDonald*, pp. 53-4.
3. G. K. A. Bell, *Randall Davidson*, pp. 1251-2.
4. *Lang Papers*, cxxxix, p. 111.
5. R. C. D. Jasper, *George Bell*, p. 33.
6. H. E. Sheen, *Canon Peter Green*, p. 88.
7. *Davidson Papers*, xi, p. 115.
8. John Barnes, *Ahead of His Age*, p. 145.
9. ibid., p. 147.
10. ibid., p. 148.
11. ibid.
12. R. C. D. Jasper, *Arthur Cayley Headlam*, p. 315.
13. *Lang Papers*, cx, p. 253.
14. Charles Smyth, *Cyril Forster Garbett*, p. 183.
15. *Lang Papers*, cx, pp. 255, 261.
16. ibid., p. 263.
17. Edward Carpenter, *Archbishop Fisher*, p. 29.
18. F. R. Barry, *Mervyn Haigh*, pp. 110-13.
19. *Lang Papers*, cxxxix, p. 62.
20. ibid., p. 93.
21. ibid., pp. 99-101.
22. ibid., pp. 105-7.
23. *Diary of A. C. Don 1935*, p. 29.
24. *Lang Papers*, cxxxix, p. 111.
25. ibid., p. 119.
26. ibid., p. 123.
27. Alan Dunstan and J. S. Peart-Binns, *Cornish Bishop*, pp. 84-5.

## Notes to Chapter 18

1. J. W. Wheeler-Bennett, *King George VI*, p. 744.
2. E. W. Kemp, *Kenneth Escott Kirk*, pp. 72-3.
3. *Lang Papers*, clx, pp. 88-90.
4. ibid., p. 92.

5. ibid., clxix, pp. 234-7.
6. ibid., pp. 241-2.
7. Edward Carpenter, *Archbishop Fisher*, pp. 55-8.
8. *Lang Papers*, clxix, p. 249.
9. ibid., p. 257.
10. Selwyn Gummer, *The Chavasse Twins*, p. 130.
11. ibid., p. 258.

*Notes to Chapter 19*

1. *Church Times*, 29 January 1965, p. 15. A variant version of this story occurs in Alistair Horne's *Macmillan: 1957–1986*, p. 611.
2. W. F. Purcell, *Fisher of Lambeth*, p. 110.
3. J. G. Lockhart, *Cosmo Gordon Lang*, p. 429.
4. *Lang Papers*, clxxxii, p. 294.
5. *Diary of A. C. Don 1941–1942*, pp. 8-9.
6. ibid., pp. 24-5.
7. ibid., p. 36.
8. ibid., p. 47.
9. *Lang Papers*, clxxxii, p. 188.
10. ibid., p. 248.
11. ibid., p. 253.
12. ibid., p. 256.
13. ibid., p. 295.
14. *Lang Papers*, clxxxii, p. 298.
15. *Don Diary*, p. 52.
16. C. E. Lysaght, *Brendan Bracken*, p. 87.
17. Andrew Boyle, *Poor, Dear Brendan*, pp. 289-90.
18. ibid., p. 290.
19. Lysaght, p. 186.
20. ibid.
21. ibid., p. 239.
22. Boyle, p. 84.
23. Lysaght, p. 185.
24. Charles Smyth, *Cyril Forster Garbett*, pp. 270-1.
25. ibid., p. 271.
26. ibid., p. 272.
27. *Don Diary*, p. 9.
28. ibid., p. 43.
29. F. A. Iremonger, *William Temple*, p. 475.
30. ibid.
31. Kenneth Harris, *Attlee*, p. 218. Other versions of this story give it as 'the only twopenny (or sixpenny) article in a penny bazaar'.
32. *Don Diary*, p. 83.
33. ibid., p. 56.
34. ibid., p. 71.
35. ibid., p. 88.
36. Smyth, p. 274.
37. *Don Diary*, p. 88.
38. ibid., p. 91.
39. Smyth, p. 276.
40. *Don Diary*, p. 91.
41. *William Temple Papers*, iv, p. 295.
42. ibid., p. 318.

43. ibid., p. 321.
44. ibid., p. 324.
45. J. W. C. Wand, *Changeful Page*, p. 155.
46. ibid.
47. J. S. Peart-Binns, *Wand of London*, p. 110.
48. F. R. Barry, *Mervyn Haigh*, p. 189.
49. Edward Carpenter, *Archbishop Fisher*, p. 129.
50. Iremonger, p. 627.
51. Purcell, p. 107.
52. Barry, p. 190.
53. Smyth, p. 296.
54. Iremonger, p. 620.
55. 'An Unknown Layman', *The Looking-Glass of Lambeth*, p. 74.
56. R. C. D. Jasper, *George Bell*, p. 285.
57. ibid., p. 284.
58. ibid., p. 286.
59. David L. Edwards, *Leaders of the Church of England*, pp. 339-40.
60. Purcell, p. 110.
61. *Theology* (March 1963), p. 102.
62. *Church Times*, 22 September 1972. The anonymous obituary was actually by Bishop Wand.
63. *Fisher Papers*, iii, p. 317.
64. ibid., pp. 320-1.
65. ibid., pp. 322-3.
66. ibid., p. 325.
67. ibid., p. 326.
68. Wand, pp. 173-4.
69. *Fisher Papers*, iii, p. 332.
70. ibid., p. 336.
71. ibid., p. 337.
72. Wand, p. 175.
73. ibid.
74. *Fisher Papers*, clxv, p. 235.
75. ibid., xcii, p. 405.
76. ibid., xcviii, p. 224.
77. ibid., p. 231.
78. ibid., p. 234.
79. Owen Chadwick, *Michael Ramsey*, p. 74.
80. ibid., p. 76.
81. *Fisher Papers*, cxix, p. 85.
82. ibid., p. 86.
83. ibid., p. 87.
84. Roy McKay, *John Leonard Wilson*, p. 122.
85. ibid., p. 123.
86. ibid.

## Notes to Chapter 20

1. Kenneth Harris, *Attlee*, p. 10.
2. ibid., pp. 563-4.
3. ibid., p. 340.
4. ibid., pp. 460-1.
5. *Fisher Papers*, clxv, p. 235.

6. Anthony Bevir Memorial Lecture, delivered at Eton College on 5 November 1980, p. 2.
7. *Fisher Papers*, clxv, pp. 235-6.
8. ibid., xiii, p. 94.
9. *George Bell Papers*, xix, p. 40.
10. *Fisher Papers*, li, p. 341.
11. ibid., p. 335.
12. ibid., iii, pp. 356-9.
13. ibid., pp. 360-3.
14. ibid., xiii, p. 38.
15. ibid., p. 48.
16. ibid., iii, pp. 378-9.
17. ibid., p. 381.
18. ibid., xiii, p. 18.
19. ibid., p. 77.
20. ibid., pp. 70-1.
21. ibid., li, p. 345.
22. ibid., xiii, pp. 22-3.

## Notes to Chapter 21

1. R. S. Essex, *Woman in a Man's World*, p. 66.
2. *Fisher Papers*, clii, p. 354.
3. Margaret Pawley, *Donald Coggan*, p. 102.
4. *Fisher Papers*, clii, p. 343.
5. ibid., p. 358.
6. ibid., p. 361.
7. ibid., p. 363.
8. Edward Carpenter, *Archbishop Fisher*, p. 224.
9. ibid., p. 225.
10. Owen Chadwick, *Michael Ramsey*, p. 88.
11. *Fisher Papers*, clxiv, pp. 132-3.
12. ibid., p. 134.
13. Chadwick, p. 91.
14. *Fisher Papers*, clxiv, p. 133.
15. ibid., p. 135.
16. ibid., p. 136.
17. Chadwick, p. 92.
18. *Fisher Papers*, clxxxii, p. 185.
19. ibid., p. 186.
20. Robert Holtby, *Robert Wright Stopford*, pp. 45-6.
21. ibid., p. 46.
22. *Fisher Papers*, clxv, pp. 235-8.

## Notes to Chapter 22

1. Alistair Horne, *Macmillan: 1957–1986*, p. 272.
2. ibid., p. 169.
3. ibid., pp. 611-12.
4. Owen Chadwick, *Michael Ramsey*, pp. 104-5.
5. Horne, p. 14.
6. *Fisher Papers*, ccxxviii, p. 172.
7. ibid., cclvii, p. 291.
8. ibid., pp. 296-7.

9. ibid., p. 344.
10. Edward Carpenter, *Archbishop Fisher*, p. 227.
11. *Fisher Papers*, ccx, p. 36.
12. ibid., p. 32.
13. ibid., p. 48.
14. Mervyn Stockwood, *Chanctonbury Ring*, p. 97.
15. *Fisher Papers*, ccxxxi, p. 288.
16. ibid., p. 303.
17. ibid., pp. 322, 326.
18. ibid., cclvii, pp. 331-2.
19. Carpenter, p. 228.
20. *Fisher Papers*, cclvii, pp. 315-16.
21. Chadwick, pp. 135-6.
22. J. S. Peart-Binns, *Ambrose Reeves*, p. 265.
23. Carpenter, p. 749.
24. ibid.
25. Chadwick, p. 107.
26. Carpenter, p. 750.
27. Carpenter, p. 750, and Chadwick, p. 107. The two accounts, while purporting to report a conversation verbatim, differ in a number of small verbal particulars.
28. Robert Holtby, *Robert Wright Stopford*, p. 55.
29. F. W. Dillistone, *The Life of Joe Fison*, p. 137.
30. *Fisher Papers*, ccx, p. 36.
31. Dillistone, pp. 137-8.

## Notes to Chapter 23

1. *Church Times*, 29 March 1974, p. 1.
2. Owen Chadwick, *Michael Ramsey*, p. 140.
3. Harold Wilson, *The Governance of Britain*, p. 108.
4. Chadwick, pp. 136-7.
5. Trevor Beeson, *The Church of England in Crisis*, p. 166.
6. ibid.
7. David L. Edwards, *Ian Ramsey*, pp. 12-13.
8. *Church Times*, 29 March 1974, p. 8.
9. ibid., 17 May 1974, p. 10.
10. Margaret Pawley, *Donald Coggan*, p. 126.
11. Margaret Duggan, *Runcie*, p. 174.
12. Chadwick, p. 137.
13. Information supplied to the author by Edward Heath, 8 September 1991.
14. Beeson, p. 105.
15. Chadwick, p. 142.
16. Beeson, p. 168.
17. Chadwick, p. 133n.
18. *Church Times*, 6 July 1973, p. 3.
19. ibid., 21 September 1973, p. 1.
20. Letter from Lord Callaghan to the author, 19 September 1991.
21. *Church Times*, 14 October 1977, p. 1.

## Notes to Chapter 24

1. Hugh Martin, 'Church and State: A Free Church Point of View', *Church Quarterly Review* (No. 245), p. 13.

2. Edward Carpenter, *Archbishop Fisher*, pp. 232-3.
3. Lord Quickswood, 'Church and State', *Church Quarterly Review* (No. 308), p. 292.
4. *Crown Appointments and the Church*, p. 31.
5. Lord Fisher of Lambeth, 'What's Best Administered', *Theology* (No. 536), p. 88.
6. Paul Welsby, *A History of the Church of England 1945–1980*, p. 220.
7. Callaghan's Commons statement, with its implications, was reported fully in the *Church Times* of 11 June 1976.

### Notes to Chapter 25

1. Margaret Duggan, *Runcie*, pp. 36-41; Jonathan Mantle, *Archbishop*, pp. 107-11; article by Douglas Brown, *Church Times*, 8 June 1979, p. 20.
2. John S. Peart-Binns, *Graham Leonard*, pp. 158-62; *Church Times*, 3 April 1981, p. 1.
3. ibid., p. 10.
4. ibid., 16 April 1987, p. 1 (article by Susan Young).
5. Quoted by Mantle, pp. 326-7.

# Bibliography

*(1) Unpublished sources in Lambeth Palace Library*

George Bell Papers.
Davidson Papers.
Diary of A. C. Don.
Fisher Papers.
Lang Papers.
William Temple Papers.

*(2) Published sources*

Ashley, Evelyn, *The Life of Henry John Temple, Viscount Palmerston*. Richard Bentley 1876.

Ashwell, A. R. and Wilberforce, R. G., *Life of the Right Reverend Samuel Wilberforce, D.D.* John Murray 1880-2.

Atlay, J. B., *The Life of the Right Rev. Ernest Roland Wilberforce, first Bishop of Newcastle-upon-Tyne and afterwards Bishop of Chichester*. Smith, Elder 1912.

Bahlman, D. W. R, ed., *The Diary of Sir Edward Walter Hamilton, 1880-1885*. Oxford, Clarendon Press, 1972.

—— , 'The Queen, Mr Gladstone, and Church Patronage', *Victorian Studies* (June 1960).

—— , 'Politics and Church Patronage in the Victorian Age', *Victorian Studies* (Spring 1979).

Balfour, Lady Frances, *The Life of George, Fourth Earl of Aberdeen, K.G., K.T.* Hodder & Stoughton 1923.

Balleine, G. R. *A History of the Evangelical Party in the Church of England*. Longmans, Green 1908.

Barnes, John, *Ahead of His Age: Bishop Barnes of Birmingham*. Collins 1979.

Barry, F. R., *Mervyn Haigh*. SPCK 1964.

Beeson, Trevor, *The Church of England in Crisis*. Davis-Poynter 1973.

Bell, G. K. A., *Randall Davidson: Archbishop of Canterbury*. Oxford University Press, 3rd edn, 1952.

Benson, A. C., *The Life of Edward White Benson, sometime Archbishop of Canterbury*. Macmillan 1899.

—— , and Esher, Viscount, eds, *The Letters of Queen Victoria: First Series, 1837-1861*. John Murray 1907.

Bentley, James, *Ritualism and Politics in Victorian Britain*. Oxford University Press 1978.

Blake, Robert, *Disraeli*. Eyre & Spottiswoode 1966.

—— , *The Unknown Prime Minister: The Life and Times of Andrew Bonar Law 1858-1923*. Eyre & Spottiswoode 1955.

Blomfield, Alfred, *A Memoir of Charles James Blomfield, D.D., Bishop of London, with selections from his correspondence*. John Murray 1863.

Boyle, Andrew, *Poor, Dear Brendan: The Quest for Brendan Bracken*. Hutchinson 1974.

Buckle, G. E., ed., *The Letters of Queen Victoria: Second Series, 1862–1885* and *Third Series, 1886–1901*. John Murray 1926, 1932.

Carpenter, Edward, *Archbishop Fisher: His Life and Times*. Norwich, Canterbury Press, 1991.

Carpenter, S. C., *Winnington-Ingram: The biography of Arthur Foley Winnington-Ingram, Bishop of London 1901–1939*. Hodder & Stoughton 1949.

Cecil, Lord David, *Lord M*. Constable 1954.

Cecil, Lady Gwendolen, *Life of Robert, Marquess of Salisbury*. Hodder & Stoughton 1932.

Chadwick, Owen, *Hensley Henson: A study in the friction between Church and State*. Oxford, Clarendon Press, 1983.

——, *Michael Ramsey: A Life*. Oxford, Clarendon Press, 1990.

——, *The Victorian Church: Parts I and II*. A. & C. Black 1966, 1970.

Christmas, Henry, *A Concise History of the Hampden Controversy*. Smith, Elder 1848.

*Church and State*: Report of the Archbishops' Commission. Church Information Office 1970.

Church, Mary C., ed., *Life and Letters of Dean Church*. Macmillan 1894.

Churchill, Winston S., *Great Contemporaries*. Fontana 1959.

Cockshut, A. O. J., *Religious Controversies of the Nineteenth Century: Selected Documents*. Methuen 1966.

Coombs, Joyce, *George and Mary Sumner: Their Life and Times*. Sumner Press 1965.

Creighton, Louise, *Life and Letters of Mandell Creighton, D.D., Sometime Bishop of London*. Longmans, Green 1904.

Crewe, Marquess of, *Lord Rosebery*. John Murray 1931.

Crowther, M. A., *Church Embattled: Religious Controversy in Mid-Victorian England*. Newton Abbot, David & Charles, 1970.

Davidson, R. T., and Benham, W., *Life of Archibald Campbell Tait, Archbishop of Canterbury*. Macmillan 1891.

Dillistone, F. W., *The Life of Joe Fison*. Oxford, Amate Press, 1983.

Dugdale, B. E. C., *Arthur James Balfour, First Earl of Balfour, K.G., O.M., F.R.S.* Hutchinson 1936.

Duggan, Margaret, *Runcie: The Making of an Archbishop*. Hodder & Stoughton 1983.

Edwards, David L., *Leaders of the Church of England 1828–1944*. Oxford University Press 1971.

——, *Ian Ramsey, Bishop of Durham: A Memoir*. Oxford University Press 1973.

Ellison, G. A., 'Church and State: the position of the Church of England today' (Anthony Bevir Memorial Lecture delivered at Eton College, 5 November 1980).

Elton, Lord, *The Life of James Ramsay MacDonald (1866–1919)*. Collins 1939.

Essex, R. S., *Woman in a Man's World*. Sheldon Press 1977.

Evans, J. H., *Churchman Militant: George Augustus Selwyn, Bishop of New Zealand and Lichfield*. Allen & Unwin 1964.

Fallows, W. G., *Mandell Creighton and the English Church*. Oxford University Press 1964.

Feiling, Keith, *The Life of Neville Chamberlain*. Macmillan 1946.

Finlayson, G. B. A. M., *The Seventh Earl of Shaftesbury, 1801–1885*. Eyre-Methuen 1981.

Fisher of Lambeth, Lord, 'What's Best Administered', *Theology* (February 1965).

Garbett, Cyril, *Church and State in England*. Hodder & Stoughton 1950.

Gooch, G. P. ed., *The Later Correspondence of Lord John Russell, 1840–1878*. Longmans, Green 1925.

Grosskurth, Phyllis, *John Addington Symonds: A Biography*. Longmans 1964.

Guedalla, Philip, ed., *Gladstone and Palmerston: being the Correspondence of Lord Palmerston with Mr Gladstone 1851–1865*. Gollancz 1928.

Gummer, Selwyn, *The Chavasse Twins*. Hodder & Stoughton 1963.

Hardie, Frank, *The Political Influence of Queen Victoria 1861–1901*. Oxford University Press 1935.

Harris, Kenneth, *Attlee*. Weidenfeld & Nicolson 1982.

Henson, H. Hensley, *Retrospect of an Unimportant Life*. Oxford University Press, 3 vols., 1942–50.

Hodder, Edwin, *The Life and Work of the Seventh Earl of Shaftesbury, K.G.* Cassell 1887.

Holtby, Robert, *Robert Wright Stopford 1901–1976*. National Society 1988.

Hopkins, C. H. G., *Bishop A. T. P. Williams: A Biography*. Great Wakering, Mayhew-McCrimmon, 1975.

Horne, Alistair, *Macmillan: 1957–1986*. Macmillan 1989.

How, F. D., *Archbishop Maclagan*. Wells, Gardner, Darton 1911.

Hughes, Dom Anselm, *The Rivers of the Flood: A personal account of the Catholic Revival in England in the Twentieth Century*. Faith Press 1961.

Hughes, Thomas, *James Fraser, Second Bishop of Manchester: A Memoir, 1818–1885*. Macmillan 1887.

Hutton, W. H., ed., *Letters of William Stubbs, Bishop of Oxford, 1825–1901*. Archibald Constable 1904.

Iremonger, F. A., *William Temple: His Life and Letters*. Oxford University Press 1948.

James, Robert Rhodes, *Anthony Eden*. Weidenfeld & Nicolson 1986.

——, *Rosebery: A Biography of Archibald Philip, Fifth Earl of Rosebery*. Weidenfeld & Nicolson 1963.

Jasper, R. C. D., *Arthur Cayley Headlam: Life and Letters of a Bishop*. Faith Press 1960.

——, *George Bell: Bishop of Chichester*. Oxford University Press 1967.

Jenkins, Roy, *Asquith*. Collins, 3rd edn., 1988.

——, *Baldwin*. Collins 1988.

Johnson, Paul, ed., *The Oxford Book of Political Anecdotes*. Oxford University Press 1986.

Jones, W. D., *Lord Derby and Victorian Conservatism*. Oxford, Blackwell, 1956.

Kemp, E. W., *Kenneth Escott Kirk*. Hodder & Stoughton 1959.

Kirk-Smith, H., *William Thomson, Archbishop of York: His Life and Times 1819–90*. SPCK 1958.

Kitchin, G. W., *Edward Harold Browne, D.D., Lord Bishop of Winchester: A Memoir*. John Murray 1895.

Knox, E. A., *Reminiscences of an Octogenarian 1847–1934*. Hutchinson 1935.

Lee, Sidney, *King Edward VII: A Biography*. Macmillan 1927.

Leveson Gower, George, *Years of Content 1858–1886*. John Murray 1940.

Lockhart, J. G., *Cosmo Gordon Lang*. Hodder & Stoughton 1949.

Longford, Elizabeth, *Victoria, R.I.* Weidenfeld & Nicolson 1964.

Lysaght, C. E., *Brendan Bracken*. Allen Lane 1979.

Macdonnell, J. C., *The Life and Correspondence of William Connor Magee, Archbishop of York, Bishop of Peterborough*. Isbister 1896.

Machin, G. I. T., *Politics and the Churches in Great Britain 1832–1868*. Oxford, Clarendon Press, 1977.

——, *Politics and the Churches in Great Britain 1869–1921*. Oxford, Clarendon Press, 1987.

McKay, Roy, *John Leonard Wilson: Confessor for the Faith.* Hodder & Stoughton 1973.

Magnus, Philip, *King Edward the Seventh.* John Murray 1964.

Mahon, Lord, and Cardwell, E., eds, *Memoirs by the Rt. Hon. Sir Robert Peel, Bart., M.P.* John Murray 1856-7.

Malden, R. H., *The English Church and Nation.* SPCK 1952.

Mantle, Jonathan, *Archbishop: The Life and Times of Robert Runcie.* Sinclair-Stevenson 1991.

Marquand, David, *Ramsay MacDonald.* Jonathan Cape 1977.

Marsh, P. T., *The Victorian Church in Decline: Archbishop Tait and the Church of England 1868-1882.* Routledge & Kegan Paul 1969.

Martin, Hugh, 'Church and State: A Free Church Point of View', *Church Quarterly Review* (Oct.–Dec. 1936).

Meacham, Standish, *Lord Bishop: The Life of Samuel Wilberforce 1805-1873.* Cambridge, Mass., Harvard University Press, 1970.

Middleman, Keith, and Barnes, John, *Baldwin: A Biography.* Weidenfeld & Nicolson 1969.

Monypenny, W. F., and Buckle, G. E., *The Life of Benjamin Disraeli, Earl of Beaconsfield.* John Murray 1920.

Morley, John, *The Life of William Ewart Gladstone.* Macmillan 1903.

Nicolson, Harold, *King George the Fifth: His Life and Reign.* Constable 1952.

Overton, J. H., and Wordsworth, Elizabeth, *Christopher Wordsworth, Bishop of Lincoln, 1807-1885.* Rivingtons 1888.

Parker, C. S., ed., *Sir Robert Peel: from his private papers.* John Murray 1899.

Pawley, Margaret, *Donald Coggan: Servant of Christ.* SPCK 1987.

Peart-Binns, J. S., *Ambrose Reeves.* Gollancz 1973.

—— , *Defender of the Church of England: The Life of Bishop R. R. Williams.* Oxford, Amate Press, 1984.

—— , *Graham Leonard, Bishop of London.* Darton, Longman & Todd 1988.

—— , *Wand of London.* Oxford, Mowbray, 1987.

—— , and Dunstan, Alan, *Cornish Bishop.* Epworth Press 1977.

Plomer, William, ed., *Kilvert's Diary: Selections from the Diary of the Rev. Francis Kilvert.* Jonathan Cape 1960 edn.

Pollock, Bertram, *A Twentieth-Century Bishop: Recollections and Reflections.* Skeffington 1944.

Prestige, G. L., *The Life of Charles Gore: A Great Englishman.* Heinemann 1935.

Prothero, R. E., and Bradley, G. G., *The Life and Correspondence of Arthur Penrhyn Stanley, D.D., late Dean of Westminster.* John Murray 1893.

Purcell, William, *Fisher of Lambeth: A Portrait from Life.* Hodder & Stoughton 1969.

Quickswood, Lord, 'Church and State', *Church Quarterly Review* (July–Sept. 1952).

Read, Donald, *Peel and the Victorians.* Oxford, Blackwell, 1987.

Rickards, E. C., *Bishop Moorhouse of Melbourne and Manchester.* John Murray 1920.

Rose, Kenneth, *King George V.* Weidenfeld & Nicolson 1983.

St Aubyn, Giles, *Edward VII: Prince and King.* Collins 1979.

Saintsbury, George, *The Earl of Derby.* Sampson Low, Marston 1892.

Sanders, L. C., ed., *Lord Melbourne's Papers.* Longmans, Green 1889.

Sandford, E. G., ed., *Memoirs of Archbishop Temple by 7 Friends.* Macmillan 1906.

Sheen, H. E., *Canon Peter Green.* Hodder & Stoughton 1965.

Simpkinson, C. H., *The Life and Work of Bishop Thorold.* Isbister 1896.

Skinner, B. G., *Robert Exon*. Bognor Regis, New Horizon, 1979.

Smith, Paul, ed., *Lord Salisbury on Politics: A selection from his articles in the Quarterly Review, 1860–1883*. Cambridge University Press 1972.

Smyth, Charles, *Cyril Forster Garbett: Archbishop of York*. Hodder & Stoughton 1959.

Spender, J. A., *The Life of the Right Hon. Sir Henry Campbell-Bannerman, G.C.B.* Hodder & Stoughton 1923.

——, and Asquith, Cyril, *Life of Herbert Henry Asquith, Lord Oxford and Asquith*. Hutchinson 1932.

Stockwood, Mervyn, *Chanctonbury Ring: An Autobiography*. Hodder & Stoughton and Sheldon Press 1982.

Temple, William, *Life of Bishop Percival*. Macmillan 1921.

Thirlwall, J. C., *Connop Thirlwall: Historian and Theologian*. SPCK 1936.

Torrens, W. T. MacCullagh, *Memoirs of William Lamb, second Viscount Melbourne*. Ward, Lock 1890.

Vidler, A. R., *The Orb and the Cross: A narrative study in the relations of Church and State with reference to Gladstone's early writings*. SPCK 1945.

Walpole, Spencer, *The Life of Lord John Russell*. Longmans, Green 1889.

Wand, J. W. C., *Changeful Page*. Hodder & Stoughton 1965.

Welch, P. J., 'Blomfield and Peel: a Study in Co-operation between Church and State, 1841–1846' *Journal of Ecclesiastical History* (1961).

Welsby, P. A., *A History of the Church of England 1945–1980*. Oxford University Press 1984.

West, F. H., *'FRB': A Portrait of Bishop Russell Barry*. Bramcote, Grove Books, 1980.

Wheeler-Bennett, J. W., *King George VI: His Life and Reign*. Macmillan 1958.

Williams, David, *Genesis and Exodus: A Portrait of the Benson Family*. Hamish Hamilton 1979.

Wilson, Harold, *The Governance of Britain*. Weidenfeld & Nicolson and Michael Joseph 1976.

Wilson, John, *CB: A Life of Sir Henry Campbell-Bannerman*. Constable 1973.

Young, G. M., *Stanley Baldwin*. Hart-Davis 1952.

Young, Kenneth, *Arthur James Balfour: The happy life of the politician, prime minister, statesman and philosopher*. Bell 1963.

# Statistical Table of Bishops

For the statistically-minded I include a few explanatory comments on the alphabetical list of bishops that follows. The list includes all the 294 bishops appointed by prime ministers from the beginning of Queen Victoria's reign up to the coming into operation of the Crown Appointments Commission.

(1) *Decorations, etc.* I have listed all wartime decorations for gallantry. These included five DSOs (one with bar) and fifteen MCs (three with bar), mostly won during the First World War. The most-decorated bishop was Noel Hudson of Newcastle and Ely (DSO and bar plus MC and bar). The knighthoods awarded include three GCVOs, twelve KCVOs, three KCMGs and one GBE. They were usually awarded in recognition of royal appointments such as Dean of the Chapels Royal or Lord High Almoner. Episcopal knights in the Church of England, however, are not customarily styled 'Sir . . .'. I have not included academic degrees or doctorates, but have listed fellowships of learned bodies such as FRS (Barnes of Birmingham) or FRHistS (Kemp of Chichester).

(2) *Schools.* The list is not complete, as in a few cases I have not, in the absence of information in the usual reference-books, been able to discover the school attended by the bishop in question. But, of the 275 bishops whose schools *were* discoverable, 135 (roughly half the total) went to what could be broadly described as major public schools. And, of these 135, no fewer than 105 (or more than a third of the total) were educated at nine particular schools: 26 at Eton, 16 at Winchester, 12 each at Rugby and Marlborough, 11 at Shrewsbury, 8 each at Westminster and Harrow, 7 at Charterhouse and 5 at St Paul's. Of the non-major-public-school half, most attended either minor public schools or provincial grammar schools. What is perhaps most significant is not so much the fact that half the bishops should have gone to a well-known school as that half should not. The scholastic background of diocesan bishops over the period 1837–1977 was by no means universally élitist.

(3) *Universities.* On the other hand, the university background of the bishops was overwhelmingly Oxbridge-orientated. 268 of the bishops went to either Oxford (147) or Cambridge (121) – about 90 per cent of the total. A long, long way behind come London (10) and Durham and Trinity College, Dublin (5 each). Some of the Oxbridge colleges were more highly favoured than others. The Oxford list is headed by Christ Church (21), New College (17), Balliol (15), Queen's (12) and Keble (11). At Cambridge by far the most prolific college is Trinity, with 37 diocesans among its alumni: the next most popular are Christ's and Corpus, with 12 each.

(4) *Theological colleges.* Here the most noteworthy fact is how few of the Victorian bishops actually patronized these institutions, though most of them were founded in the nineteenth century. The reason would appear to be that (except perhaps for Cuddesdon) they were in the main, to begin with, intended for those who could not afford to go to Oxbridge. It was not until towards the end of the nineteenth century that it began to be considered vital for all ordinands to attend a theological college, though even then some people regarded the colleges as almost like 'finishing schools' to round off an Oxbridge education.

Some colleges, like Cuddesdon and Wells, were founded with a bias towards university-educated men; others, like Salisbury, were established to help working and lower-middle-class men enter the ministry. It is not surprising therefore that Cuddesdon and Wells should both have produced a fair number of English diocesans and Salisbury only one (Curzon of Exeter). In fact Cuddesdon comes easily top of the list with 31; next come the two Cambridge colleges, Westcott House with 25 and Ridley Hall with 23. Wells produced 16, Wycliffe Hall 11 and the others only 33 between them.

(5) *Suffragan and overseas sees.* Although seventeen suffragan bishops were consecrated in the sixteenth century under an Act of 1534, the Act lapsed in 1592 and was not revived until 1870, in the face of strong demands by diocesans for episcopal assistance. Since then more and more suffragan sees have been created, until now almost every diocese in the Church of England has one or more. It has become increasingly common for suffragans to be promoted to dioceses of their own. 66 of the diocesans on my list had previously held one suffragan see; five had held two such sees; one (Baddeley of Blackburn) had held both an overseas see and a suffragan see before his translation to an English diocese. 15 other English diocesans had previously held an overseas see.

(6) *Consecrations.* These usually took place in either Westminster Abbey or St Paul's Cathedral, though in Victorian times a number of bishops were consecrated in the chapel of Lambeth Palace. Bishops for the northern province have for many years been consecrated in York Minster. Southwark Cathedral has latterly also become a regular venue for southern consecrations. The date chosen has usually been a saint's day, but by no means invariably so.

(7) *Diocesan sees.* Of the 294 bishops on the list, 58 have held two diocesan sees and 11 three such sees. The two-translation men have usually been archbishops (Longley, Frederick Temple, Davidson, William Temple, Fisher, Garbett, Ramsey and Coggan); the other three were Gore, Talbot and Warman. Longley was actually translated three times, but his appointment to Ripon in 1836 was made before the period of this book begins.

(8) *Year appointed.* This means the year in which the prime minister's offer was actually made, and may not be the same year as that in which a candidate had his election confirmed and so legally became the bishop of the diocese. There might well be an interval of two or three months between appointment and confirmation, with a further interval (for those not yet in episcopal orders) between confirmation and consecration.

(9) *Prime ministers.* The palm goes to Salisbury, who awarded no fewer than 38 diocesan mitres during his three premierships. Next come Baldwin and Churchill (32 each), followed by Macmillan and Wilson (25 each), Gladstone (22) and Lloyd George and Attlee (20 each). These eight prime ministers were responsible between them for 214 out of the 374 appointments made during the period under review. The tallies of the remaining 18 premiers, totalling 160 appointments between them, are Palmerston and Asquith (19 each), Heath (18), Balfour and MacDonald (15 each), Disraeli (13), Russell and Eden (10 each), Melbourne (9), Chamberlain (8), Peel (5), Aberdeen and Campbell-Bannerman (4 each), Derby and Callaghan (3 each), Rosebery and Douglas-Home (2 each) and Bonar Law (1). (Melbourne's period begins on 6 May 1837; Callaghan's ends on 31 May 1977.) It should of course be remembered that the number of dioceses in the Church of England (excluding the four Welsh sees) nearly doubled during the period under review: from 24 in 1837 to 43 in 1977. 12 of the 19 new sees were created during the first quarter of the twentieth century.

(10) *Tenure of see.* Long periods in office were common in early and mid

Victorian times, until an Act passed in 1869 permitted bishops to retire rather than soldier on until death finally released them from their duties. But even after then lengthy episcopates were recorded. The first prize goes to Edwards of St Asaph, who was appointed by Salisbury in 1889 and survived well into the disestablishment period, becoming the first Archbishop of Wales and not finally bowing out until 1934, by when he had been in office for 45 years. A close runner-up was Ellicott of Gloucester and Bristol, with a 42-year span to his credit, though for his last eight years he was Bishop of Gloucester only. Other lengthy reigns were those of Winnington-Ingram of London (38 years), Pelham of Norwich (36), Thirlwall of St Davids (34), Ollivant of Llandaff (33), Pollock of Norwich (32), Campbell of Bangor and Eden of Wakefield (31 each), and Jayne of Chester and Philpott of Worcester (30 each). A further 57 bishops served between 20 and 30 years in a single diocese, two notable modern examples being Bell of Chichester (28) and Say of Rochester (27). Davidson's 25-year spell as Archbishop of Canterbury set a record for the period.

| Name of bishop | Dates | Public or secondary school | University and college | Theological college | Suffragan/ overseas see(s) held | Date of consecration | Diocesan see(s) held | Year appd. | Prime Mnstr responsible | Years held |
|---|---|---|---|---|---|---|---|---|---|---|
| 1. *Allen,* Geoffrey Francis | 1902–82 | Rugby | Oxford (Univ. Coll.) | Ripon Hall | *Egypt* (res. 1952) | 25 Jan. 1947 | Derby | 1959 | Macmillan | 10 |
| 2. *Allison,* Sherard Falkner | 1907– | Dean Close, Cheltenham | Cambridge (Jesus) | Ridley Hall | | 2 Feb. 1951 | Chelmsford Winchester | 1950 1961 | Attlee Macmillan | 10 13 |
| 3. *Anderson,* William Louis, DSC | 1892–1972 | St Paul's | Cambridge (Gonville and Caius) | Ridley Hall | Croydon | 18 Oct. 1937 | Portsmouth Salisbury | 1941 1949 | Churchill Attlee | 7 13 |
| 4. *Ashdown,* Hugh Edward | 1904–77 | St John's, Leatherhead | Oxford (Keble) | Lincoln | | 1 May 1957 | Newcastle | 1957 | Macmillan | 15 |
| 5. *Askwith,* Wilfred Marcus, KCMG | 1890–1962 | Bedford | Cambridge (Corpus Christi) | Ridley Hall | | 30 Nov. 1942 | Blackburn Gloucester | 1941 1953 | Churchill Churchill | 12 8 |
| 6. *Atlay,* James | 1817–94 | Oakham | Cambridge (St John's) | | | 24 June 1868 | Hereford | 1868 | Disraeli | 26 |
| 7. *Baddeley,* Walter Hubert, DSO, MC and bar | 1894–1960 | Varndean G.S., Brighton | Oxford (Keble) | Cuddesdon | *Melanesia* Whitby (1947) | 30 Nov. 1932 | Blackburn | 1954 | Churchill | 6 |
| 8. *Bagot,* Richard | 1782–1854 | Rugby | Oxford (Christ Church) | | | 23 Aug. 1829 (for Oxford) | Bath and Wells | 1845 | Peel | 9 |
| 9. *Bardsley,* Cuthbert Killick Norman, CBE | 1907–91 | Eton | Oxford (New Coll.) | Westcott House | Croydon | 1 Nov. 1947 | Coventry | 1956 | Eden | 20 |
| 10. *Bardsley,* Cyril Charles Bowman | 1870–1940 | Marlborough | Oxford (New Coll.) | Wycliffe Hall | | 2 Feb. 1924 | Peterborough Leicester | 1924 1926 | Baldwin Baldwin | 2 13 |
| 11. *Bardsley,* John Wareing | 1835–1904 | Manchester G.S. | Dublin (Trinity) | | | 24 Aug. 1887 | Sodor and Man Carlisle | 1887 1891 | Salisbury Salisbury | 5 12 |
| 12. *Baring,* Charles | 1807–79 | (Educated privately) | Oxford (Christ Church) | | | 10 Aug. 1856 | Gloucester and Bristol Durham | 1856 1861 | Palmerston Palmerston | 5 18 |

| Name of bishop | Dates | Public or secondary school | University and college | Theological college | Suffragan/ *overseas* see(s) held | Date of consecration | Diocesan see(s) held | Year appd. | Prime Mnstr responsible | Years held |
|---|---|---|---|---|---|---|---|---|---|---|
| 13. *Barnes*, Ernest William, FRS | 1874–1953 | King Edward's, Birmingham | Cambridge (Trinity) | | | 29 Sep. 1924 | Birmingham | 1924 | MacDonald | 29 |
| 14. *Barry*, Frank Russell, DSO | 1890–1976 | Bradfield | Oxford (Oriel) | Wells | | 18 Oct. 1941 | Southwell | 1941 | Churchill | 22 |
| 15. *Bell*, George Kennedy Allen | 1883–1958 | Westminster | Oxford (Christ Church) | Wells | | 11 June 1929 | Chichester | 1929 | Baldwin | 28 |
| 16. *Benson*, Edward White | 1829–96 | King Edward's, Birmingham | Cambridge (Trinity) | | | 25 April 1877 | Truro **Canterbury** | 1876 1882 | Disraeli Gladstone | 6 13 |
| 17. *Bickersteth*, Edward Henry | 1825–1906 | (Educated at home) | Cambridge (Trinity) | | | 25 April 1885 | Exeter | 1885 | Gladstone | 16 |
| 18. *Bickersteth*, John Monier, KCVO | 1921– | Rugby | Oxford (Christ Church) | Wells | Warrington | 7 April 1970 | Bath and Wells | 1975 | Wilson | 12 |
| 19. *Bickersteth*, Robert | 1816–84 | (Some medical training) | Cambridge (Queens') | | | 18 June 1857 | Ripon | 1856 | Palmerston | 27 |
| 20. *Bilbrough*, Harold Ernest | 1867–1950 | Winchester | Oxford (New Coll.) | | Dover | 24 Feb. 1916 | Newcastle | 1927 | Baldwin | 14 |
| 21. *Blagden*, Claude Martin | 1874–1952 | Bradfield | Oxford (Corpus Christi) | | | 25 Mar. 1927 | Peterborough | 1927 | Baldwin | 22 |
| 22. *Blanch*, Stuart Yarworth | 1918– | Alleyn's, Dulwich | Oxford (St Catherine's) | Wycliffe Hall | | 25 Mar. 1966 | Liverpool **York** | 1965 1974 | Wilson Wilson | 9 8 |
| 23. *Bloomer*, Thomas | 1894–1984 | Royal School, Dungannon, N.I. | Dublin (Trinity) | | | 18 Oct. 1946 | Carlisle | 1946 | Attlee | 20 |

| No. & Name | Dates | School | University (College) | Theological College | Missionary/Suffragan | Consecration | Diocese | Year | Prime Minister | No. |
|---|---|---|---|---|---|---|---|---|---|---|
| 24. *Blunt*, Alfred Walter Frank | 1879–1957 | Marlborough | Oxford (Exeter) | | | 25 July 1931 | Bradford | 1931 | MacDonald | 24 |
| 25. *Bowlby*, Ronald Oliver | 1926– | Eton | Oxford (Trinity) | Westcott House | | 6 Jan. 1973 | Newcastle | 1972 | Heath | 7 |
| 26. *Bowles*, Cyril William Johnston | 1916– | Brentwood | Cambridge (Emmanuel and Jesus Colls.) | Ridley Hall | | 1 Nov. 1969 | Derby | 1969 | Wilson | 18 |
| 27. *Bowstead*, James | | | Cambridge (Corpus Christi) | | | 22 July 1838 | Sodor and Man / Lichfield | 1838 / 1840 | Melbourne / Melbourne | 2 / 3 |
| 28. *Bradfield*, Harold William | 1898–1960 | Alleyn's, Dulwich | London (King's) | | | 1 May 1946 | Bath and Wells | 1946 | Attlee | 14 |
| 29. *Brook*, Richard | 1880–1969 | Bradford | Oxford (Lincoln) | Leeds Cl. Sch. | | 1 Nov. 1940 | St Edmundsbury and Ips. | 1940 | Churchill | 13 |
| 30. *Brown*, David Alan | 1922–82 | Monkton Combe | London | London Coll. of Div. | | 1 Nov. 1973 | Guildford | 1973 | Heath | 9 |
| 31. *Brown*, Laurence Ambrose | 1907– | Luton G.S. | Cambridge (Queens') | Cuddesdon | Warrington | 30 Nov. 1960 | Birmingham | 1969 | Wilson | 8 |
| 32. *Brown*, Leslie Wilfrid, CBE | 1912– | Enfield G.S. | London | London Coll. of Div. | *Uganda Namirembe* (1960) | 6 Jan. 1953 | St Edmundsbury and Ips. | 1966 | Wilson | 12 |
| 33. *Browne*, Edward Harold | 1811–91 | Eton | Cambridge (Emmanuel) | | | 29 Mar. 1864 | Ely / Winchester | 1864 / 1873 | Palmerston / Gladstone | 9 / 18 |
| 34. *Browne*, George Forrest | 1833–1930 | St Peter's, York | Cambridge (St Catharine's) | | Stepney | 21 April 1895 | Bristol | 1897 | Salisbury | 17 |
| 35. *Bulley*, Sydney Cyril | 1907–89 | Newton Abbot G.S. | Durham (St Chad's) | | Penrith | 24 Feb. 1959 | Carlisle | 1966 | Wilson | 6 |
| 36. *Burge*, Hubert Murray | 1862–1925 | Marlborough | Oxford (Univ. Coll.) | | | 25 May 1911 | Southwark / Oxford | 1911 / 1919 | Asquith / Lloyd George | 8 / 6 |

| Name of bishop | Dates | Public or secondary school | University and college | Theological college | Suffragan/ *overseas* see(s) held | Date of consecration | Diocesan see(s) held | Year appd. | Prime Mnstr responsible | Years held |
|---|---|---|---|---|---|---|---|---|---|---|
| 37. *Burroughs*, Edward Arthur | 1882–1934 | Harrow | Oxford (Balliol) | | | 6 Jan. 1926 | Ripon | 1925 | Baldwin | 8 |
| 38. *Burrows*, Leonard Hedley | 1857–1940 | Charterhouse | Oxford (New Coll.) | | Lewes | 11 July 1909 | Sheffield | 1914 | Asquith | 25 |
| 39. *Burrows*, Winfrid Oldfield | 1858–1929 | Eton | Oxford (Corpus Christi) | Cuddesdon | | 25 July 1912 | Truro Chichester | 1912 1919 | Asquith Lloyd George | 7 10 |
| 40. *Campbell*, James Colquhoun | 1813–95 | | Cambridge (Trinity) | | | 14 June 1859 | Bangor | 1859 | Derby | 31 |
| 41. *Carpenter*, Harry James | 1901– | Churchers' Petersfield | Oxford (Queen's) | Cuddesdon | | 25 Jan. 1955 | Oxford | 1954 | Churchill | 15 |
| 42. *Carpenter*, William Boyd | 1841–1918 | Royal Instit., Liverpool | Cambridge (St Catharine's) | | | 25 July 1884 | Ripon | 1884 | Gladstone | 27 |
| 43. *Carr*, Charles Lisle | 1871–1942 | Liverpool Coll. | Cambridge (St Catharine's) | Ridley Hall | | 24 June 1922 | Coventry Hereford | 1922 1930 | Lloyd George MacDonald | 9 10 |
| 44. *Cash*, William Wilson, DSO, OBE | 1880–1955 | Cambridge School, Sale | | | | 1 Nov. 1941 | Worcester | 1941 | Churchill | 14 |
| 45. *Cecil*, Lord Rupert Ernest William Gascoyne | 1863–1936 | Eton | Oxford (Univ. Coll.) | | | 28 Dec. 1916 | Exeter | 1916 | Asquith | 20 |
| 46. *Charles-Edwards*, Lewis Mervyn | 1902–83 | Shrewsbury | Oxford (Keble) | Lichfield | | 6 Jan. 1956 | Worcester | 1955 | Eden | 14 |
| 47. *Chase*, Frederic Henry | 1853–1925 | King's Coll. Sch., London | Cambridge (Christ's) | | | 18 Oct. 1905 | Ely | 1905 | Balfour | 19 |
| 48. *Chase*, George Armitage, MC* | 1886–1971 | Rugby | Cambridge (Queens') | Bishop's Hostel, Farnham | | 1 Nov. 1946 | Ripon | 1946 | Attlee | 13 |

| No. & Name | Dates | School | University | Theological College | | Consecrated | See | Year | Prime Minister | Yrs |
|---|---|---|---|---|---|---|---|---|---|---|
| 49. *Chavasse*, Christopher Maude, OBE, MC, TD† | 1884–1962 | Liverpool Coll. | Oxford (Trinity) | Bishop's Hostel, Liverpool | | 25 April 1940 | Rochester | 1939 | Chamberlain | 22 |
| 50. *Chavasse*, Francis James | 1846–1928 | Chesterfield G.S. | Oxford (Corpus Christi) | | | 25 April 1900 | Liverpool | 1900 | Salisbury | 23 |
| 51. *Claughton*, Thomas Legh | 1808–92 | Rugby | Oxford (Trinity) | | | 11 June 1867 | Rochester<br>St Albans | 1867<br>1877 | Derby<br>Disraeli | 10<br>13 |
| 52. *Claxton*, Charles Robert | 1903– | Weymouth Coll. | Cambridge (Queens') | Ridley Hall | Warrington | 7 April 1946 | Blackburn | 1960 | Macmillan | 11 |
| 53. *Cockin*, Frederick Arthur | 1888–1969 | Marlborough | Oxford (Univ. Coll.) | Cuddesdon | | 24 June 1946 | Bristol | 1946 | Attlee | 12 |
| 54. *Coggan*, Frederick Donald | 1909– | Merchant Taylors' | Cambridge (St John's) | Wycliffe Hall | | 25 Jan. 1956 | Bradford<br>**York**<br>**Canterbury** | 1955<br>1961<br>1974 | Eden<br>Macmillan<br>Wilson | 5<br>13<br>5 |
| 55. *Compton*, Lord Alwyne | 1825–1906 | Eton | Cambridge (Trinity) | | | 2 Feb. 1886 | Ely | 1886 | Salisbury | 19 |
| 56. *Creighton*, Mandell | 1843–1901 | Durham G.S. | Oxford (Merton) | | | 25 April 1891 | Peterborough<br>London | 1891<br>1896 | Salisbury<br>Salisbury | 5<br>5 |
| 57. *Crick*, Douglas Henry | 1884–1973 | Winchester | Oxford (New Coll.) | Bishop's Hostel, Liverpool | Stafford | 30 Nov. 1934 | Chester | 1939 | Chamberlain | 16 |
| 58. *Curzon*, Charles Edward | 1877–1954 | Lancaster G.S. | Cambridge (Christ's) | Salisbury | Stepney | 18 Oct. 1928 | Exeter | 1936 | Baldwin | 12 |
| 59. *David*, Albert Augustus | 1867–1950 | Exeter | Oxford (Queen's) | | | 25 July 1921 | St Edmundsbury and Ips.<br>Liverpool | 1921<br>1923 | Lloyd George<br>Baldwin | 2<br>21 |
| 60. *Davidson*, Randall Thomas, GCVO | 1848–1930 | Harrow | Oxford (Trinity) | | | 25 April 1891 | Rochester<br>Winchester<br>**Canterbury** | 1890<br>1895<br>1903 | Salisbury<br>Salisbury<br>Balfour | 4<br>8<br>25 |

* 3rd son of Bishop F. H. Chase.
† Twin son of Bishop F. J. Chavasse.

| Name of bishop | Dates | Public or secondary school | University and college | Theological college | Suffragan/ *overseas* see(s) held | Date of consecration | Diocesan see(s) held | Year appd. | Prime Mnstr responsible | Years held |
|---|---|---|---|---|---|---|---|---|---|---|
| 61. *Davys*, George | 1780–1864 | | Cambridge (Christ's) | | | 16 June 1839 | Peterborough | 1839 | Melbourne | 25 |
| 62. *Diggle*, John William | 1847–1920 | Manchester G.S. | Oxford (Wadham) | | | 2 Feb. 1905 | Carlisle | 1904 | Balfour | 15 |
| 63. *Donaldson*, St Clair George Alfred | 1863–1935 | Eton | Cambridge (Trinity) | Wells | *Brisbane* | 28 Oct. 1904 | Salisbury | 1921 | Lloyd George | 14 |
| 64. *Drury*, Thomas Wortley | 1847–1926 | King William's Coll., IoM | Cambridge (Christ's) | | | 30 Nov. 1907 | Sodor and Man / Ripon | 1907 / 1911 | Campbell-Bannerman / Asquith | 5 / 8 |
| 65. *Durnford*, Richard | 1802–95 | Eton | Oxford (Pembroke and Magdalen) | | | 8 May 1870 | Chichester | 1870 | Gladstone | 25 |
| 66. *Eastaugh*, Cyril, MC | 1897–1988 | Abp Tenison G.S. | Oxford (Christ Church) | Cuddesdon | Kensington | 1 Nov. 1949 | Peterborough | 1961 | Macmillan | 11 |
| 67. *Eastaugh*, John Richard Gordon | 1920–90 | | Leeds | Mirfield | | 24 Jan. 1974 | Hereford | 1973 | Heath | 16 |
| 68. *Eden*, George Rodney | 1853–1940 | Richmond School, Yorks, and Reading | Cambridge (Pembroke) | | Dover | 18 Oct. 1890 | Wakefield | 1897 | Salisbury | 31 |
| 69. *Eden*, Robert John, Lord Auckland | 1799–1870 | Eton | Cambridge (Magdalene) | | | 23 May 1847 | Sodor and Man / Bath and Wells | 1847 / 1854 | Russell / Aberdeen | 7 / 15 |
| 70. *Edwards*, Alfred George | 1848–1937 | Llandovery | Oxford (Jesus) | | | 25 Mar. 1889 | St Asaph | 1889 | Salisbury | 45 |

| | | | | | | | | | |
|---|---|---|---|---|---|---|---|---|---|
| 71. *Ellicott*, Charles John | 1819–1905 | Oakham and Stamford G.S.s | Cambridge (St John's) | | 25 Mar. 1863 | Gloucester and Bristol | 1863 | Palmerston | 42* |
| 72. *Ellison*, Gerald Alexander, KCVO | 1910– | Westminster | Oxford (New Coll.) | Westcott House | 21 Sep. 1950 | Chester / London | 1954 / 1973 | Churchill / Heath | 18 / 8 |
| 73. *Fallows*, William Gordon | 1913–79 | Barrow G.S. | Oxford (St Edmund Hall) | Ripon Hall | 11 June 1968 | Sheffield | 1971 | Heath | 8 |
| 74. *Feaver*, Douglas Russell | 1914– | Bristol G.S. | Oxford (Keble) | Wells | 1 Nov. 1972 | Peterborough | 1972 | Heath | 12 |
| 75. *Festing*, John Wogan | 1837–1902 | King's Coll. School, London | Cambridge (Trinity) | | 24 June 1890 | St Albans | 1890 | Salisbury | 13 |
| 76. *Fisher*, Geoffrey Francis, GCVO | 1887–1972 | Marlborough | Oxford (Exeter) | Wells | 21 Sep. 1932 | Chester / London / **Canterbury** | 1932 / 1939 / 1945 | MacDonald / Chamberlain / Churchill | 7 / 6 / 16 |
| 77. *Fison*, Joseph Edward | 1906–72 | Shrewsbury | Oxford (Queen's) | Wycliffe Hall | 25 April 1963 | Salisbury | 1963 | Macmillan | 9 |
| 78. *Fleming*, William Launcelot Scott, KCVO, FRSE | 1906–90 | Rugby | Cambridge (Trinity Hall) | Westcott House | 18 Oct. 1949 | Portsmouth / Norwich | 1949 / 1959 | Attlee / Macmillan | 10 / 12 |
| 79. *Fraser*, James | 1818–85 | Shrewsbury | Oxford (Lincoln) | | 25 Mar. 1870 | Manchester | 1870 | Gladstone | 15 |
| 80. *Frere*, Walter Howard, CR | 1863–1938 | Charterhouse | Cambridge (Trinity) | Wells | 30 Nov. 1923 | Truro | 1923 | Baldwin | 12 |
| 81. *Furse*, Michael Bolton | 1870–1955 | Eton | Oxford (Trinity) | *Pretoria* | 29 June 1909 | St Albans | 1920 | Lloyd George | 24 |
| 82. *Garbett*, Cyril Forster | 1875–1955 | Portsmouth G.S. | Oxford (Keble) | Cuddesdon | 18 Oct. 1919 | Southwark / Winchester / **York** | 1919 / 1932 / 1942 | Lloyd George / MacDonald / Churchill | 13 / 10 / 13 |

* Gloucester only 1897–1905

| Name of bishop | Dates | Public or secondary school | University and college | Theological college | Suffragan/ *overseas* see(s) held | Date of consecration | Diocesan see(s) held | Year appd. | Prime Mnstr responsible | Years held |
|---|---|---|---|---|---|---|---|---|---|---|
| 83. *Gibbs*, John | 1917– | Bristol and London | Lincoln | Bradwell | | 19 June 1973 | Coventry | 1976 | Wilson | 9 |
| 84. *Gibson*, Edgar Charles Sumner | 1848–1924 | Charterhouse | Oxford (Trinity) | Wells | | 1 June 1905 | Gloucester | 1905 | Balfour | 18 |
| 85. *Gilbert*, Ashurst Turner | 1786–1870 | Manchester G.S. | Oxford (Brasenose) | | | 27 Feb. 1842 | Chichester | 1842 | Peel | 28 |
| 86. *Glyn*, Hon. Edward Carr | 1843–1928 | Harrow | Oxford (Univ. Coll.) | | | 24 Feb. 1897 | Peterborough | 1896 | Salisbury | 19 |
| 87. *Goodwin*, Harvey | 1818–91 | Private school in High Wycombe | Cambridge (Gonville and Caius) | | | 30 Nov. 1869 | Carlisle | 1869 | Gladstone | 22 |
| 88. *Gordon*, Archibald Ronald McDonald | 1927– | Rugby | Oxford (Balliol) | Cuddesdon | | 23 Sep. 1975 | Portsmouth | 1975 | Wilson | 9 |
| 89. *Gordon*, George Eric | 1905–92 | St Olave's, London | Cambridge (St Catharine's) | Wycliffe Hall | | 29 Sep. 1966 | Sodor and Man | 1966 | Wilson | 8 |
| 90. *Gore*, Charles | 1853–1932 | Harrow | Oxford (Balliol) | | | 23 Feb. 1902 | Worcester Birmingham Oxford | 1901 1905 1911 | Salisbury Balfour Asquith | 3 6 8 |
| 91. *Gorton*, Neville Vincent | 1888–1955 | Marlborough | Oxford (Balliol) | | | 2 Feb. 1943 | Coventry | 1943 | Churchill | 12 |
| 92. *Gott*, John | 1830–1906 | Winchester | Oxford (Brasenose) | | | 29 Sep. 1891 | Truro | 1891 | Salisbury | 15 |
| 93. *Graham*, John | 1794–1865 | Durham G.S. | Cambridge (Christ's) | | | 14 May 1848 | Chester | 1848 | Russell | 17 |

| No. | Name | Dates | School | University | Theological college | Birthplace | Consecrated | See | Year | Prime Minister |
|---|---|---|---|---|---|---|---|---|---|---|
| 94. | *Greer*, William Derrick Lindsay | 1902–72 | St Columba's Coll., Co. Dublin | Dublin (Trinity) | Westcott House | | 29 Sep. 1947 | Manchester | 1947 | Attlee | 23 |
| 95. | *Greig*, John Harold | 1865–1938 | | Cambridge (Pembroke) | | *Gibraltar* | 25 Jan. 1921 | Guildford | 1927 | Baldwin | 7 |
| 96. | *Guy*, Basil Tudor | 1910–75 | Forest School | Oxford (Keble) | Wells | Bedford | 25 July 1957 | Gloucester | 1962 | Macmillan | 13 |
| 97. | *Habgood*, John Stapylton | 1927– | Eton | Cambridge (King's) | Cuddesdon | | 1 May 1973 | Durham | 1973 | Heath | 10 |
| 98. | *Haigh*, Mervyn George | 1887–1962 | Clifton | Oxford (New Coll.) | | | 24 Feb. 1931 | Coventry<br>Winchester | 1930<br>1942 | MacDonald<br>Churchill | 11<br>10 |
| 99. | *Halsey*, Henry David | 1919– | KCS, Wimbledon | London (King's) | Wells | Tonbridge | 2 Feb. 1968 | Carlisle | 1972 | Heath | 17 |
| 100. | *Hamilton*, Walter Kerr | 1808–69 | Eton | Oxford (Christ Church) | | | 14 May 1854 | Salisbury | 1854 | Aberdeen | 15 |
| 101. | *Hampden*, Renn Dickson | 1793–1868 | (Educated privately) | Oxford (Oriel) | | | 26 Mar. 1848 | Hereford | 1847 | Russell | 20 |
| 102. | *Harland*, Maurice Henry | 1896–1986 | St Peter's, York | Oxford (Exeter) | Leeds Clergy School | Croydon | 25 July 1942 | Lincoln<br>Durham | 1947<br>1956 | Attlee<br>Eden | 9<br>10 |
| 103. | *Harmer*, John Reginald | 1857–1944 | Eton | Cambridge (King's) | | *Adelaide* | 23 May 1895 | Rochester | 1905 | Balfour | 25 |
| 104. | *Headlam*, Arthur Cayley, CH | 1862–1947 | Winchester | Oxford (New Coll.) | | | 25 Jan. 1923 | Gloucester | 1922 | Bonar Law | 22 |
| 105. | *Henderson*, Edward Barry, DSC | 1910–86 | Radley | Cambridge (Trinity) | Cuddesdon | Tewkesbury | 11 June 1955 | Bath and Wells | 1960 | Macmillan | 15 |
| 106. | *Henson*, Herbert Hensley | 1863–1947 | (Educated privately) | Oxford | | | 2 Feb. 1918 | Hereford<br>Durham | 1917<br>1920 | Lloyd George<br>Lloyd George | 3<br>19 |
| 107. | *Herbert*, Percy Mark | 1885–1968 | Rugby | Cambridge (Trinity) | | Kingston-upon-Thames | 25 Jan. 1922 | Blackburn<br>Norwich | 1926<br>1941 | Baldwin<br>Churchill | 16<br>17 |

| Name of bishop | Dates | Public or secondary school | University and college | Theological college | Suffragan/ overseas see(s) held | Date of consecration | Diocesan see(s) held | Year appd. | Prime Mnstr responsible | Years held |
|---|---|---|---|---|---|---|---|---|---|---|
| 108. *Hervey*, Lord Arthur Charles | 1808–94 | Eton | Cambridge (Trinity) | | | 21 Dec. 1869 | Bath and Wells | 1869 | Gladstone | 25 |
| 109. *Heywood*, Bernard Oliver Francis | 1871–1960 | Harrow | Cambridge (Trinity) | | Hull (1931) | 25 Mar. 1926 | Southwell / Ely | 1926 / 1934 | Baldwin / MacDonald | 2 / 6 |
| 110. *Hicks*, Edward Lee | 1843–1919 | Magdalen Coll. Sch., Oxford | Oxford (Brasenose) | | | 24 June 1910 | Lincoln | 1910 | Asquith | 9 |
| 111. *Hicks*, Frederick Cyril Nugent | 1872–1942 | Harrow | Oxford (Balliol) | Cuddesdon | *Gibraltar* | 18 Oct. 1927 | Lincoln | 1932 | MacDonald | 9 |
| 112. *Hill*, Rowley | 1836–87 | Christ's Hospital | Cambridge (Trinity) | | | 24 Aug. 1877 | Sodor and Man | 1877 | Disraeli | 10 |
| 113. *Hinds*, Samuel | 1793–1872 | 'A school near Bristol' | Oxford (Queen's) | | | 2 Dec. 1849 | Norwich | 1849 | Russell | 8 |
| 114. *Hodgson*, Henry Bernard | 1856–1921 | Shrewsbury | Oxford (Queen's) | | | 24 Feb. 1914 | St Edmundsbury and Ips. | 1914 | Asquith | 7 |
| 115. *Hodson*, Mark Allin | 1907–85 | Enfield G.S. | London (Univ. Coll.) | Wells | Taunton | 6 Jan. 1956 | Hereford | 1961 | Macmillan | 12 |
| 116. *Hone*, Campbell Richard | 1873–1967 | Blackheath | Oxford (Wadham) | Leeds Clergy School | Pontefract | 2 Feb. 1931 | Wakefield | 1938 | Chamberlain | 7 |
| 117. *Hook*, Ross Sydney, MC | 1917– | Christ's Hospital | Cambridge (Peterhouse) | Ridley Hall | Grantham | 30 Nov. 1965 | Bradford | 1972 | Heath | 8 |
| 118. *Hoskyns*, Sir Edwyn, Bart. | 1851–1925 | Haileybury | Cambridge (Jesus) | | Burnley | 18 Oct. 1901 | Southwell | 1904 | Balfour | 21 |

| | Dates | School | University (College) | Theological College | First See | Consecration | See | Year | Prime Minister | No. |
|---|---|---|---|---|---|---|---|---|---|---|
| 119. *How*, William Walsham | 1823–97 | Shrewsbury | Oxford (Wadham) | | Bedford | 25 July 1879 | Wakefield | 1888 | Salisbury | 9 |
| 120. *Hudson*, Noel Baring, DSO and bar, MC and bar | 1893–1970 | St Edward's, Oxford | Cambridge (Christ's) | Westcott House | *Labuan and Sarawak* (res. 1938) | 28 Oct. 1931 | Newcastle / Ely | 1941 / 1956 | Churchill / Eden | 16 / 6 |
| 121. *Hughes*, Joshua | 1807–89 | Ystradmeurig G.S. | Lampeter (St David's) | | | 8 May 1870 | St Asaph | 1870 | Gladstone | 19 |
| 122. *Hughes*, Joshua Pritchard* | 1847–1938 | Llandovery and Shrewsbury | Oxford (Balliol) | | | 1 June 1905 | Llandaff | 1905 | Balfour | 26 |
| 123. *Hunkin*, Joseph Wellington, OBE, MC and bar | 1887–1950 | Truro and Leys | Cambridge (Gonville and Caius) | Ridley Hall | | 11 June 1935 | Truro | 1935 | MacDonald | 15 |
| 124. *Hunter*, Leslie Stannard | 1890–1983 | Kelvinside | Oxford (New Coll.) | | | 29 Sep. 1939 | Sheffield | 1939 | Chamberlain | 23 |
| 125. *Jackson*, John | 1811–85 | Reading | Oxford (Pembroke) | | | 5 May 1853 | Lincoln / London | 1853 / 1868 | Aberdeen / Disraeli | 16 / 16 |
| 126. *Jacob*, Edgar | 1844–1920 | Winchester | Oxford (New Coll.) | | | 25 Jan. 1896 | Newcastle / St Albans | 1895 / 1903 | Salisbury / Balfour | 7 / 17 |
| 127. *Jacobson*, William | 1803–84 | Homerton | Oxford (St Edmund Hall and Lincoln) | | | 24 Aug. 1865 | Chester | 1865 | Palmerston | 19 |
| 128. *James*, Colin Clement Walter | 1926– | Aldenham | Cambridge (King's) | Cuddesdon | Basingstoke | 2 Feb. 1973 | Wakefield | 1976 | Callaghan | 8 |
| 129. *Jayne*, Francis John | 1845–1921 | Rugby | Oxford (Wadham) | | | 24 Feb. 1889 | Chester | 1889 | Salisbury | 30 |
| 130. *Jeune*, Francis | 1806–68 | St Servan's Coll., Rennes | Oxford (Pembroke) | | | 29 June 1864 | Peterborough | 1864 | Palmerston | 4 |

*3rd son of Bishop J. Hughes.

| Name of bishop | Dates | Public or secondary school | University and college | Theological college | Suffragan/ *overseas* see(s) held | Date of consecration | Diocesan see(s) held | Year appd. | Prime Mnstr responsible | Years held |
|---|---|---|---|---|---|---|---|---|---|---|
| 131. *Jones*, Edward Michael Gresford, KCVO | 1901–82 | Rugby | Cambridge (Trinity) | Westcott House | Willesden | 25 Mar. 1942 | St Albans | 1950 | Attlee | 19 |
| 132. *Jones*, William Basil Tickell | 1822–97 | Shrewsbury | Oxford (Trinity) | | | 24 Aug. 1874 | St Davids | 1874 | Disraeli | 23 |
| 133. *Jones*, William Stanton | 1866–1951 | | Durham | St Aidan's, Birkenhead | | 11 June 1928 | Sodor and Man | 1928 | Baldwin | 14 |
| 134. *Kemp*, Eric Waldram, FRHistS | 1915– | Brigg G.S. | Oxford (Exeter) | St Stephen's House | | 23 Oct. 1974 | Chichester | 1974 | Wilson | |
| 135. *Kempthorne*, John Augustine | 1864–1946 | Haileybury | Cambridge (Trinity) | | Hull | 16 May 1910 | Lichfield | 1913 | Asquith | 24 |
| 136. *Kennion*, George Wyndham | 1845–1922 | Eton | Oxford (Oriel) | | *Adelaide* | 30 Nov. 1882 | Bath and Wells | 1894 | Rosebery | 27 |
| 137. *Key*, John Maurice | 1905–84 | Rossall | Cambridge (Pembroke) | Westcott House | Sherborne | 1 Nov. 1947 | Truro | 1959 | Macmillan | 13 |
| 138. *King*, Edward | 1829–1910 | (Educated privately) | Oxford (Oriel) | | | 25 April 1885 | Lincoln | 1885 | Gladstone | 25 |
| 139. *Kirk*, Kenneth Escott | 1886–1954 | Sheffield G.S. | Oxford (St John's) | Cuddesdon | | 30 Nov. 1937 | Oxford | 1937 | Chamberlain | 17 |
| 140. *Knox*, Edmund Arbuthnott | 1847–1937 | St Paul's | Oxford (Corpus Christi) | | Coventry | 28 Dec. 1894 | Manchester | 1903 | Balfour | 18 |
| 141. *Lang*, Cosmo Gordon, GCVO | 1864–1945 | Park School, Glasgow | Glasgow and Oxford (Balliol) | Cuddesdon | Stepney | 1 May 1901 | York Canterbury | 1908 1928 | Asquith Baldwin | 20 14 |

| | | | | | | | | | |
|---|---|---|---|---|---|---|---|---|---|
| 142. *Lee*, James Prince | 1804–69 | St Paul's | Cambridge (Trinity) | | 23 Jan. 1848 | Manchester | 1847 | Russell | 21 |
| 143. *Leeson*, Spencer Stottisbury Gwatkin | 1892–1956 | Winchester | Oxford (New Coll.) | | 1 Nov. 1949 | Peterborough | 1949 | Attlee | 7 |
| 144. *Legge*, Hon. Augustus | 1839–1913 | Eton | Oxford (Christ Church) | Lichfield | 29 Sep. 1891 | Lichfield | 1891 | Salisbury | 22 |
| 145. *Leonard*, Graham Douglas, KCVO | 1921– | Monkton Combe | Oxford (Balliol) | Westcott House / Willesden | 21 Sep. 1964 | Truro | 1973 | Heath | 8 |
| 146. *Lewis*, Richard | 1821–1905 | Haverfordwest G.S. and Bromsgrove | Oxford (Worcester) | | 25 April 1883 | Llandaff | 1883 | Gladstone | 22 |
| 147. *Lightfoot*, Joseph Barber | 1828–89 | King Edward's Birmingham | Cambridge (Trinity) | | 25 April 1879 | Durham | 1879 | Disraeli | 10 |
| 148. *Lloyd*, Arthur Thomas | 1845–1907 | Magdalen Coll., School, Oxford | Oxford (St Edmund Hall) | Thetford | 18 Oct. 1894 | Newcastle | 1903 | Balfour | 4 |
| 149. *Lloyd*, Daniel Lewis | 1843–99 | Lampeter G.S. | Oxford (Jesus) | | 24 June 1890 | Bangor | 1890 | Salisbury | 8 |
| 150. *Longley*, Charles Thomas | 1794–1868 | Westminster | Oxford (Christ Church) | | 6 Nov. 1836 (for Ripon) | Durham / York / Canterbury | 1856 / 1860 / 1862 | Palmerston / Palmerston / Palmerston | 4 / 2 / 6 |
| 151. *Longworth*, Tom | 1891–1977 | Shrewsbury | Oxford (Univ. Coll.) | Cuddesdon / Pontefract | 2 Feb. 1939 | Hereford | 1949 | Attlee | 12 |
| 152. *Lonsdale*, John | 1788–1867 | Eton | Cambridge (King's) | | 3 Dec. 1843 | Lichfield | 1843 | Peel | 24 |
| 153. *Lovett*, Ernest Neville, CBE | 1869–1951 | Sherborne | Cambridge (Christ's) | | 25 July 1927 | Portsmouth / Salisbury | 1927 / 1936 | Baldwin / Baldwin | 9 / 10 |

| Name of bishop | Dates | Public or secondary school | University and college | Theological college | Suffragan/ *overseas* see(s) held | Date of consecration | Diocesan see(s) held | Year appd. | Prime Mnstr responsible | Years held |
|---|---|---|---|---|---|---|---|---|---|---|
| 154. *Loyd*, Philip Henry | 1884–1952 | Eton | Cambridge (King's) | Cuddesdon | *Nasik*, India | 22 Mar. 1925 | St Albans | 1944 | Churchill | 6 |
| 155. *Lunt*, Geoffrey Charles Lester, MC | 1885–1948 | Sherborne | Oxford (Exeter) | | | 25 Jan. 1935 | Ripon **Salisbury** | 1934 1946 | MacDonald Attlee | 11 2 |
| 156. *McGowan*, Henry | 1891–1948 | Bristol G.S. | Cambridge (St Catharine's) | Ridley Hall | | 2 Feb. 1946 | Wakefield | 1945 | Attlee | 2 |
| 157. *Mackarness*, John Fielder | 1820–89 | Eton | Oxford (Merton) | | | 25 Jan. 1870 | Oxford | 1869 | Gladstone | 19 |
| 158. *Maclagan*, William Dalrymple | 1826–1910 | Edinburgh H.S. | Edinburgh and Cambridge (Peterhouse) | | | 24 June 1878 | Lichfield **York** | 1878 1891 | Disraeli Salisbury | 13 17 |
| 159. *Macmillan*, John Victor, OBE | 1877–1956 | Eton | Oxford (Magdalen) | Bishop's Hostel, Farnham | Dover | 1 Nov. 1927 | Guildford | 1934 | MacDonald | 15 |
| 160. *Magee*, William Connor | 1821–91 | Kilkenny Coll. | Dublin (Trinity) | | | 15 Nov. 1868 | Peterborough **York** | 1868 1891 | Disraeli Salisbury | 22 3 mths |
| 161. *Martin*, Clifford Arthur | 1895–1977 | | Cambridge (Fitzwilliam) | Ridley Hall | | 25 July 1944 | Liverpool | 1944 | Churchill | 21 |
| 162. *Martineau*, Robert Arthur Schurhoff | 1913– | King Edward's, Birmingham | Cambridge (Trinity Hall) | Westcott House | Huntingdon | 6 Jan. 1966 | Blackburn | 1971 | Heath | 9 |
| 163. *Mercer*, Eric Arthur John | 1917– | Dover G.S. | | Kelham | Birkenhead | 7 Nov. 1965 | Exeter | 1973 | Heath | 12 |
| 164. *Moberly*, George | 1803–85 | Winchester | Oxford (Balliol) | | | 28 Oct. 1869 | Salisbury | 1869 | Gladstone | 16 |

| | Dates | School | University | Theological College | Consecrated | Suffragan see | Diocesan see | Year | Prime Minister | No. |
|---|---|---|---|---|---|---|---|---|---|---|
| 165. *Montgomery-Campbell*, Henry Colville, KCVO, MC | 1887–1970 | Malvern | Oxford (Brasenose) | Wells | 25 July 1940 | Willesden Kensington (1942) | Guildford London | 1949 1955 | Attlee Eden | 7 5 |
| 166. *Moorhouse*, James | 1826–1915 | (Educated privately) | Cambridge (St John's) | | 22 Oct. 1876 | *Melbourne* | Manchester | 1886 | Salisbury | 17 |
| 167. *Moorman*, John Richard Humpidge | 1905–89 | Gresham's, Holt | Cambridge (Emmanuel) | Westcott House | 11 June 1959 | | Ripon | 1959 | Macmillan | 16 |
| 168. *Morgan*, Edmund Robert | 1888–1979 | Winchester | Oxford (New Coll.) | Bishop's Hostel, Farnham | 3 June 1943 | Southampton | Truro | 1951 | Attlee | 8 |
| 169. *Morris*, Arthur Harold | 1898–1977 | Cambridge and County High S. for Boys | Cambridge (Fitzwilliam) | Ridley Hall | 1 Nov. 1949 | Pontefract | St Edmundsbury and Ips. | 1954 | Churchill | 11 |
| 170. *Mortimer*, Robert Cecil | 1902–76 | St Edward's, Oxford | Oxford (Keble) | Wells | 25 April 1949 | | Exeter | 1949 | Attlee | 24 |
| 171. *Mosley*, Henry | 1868–1948 | | Oxford (Keble) | Ely | 18 Oct. 1919 | Stepney | Southwell | 1928 | Baldwin | 13 |
| 172. *Moule*, Handley Carr Glyn | 1841–1920 | (Educated at home) | Cambridge (Trinity) | | 18 Oct. 1901 | | Durham | 1901 | Salisbury | 19 |
| 173. *Musgrave*, Thomas | 1788–1860 | Richmond G.S., Yorks | Cambridge (Trinity) | | 1 Oct. 1837 | Hereford York | | 1837 1847 | Melbourne Russell | 10 12 |
| 174. *Nicholls*, Vernon Sampson | 1917– | Truro | Durham | Clifton | 11 June 1974 | | Sodor and Man | 1974 | Wilson | 9 |
| 175. *Nickson*, George | 1864–1949 | Southport | TCD and Cambridge (Corpus Christi) | Ridley Hall | 29 June 1906 | Jarrow | Bristol | 1914 | Asquith | 19 |
| 176. *Ollivant*, Alfred | 1798–1882 | St Paul's | Cambridge (Trinity) | | 2 Dec. 1849 | | Llandaff | 1849 | Russell | 33 |
| 177. *Owen*, John | 1854–1926 | Bottwnog G.S. | Oxford (Jesus) | | 1 May 1897 | | St Davids | 1897 | Salisbury | 29 |

| Name of bishop | Dates | Public or secondary school | University and college | Theological college | Suffragan/ *overseas* see(s) held | Date of consecration | Diocesan see(s) held | Year appd. | Prime Mnstr responsible | Years held |
|---|---|---|---|---|---|---|---|---|---|---|
| 178. *Owen*, Leslie | 1886–1947 | Merchant Taylors' | Oxford (St John's) | Ely | Jarrow Maidstone (1944) | 2 Feb. 1939 | Lincoln | 1946 | Attlee | 1 |
| 179. *Paget*, Francis | 1851–1911 | Shrewsbury | Oxford (Christ Church) | Cuddesdon | | 29 June 1901 | Oxford | 1901 | Salisbury | 10 |
| 180. *Paget*, Henry Luke* | 1853–1937 | Shrewsbury | Oxford (Christ Church) | | Ipswich Stepney (1909) | 25 April 1906 | Chester | 1919 | Lloyd George | 13 |
| 181. *Parker*, Clement George St Michael | 1900–80 | | Oxford (Christ Church) | Ely | Aston | 18 Oct. 1954 | Bradford | 1961 | Macmillan | 10 |
| 182. *Parsons*, Richard Godfrey | 1882–1948 | Durham | Oxford (Magdalen) | Cuddesdon | Middleton | 25 Jan. 1927 | Southwark Hereford | 1932 1941 | MacDonald Churchill | 9 7 |
| 183. *Partridge*, Frank | 1877–1941 | (Educated privately) | London | Cuddesdon | | 24 June 1936 | Portsmouth | 1936 | Baldwin | 5 |
| 184. *Pearce*, Edmund Courtenay† | 1870–1935 | Christ's Hospital | Cambridge (Corpus Christi) | | | 18 Oct. 1927 | Derby | 1927 | Baldwin | 8 |
| 185. *Pearce*, Ernest Harold, CBE | 1865–1930 | Christ's Hospital | Cambridge (Peterhouse) | | | 24 Feb. 1919 | Worcester | 1919 | Lloyd George | 11 |
| 186. *Pelham*, John Thomas | 1811–94 | Westminster | Oxford (Christ Church) | | | 11 June 1857 | Norwich | 1857 | Palmerston | 36 |
| 187. *Pepys*, Henry | 1783–1860 | | Cambridge (Trinity) | | | 1 Mar. 1840 | Sodor and Man Worcester | 1840 1841 | Melbourne Melbourne | 1 19 |
| 188. *Percival*, John | 1834–1918 | Appleby G.S. | Oxford (Queen's) | | | 25 Mar. 1895 | Hereford | 1895 | Rosebery | 22 |

| No. Name | Dates | School | University | Theol. College | Consecrated | See | Year | Prime Minister | |
|---|---|---|---|---|---|---|---|---|---|
| 189. *Perowne*, Arthur William Thomson‡ | 1867–1948 | Haileybury | Cambridge (King's) | Ridley Hall | 2 Feb. 1920 | Bradford<br>Worcester | 1920<br>1931 | Lloyd George<br>MacDonald | 11<br>10 |
| 190. *Perowne*, John James Stewart | 1823–1904 | Norwich G.S. | Cambridge (Corpus Christi) | | 2 Feb. 1891 | Worcester | 1890 | Salisbury | 10 |
| 191. *Phillips*, John Henry Lawrence | 1910–85 | Weymouth | Cambridge (Trinity Hall) | Ridley Hall | 25 Mar. 1960 | Portsmouth | 1959 | Macmillan | 15 |
| 192. *Philpott*, Henry | 1807–92 | Chichester Cath. School | Cambridge (St Catharine's) | | 25 Mar. 1861 | Worcester | 1860 | Palmerston | 30 |
| 193. *Phipps*, Simon Wilton, MC | 1921– | Eton | Cambridge (Trinity) | Westcott House | 25 April 1968 | Horsham<br>Lincoln | 1974 | Wilson | 11 |
| 194. *Pollard*, Benjamin, TD | 1890–1967 | Manchester G.S. | Victoria Univ. of Manchester | Egerton Hall | 21 Sep. 1936 | Lancaster<br>Sodor and Man | 1954 | Churchill | 12 |
| 195. *Pollock*, Bertram, KCVO | 1863–1943 | Charterhouse | Cambridge (Trinity) | | 25 April 1910 | Norwich | 1909 | Asquith | 32 |
| 196. *Powys*, Horatio | 1805–77 | Harrow | Cambridge (St John's) | | *25 July 1854 | Sodor and Man | 1854 | Aberdeen | 23 |
| 197. *Price*, Stuart Hetley | 1922–77 | Loughborough G.S. | Cambridge (Corpus Christi) | Westcott House | 1 May 1972 | Doncaster<br>Ripon | 1975 | Wilson | 1 |
| 198. *Ramsbotham*, John Alexander | 1906–89 | Haileybury | Cambridge (Corpus Christi) | Wells | 2 Feb. 1950 | Jarrow<br>Wakefield | 1958 | Macmillan | 9 |
| 199. *Ramsey*, Arthur Michael | 1904–88 | Repton | Cambridge (Magdalene) | Cuddesdon | 29 Sep. 1952 | Durham<br>**York**<br>**Canterbury** | 1952<br>1955<br>1961 | Churchill<br>Eden<br>Macmillan | 4<br>5<br>13 |
| 200. *Ramsey*, Ian Thomas | 1915–72 | Farnworth G.S. | Cambridge (Christ's) | Ripon Hall | 1 Nov. 1966 | Durham | 1966 | Wilson | 6 |

* Younger brother of Bishop F. Paget.
† Younger brother of Bishop E. H. Pearce.
‡ 4th son of Bishop J. J. S. Perowne.

| Name of bishop | Dates | Public or secondary school | University and college | Theological college | Suffragan/overseas see(s) held | Date of consecration | Diocesan see(s) held | Year appd. | Prime Mnstr responsible | Years held |
|---|---|---|---|---|---|---|---|---|---|---|
| 201. *Rawlinson*, Alfred Edward John | 1884–1960 | Dulwich | Oxford (Corpus Christi) | Cuddesdon | | 24 Feb. 1936 | Derby | 1935 | Baldwin | 23 |
| 202. *Reeve*, Arthur Stretton | 1907–81 | Brighton | Cambridge (Selwyn) | Westcott House | | 29 Sep. 1953 | Lichfield | 1953 | Churchill | 21 |
| 203. *Reindorp*, George Edmund | 1911–90 | Felsted | Cambridge (Trinity) | Westcott House | | 25 Mar. 1961 | Guildford Salisbury | 1961 1972 | Macmillan Heath | 12 8 |
| 204. *Riches*, Kenneth | 1908– | Colchester G.S. | Cambridge (Corpus Christi) | Cuddesdon | Dorchester | 25 July 1952 | Lincoln | 1956 | Eden | 18 |
| 205. *Ridding*, George | 1828–1904 | Winchester | Oxford (Balliol) | | | 1 May 1884 | Southwell | 1884 | Gladstone | 20 |
| 206. *Ridgeway*, Charles John | 1841–1927 | St Paul's | Cambridge (Trinity) | | | 25 Jan. 1908 | Chichester | 1907 | Campbell-Bannerman | 11 |
| 207. *Ridgeway*, Frederic Edward* | 1848–1921 | Tonbridge | Cambridge (Clare) | | Kensington | 17 Feb. 1901 | Salisbury | 1911 | Asquith | 10 |
| 208. *Roberts*, Edward James Keymer | 1908– | Marlborough | Cambridge (Corpus Christi) | Cuddesdon | Malmesbury Kensington (1962) | 1 Nov. 1956 | Ely | 1963 | Douglas-Home | 13 |
| 209. *Robertson*, Archibald | 1853–1931 | Bradfield | Oxford (Trinity) | | | 1 May 1903 | Exeter | 1903 | Balfour | 13 |
| 210. *Rodger*, Patrick Campbell | 1920– | Rugby | Oxford (Christ Church) | Westcott House | | 24 June 1970 | Manchester | 1970 | Wilson | 8 |
| 211. *Runcie*, Robert Alexander Kennedy, MC | 1921– | Merchant Taylors', Crosby | Oxford (Brasenose) | Westcott House | | 24 Feb. 1970 | St Albans | 1969 | Wilson | 10 |
| 212. *Ryle*, Herbert Edward† | 1856–1925 | Eton | Cambridge (King's) | | | 25 Jan. 1901 | Exeter Winchester | 1900 1903 | Salisbury Balfour | 2 8 |

| No. Name | Dates | School | University (College) | Theological College | Consecrated | Suffragan See | Diocese | Year | Prime Minister | Years |
|---|---|---|---|---|---|---|---|---|---|---|
| 213. *Ryle*, John Charles | 1816–1900 | Eton | Oxford (Christ Church) | | 11 June 1880 | | Liverpool | 1880 | Disraeli | 20 |
| 214. *Savage*, Gordon David | 1915–90 | Reading | Oxford (St Catherine's) | Tyndale Hall | 18 Oct. 1960 | Buckingham | Southwell | 1963 | Douglas-Home | 6 |
| 215. *Say*, Richard David, KCVO | 1914– | Univ. Coll. School | Cambridge (Christ's) | Ridley Hall | 6 Jan. 1961 | | Rochester | 1960 | Macmillan | 27 |
| 216. *Seaton*, James Buchanan | 1868–1938 | Leeds G.S. | Oxford (Christ Church) | | 1 Nov. 1928 | | Wakefield | 1928 | Baldwin | 10 |
| 217. *Selwyn*, George Augustus | 1809–78 | Eton | Cambridge (Trinity) | | 17 Oct. 1841 | *New Zealand* | Lichfield | 1867 | Derby | 11 |
| 218. *Sheepshanks*, John | 1834–1912 | | Cambridge (Christ's) | | 29 June 1893 | | Norwich | 1893 | Gladstone | 16 |
| 219. *Sheppard*, David Stuart | 1929– | Sherborne | Cambridge (Trinity Hall) | Ridley Hall | 18 Oct. 1969 | Woolwich | Liverpool | 1975 | Wilson | |
| 220. *Shirley*, Walter Augustus | 1797–1847 | Winchester | Oxford (New Coll.) | | 10 Jan. 1847 | | Sodor and Man | 1846 | Russell | 4 mths |
| 221. *Short*, Thomas Vowler | 1790–1872 | Exeter G.S. and Westminster | Oxford (Christ Church) | | 6 June 1841 | | Sodor and Man<br>St Asaph | 1841<br>1846 | Melbourne<br>Russell | 5<br>24 |
| 222. *Shuttleworth*, Philip Nicholas | 1782–1842 | Winchester | Oxford (New Coll.) | | 20 Sep. 1840 | | Chichester | 1840 | Melbourne | 1 |
| 223. *Simpson*, Bertram Fitzgerald, MC | 1883–1971 | | Durham and London (Univ. Coll.) | | 24 June 1932 | Kensington | Southwark | 1941 | Churchill | 16 |
| 224. *Skelton*, Henry Aylmer | 1884–1959 | Felsted | Oxford (Keble) | Bishops Coll., Cheshunt | 24 Feb. 1939 | Bedford | Lincoln | 1942 | Churchill | 4 |

* Younger brother of Bishop C. J. Ridgeway
† 2nd son of Bishop J. C. Ryle.

| Name of bishop | Dates | Public or secondary school | University and college | Theological college | Suffragan/ overseas see(s) held | Date of consecration | Diocesan see(s) held | Year appd. | Prime Mnstr responsible | Years held |
|---|---|---|---|---|---|---|---|---|---|---|
| 225. *Skelton*, Kenneth John Fraser, CBE | 1918– | Dulwich | Cambridge (Corpus Christi) | Wells | *Matabeleland* (res. 1970) | 25 July 1962 | Lichfield | 1974 | Wilson | 9 |
| 226. *Smith*, Guy Vernon, MC | 1880–1957 | Winchester | Oxford (New Coll.) | Wells | Willesden | 25 July 1929 | Leicester | 1940 | Chamberlain | 13 |
| 227. *Smith*, Martin Linton, DSO | 1869–1950 | Repton | Oxford (Hertford) | Wycliffe Hall | Warrington | 1 Nov. 1918 | Hereford Rochester | 1920 1930 | Lloyd George MacDonald | 10 9 |
| 228. *Stockwood*, Arthur Mervyn | 1913– | Kelly Coll., Tavistock | Cambridge (Christ's) | Westcott House | | 1 May 1959 | Southwark | 1958 | Macmillan | 21 |
| 229. *Stopford*, Robert Wright, KCVO, CBE | 1901–76 | Liverpool Coll. | Oxford (Hertford) | Cuddesdon | Fulham | 11 June 1955 | Peterborough London | 1956 1961 | Eden Macmillan | 5 12 |
| 230. *Straton*, Norman Dumenil John | 1840–1918 | | Cambridge (Trinity) | | | 25 Mar. 1892 | Sodor and Man Newcastle | 1891 1907 | Salisbury Campbell-Bannerman | 15 8 |
| 231. *Strong*, Thomas Banks, GBE | 1861–1944 | Westminster | Oxford (Christ Church) | Cuddesdon | | 24 Aug. 1920 | Ripon Oxford | 1920 1925 | Lloyd George Baldwin | 5 12 |
| 232. *Stubbs*, Charles William | 1845–1912 | Royal Instit. School, Liverpool | Cambridge (Sidney Sussex) | | | 30 Nov. 1906 | Truro | 1906 | Campbell-Bannerman | 6 |
| 233. *Stubbs*, William | 1825–1901 | Ripon G.S. | Oxford (Christ Church) | | | 25 April 1884 | Chester Oxford | 1884 1888 | Gladstone Salisbury | 4 12 |
| 234. *Sumner*, John Bird | 1780–1862 | Eton | Cambridge (King's) | | | 14 Sep. 1828 (for Chester) | Canterbury | 1848 | Russell | 14 |
| 235. *Swayne*, William Shuckburgh | 1862–1941 | St Paul's, Stony Stratford | Oxford (New Coll.) | | | 6 Jan. 1920 | Lincoln | 1919 | Lloyd George | 12 |

| No. | Name | Dates | School | University | Theological College | Consecration | See(s) | Year | Prime Minister | |
|---|---|---|---|---|---|---|---|---|---|---|
| 236. | *Tait*, Archibald Campbell | 1811–82 | Edinburgh H.S. | Glasgow and Oxford (Balliol) | | 23 Nov. 1856 | London **Canterbury** | 1856 1868 | Palmerston Disraeli | 12 14 |
| 237. | *Talbot*, Edward Stuart | 1844–1934 | Charterhouse | Oxford (Christ Church) | Cuddesdon | 18 Oct. 1895 | Rochester Southwark **Winchester** | 1895 1905 1911 | Salisbury Balfour Asquith | 10 6 13 |
| 238. | *Taylor*, Francis John | 1912–71 | Hymers' Coll., Hull | Oxford (Queen's) | Wycliffe Hall | 25 July 1962 | Sheffield | 1962 | Macmillan | 9 |
| 239. | *Taylor*, John Ralph Strickland | 1883–1961 | Marlborough | Cambridge (Pembroke) | Ridley Hall | 6 Jan. 1943 | Sodor and Man | 1942 | Churchill | 12 |
| 240. | *Taylor*, John Vernon* | 1914– | St Lawrence Coll., Ramsgate | Cambridge (Trinity) and Oxford (St Catherine's) | Wycliffe Hall | 31 Jan. 1975 | Winchester | 1974 | Wilson | 10 |
| 241. | *Temple*, Frederick | 1821–1902 | Blundell's | Oxford (Balliol) | | 21 Dec. 1869 | Exeter London **Canterbury** | 1869 1885 1896 | Gladstone Gladstone Salisbury | 16 11 6 |
| 242. | *Temple*, William† | 1881–1944 | Rugby | Oxford (Balliol) | | 25 Jan. 1921 | Manchester York **Canterbury** | 1920 1928 1942 | Lloyd George Baldwin Churchill | 8 13 2 |
| 243. | *Thirlwall*, Connop | 1797–1875 | Charterhouse | Cambridge (Trinity) | | 9 Aug. 1840 | St Davids | 1840 | Melbourne | 34 |
| 244. | *Thompson*, James Denton | 1856–1924 | Liverpool Inst. and Coll. | Cambridge (Corpus Christi) | | 25 Mar. 1912 | Sodor and Man | 1911 | Asquith | 12 |
| 245. | *Thomson*, William | 1819–90 | Shrewsbury | Oxford (Queen's) | | 1 Dec. 1861 | Gloucester and Bristol **York** | 1861 1862 | Palmerston Palmerston | 1 28 |
| 246. | *Thornton-Duesbery*, Charles Leonard | 1867–1928 | Shattallan Hall, IoM | Dublin (Trinity) | | 24 Feb. 1925 | Sodor and Man | 1925 | Baldwin | 3 |

* Son of Bishop J. R. S. Taylor.
† 2nd son of Archbishop Frederick Temple.

| Name of bishop | Dates | Public or secondary school | University and college | Theological college | Suffragan/ overseas see(s) held | Date of consecration | Diocesan see(s) held | Year appd. | Prime Mnstr responsible | Years held |
|---|---|---|---|---|---|---|---|---|---|---|
| 247. *Thorold*, Anthony Wilson | 1825–95 | Stanmore | Oxford (Queen's) | | | 25 July 1877 | Rochester Winchester | 1877 1890 | Disraeli Salisbury | 13 4 |
| 248. *Tarks*, John Gerhard | 1903–74 | Westminster | Cambridge (Trinity) | Ridley Hall | | 24 Feb. 1962 | Chelmsford | 1962 | Macmillan | 9 |
| 249. *Tinsley*, Ernest John | 1919– | | Durham (St John's) | Westcott House | | 6 Jan. 1976 | Bristol | 1975 | Wilson | 9 |
| 250. *Tomkins*, Oliver Stratford | 1908– | Trent | Cambridge (Christ's) | Westcott House | | 6 Jan. 1959 | Bristol | 1958 | Macmillan | 16 |
| 251. *Treacy*, Eric, MBE | 1907–78 | Haberdashers' | London (King's) | St Aidan's, Birkenhd | Pontefract | 18 Oct. 1961 | Wakefield | 1968 | Wilson | 8 |
| 252. *Trillo*, Albert John | 1915– | The Quintin | London (King's) | | Bedford Hertford (1968) | 2 Feb. 1963 | Chelmsford | 1971 | Heath | 14 |
| 253. *Turton*, Thomas | 1780–1864 | | Cambridge (Queens' and St Catharine's) | | | 4 May 1845 | Ely | 1845 | Peel | 19 |
| 254. *Underhill*, Francis | 1878–1943 | Shrewsbury | Oxford (Exeter) | Cuddesdon | | 30 Nov. 1937 | Bath and Wells | 1937 | Baldwin | 6 |
| 255. *Villiers*, Henry Montagu | 1813–61 | | Oxford (Christ Church) | | | 13 April 1856 | Carlisle Durham | 1856 1860 | Palmerston Palmerston | 4 1 |
| 256. *Wakefield*, Henry Russell | 1854–1933 | Tonbridge | Paris and Bonn | Cuddesdon | | 28 Oct. 1911 | Birmingham | 1911 | Asquith | 13 |
| 257. *Wakeling*, John Denis, MC | 1918– | Dean Close, Cheltenham | Cambridge (St Catharine's) | Ridley Hall | | 29 Sep. 1970 | Southwell | 1970 | Wilson | 15 |

| No. Name | Dates | School | University | Theological college | | Consecration | See | Year | Prime Minister | |
|---|---|---|---|---|---|---|---|---|---|---|
| 258. *Waldegrave*, Samuel | 1817–69 | Pestallozzian school at Cheam | Oxford (Balliol) | | | 11 Nov. 1860 | Carlisle | 1860 | Palmerston | 9 |
| 259. *Walker*, Peter Knight | 1919– | Leeds G.S. | Oxford (Queen's) | | Dorchester | 13 July 1972 | Ely | 1977 | Callaghan | 12 |
| 260. *Wand*, John William Charles, KCVO | 1885–1977 | King's School, Grantham | Oxford (St Edmund Hall) | Bp Jacob's Hostel, Newcastle | *Brisbane* | 1 May 1934 | Bath and Wells / London | 1943 / 1945 | Churchill / Churchill | 2 / 10 |
| 261. *Warman*, Frederic Sumpter Guy | 1872–1953 | Merchant Taylors' | Oxford (Pembroke) | | | 18 Oct. 1919 | Truro / Chelmsford / Manchester | 1919 / 1923 / 1928 | Lloyd George / Baldwin / Baldwin | 4 / 6 / 18 |
| 262. *Watkins*, Ivor Stanley | 1896–1960 | Hereford Cath. School | Cambridge (Trinity Hall) | Cuddesdon | Malmesbury | 1 Nov. 1946 | Guildford | 1956 | Eden | 4 |
| 263. *Watts-Ditchfield*, John Edwin | 1861–1923 | | Victoria Univ. of Manchester | London Coll. of Div. | | 24 Feb. 1914 | Chelmsford | 1914 | Asquith | 9 |
| 264. *Westcott*, Brooke Foss | 1825–1901 | King Edward's, Birmingham | Cambridge (Trinity) | | | 1 May 1890 | Durham | 1890 | Salisbury | 11 |
| 265. *White-Thomson*, Leonard Jauncey | 1863–1933 | Eton | Cambridge (King's) | | | 25 Mar. 1924 | Ely | 1924 | Baldwin | 9 |
| 266. *Whitsey*, Hubert Victor | 1916–87 | Blackburn G.S. | Oxford (St Edmund Hall) | Westcott House | Hertford | 1 Nov. 1971 | Chester | 1973 | Heath | 8 |
| 267. *Whittingham*, Walter Godfrey | 1862–1941 | | Cambridge (Peterhouse) | | | 1 Nov. 1923 | St Edmundsbury and Ips. | 1923 | Baldwin | 17 |
| 268. *Wigram*, Joseph Cotton | 1798–1867 | (Educated privately) | Cambridge (Trinity) | | | 17 May 1860 | Rochester | 1860 | Palmerston | 7 |
| 269. *Wilberforce*, Ernest Roland* | 1840–1907 | Harrow | Oxford (Exeter) | Cuddesdon | | 25 July 1882 | Newcastle / Chichester | 1882 / 1895 | Gladstone / Salisbury | 13 / 12 |

*Son of Bishop Samuel Wilberforce.

| Name of bishop | Dates | Public or secondary school | University and college | Theological college | Suffragan/ overseas see(s) held | Date of consecration | Diocesan see(s) held | Year appd. | Prime Mnstr responsible | Years held |
|---|---|---|---|---|---|---|---|---|---|---|
| 270. *Wilberforce*, Samuel | 1805-73 | (Educated privately) | Oxford (Oriel) | | | 30 Nov. 1845 | Oxford / Winchester | 1845 / 1869 | Peel / Gladstone | 24 / 4 |
| 271. *Wild*, Herbert Louis | 1865-1940 | Charterhouse | Oxford (Exeter) | | | 30 Nov. 1915 | Newcastle | 1915 | Asquith | 12 |
| 272. *Wilkinson*, George Howard | 1833-1907 | Durham G.S. | Oxford (Brasenose) | | | 25 April 1883 | Truro | 1883 | Gladstone | 8* |
| 273. *Williams*, Alwyn Terrell Petre | 1888-1968 | Rossall | Oxford (Jesus) | | | 25 Mar. 1939 | Durham / Winchester | 1938 / 1952 | Chamberlain / Churchill | 13 / 9 |
| 274. *Williams*, Henry Herbert, CH | 1872-1961 | St Peter's, York | Oxford (Queen's) | | | 24 Aug. 1920 | Carlisle | 1920 | Lloyd George | 26 |
| 275. *Williams*, Ronald Ralph | 1906-79 | Judd School, Tonbridge | Cambridge (Gonville and Caius) | Ridley Hall | | 28 Oct. 1953 | Leicester | 1953 | Churchill | 25 |
| 276. *Williams*, Watkin Herbert | 1845-1944 | Westminster | Oxford (Christ Church) | | | 2 Feb. 1899 | Bangor | 1899 | Salisbury | 25 |
| 277. *Willson*, St John Basil Wynne | 1868-1946 | Cheltenham | Cambridge (St John's) | | | 1 Nov. 1921 | Bath and Wells | 1921 | Lloyd George | 16 |
| 278. *Wilson*, Henry Albert, CBE | 1876-1961 | | Cambridge (Corpus Christi) | | | 25 Jan. 1929 | Chelmsford | 1928 | Baldwin | 22 |
| 279. *Wilson*, John Leonard, KCMG | 1897-1970 | St John's, Leatherhead | Oxford (Queen's) | Wycliffe Hall | *Singapore* (res. 1949) | 22 July 1941 | Birmingham | 1953 | Churchill | 16 |
| 280. *Wilson*, Roger Plumpton, KCVO | 1905- | Winchester | Oxford (Keble) | Westcott House | | 25 April 1949 | Wakefield / Chichester | 1949 / 1957 | Attlee / Macmillan | 9 / 16 |
| 281. *Winnington-Ingram*, Arthur Foley, KCVO | 1858-1946 | Marlborough | Oxford (Keble) | | Stepney | 30 Nov. 1897 | London | 1901 | Salisbury | 38 |

| No. & Name | Dates | School | University (College) | Theological College | Date | Suffragan | See(s) | Year(s) | Prime Minister | |
|---|---|---|---|---|---|---|---|---|---|---|
| 282. *Wood*, Maurice Arthur Ponsonby, DSC | 1916– | Monkton Combe | Cambridge (Queens') | Ridley Hall | 29 Sep. 1971 | | Norwich | 1971 | Heath | 14 |
| 283. *Woodford*, James Russell | 1820–85 | Merchant Taylors' | Cambridge (Pembroke) | | 14 Dec. 1873 | | Ely | 1873 | Gladstone | 12 |
| 284. *Woods*, Edward Sydney* | 1877–1953 | Marlborough | Cambridge (Trinity) | Ridley Hall | 1 May 1930 | Croydon | Lichfield | 1937 | Baldwin | 16 |
| 285. *Woods*, Frank Theodore | 1874–1932 | Marlborough | Cambridge (Trinity) | Ridley Hall | 21 Sep. 1916 | | Peterborough / Winchester | 1916 / 1923 | Asquith / Baldwin | 8 / 8 |
| 286. *Woods*, Robert Wylmer, KCMG, KCVO† | 1914– | Gresham's | Cambridge (Trinity) | Westcott House | 20 Feb. 1971 | | Worcester | 1970 | Heath | 11 |
| 287. *Woodward*, Clifford Salisbury, MC | 1878–1959 | Marlborough | Oxford (Jesus) | Wycliffe Hall | 25 May 1933 | | Bristol / Gloucester | 1933 / 1945 | MacDonald / Attlee | 13 / 7 |
| 288. *Woollcombe*, Kenneth John | 1924– | Haileybury | Oxford (St John's) | Westcott House | 16 Mar. 1971 | | Oxford | 1970 | Heath | 7 |
| 289. *Wordsworth*, Christopher | 1807–85 | Winchester | Cambridge (Trinity) | | 24 Feb. 1869 | | Lincoln | 1868 | Disraeli | 16 |
| 290. *Wordsworth*, John‡ | 1843–1911 | Winchester | Oxford (New Coll.) | | 28 Oct. 1885 | | Salisbury | 1885 | Salisbury | 26 |
| 291. *Wynn*, Harold Edward | 1889–1956 | Mercers' | Cambridge (Trinity Hall) | Ely | 25 July 1941 | | Ely | 1941 | Churchill | 16 |
| 292. *Yates*, John | 1925– | Battersea and Blackpool G.S.s | Cambridge (Jesus) | Lincoln | 25 Jan. 1972 | Whitby | Gloucester | 1975 | Wilson | 16 |
| 293. *Yeatman-Biggs*, Huyshe Wolcott, FSA | 1845–1922 | Winchester | Cambridge (Emmanuel) | | 29 Sep. 1891 | Southwark | Worcester / Coventry | 1905 / 1918 | Balfour / Lloyd George | 13 / 4 |
| 294. *Young*, David Nigel de Lorentz | 1931– | Wellington | Oxford (Balliol) | Wycliffe Hall | 21 Sep. 1977 | | Ripon | 1977 | Callaghan | |

* Younger brother of Bishop F. T. Woods.
† Son of Bishop E. S. Woods.
‡ Eldest son of Bishop Christopher Wordsworth.

* Resigned see 1891; Bishop of St Andrews, Scotland, 1893–1907.

# Index